ISBN 978-0-483-12516-2
PIBN 10604003

This book is a reproduction of an important historical work. Forgotten Books uses
state-of-the-art technology to digitally reconstruct the work, preserving the original format
whilst repairing imperfections present in the aged copy. In rare cases, an imperfection in
the original, such as a blemish or missing page, may be replicated in our edition. We do,
however, repair the vast majority of imperfections successfully; any imperfections that
remain are intentionally left to preserve the state of such historical works.

THE

M^CMASTER UNIVERSITY

MONTHLY

VOL. V.

JUNE, '95 TO MAY, '96·

TORONTO :

DUDLEY & BURNS, PRINTERS.

1896.

CONTENTS.

ENGRAVINGS.

POETRY.

STUDENTS' QUARTER.

CONTRIBUTED ARTICLES.

XIII

CHAS N SCHUTT

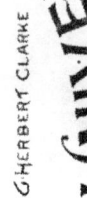

A P McDONALD

G HERBERT CLARKE

UNIVERSITY.

O G LANGFORD

STAMBURY R TARR

D·NIMMO·

R ROUTLEDGE

G R MACFAUL

McMASTE

G   A PINE

W R SMITH

THE

McMASTER UNIVERSITY MONTHLY

JUNE, 1895.

GRADUATES IN ARTS, 1895.

GEORGE HERBERT CLARKE.

George Herbert Clarke, B.A., was born on the 27th of August, 1873. The charming English sea-port of Gravesend, in the ancient county of Kent, lays authentic claim to the honour of being his birth-place. Doubtless, the natural beauties and historic associations of the scenes of his childhood already had their influence in moulding the latent poetic temperament, and fostering the inborn patriotism of the lad when, in his eighth year, he left his native shores to reside in Canada. Arriving in Toronto, from then to the present the home of his father's family, he attended various public schools, and at twelve entered the Jarvis Street Collegiate Institute. Here he gained many prizes, chiefly in English. When fifteen, he entered Woodstock College, and in the succeeding two years, completed with credit the matriculation course for McMaster University. He looks upon Woodstock and its influences with gratitude and affection, for there many crises were passed and essential habits formed. Under the inspiration of the late Principal Huston's teaching at the Collegiate and at Woodstock, Herb., from a child a lover of literature, laid the foundation of the careful English scholarship which has characterized his subsequent career. Among his first literary efforts were several contributions to the *Woodstock College Monthly*—fitting precursors to the more finished productions which have since appeared in that journal's successor, THE MC-MASTER UNIVERSITY MONTHLY, as well as in *The Canadian Magazine, Saturday Night, Buffalo Express,* etc. Among the numerous offices which "G. H," has ably filled during his course at McMaster, space permits mention only of his presidency of the Camelot Club, and his position, for nearly three years, upon the staff of the MONTHLY. This magazine, indeed, owes no small debt to the energetic ability and high journalistic talent which he has so untiringly displayed in its service. Mr. Clarke's work in all departments of study has been marked by a thoroughness of method which has had its due reward, not only in high examination standings, but in a well-balanced intellectual growth. In subjects connected with his beloved specialty, English, his success has been unsurpassed. Herb. holds high place in the esteem of professors and students alike, and among his classmates, as class-bard, is the poet-exponent of the strong fellow-feeling which binds together the members of '95·

FREDERICK EBY.

Frederick Eby, B.A., the youngest son of Dr. Eby of Sebring-ville, was born in October, 1874. He has inherited that earnest disposition of his Waldensian forefathers whose religious zeal caused them to be driven from the north of Italy into Switzerland, in the sixteenth century, and on account of which they received, in their new home, the name Mennonites. His public school days were spent in Sebringville. When fourteen he went to the Stratford Collegiate Institute, and after two years matriculated into Toronto University. He early desired a broad intellectual culture, and finding at McMaster a course more adapted to the fuller development of his mind, he entered the class of '95· In this choice he was moved, probably, by the spirit of his ancestors, who were all men of broad minds; one of his maternal fore-fathers being the printer and editor of the first German Bible published in America. At McMaster he has evinced a strong intellect with his maturing years. Few indeed thought, at the first assembling of '95, that the youngest-looking member would take so high a standing in his final year; but such has been his earnestness, combined with natural ability, that he has excelled not only in the classics, in which he specialized, but also in the mental and moral sciences. Frederick Eby is one of the most promising of the graduates for a life devoted to the acquirement of a true and high scholarship.

ONESIMUS GEORGE LANGFORD.

Onesimus George Langford, B.A., familiarly known as "O.G." was born at Parsons' Farm, Stanstead, Wrotham, Kent, England, Aug. 25th, 1861. His father was a farmer, but in 1866 went into business, so young George was early initiated into practical life. George left the common school at 12 years of age, his father dying the following year. Young Langford early took to music, and from 1877 to 1881, while still in business, conducted a Philharmonic Society. During this period he several times presented to the public Handel's *Messiah* with a large company trained and led by himself. He came to Canada in 1881, and was in business in Peterboro for two years. He began preaching in August, 1882, and entered Woodstock College, Sept., 1883. In 1885, he took the Hagersville church for one year, and while there entirely removed the large church debt, and brought great spiritual blessing to the people. He went in 1886 to Hartford, Ont. Here, also, great blessing attended his ministry. On leaving Hartford, Mr. Langford travelled for 18 months, lecturing and singing in the interests of the temperance cause, and meeting with great success; but he is a man with a purpose: to preach the gospel. So he returned to Woodstock in September, 1889, and matriculated in 1891. During this period he was the loved and honored pastor of the church at Beachville, with many consequent conversions. His coming to McMaster necessitated a change of pastorate. Grimsby called him. He held this pastorate during his entire Arts Course, his work being blessed by the baptism of 40 souls. He is now pastor at Georgetown, and intends entering Theology at McMaster next fall. Mr. Langford is a married man and has six sweet children. "O.G." fondly says that his success is due largely to the faithful assistance of his wife. The writer has visited the home of Mr. and

Mrs. Langford. She is a true and devoted wife whose sky is never dim, whose heart is ever buoyant with hope. Their home life is simple and sweet and strong. Mr. Langford is an author of no men standing. In *The Examiner, The Sunday School Times* and *The Chicago Standard*, the products of his pen are always welcomed. As a fellow-student I cannot refrain from paying a tribute also to the faithful and efficient service which "O.G." has rendered to our own college magazine. As a preacher Mr. Langford is strong, clear and simple in style. His utterance is graced by delicate and appropriate imagery, feeling and pathos. He is a speaker of deep conviction and over-mastering purpose. As a Christian his life speaks for itself. The man who with a family to support and educate, and the duty of preaching every Sunday, can do what "O.G." has done knows what Paul meant when he said "I press." As a friend he is constant and true. The future of such a man cannot be other than bright in the best sense. Go on, "O.G.," we are listening for your voice. We are waiting for your footsteps, at the head of your calling.

WALTER SYM SCOTT McALPINE.

Walter S. Scott McAlpine, B.A., was born in the Township of Sarnia, County of Lambton, on Christmas Day, 1862. When he was thirteen his father moved to Sarnia, where Mac. attended the High School. After securing a teacher's certificate he taught three years in the Township of Enniskillen. In '86 he attended the Toronto Normal School, then taught for three years at Chatham. In 1890 he became pastor of the Dresden Baptist Church, and the following year entered McMaster University. In college and out Mac. has been a universal favourite. The confidence that is gained by geniality and character has been given to him. During the last year he has been High Kakiac, the head of our college administration. The High Kakiac carries the influence of his birthday with him. He is broad and deep in all qualities of affection. "The milk of human kindness" has not been soured in him. It is only on the rarest occasions that he strikes fire, and then it is but a "hasty spark and straight is cold again," or rather warm with forgiveness and love. He is fond of flowers, birds and babies and so is as good

as men are generally made. Mac. is a musical genius. His soul
was poured into the mould of harmony. He is a citizen of the
world where the great musical geniuses have congregated and
found the full development of their gifts. On numberless occasions in room fifteen we have beheld McAlpine and Langford
ascending like sons of kings the golden stairway of the musical
scale, "trailing clouds of glory" after them. They were soon
in their element, in that heaven of song that is just above us for
all such gifted souls. After a hard week McAlpine's soul would
find expression in these words of Shelley :

> "Let me drink of the spirit of that sweet sound,
>   More, O more, I am thirsting yet,
> It loosens the serpent which 'study' has bound
>   Upon my heart to stifle it ;
> The dissolving strain, through every vein
> Passes into my heart and brain."

A. P. McDONALD.

Mr. A. P. McDonald, B.A., B. Th., is of Scotch parentage, and
was born in Osgoode, Carleton Co., on the 4th of August, 1861.
He professed to be converted when about 13 years of age, was
baptised by the Rev. P. H. McEwen and united with the Ormond
Baptist Church. From earliest youth he was the subject of deep
religious impressions, and was most conscientious in all his
actions. He is now just what we should expect a youth of such
characteristics to become, a man of strong convictions in regard
to moral and religious truth. After attending the public school
at home, he went to Woodstock College, from which he graduated
in 1885, matriculating into the University of Toronto. After
taking three years of the Arts Course in that institution, which
was interrupted somewhat by ill-health, he entered upon his Theology in McMaster, from which he graduated with the degree of
B.Th., in '92· He immediately accepted a call to the Baptist
church in Forest, Ontario, where he spent a very happy and successful pastorate of a little less than three years. Last fall, Mr.
McDonald returned to take his final year in Arts in McMaster,
and graduated this spring. Mr. McDonald always took an active
part in college sports, and his popularity is clearly shown by the

oilices and honors his fellow students have thrust upon him. During his last year in residence, he was captain of the football team, as well as chairman of the student body. At the recent meeting of the Alumni Association of McMaster University, Mr. McDonald was appointed one of the representatives of the Arts Graduates in the Senate. His work for the present will be in the beautiful rural town of Dundas.

GEORGE RAINBOTH McFAUL.

George Rainboth McFaul, B.A., was born in 1869 at Point Fortune, county of Vaudreuil, Province of Quebec. His father was a farmer whose home overlooked the fair Ottawa. He was fourteen years of age when his father sold his farm and removed to Niagara Falls, Ontario. George attended the High School at Niagara Falls South for three terms, and at the age of sixteen he was converted, during special services held in the Baptist church of that place. He was afterwards baptized and united with the church. Even before George was converted he thought the ministry was his life's work and he never afterwards swerved from this conviction. At the age of eighteen he went to Grande Ligne Institute to prepare for the French work. Here he laboured with great success for four years, winning the hearts both of professors and of pupils by his diligence in study, his fidelity to the truth, and by the marked spirituality which regulated his actions. Matriculating from Grande Ligne Institute, he now entered McMaster University. During most of his course he preached weekly upon various fields; notably spending his last year and a half as pastor of Kenilworth Avenue Baptist Church, Toronto. He made good progress in his studies and accomplished altogether as much work as any man in '95. He is an honour not only to his class, but also to his *Alma Mater.* At present C. R. McFaul is labouring at Rockland and Clarence, about thirty miles from Ottawa. He preaches every Sunday afternoon in French at Canaan and may eventually fully enter the French work. Our friend is an eloquent preacher, and an enthusiastic and consecrated Christian student and worker. He may yet rival even the silver-tongued Laurier in his command over Canada's two tongues.

DAVID NIMMO.

David Nimmo, B.A., was born July 13th, 1865, in Linlithgow, Scotland. When David was three years of age his parents emigrated to Canada, and eventually settled in Mount Forest. It was there that David got most of his early schooling, and it was there also that he began to learn his trade as a machinist, which he finished at the London Tool Works. While in Woodstock in 1886, he was converted and baptized by Rev. W. H. Porter, then pastor of Talbot St. Baptist Church, London. In 1888 he decided to return to school that he might be better fitted to preach the Gospel which he felt called to proclaim. So he entered Woodstock College in September of that year. It was there that he laid the foundations of the student habits which have proved so serviceable to him since. In June of 1891 he graduated and in October of the same year entered on his Arts Course in McMaster. After four years of diligent application to his work he shares in the glory of being one of the graduates of the famous Class of '95· There is only one David Nimmo, but how can he be sketched ? As a student he is not what might be termed brilliant, but he has remarkable powers of concentration, whereby he can apply himself almost constantly to his books. He has read quite widely in both prose and poetry ; of the latter that of Shelley is most admired. As a result of this reading his public speaking abounds in poetic expressions, evidencing as well much original thought of real practical character. By his natural gift of speaking he has won the title of orator, and it is conceded by all that it is no misnomer. As to his character—it is irreproachable. He is possessed of a large heart, is truly sympathetic for the poor and suffering and is a most reliable friend. His ideals are high and noble and he is constantly striving to attain them. The ambition of his life is to reach the masses of the poor with the Gospel of Jesus. May he never lose sight of this goal !

ROBERT ROUTLEDGE.

Robert Routledge, B.A., of English and Irish parentage, was born in Brant Township, 6th concession, in the County of Bruce. From earliest youth he was a great lover of flowers and animals, and was always crazy for fishing, swimming and boating. He could dive "double the distance of any other fellow" in the Walkerton High School. He enjoyed very much his public school days. During the summer months his mother, of whom he always speaks most affectionately, would permit him to remain at home occasionally to spend the day fishing. At the age of 13 he passed the entrance into the High School. When 15 he spent part of a year at the High School, and similarly when about 17. The rest of the time was spent at home on the farm. Robert was converted during his first year at the High School. He gained his 2nd class certificate at the end of the second year. After three months at the Model, he taught in the home school for two years. He then spent five months at the Walkerton High School and took up the matriculation work. At the age of 21 he entered McMaster University; here he has made many warm friends, and was graduated this year with high honors in several departments. He was always very fond of botany, and the natural sciences generally, as would be expected from his early inclinations. He had also a lively regard for mathematics during his course. Metaphysics to him was easy reading, but he had no particular love for the languages. As all his class-mates testify, Rob is a warm friend, a man of strong and earnest character, and, in brief, a right royal fellow. Outside of his regular work he did good service as president of the Natural Science Club. He is a young man, well endowed naturally, so that the training he received in McMaster, the excellence of which is indicated in his high record as a student, should well fit him to realize our predictions of a bright and useful future for him. He is located for the present at Neepawa, Manitoba.

JOHN WILLIAM RUSSELL.

John William Russell, **B.A.**, first mathematician of the year which has recently been graduated, was born near the village of Millbrook, Durham Co., in December, 1870. His ancestors were from England; his paternal grandfather, coming to this Province when it was yet largely unpeopled, settled upon the old homestead. Here amid the tranquil beauties of rural scenery, Mr. Russell spent his boyhood days, early gaining a love for nature

and the advantages of country life. At the usual age he commenced his education, early exhibiting those qualities which
have in after years marked him as a thorough student. From
the public. school of Millbrook at the age of fifteen he took a
third-class certificate. Subsequently, for two years, he attended
the Port Hope High School, from which he matriculated with
high honours into Toronto University. Mr. Russell then turned
his attention to teaching, holding for three years the school in
his native district. As might be expected, the greatest degree
of success followed his efforts in this line. At the end of this
time he desired still further to investigate the realm of knowledge, and accordingly entered McMaster University, where he
was soon distinguished as a student of rare abilities in mathematical and scientific studies. During the four years of his course,
he has always maintained a first place in the class-room and a
high standing on the examination lists. Not merely as a student,
however, but also as a genial classmate and generous fellow-
student, " Jack " will be ever remembered in the hearts of his
comrades. His popularity was proved when he received the
election to the presidency of the Literary and Scientific Society,
one of the highest marks of esteem the student body confer. He
has filled this position admirably, and has shown those qualities which make the truly successful public man. His friends
have noticed with pleasure the proficiency Mr. Russell has
attained in public speaking. They are assured of his success in
this regard. Mr. Russell will find the largest field for the exercise of his powers in the profession he has chosen as the province
of his future activities. He will enter the teaching ranks, at
least for a time. Of his success in this department we are certain, and can feel sure his excellent Christian character and earnest endeavours will make his name an ornament to his *Alma
Mater.*

CHARLES HIRAM SCHUTT.

Charles Hiram Schutt, B.A., was born in 1873, at Champlain,
State of New York. When Charles was three years of age his
father crossed the lines to Canada and settled on a farm at Lacolle, Quebec, a beautiful and. historical spot overlooking the
Richelieu River, near Lake Champlain. After attending the

Public School and the Lacolle Academy, he went at the age of fourteen to Grande Ligne Institute, where he studied for about five years, winning the respect and love of all who knew him. While there he was led to receive Christ as his Saviour and, after baptism, united with the French Baptist Church. Matriculating from Grande Ligne Institute, he entered McMaster University, where he soon won the esteem of all his classmates by his geniality, his fidelity to truth and his diligence in study. No student of class '95 has made greater progress than Charles during the four years of his course. He is known to all as a man who is not afraid of work. While at McMaster he decided to enter the ministry. Although he had thought of doing so previously, it was only now that he became firmly convinced that this was the work which God had for him to do. Charles is not only a fluent speaker of our English language but also of the French; he is a profound thinker, as his standing in philosophy and metaphysics will show, a consecrated Christian, and a firm believer in the old Gospel as preached by the apostles. We predict for him a very useful and successful life in the Master's service. He is now pastor of the Baptist Church at Cobourg, Ontario, where his work is already achieving its wonted good results.

WILSON R. SMITH.

Wilson R. Smith, B.A., was born in the County of Norfolk, his father being the late Rev. R. B. Smith. From his ancestors Wilson inherited any number of virtues, which are to be left for his tombstone to record. After obtaining a certificate while still almost a boy, he began teaching at Carlton and Port Burwell. In 1886 he attended the Normal School, where he succeeded in winning the Prince of Wales' Gold Medal. Afterwards he taught in Tilsonburg High School for a few months, and then in Aylmer Collegiate Institute for three and a half years. In 1889 Mr. Smith married Miss Hattie Brown of Newbury. They have one child, who is said by his parents to be the finest and brightest boy in the province. Mr. Smith took the second year of his arts course at the University of Toronto and the third and fourth years at McMaster University. In 1891 Mr. Smith was appointed to the position of science master in Woodstock College, where he is now achieving marked success.

STAMBURY RYRIE TARR.

Stambury Ryrie Tarr, B.A., was born in Toronto, on June 26th, 1875. His nature happily embodies the best characteristics of both Scotch and English blood. Stambury grew up in the beautiful city of Ottawa, and spent an industrious boyhood at the public schools of that city ; not, of course, unaccompanied by a more than moderate amount of " fun." Before long he entered the Ottawa Collegiate Institute, where he distinguished himself as president of the Literary Society and associate editor of the school paper. Truly an earnest of future events ! In due course of time, our hero matriculated, and carried away from the Institute not only several prizes for mathematics and public speaking, but also the good wishes and the hearty esteem of all who remained behind. In October, 1891, he entered McMaster as a full-fledged freshman, ambitious, industrious and elate. He took a good stand in all exams., and, apart from orthodox astronomy, never knew a "star." Indeed, he has fully proved his ability to take "first all round," and ill health alone prevented that consummation this year. He has specialized in English and Mathematics. Stambury has always been thoroughly popular with the boys, his classmates especially, and has held many offices with great success. As a member of the MONTHLY staff last year, he did praiseworthy service ; and as president of the Literary and Scientific Society has certainly proved himself a very efficient leader. His love of books has awakened a decided literary taste and this, coupled with his mathematical ability, ensures a degree of balance and ready interest to his writings that may well attract attention. Nor is the Muse herself unknown to this versatile youth. With all this promise of future high achievement, Stambury contents himself during the present vacation, with characteristic inquisitiveness, by making experimental researches in agriculture on a Fonthill farm. He carries with him the affection of all his fellows.

WILLIAM JAMES THOROLD.

William James Thorold, B.A., was born in Toronto on the 7th of October, 1871, where after passing through the city Public Schools he was engaged for about four years at the Head Offices

of the Northern and North-Western Railway. Then a year at
Woodstock College, followed by two years at the Parkdale Collegiate Institute, furnished him with the literary attainments
prerequisite to a successful matriculation examination which
followed in 1891. He now entered upon the Arts Course at Mc-
Master University, which he has faithfully and successfully pursued during the last four years, graduating at the recent commencement. The literary features of the course more especially
have been attractive to Mr. Thorold's mind and tastes, and in
them he has found not only models for study and practice, but
strong incentives to independent work. And so during his course
at McMaster, contributions from his ever busy pen, in the form
of short stories or dramatic sketches, have appeared from time to
time in the University Monthly Magazine, The Daily Mail, as
well as in papers published in Kingston, in San Francisco, and
New York. He has also been requested by two leaders
in the histrionic world to write dramas for their repertoires.
Mr. Thorold has likewise been an ardent student of elocution,
and possessing a rich and well-trained voice, he has always been
a favorite with the students upon the platform. At present he
is engaged as assistant in elocution to Mr. H. N. Shaw, B.A., at
the Toronto Conservatory of Music, where he recently took a
prominent part in the representation of " Electra" and won high
encomiums for his elocutionary power. We understand that Mr.
Thorold is strongly inclined to devote himself to journalism, in
which his many eminent qualifications cannot fail to secure for
him a brilliant career.

GRADUATES IN THEOLOGY.

ROBERT GARSIDE.

In Headingly, a pretty suburb of Leeds, England, Robert Garside, B.A., B.Th., was born in 1857. He was named after his uncle, an alderman in the town. Boyhood days passed quickly and pleasantly in a home which was populous with books and presided over by a gentle mother. Memories of summer visits with his father and the rest, the services of the Episcopal church, fragments of conversations, the visits of friends and relatives, the busy streets of Leeds, are all that remain of childhood's happy days. He at first attended private schools, and then others under denominational guidance. In 1867 the family moved to Canada. Here the principal cities were visited and Belleville was selected as an abode; but when November came again the return voyage was taken to England. After three years we find the whole family again in Canada and this time on a farm in North Orillia. Robert passed two years here and then tried town life in Orillia, working as boy in a store, as clerk and then as book-keeper. Next we see him as a clerk in Brantford. Though up to this time he had attended the Episcopal church, yet here he was led to go to the Tabernacle Baptist Church. He was converted under the ministry of the Rev. R. Cameron and became an active worker in the church and Y.M.C.A. He was often heard preaching upon the streets, in the jail and the school-houses of the district, and sometimes in the Baptist churches of Burtch, Wolverton, Scotland and Burford. Mr. Garside now decided to study for the ministry, and in 1879 went to Woodstock College where he spent four happy and profitable years. Then he entered the University of Toronto, and took the honor course in metaphysics. In 1886 he took the degree of B A. One year of theological study was completed in McMaster, and then in obedience to the call of the Lord he hastened to India in 1887 as His missionary. Previous to embarking he was married to Miss Margaret Denovan of Toronto. During his stay in India he travelled some 8,090 miles in oxcart, on horseback, in jinrickshaw, and on foot, for the purpose of proclaiming the gospel in Telugu and prosecuting mission work. The girls' boarding-schools in Tuni and village schools in the district were established The Tuni church, and the girls' school dormitories were built, and a bungalow reconstructed, Mr. Garside attending to the purchase of material and the details of construction. He wrote three tracts in Telugu, one against the infamous opium traffic. He baptized between 50 and 60 converts and started the work among the caste people near Narsapatnam as well as new work in many other villages. After more than six years of hard, faithful work, return was found imperative. Since last October he has been engaged in concluding his theological course in McMaster University, where he has just taken the degree of B.Th.

WILLIAM HARYETT.

Between the ages of 8 and 10, William Haryett often experienced deep religious conviction, owing, probably, to the conversion of both his parents while he was yet a lad. It was in Sunday-school one day that he first felt called to the ministry, and longed to preach the gospel to the negroes. The fluctuations to which youth is so susceptible followed; until, when 19, he became actually converted and was baptized two years later. After undergoing the transition from faltering testimony to confident exhortation, he began open-air preaching at the seaside, in Hyde Park, London, Eng., on bridges, street-corners, etc. He was occasionally sent out to fill appointments, and the work thus grew upon him until he felt constrained to enter the East London Institute for Home and Foreign Missions. While here he frequently preached on the Mile End Waste, and in surrounding Mission Halls, and in October of 1878, graduated and went to Jamaica to labour among the negroes. After spending nearly two years of very happy service, he was compelled to return to his native land, nearly blind and much reduced through fever and nervous prostration. A rest of about nine months, native air, and proper medical treatment, under the blessing of God so far restored him that in March, 1881, he was engaged by General Carr Tate to do mission work among the poor and neglected in the villages near the town of Ryde, Isle of Wight. After numerous conversions, he finally resigned, and on the 29th of August,

1882, set sail for Canada. During the first five months' abode in this fair Dominion he supplied the Sparta and First Yarmouth churches, and for the next two-and-a-half years was pastor of the Barrie church. During this pastorate over 30 were baptized and $1500 of the debt paid off the church property. The next five years he was pastor of First Avenue Church, during which time seventy were baptized, the church membership more than doubled, and the present handsome edifice was built. His next pastorate was at Burgessville, where he laboured for two-and-a-half years; while here 28 were baptized and eight others received. In October, 1893, he resigned to come to Toronto, when he re-entered McMaster University to finish a four years Theology Course, begun in 1886, but unhappily broken through sickness and bereavement, from which he graduated in May of this year. His present charge is at Ossington Avenue, Toronto, which he assumed twelve months ago last March; during this time 21 have been added to the church.

JOHN McKINNON.

The subject of this sketch, John McKinnon, was born in the township of Greenock, Bruce Co., Ont. The years of his youth and early manhood were spent on his father's farm, where his strong physique was developed. The religious instruction received in his home early awakened in his mind serious thoughts of spiritual matters. He also had the benefit of the soul-stirring preaching of such men of God as Father Stewart, N. Sinclair, Elder Tapscott and others. It was not, however, until he reached the years of manhood that he fully trusted in Christ as his personal Saviour, and united with the church at Greenock. Even before his conversion he often thought of the work of the ministry, so it is not strange that immediately after his conversion he felt drawn to that calling. He at once engaged in such Christian work as Sunday School teaching, and leading prayer-meetings, and after a time attempted to preach. Seeing the need of further mental training he went for a short time to a public school, from which he passed the entrance to the High School. After spending a short time in Woodstock College, he entered Walkerton High School, where so many McMaster students from Bruce

Co. have studied, under the wise leadership and Christian influence of the principal, Mr. Jos. Morgan. Having spent two years at Walkerton, in the autumn of 1892 Bro. McKinnon came to McMaster to pursue a course of study in Theology. After three years of faithful work in that department he goes forth well prepared for his work. He has spent his vacations in successful missionary work. The summer of '93 he spent at Tobermory, North Bruce; and the following summer at Blue Mountain, in the Northern Association. His strong sympathy, and his fearless presentation of the truth, won for him the love and confidence of the people to whom he ministered. Our brother's gentle disposition, and beautiful Christian character, have won the affection and respect of all his fellow students. He goes forth to his work with a lofty conception of the spirit and character of the Christian ministry, possessing a love for souls, and unswerving loyalty to the truth. In his work with the Keady and Sullivan churches we predict for him even a greater measure of success than has attended his ministry elsewhere.

CHARLES SEGSWORTH.

Charles Segsworth, was born at Monck, in the Township of Luther, Wellington Co. His boyhood was spent on the farm where he was early trained to habits of industry. At the age of eighteen he left home, and after labouring with a farmer for the summer, began to prepare for entrance to the High School. In the autumn of 1888, he entered Orangeville High School, with a view towards qualifying for teaching. When about ten years of age, brother Segsworth was the subject of deep religious impressions, and was keenly sensible of his need of a Saviour, but it was not until the time of his attendance at Orangeville High School, that he dared call himself a Christian. Very soon after this his mind became exercised on the matter of baptism and church membership. Previous to this his sympathies were with the Methodist body, but a study of the Scriptures showed him that immersion of believers was the only baptism known to early Christians. At length he was convinced of his duty to be baptized and unite with those keeping the ordinances as they were delivered. He was baptized into the fellowship of the Orangeville Baptist Church by Rev. W. T. Tapscott, then of Brampton. In the spring of 1890, he went to Buffalo, and while there devoted his Sunday evenings to preaching to a small congregation on the outskirts of the city. The following autumn he went to Woodstock College, where he remained for two years. In 1892, he came to McMaster and began the English theological course which he has just completed. The summer months, during his college course at both Woodstock and McMaster were spent in pastoral work, so that he has had considerable practical experience. He was first led to think of the ministry by reading Stanley's travels in Africa. His heart was so stirred on becoming acquainted with the spiritual needs of that country, that he resolved to give his life to the work of foreign missions, if God would open the way. At present his work seems to be in the home field, though he still looks in the direction of foreign work. His is a true conception of the Christian ministry. He seeks not high things, but is ready to "endure hardness as a good soldier of Jesus Christ." His faithfulness and unselfishness, combined with strong common sense and sound judgment, are qualities which give promise of abundant success in the noble work to which he has given his life.

RALPH WILBERFORCE TROTTER.

Ralph Wilberforce Trotter, B.Th., is the youngest of the now famous Trotter brothers. He was born at Thurlaston, Leicestershire, Eng., Sept. 10th, 1865. The Trotter family came to Canada in 1870, and upon the death of the father, in 1874, removed to Woodstock, where they will ever be known and loved. At 12 years of age, Ralph was apprenticed to Messrs. J. and T. Grant, the largest boot and shoe firm in Woodstock. He served two or three years, and was then promoted to the management of a large branch shoe business in the store now occupied by J. White & Co. After two successful years he took the entire charge of Mr. Grant's outside business, and b came head traveller and buyer for Messrs. Sterling Bros., wholesale boot and shoe dealers. After six years of phenomenal success he resigned this position to enter Woodstock College in preparation for the ministry. Financial crises here met him and diverted his purpose,

2

so that he was forced to accept for a time a call to the church in Paris. This work of only a few months resulted in a large ingathering. When he left, the church presented him with a very appreciative address and a large purse. Recognizing his special fitness for new work, the Home Mission Board called him to undertake the newly-established mission at the Sault. Here in a very short time a church was erected and the membership increased from 13 to 84. His next work was with the Ossington Avenue Church, Toronto, while he was at McMaster; here 40 more were added in seven months. The Barrie pastorate followed, and for two and a half years he pursued his course in the college and did a great work. The membership quadrupled. The building had to be greatly enlarged. For 14 years the church had been receiving $350 a year from the Home Mission Board and was heavily in debt besides. In six months it was self-supporting, paying its pastor $900 a year and contributing largely to missions. The strain of so heavy a pastorate led to his resigning, and he accepted the call of the church in Lindsay. Here 43 were added to the church in a few months, and a new Sunday School erected which is a model of convenience and modern beauty. Here, also, he received ordination. Ralph Trotter is an outstanding man, he will never be a man of the ranks. Possessed with a more than ordinary share of enthusiasm, a freedom born of fearless conviction, with no undue reverence for established customs, his career has been brilliant. He is a most striking preacher—dashing, vivid, picturesque. He has a marvellous power of imaginative description. His themes are simple gospel themes, ever culminating in the cross. He does not aim at merely pleasing the eye or the ear, but ever points to Calvary as the only remedy for sin. That he should have succeeded in obtaining the degree of B.Th. under so many adverse circumstances is due to a keenness of intellect and excellent gifts which we are not afraid to predict will all be used in the service of the gospel. Immediately upon graduating he received a call to the pastorate of the first church in Victoria, B.C. A difficult work here awaits him, but already the newspaper reports are encouraging and promising. We expect to see Ralph win his way to eminence, as we are sure he will, not less by his splendid gifts than by his large, loving heart.

TO A FLOWER.

"I fain would know thy name
　My pretty little flower;
You look so cosy and so fair
　In your dainty little bower."

　　"*But wherefore know my name?*
　　　The rose smells just as sweet
　　To him who never chanced at all
　　　Its common name to meet."

"And yet, despite the word
　Of poet or of flower,
The thing without the name, I ween,
　Is scarcely in one's power."

　　"*The name without the thing*
　　　Is emptiness itself,
　　And only lays a useless weight
　　　On memory's burdened shelf"

"Not useless when I wish
　To tell my friend of thee;
With this supplied, 'tis easier far
　To do such courtesy.

"I wish to be your friend
　And you a friend to me,
And as my other friends have names
　I wish a name for thee."

　　"*If you will be my friend*
　　　And I thy friend may be,
　　If henceforth it be mutual joy
　　　Each other's face to see,

　　"*I'll gladly tell my name*
　　　Thy knowledge to complete,
　　And trust that oft in future days
　　　We may each other greet."

J. H. F.

INFLUENCE OF THE CRUSADES ON EUROPEAN CIVILIZATION.

I.

About the middle of the eleventh century, there was born in the town of Amiens in the French province of Picardy, a male child to whom was given the unpretentious name of Peter. In due time this child became a man; and being of good family was enlisted in the service of the neighboring Counts of Boulonge. But Peter was not content to abide under the galling yoke of military service, so left his sword and his wife as well, and retired to a hermitage to spend his time in meditation and prayer. It was a season of peculiar spiritual development. The Christianity of that day was largely tainted with a localizing spirit imported from the preceding heathenism, that led its adherents to attach special sanctity to certain places and scenes.

This tendency to associate incidents in the life of god or hero with some locality "is the most prominent characteristic of heathen religions," and Roman writers assure us that there was scarcely one such but had its votaries at Rome when that city was mistress of the world. The Egyptian Isis and Osiris, the Greek Sarpedon and Memnon, the Teutonic Baldur and Woden, and many others, were represented in the Western metropolis, when the "sect of the Nazarene" began to attract followers and make disciples.

It is not surprising that these people, coming into the profession of Christianity, should bring with them this propensity to reverence special places and events; and that the whole current of their desires should set in the direction of Palestine, every hill, valley and plain of which had been made sacred by the presence of the Son of Man.

Especially was this the case with regard to the cave of Bethlehem and the sepulchre at Jerusalem over which Constantine and his mother Helena had erected churches of elaborate architecture. This condition of the public mind made itself known by the frequent journeys of pilgrims to the "Holy Land," and each year saw thousands of persons toiling over land and sea to look with reverent eyes on the scene of the nativity, the

Garden of Gethsemane, the Mount of the Ascension, and the
place where the Lord lay.

As might be expected, the pilgrimage spirit reached Peter
in his retreat. It was to him a heavenly vision. He was not
disobedient unto it. With joy unspeakable he set out and found
himself at length with hundreds of others at the shrine of the
Christian Mecca. Alas! on what sad times had the disciples of
the true God fallen. What consternation and righteous wrath
did the hermit feel as he saw the outrages perpetrated by the
Turks, who for twenty years had been masters of Palestine !
the sanctuary defiled ; the Patriarch enslaved ; the pilgrims buf-
feted, humiliated, oppressed—these like irons entered into his
soul, and he vowed to God that he would rouse Christendom to
a sense of their enormity. One day while prostrated in the
Temple he thought the voice of the Lord called to him " Rise
Peter, go forth to make known the tribulations of my people !"
and Peter hastened to obey.

On his way home he visited the Patriarch Simeon. The
Prelate's tale was pitiful. " The nations of the West shall take
up arms in your behalf," said Peter, and from that day he became a preacher of the Crusades. On this errand he scaled
mountains, and descended into valleys; visited cities and traversed plains ; preached in pulpits, roads and market-places. The
appearance of the man is thus described by William of Tyre :
" Pusillus persona contemptibilis, vivacis ingenii, et oculum ha-
bens perspicacem gratumque, et sponte fluens ei non delrat elo-
quium." Notwithstanding these physical defects, the preaching
of this zealot moved the people mightily. They listened attentively to his story. They shared his indignation and his tears.
They vowed the direst vengeance on the infidel foe ; and as he
went from place to place, " a nerve was touched of exquisite feeling, and the sensation vibrated to the heart of Europe."

II.

No man, however capable of moving his fellow men, could
have brought about such a movement without the aid of some
higher power. The popular frenzy aroused l y the preaching of
Peter the Hermit, would soon have been dissipated like the foam
of a storm-lashed billow, had not some mightier agency been at

work organizing and shaping the general commotion into a definite and practical enterprise.

Such agencies had been operating for some twenty years before this (1074). Gregory VII., better known as Hildebrande, had issued a circular calling for the defence of the Holy Sepulchre and for the repelling of the Seljukian Turks then threatening the city of Constantinople.

Above and beyond the glory of contending for the faith there rose before the vision of Gregory the still more glorious prospect of bringing Nicephorus III. and Simeon the Patriarch under vassalage to Rome; thus making the Pope absolute lord of East and West. But such a plan with such a purpose touched no sympathetic chord in the public breast. What cared the Latin Christians for the woes of the Byzantine emperor or the distresses of the Patriarch? No religious associations had been awakened, no mention made of abominable outrages committed within the sanctuary, no harrowing description given of the sufferings inflicted upon the pilgrims, not a word uttered as to the merits that would accrue from a journey to the shrine. It is not surprising then that Hildebrande failed to see the West girding itself for conflict with the enemies of the faith.

Nevertheless the circular was not utterly fruitless. In 1081 Robert Guiscard, conqueror of Southern Italy and founder of the kingdom of Naples, set sail with a fleet of 130 ships and 30,000 men, and besieged Dyrrachium on the Adriatic. The fleet under Bohemund, Robert's son, was disastrously defeated, and but for the jealousy existing between Alexios, the supplanter of Nicephorus and Paleologus his general, the army had met a similar fate. Robert had scarcely rallied from these reverses when (1082) he was called home to defend the Pope from the armies of Henry IV. of Germany.

Bohemund continued the warfare in his father's stead and succeeded in over running Epirus and the Thessalian province of Larissa; but a lack of means compelled his return to Italy (1083) and Brienne, constable of Apula, was left as his deputy. The latter fared not well. Alexios forced him to raise the siege of Kastoria and bind himself to abandon the invasion of his dominions. Several months later Robert made another attempt to conquer the East. He besieged Corfu, pressed on to Cephalonia, and might have gained a foothold there but a greater foe than all, and one not to be resisted laid him low and snatched him out of life. Thus ended the futile measures projected by Gregory VII.

The next occupant of the Papal chair, Victor III., made a proclamation of war against the Mohammedan powers, attaching thereto a promise of forgiveness of sins for all who might enlist. But no enthusiasm was awakened. The only response was a piratical expedition made by the fleets of Genoa and Pisa, and the only result was a harvest of plunder reaped from the coasts of Northern Africa.

Eight years passed by. The Pontificate was contended for by Urban II. and Clement III. Latin Christendom sided with Urban, save Germany, where Henry and the clergy supported Clement ; and England, which under William II. remained neutral. Twice during the years 1088-1093 was the Bishop of Ravenna unseated and 1095 saw Urban victorious. Other questions—the celibacy of the clergy, the power of laymen to bestow benefices, the separation of the Greek and Latin churches—demanded his attention, and as a means of their settlement a council was called at Piacenza, capital of the Province of the same name, for March, 1095. Urban's popularity was evidenced by the fact that 200 bishops, 4,000 clergy, and 30,000 laymen responded to his summons. No building could afford standing room for so great a throng. Where could they assemble ? The plain surrounding the city spread its broad acres invitingly, the southern sun shone brightly, and out through the gates poured the multitude to encamp for seven days in solemn conclave.

Prominent among the delegates were the envoys of Alexios, come to plead the cause of their master. These pressed their suit vigorously. They described the pitiful condition of their land. They enlarged upon the jeopardy of their king. They finished their plea by urging the policy of checking the Turks, while yet far from the borders of Italy. The multitude heard them with a ready sympathy. The statesmen were moved by the last suggestion, the warriors were touched by the former ; all were ready to be led forth at once. Not so the Pope. There were internal feuds to be healed at home ; Henry IV. and the stubborn clergy must be brought to terms, and his own position made more secure. It was then with consummate shrewdness that he postponed a decision of the matter, and dismissed the ambassadors with a promise that Constantinople should not be forgotten on the way to Palestine.

The succeeding months were fully occupied with the above named tasks, and spring had ripened into summer and summer into autumn when another council met at Clermont, a city of Auvergne.

This convention was even more thronged than the former. The city was full and thousands of tents were pitched outside the walls to receive the overflow. If Urban had had any doubts as to the security of his position, he was certainly reassured now, for he saw coming to his support 13 archbishops, 225 bishops, 400 prelates, and a host of lay dignitaries from the adjoining countries. Eight days were consumed in disposing of various matters touching public and private conduct, and on the ninth day Urban ascended a scaffold in the market place to address the council on the one great topic that engrossed the attention of all.

His oration has been preserved by three writers; William of Tyre, William of Malmesbury, and an anonymous author whose manuscript is stored in the Vatican library. All three reports are substantially the same. The cowardice of the Turks contrasted with the courage of the warriors present. The physical inferiority of the barbarian plunderers of Syria was dwelt upon. The certainty of glory here and hereafter was emphasized. Sufferings would no doubt be the portion of many, but they would be light afflictions and not to be compared with the crown of martyrdom that would surely deck the brow of all who might die in defence of the sepulchre of their Lord. At this point a great shout went up. "Deus vult," cried the clergy in the pure Latin idiom ; " Diex el volt," echoed the laity in their provincial patois. "It is indeed the will of God," answered the speaker " and let these words be your watch-cry when you unsheathe " your swords against the enemy." At this the enthusiasm overleaped all restraints. Cheer upon cheer rent the air, and clergy and laity were commingled in one wild rush to receive the pontifical blessing and the red cross badge at the hands of the Pope.

The Bishop of Puy was chosen leader of the clericals, and

Raymond, Count of Toulouse, took command of the army; and the fifteenth of the following August was appointed as the day of the exodus. Then, as two streams unite to form the volume of a mighty river, so at the Council of Clermont, the deliberate planning of the Pope, and the vehement preaching of the Hermit combined in one torrent of enthusiasm that swept the nations through a series of nine savage wars, that stained the pages of history with blood, that drained nineteen states of six millions of their population, and wrought a radical change in the condition of all Europe.

III.

Coming to the consideration of the effects of the Crusades upon the progress of civilization, we find them naturally falling under three heads.

I. Commercial.

Long before the Crusades began, there had been a small trade established by returning pilgrims. Palestine was a sacred spot, any article coming from that land shared its sanctity. The pilgrim would bring home some token of his visit—a splinter of the true cross, a bone of the Apostle Peter, a shred from the robe of saint or martyr, a head of John the Baptist, a relic of the Virgin. It soon became apparent that these commanded a high price at home. Those who had been unable to see the Holy Land, were glad to own some of the articles that had come from there; and gradually a commerce had sprung up. Why stop at that? If old bones and splinters, nails and rags, sold readily, why not other commodities?

The trial was made and made successfully. Soon the pious though thrifty merchant combined religious and secular speculation and added to his store of relics such articles as silks, jewels and paper. Little by little the demands increased. Avenues of trade opened up, and the East began to pour its luxuries into the lap of the West. To this quiet and steady commerce the Crusades gave a great and sudden impetus. It is evident that large bodies of men and women cannot be moved from place to place without expense. True, the heedless rabble who followed Peter the Hermit and Walter the Penniless as the vanguard of the first Crusade, did not take that very essential fact into consideration, and

toiled amid untold sufferings from the banks of the Meuse and Mosette to the shores of the Bosphorus, the leaders of succeeding expeditions being forewarned contracted with the fleets of the above named cities for provisions and transportation from their own ports to Dalmatia on the Adriatic.   These contracts were largely accepted and regularly fulfilled.   Thus a strong impulse was given to the already lucrative carrying trade, and "the most destructive frenzy that ever befell the European nations became a source of opulence to these republics."

II.   Social.

The inception of the Crusades brought about a disturbance of the existing conditions of society that led to a complete break down of the feudal system.   A landed proprietor enlisting as a Crusader, must of necessity sell his fief and his peculiar privileges to supply the expenses of himself and his retainers.   In the majority of cases some speculator bought the one and the nearest community purchased the other.   In this way the numbers of petty lords and of small domains were materially decreased and property became concentrated in fewer hands.   If the baron retained his lands and came again to his castle, he lived in a much more social condition.   During the Crusades he had been followed by his own retinue or had attached himself to some more powerful princeling.   Through many a conflict or wearisome siege, over many a toilsome march had he gone with his comrades, learning all the while the value of human sympathy and companionship.   On his return this man would be unwilling to take up his old life of solitude, and would gather about him as many as possible of those who would be congenial spirits; people then began to draw nearer to one another and the old state of isolation gave way to something more like society.

Equally remarkable was the reflex action upon those who remained at home.   Passing through many cities larger and wealthier than they had left, the Crusaders could not but be made to feel the difference between their own rusticity and the refinement of their neighbors.   Their ideas would be enlarged, their prejudices uprooted, their eyes opened to a state of living and doing far above anything they had known.   Not only so, but the sojourn in foreign lands was in itself a process of education.   Rome, at that time a city of striking magnificence, was a favorite halting place for a large number who thus became spectators of its manners, customs, politics, and religion. In the East, Greece shed upon them the light of a civilization which though effete and waning "gave the Crusaders the impression of something more advanced than their own." Even on the battle-field they were brought face to face with the Musselman race, than which none could be found more elegant in manners, or possessed of a more graceful deportment; while the wealth displayed in the Saracen camp was in very truth dazzling. Impressions such as these were too vivid to be easily effaced; armies were continually passing to and fro; closer communications were opened up between countries heretofore mutually strange; and many adventurers returning home brought with them customs and comforts with which they had become familiar by a long residence abroad.

Accordingly we see, soon after the Crusades began, more splendor in the courts, more of pomp in public assemblies, more tas efulness in pleasures, and more romance in enterprises, pervading middle and southern Europe; and to these wild expeditions, the offspring of folly and superstition, are we indebted for the first influences that lifted European civilization out of the slough in which it had lain for centuries.

From this social upheaval there came liberty to the nations. During the two hundred years of crusading, the estates of the barons were divided or wasted, the feudal yoke gradually fell from the shoulders of men, and there was a general advancement in prosperity and in enlightenment. The Crusades over, the people were in no mood for submitting to the dictation of the nobility and began to form new municipalities in Italy, Germany, Flanders and elsewhere. In fact "the period of feudalism, picturesque and poetical in itself, and in many of its aspects, was incompatible with freedom; and its decline ushered in a new era of social and political enfranchisement."

III. Religious.

Ecclesiastically speaking, the feudal system had worked well. It had exercised the same disintegrating influence upon the church that was wrought upon society; so that while the nobles dwelt each upon his hilltop, the bishops, prelates and abbots isolated themselves in their several dioceses and monastries.

From this condition of affairs, abuses and disorders grew; " at no time was the crime of simony carried to a greater extent ; at no time were benefices disposed of in a more arbitrary manner; never were the morals of the clergy more loose and disorderly." The evil, however, began to work its own cure. The better portion of people and clergy were scandalized and there sprang up a desire for reform. But reform could come in only one way— there must be a central power about which the better feeling of the church itself could rally and which would be able to restrain those not so amenable to conscience. Some of the bishops, e. g., Claude of Turin, and Agobarde of Lyons, thought to become this authority for their own dioceses, but the attempt failed. There was but one organization in all the church able to cope with so great a task, and that was the See of Rome. With that task that See did cope, and " in the course of the eleventh century the church entered upon its fourth state, that of a theocracy, supported by monastic institutions"; reaching its full ascendancy under the pontificate of Gregory VII. Thus it came to pass that the Crusades began under the patronage of Rome ; and Rome was not slow to perceive in them a means of further enlarging her power.

(a). Increased wealth.

By a decree of the Council of Clermont the lands of all crusading noblemen were placed under the care of the church. In this way the church, or the Pope the head of the church, became the guardian of vast estates left solely at his own disposal. Of the many who thus entrusted property to the clerical power, hundreds died by the way, fell in wild charge on Saracen ranks, perished under the walls of some beleagured city or succumbed to the ravages of fever at Antioch, and never returned to claim their own. So through the two centuries during which this traffic continued, the church ever receiving and never giving, was the one speculator who never made a losing bargain ; but silently absorbed personal and landed property, estate, domain and fief, withdrawing them all from the jurisdiction of the sovereign and making of them a kingdom within a kingdom, owing allegiance to none but the occupants of the chair of Saint Peter at Rome.

(b). Personal power.

Still more despotic was the power gained over the persons

of men. The vows of the Crusaders were often taken under the pressure of remorse, illness, or misfortune; and were never carried out in any practical way. But the votary thus pledging himself was absolved from all civil and social allegiance and became the vassal of the Pope, bound to him by fetters of iron. As the years went by and the crusading frenzy maintained its power, the influence of the Pope continued to grow. The holy war was at first proclaimed as an avenue to salvation opened by God for those who could not see their way clear to taking the vows of monastic life; and this induced hundreds to enlist. From this it was but a step to preaching the Crusades as a duty binding on all the faithful, to neglect which was to be guilty of the grossest recreancy; and they would be few indeed who would dare refuse at least to adopt the badge, if not to enter upon active service. Thus the call to enlist became the test by which the Pope could determine the fidelity of any doubtful one and the means by which he enslaved all Christendom. In this way, and by these steps, there grew up in Europe a hierarchy having its roots in every soil and drawing its life from every land—a priestly kingdom that more and more enslaved the minds of men until it was opposed by the Monk of Erfurt and crushed by the slow but sure grinding of the wheels of the Reformation.

(c). The sending of Legates.

Heretofore a prelate of fame and rank had occasionally been sent to attend a council, investigate a controversy, arbitrate a dispute, or negotiate with a sovereign; on every occasion invested with full papal authority. But such had been the exception, not the rule. The Crusades however afforded plausible excuse for sending special legates into all countries for the purpose of preaching, recruiting, and gathering contributions. Gradually the public became accustomed to seeing the representative of the Pope everywhere. to hearing his voice and feeling his authority in all enterprises, and soon that authority was considered supreme. The contributions became a tax, the call to arms a threat, the appeal to enlist a demand, and the " Vicar of God " was liege lord of Latin Christendom. As the Crusaders conquered Palestine, sees were established there. When the Mohammedans recaptured the land the bishops ruling those dioceses fled to Rome. Having been invested with episcopal authority and being without territory, they were appointed "in partibus fidelium" and sent as vicars-general to foreign powers; an office of great importance to the Pope; and one that gave him unlimited opportunities for diplomatic interference. Slowly and insidiously did this power advance; step by step were the precincts of national liberty invaded; little by little did this paralysing influence creep ever nearer and nearer the national heart; until the life blood of freedom well nigh ceased to circulate. The Crusades now made the Western world subject to the Pontiff. The taxation of the clergy on his authority could not be refused. A tenth of all the wealth of the hierarchy passed through his hands. By the year 1200 we find him arbiter of the nations.

(d). Familiarity with war.

The Crusades exerted a far-reaching influence by accustoming the European nations to the waging of war, and by throwing about the most cruel of bloodshed the glamour of piety. When the first Crusades went out their mission was truly one of defence. They were truly actuated by a desire to rescue the Sepulchre from those who were profaning it. The Saracens had been for centuries the aggressors. The genius of Islam was fierce and intolerant warfare against all who did not receive the Koran and bow to the authority of the Prophet. In this spirit the Moslems had swept from land to land until Arabia, Asia, Persia, Africa, Egypt, India, Spain, had been subdued; the Holy Land conquered, and the Mediterranean covered with their fleets. Their presence in any country meant subjugation and degradation to the inhabitants thereof, and it is not surprising that the very name of Mahomet became a synonym of scorn and hatred. "But it is easier in theory than in fact to draw the line between wars for the defense and for the propagation of the faith, and the Crusaders had not begun before they were diverted from their declared object—before they threw off all pretence to be considered defensive warriors." If one class of foes should be exterminated why not another? If the Saracen, why not the Jew? So with the remembrance of years of extortion rankling in their hearts these soldiers of the Cross fell upon the Jewish populations of Germany and along the Rhine, and put them to frightful massacre, at Verdun, Treves, Maintz, Spires and Worms.

As time went by the distinction between foes became more and more obliterated, and heretics began to be regarded as legitimate objects of attack. The decrees of the Pope letting loose the soldiery against the Albigenses, the Waldenses, the Lollards, and the other schismatics, were backed by public sentiment; and there had begun a refulfilment of our Lord's words, "The time cometh when whosoever killeth you will think that he doeth God service." From the attacking of communities it was but a step to the persecution of individuals. When that point was reached the Inquisition became a fact. It did not take the Pope long to see that here was a means of crushing opposition. Let the refractory subject, or any one who had dared to thwart the plans of the Pontiff or to hinder the encroachments of Rome, be once declared an enemy to the church, and it became the duty of the faithful Catholic to take up arms against him. So went Philip of France against John of England. Nay, more; the intention of the word "crusade" was broadened until it included all non-catholics, and with the enlarged meaning of the word as a cloak, Cortes invaded Mexico, the Duke of Alva attacked the Netherlands, and Philip II. sent out the Armada. Thus for five centuries the history of Europe was a perpetual crusade; and out of the defence of the Sepulchre grew the idea that war was not only praiseworthy but obligatory if waged against one who was on any pretence whatever accused of idolatry, infidelity, heresy, or the slightest opposition to the church of Rome.

The question presents itself, were the Crusades beneficial or hurtful in their results? This question has been variously answered as different writers have fixed their attention upon different facts. The main arguments for the negative seem to be the drainage of men and money of which they were the cause, the sudden occasion of power given to the Papacy, and the fanatical zeal developed in the minds of men. But on the other hand it must be remembered that the continent was relieved of no little amount of social congestion in the persons of restless spirits who, being drawn off and employed abroad were prevented from working mischief at home; that the financial loss was more than compensated by the opening up of the avenues of trade ; and that the spirit of enterprise remained long after the fanaticism had died away.

Moreover, it cannot be disputed that these expeditions brought to a semi-barbarous people a desire for the refinement of civilized life; they hastened the day of intelligent self-government; they broke the power of feudal tyranny, and delivered society from the cast-iron rigidity in which it had lain bound for centuries.   In a word, they opened the prison houses of mediæval darkness, and set free the forces of enlightenment and of progress to lay the foundation of the Europe of the Revival of Learning, the Europe of the Reformation, and the Europe of the Nineteenth Century.

P. K. Dayfoot.

THE ELEMENTS OF TRUE CULTURE.

I would have you notice that the topic on which it is my privilege to speak is the elements of *true* culture.   There is a false, a spurious culture abroad; a culture that finds its highest satisfaction in quoting Emerson and Browning without any real understanding of the philosophy of the one or the poetry of the other; a culture in which there is much profession of refinement, whether there is any possession or not ; a culture that is past master of the art of bowing and smiling, though the smiler may be one of the most vulgar of creatures at heart ; a culture that is well and truly called " polish," for that after all is what it is.   With this superficial thing we have nothing to do—our search is after the genuine commodity ; and the elements that enter into its composition and by which its genuineness may be easily tested are not far to seek.   True culture is :—

1.   Thorough.—The etymology of the word will teach us that Culture is from the Latin ' colere ' to till, and involves the idea of deep soil ploughing in the mental field.   Culture and agriculture are alike, in that they both demand a going down beneath a surface, a turning up the sod, an exposing of the underside to the fructifying influences of heat, light and moisture.   In

3

the light of this fact it will become evident that one may be truly cultured without being filled like a dictionary with a mass of unorganized, disconnected facts. There are men and women who imagine that in order to be cultured people they must be walking encyclopædias, store houses of information concern'ng every subject under the sun, but having no exhaustive knowledge of anything.

This is a mistake peculiar to these days, when the morning paper in a single issue discusses all manner of subjects, from Home Rule and the last war scare in Europe, to Theosophy and the latest Ethical theory ; but it is a mistake nevertheless. From the days of Aristotle until now the most truly cultured have been those who first of all have secured a thorough knowledge of some one department of human learning. Compare the curriculum of the Collegiate Institute of to-day with that of a University in the days of Roger Bacon, and John Wycliffe, and the list would include many topics unheard of by scholars of that time ; yet we in this age are establishing ourselves upon the deep and solid foundations which they so carefully laid.

It is possible for each one of us to attain to this culture. I know all about the difficulty of prosecuting one special line of research amid the many demands that our life work will make upon us. I know also the possibility of the careful gathering up of fragments of time that generally lie neglected in the working hours of each day, and the using of them for the cultivation of some particular subject.

The busiest of people do this. Mr. W. R. Meredith is an accomplished French scholar and is rarely without a French author in his pocket. I should like to hear Dr. McCook, of New York, preach on the text "Go to the ant, thou sluggard," for in the midst of a busy pastorate he has found time to cultivate an intimate acquaintance with the various species of ants. Hugh Miller, while his fellow stone-masons were drinking beer or sleeping off the effects of it, spent his nights and mornings studying the rocks until he became one of the first geologists of the United Kingdom. It is astonishing what we can accomplish when we set ourselves with full purpose of mind in any one direction.

II. INCLUSIVE.—It must include :— (1) An acquaintance

with various branches of knowledge. While it is true that the ideally cultured person is thoroughly conversant with some one department of learning, it is also true that this specialty should be supplemented by a general knowledge of those events and facts that are of most importance in the time in which that person lives. That a theologian should know all about Church History and nothing of British History ; that a physician should be perfectly acquainted with Medical Science and hardly know the names of the standard English authors; that a lawyer should be versed in Blackstone, Coke, and Lorimer's Institutes, and be ignorant of the social movements of his day ; that any one should f il to be in touch with current events, argues a most imperfect culture ; a culture that will be seriously crippled in the attempt to make an impression upon its own generation. Yet there are those—we have all met them—who have surprised us by the lamentable darkness of their minds as to the commonest happenings of the day. Herein lies one difference between the culture of the Old World and that of the New. In the older countries men : un more to specialism. If a man is a soldier, he can march and countermarch and poise a musket without diverging by a hair's breadth from the proper angle; but put him in the fie d and ask him to build a cabin to shelter him from the storm and he is helpless. The same principle obtains even among those matchless specialists, the German Professors, who know all that can be known about Hebrew or Greek, Metaphysics or Electricity, and are hopelessly, helplessly ignorant outside their own department. Without boasting, we may claim to have avoided that mistake in America. We recognize the fact that the foreigners of fifty years ago are our neighbors today : that the Atlantic and Pacific are joined by iron bands ; that London, England, is distant less than a week's sail ; that a midsummer holiday now includes a trip round the world, and that the journey has actually been made in fifty-six days. Not content with communication on land and sea, we have got beneath the sea, and the cable will bring a message from India, with all its changes and repetitions, in a little less than two hours. To be without a working knowledge of the transactions in progress all about us would be to hermitize one's self, and the day demands a generation of people all alive to the questions of world-wide

interest. I repeat the statement, that we in America recognize
this demand and respond to it. The average man here is a well
informed man; he has an interest in all that transpires in his
own land, and also in the important questions of other lands;
and by so much has American culture the advantage of European culture.

(2) It must include a developing of all parts of the man.
Man is a threefold being. He is a living illustration of the doctrine of the Trinity. He consists of body, intellect and spirit.
An ideal culture develops all three parts of man's being, just as
a perfect tilling of a field will plough and harrow the fence corners and the hillocks as well as the plain open area. Yet how
one-sided is much of the culture of to-day! John L. Sullivan's
body is so perfectly cultured that he is exhibited on the stage as
a model of physical manhood. As for his intellect and spirit,
who ever heard if he possessed them? Thomas Carlyle's intellect was mighty, his body was racked with dyspepsia, and as to
his spiritual being, let the story of his domestic life be its own
witness. General Gordon's spiritual faculty was abnormally
developed (if such be possible). He was all heart. His physique
was but ordinary, and his mental powers were erratic and un-
governed in the extreme. These are pre-eminent examples of
what can be seen every day. The ordinary individual is like
Ephraim, of whom Hosea says, that he was a "cake not turned,"
—one side of his nature was raw. We shall all be Ephraims
unless we guard ourselves.

Look now at a specimen of symmetrical, inclusive culture.
I refer to Dr. Phillips Brooks of Boston. Physically, he towers
like Saul above his brethren. Intellectually, he is unsurpassed
in the Episcopalian ministry. Spiritually, he is a king among
men. Such is complete culture. It is "perfect and entire, wanting nothing."

III. REFINED.—So essential is this quality, that the words
"culture" and "refinement" are fast becoming synonyms in our
language, and the ideas they convey are becoming identical in
our thought. One may be scholarly, but if his scholarship be
not adorned by the graces of a refined nature, he will be but a
vulgar fellow after all. Samuel Johnson was the leader of public sentiment in his day, and by all odds the intellectual giant of

his time; but he was far from being cultured. How could he be worthy the name, when his gluttony in eating, his untidiness in dress, and his boorishness in manner made him an object of dread to every one save a few who, like Boswell, worshipped at the shrine of his genius?

Now, refinement is the attractive element of culture. A diamond is a valuable stone always and everywhere; but not until it has been cut and drilled and polished to the highest degree of brilliancy is it considered worthy a golden setting, and a place upon the hand of beauty.

So with men. Learning and ability command appreciation at all times; but the character in which they inhere is dull and lustreless, without form or comeliness, until it is made to reflect the light of true refinement.

I need hardly remind you that the fountain of all refinement is a pure heart. Given that, and the refined disposition will show itself, however unfavorable the surroundings may be. In the wildernesses of Eastern Ontario, amid swamps and woods, I have met people as truly refined in speech and sentiment as though they had been reared in king's houses and had worn purple and fine linen all their days. Indeed the revelations of the past summer, show beyond a doubt, that an entrance to the Queen's drawing room is no guarantee of a refined spirit; and the expositions of the doings in high life in all lands assure us that the upper crust of the social pie is quite likely to be as unpalatable as the lower.

In conclusion, I would say that the spring of all the best culture the world has ever seen is found in the word of God. Look where you will, that is apparent. Go to the library. There you have "Milton's Paradise Lost," every line of which is saturated with Biblical thought. There is Spenser's "Faerie Queene," and the heroic Red Cross Knight is but an incarnation of Paul's Christian soldier, described in Eph. 6: 11, 17. There is Cowper's "Task," and any one acquainted with Isaiah's prophecy will recognize the imagery of the prophet in the language of the later poem. There is Wordsworth, and his "Ode on Immortality," is an echo of the 15th chapter of I Cor. There is Shakespeare, and his Lady Macbeth is Jezebel the wife of Ahab arrayed in modern garb, while his profoundest utterances are as might be expected, they had cause for bitter repentance when they found themselves in a hostile country, all supplies cut off, and hundreds of their companions perishing of fever, famine and war. Those who followed took warning by the "long line of bones that whitened the road through Hungary to the East," and learned that though bent on a sacred errand they could not expect to be fed like the ravens nor clothed like the lilies of the field; but that he who went upon this mission would do well to count the cost and be prepared to pay it. How was this to be done? The only persons capable of raising money were the noblemen and the possessors of fiefs. The peasantry and serfs who composed the remainder of the social fabric were but dependents on the bounty of their masters. The nobility, then, were compelled to mortgage their lands in order to fit out their expeditions, purchase arms and horses, and supply members of their retinue. The private adventurer, too, must have coin with which to procure his Milan and Damascus steel, make provision for transport and raise a fund for his maintenance while abroad.

There were not wanting those who were ready to supply all pecuniary needs. The Jews were always on hand to pawn or purchase. The cautious traders, the keen-eyed brokers, the small land-owners, anxious to broaden their acres, frugal nobles, and even kings, were not slow to seize the opportunity of gain. Thus Rufus of England for the sum of 10,000 marks bought the Norman dukedom of his brother Robert, and many a smaller domain changed hands in an altogether unlooked for manner. But a more important result was the immediate harvest reaped by the civic republics of Venice, Genoa, and Pisa; which cities formed the main trade centres of Italy. Of these Venice ranked first; excelling her rivals in the size and numbers of fleets, the skill and boldness of her sailors, the energy and enterprise of her merchants. This city was then in the best position to profit by the opportunities the Crusades afforded; and to such purpose did she use these opportunities, that after the fall of Constantinople, Dandolo the nonegenarian Doge became ruler of Romania the carrying trade was virtually monopolised by her citizens and the islands of the Levant became filled with Venetian princes. The others, however, were not far behind. After the first army of 22,000 horse and foot under Godfrey of Bouillon had reflections of scriptural truths. There is Walter Scott, and who is his famous Meg Merrilies, but the Witch of Endor whose story is told in I Samuel 28th chapter ? John Bunyan's "Pilgrims Progress" is now an English classic, but a greater John than the Bedford preacher first saw the vision 2000 years ago and gave us the record of it in the book of Revelation.

Let us sit in the music hall and listen to the compositions of the great masters. What do we hear ? Handel's "Messiah," Haydn's "Creation," Mozart's "Twelfth Mass," Bach's "Five Passions," all based upon scripture narrative. Let us visit the art galleries. What are these marvellous paintings before which the people stand in throngs enraptured ? Raphael's "Madonna," Angelo's "Last Judgment," Murrillo's "Descent from the Cross," Da Vinci's "Last Supper," Gabriel Max's "Christ before Pilate," not one of which would ever have been produced but for the inspiration of the four gospels. Read the master pieces of the time in the writings of John Ruskin, James Anthony Froude, John Bright, Thomas Macaulay, and there you find the strong, vigorous, yet simple Saxon of the English Bible ; and it is no secret that these men made that book their model of a pure and cultivated style.

Such then is true culture—thorough, inclusive, refined, inspired and developed by that power for all good, the word of God. May such culture be ours ; and if we would find an example of its fullness, let us seek it in the man Christ Jesus of Nazareth whom one writer has well described as "The truest gentleman the world has ever seen."

D.

EDITORIAL NOTES.

Following the example of last year, the McMASTER MONTHLY again devotes a large share of the June number to biographical notes of the recent graduates in Arts and Theology. It is hoped that this feature will prove even more acceptable than last year, as the notes have been prepared with more care and no effort has been spared to secure variety of treatment. Mr. Dayfoot's essay on the Crusaders is the result of long and patient reading and very careful writing, and has been spoken of already by several who have read it in manuscript as a remarkable production. We bespeak for it many readers and careful study.

Friends of the University can materially aid our Faculty and students by making donations of books to the University library. Many of our readers have duplicate copies of valuable books, and these, while of little use to them, might be of very great service to us. Others have bound and unbound copies of the leading magazines and reviews. Our files of the *Forum, Nineteenth Century, North American, Contemporary, Edinburgh, Blackwood's, Westminster* and the *Quarterly* are incomplete and any gift that would help to complete them would be gladly received. Old magazines are, for the most part, consigned to the dusty recesses of the library in the home and are seldom or never opened. In the University, however, they are, in many cases, both interesting and valuable. We doubt not but that many of our students know of collections of books out of which, without detriment to the owners, donations might be made to the University. It is to be hoped that they will not forget our needs, and that they will therefore lose no opportunity of supplying them. Much might be done in this way.

WHEN one looks at the handsome and comfortable rooms in all departments of Woodstock College to-day, at its well-filled library, its splendid apparatus for scientific pursuits, at its long and generous prize list, its complete manual training facilities, and the wonderful results thereof, and knows something of the spirit of the young men who filled the College chapel at the recent closing exercises, one cannot help thinking that now are the "palmy days" rather than some decades ago, when there were good men and women, to be sure, and some of the noblest of teachers in the class-rooms, but when class accommodation or scientific apparatus reminded one of the luxuries of the old-time district school. The College of to-day, so magnificently equipped at every point, sending out from year to year its large graduating classes of earnest and thoroughly trained Christian young men, is surely a possession of which all Canadian Baptists should be proud, and use every effort to take advantage, either for themselves or for any whom they can persuade to attend its classes. Every young Baptist in Ontario and Quebec should have the privilege of living for a time in the Christian atmosphere and amid the hallowed associations of Woodstock College.

"MOULTON COLLEGE is doing splendid work," appears to have been the unanimous testimony of those who attended the various closing exercises recently conducted in Bloor Street Baptist chapel. So long as the present high standard in all departments is maintained, Moulton will continue, as in past years, to draw students from all denominations in every province of the Dominion. The number of Baptist parents who think they can afford their daughters the exceptional privileges of attendance at the art and music classes, and of life in the healthy Christian atmosphere of Moulton College, is, of course, comparatively limited, but that number is bound to increase with better times and the rapid improvement in the desires and tastes of the people everywhere. Even now there are Baptist parents in every county and town in Ontario who can well afford their girls such an education as is alone worth paying for, namely, the very best that can be had for the outlay ; and if these would patronize their own institution, its halls would soon be crowded. This they certainly will do, once they realize that only such a high quality of instruction as Moulton affords will enable their girls to do themselves justice in such positions in life as they may reasonably expect to fill some day. What matter then a few extra dollars, when it is a question of giving them the one opportunity in life of making the very most of their natural endowments ?

COLLEGE NEWS.

MOULTON COLLEGE.

THE closing exercises of the College were largely attended throughout and pronounced by all to be highly interesting. The weather was delightfully cool, a great relief after the extreme heat of the previous weeks, when the students were undergoing the strain of written examinations. The work has gone on very smoothly and earnestly during the past year and the papers show that creditable results have been accomplished.

On the afternoons of Thursday and Friday, the 6th and 7th days of June, the work of the students in the Art Department was inspected by the friends of the College. Mrs. Dignam is to be congratulated upon the marked progress which was shown to have been made under her able instruction.

On Friday evening the College chapel was crowded, when a Recital was given under the direction of Miss Hart. Special mention must be made of the " Tableaux Mouvants," which were heartily encored. The enunciation of those who gave recitations was very distinct and pleasing. The entire entertainment reflected great credit upon the performers and their teacher.

THERE are three musical graduates this year, Miss Carrie Fisher, Miss Isabel Matthews and Miss Lily Pollard These gave a piano recital on Saturday afternoon before a delighted audience. Their success and the pleasure they gave to their many friends must have been full recompense for the many hours of practising.

THE sermon before the graduating class was preached in the Bloor St. Baptist Church, on Sunday evening, June 9th. On this occasion more than ordinary interest was felt, as the speaker, the Rev. T. S. Johnson, pastor of the First Baptist Church, of Brantford, was the father of one of the members of the Class of '95. His text was " None of us liveth unto himself " (Romans xiv : 7), and the discourse which followed was appropriate and inspiring.

ON Monday evening about sixty of the students of the College, under Miss Smart's leadership, gave the beautiful cantata, " The Lady of Shalott." The music, so fittingly set to the words of the poem, is by Bendall. The chief solo, wherein the climax of the theme is reached, was sung by Miss Smart most acceptably. Other solo parts were taken by Misses Johnson, Boehmer and Taylor. The very efficient manner in which the choruses were rendered, revealed careful, painstaking training. The accompaniment was played by Miss Helmer, a former student, who has given valuable assistance on other occasions and is always welcomed heartily.

ON Tuesday afternoon the Alumnæ Society met in the College chapel and celebrated the first anniversary of its birthday. The programme was most enjoyable.

The officers for the ensuing year are : President, Miss Carrie Porter, Vice-President, Miss M. E. Dryden ; Secretary, Miss Bessie Newman ; Treasurer, Miss Gertrude Scarfe. Executive Committee, Miss Pollard, Miss Edith Wilkes, Miss Maud Holmes.

THE Bloor Street Church was beautifully decorated on Tuesday night, the occasion of the greatest interest when the graduating exercises took place. The class numbered twelve, six in the Matriculation course, two in the English Scientific, one in the Modern Language, and three in the Musical course. In the programme which is given below, one number is omitted, namely, the address by the Principal. Miss Fitch, in well-chosen words, gave a most heart-felt farewell speech to the young ladies who just a few moments before had received their diplomas. The entire audience must have been profited by her elevating and ennobling remarks. The music, which was under Mr. Vogt's direction, was given by members of the Jarvis St. choir and was very appropriate and pleasing. Short sketches of our graduating class follow.

PROGRAMME.

Processional March.

Prayer.

Quartette,   .   .   .   "Sun of my Soul."   .   .   .   .   Holden
MISSES JAMES AND LUGSDIN, MESSRS. LYE AND DAVIES.

Essay, ...   "The Jew in Fiction."
ETHEL M. BOTTERILL.

Essay, ...   "Excalibur."
REBECCA R. DUBENSKY.

Essay, ...   "National Emblems."
AMELIA A. IRVINE.

Trio, ...   "Praise ye the Lord."   .   .   .   Geibel
MISS FINDLEY, MESSRS. LYE AND DAVIES.

Essay,   .   .   "The Days of the Spinning Wheel."
EDITH L. JOHNSON.

Essay,   .   .   .   "The Value of Expression."
LILLIA M. KIRK.

Essay,   .   "The Golden Age of the Hebrew Monarchy."
MARGARET M. LAIDLAW.

Quartette,   .   .   .   "Even Me."   .   .   .   .   Warren
MISSES JAMES AND ROSEBRUGH. MESSRS. LYE AND DAVIES.

Essay, ...   "It is the Fashion."
OLIVE C. MATTHEWS.

Essay,   .   .   .   "An Obsolete Commandment."
MARGARET M. POLLARD.

Essay,   ,   .   .   "The Gifts of Florence."
F. MAUD HOLMES.

Presentation of Diplomas.

Sextette,   .   .   .   "List, the Cherubic Host."   .   .   .   Gaul
MISSES FINDLEY, JAMES, PLUMTREE, LUGSDIN AND ROSEBRUGH,
AND MR. DAVIES.

Benediction.

THE GRADUATING CLASS OF MOULTON COLLEGE.

ETHEL MARION BOTTERILL.—Ethel's home is in Glenolden, Penn. After three years of faithful work, she has successfully completed the Matriculation course. Her forte is English Literature and our "Heliconian" will sorely miss her bright little paragraphs. However, we are hoping that the autumn months may again find her here pursuing her studies at McMaster.

REBECCA HARPER DUBENSKY.—Rebecca is our little English girl. We have had among us representatives from many parts of the globe, but it is not often that our graduating class has had a member from merry old England. Moulton has been Rebecca's home for five years, during which time she has steadily climbed through each year of our course from the preparatory to the graduating class.

FLORENCE MAUD HOLMES.—As a boarder and as a day pupil we have known Maud. Her home is in Toronto, and her school life for four years has been spent at Moulton. Her work has always been well and faithfully done, and she has, now in leaving College, won the honor that her hard work and earnest efforts so richly deserve.

AMELIA ANNIE IRVING.—We welcomed Miss Irvine, a Lobo girl, among us at Christmas, when she took examinations for entrance into the fourth year of the graduating class. During the six months intervening, she has done admirable work, having, against so many difficulties, very successfully passed her final examinations.

EDITH LYNETTE JOHNSON.—"Work while you work, and play while you play," might be said to have been Edith's motto during her Moulton life. Study hour found her doing earnest work, but she was always among the first to enter into College fun when the close of the hour was announced. Brantford has always been kind to Moulton, and each year as someone goes away, we feel we have lost, as in Edith, a bright and earnest spirit.

LILLIA MILDRED KIRK.—In Lillia, we have a representative of Bracebridge, Muskoka. She has been in Moulton for three years, and during that time has been absorbed in her work. Those of us, who have been visited by la grippe and other maladies, will remember Lillia with very kindly feeling, for the ever-ready and cheerful care she always had for those in need.

MARGARET MAY LAIDLAW.—Margaret came to Moulton from her home in Sparta, two years ago, and now leaves us, after completing the fourth year of the English Scientific course. During her stay here, she has won a warm place in the hearts of all by her kind and genial manner, and the strong stand she has always taken for the right and honorable.

OLIVE CLARA MATTHEWS.—This year we have three Toronto girls in our graduating class, and Olive is, one. Her life amongst us has been that of a day pupil, and we all feel that, though sometimes as boarders we do not become so well acquainted with those from outside, we have found in Ollie a very pleasant and kind friend.

CAROLINE MARY FISHER.—Carrie comes from Wingham, and has spent two years here. Next year we shall miss those charming strains of music, which have all this year descended from Carrie's music room, regularly and promptly at every practice period. In her musical studies, she has been wonderfully successful, and has in the midst of it all, by her quiet, modest manner, endeared herself to her fellow-students.

MARGARET MAY POLLARD.—May is another Toronto girl, and day pupil. With her, too, our intercourse has been of the most pleasant character. She has studied long and well in Moulton and now we congratulate her upon achieving the prize which she so well deserved.

ANNIE ISABEL MATTHEWS.—Of all our musical graduates, we are more than proud, for we feel they have done such good work. Every day for hours at a time we might hear Isabel's piano overhead; but always, even after a hard day of practice and lessons, she never failed to have a pleasant smile for her interested friends.

ELIZABETH POLLARD.— This is Lillie's second experience as a Moulton graduate. Last year she passed the Matriculation examination, and now has completed the Musical course. We will miss Lillie and our other graduates next year in our literary and musical programmes, for they were always ready to lend cheerful and valuable assistance.

CLOSING AT WOODSTOCK.

The Commencement this year began with the annual sermon to the graduating class on the evening of Sunday, June 2nd. Rev. W. H. Cline, B.A., B.D., was the preacher, and the sermon was clear, impressive, and in every way suitable to the occasion.

On Monday at 4 p. m. the alumni and alumnæ with many friends from the town gathered in the beautiful dining-hall of the College for the annual collation. After dinner two and a half hours were pleasantly and profitably spent in speech and song.

In the evening at 8 o'clock the annual public meeting of the Association took place. Several questions of public and denominational interest were ably discussed by speakers chosen for the occasion. A short time was allowed for free discussion of each question, and in this way valuable information was elicited, and the interest maintained.

On Tuesday morning at 10 o'clock a large audience assembled to enjoy the graduating exercises proper. The class of '95 was unusually large, and was well represented by the several essayists. The competition in public speaking was spirited and much enjoyed; the prize winners were many and were much applauded by their fellows. D. E. Thomson, Esq., in a few appropriate words presented the prizes to the winners. Principal Bates spoke to the class in a brief but beautiful farewell address. Rev. Dr. Dadson, on behalf of the Senate, presented the diplomas of the University. Our returned missionary, Rev. H. F. Laflamme, and other friends, were heard with much pleasure.

It would be unfair to close without mentioning the beautiful service of music and song provided for all the meetings; what with the College quartette, the choruses, the orchestra, and especially the Whyte Brothers, it was a continual feast of song.

The following, having passed the required examinations, were presented with Diplomas :—

David Bovington, Charles M. Clarke, Joshua Knechtel, Archie M. MacDonald, John C. McFarlane, Harley C. Newcombe, Thomas Scarlett, Freeman J. Scott, Benjamin R. Simpson, Thomas A. Surtees, William B. Tighe, Arthur John Thompson, Alexander W. Torrie, James Weir, George W. Welch, David C. Welch.

The following awards of scholarships and prizes were made :—

General Proficiency Prizes—Third Year—(The Hiram Calvin Scholarship)—D. Bovington. Second Year—(The S. J. Moore Scholarship)—S. E. Grigg and Wm. H. Walker (equal). First Year (Senior)—First Prize—Frank H. Phipps ; Second Prize—Herbert Arkell. First Year (Junior)—First Prize—De Loyd Schell ; Second Prize—Sam. McLay and Wm. Pembleton (equal).

Preparatory—First Prize—W. Damen and C. Mara (equal).

Manual Training Prizes—(Senior Year)—Gold Medal, S. J. Whittaker ; Silver Medal, A. W. Canfield. Middle Year—First Prize—Clarke Wallis ; Second Prize—Richard Guyatt. Junior Year—First Prize—E. Scarlett ; Second Prize—A. N. Wolverton.

Special Prizes.—Prize for Drawing—D. Bagshaw. First Prize for Essay Writing—G. R. Welch ; Second Prize—H. C. Newcombe. Prize for Public Speaking—W. F. Spidle.

JOSHUA Knechtel came to us from the town of Hanover. His course all through has been very creditable. Last year he was gold medalist in manual training, and we can always feel assured that while he is not given to making a commotion, accurate thorough intelligence will characterize everything he does.

EDGAR Wenger claims the northern town of Ayton as his home. He came to Woodstock as a very small boy and his development, both mental and physical, has been very marked. Edgar is a born engineer and the electrical apparatus, in the construction of which he has whiled away many a pleasant leisure hour in College, gives promise that we will hear honorable mention of his name in the future.

FREEMAN J. Scott is a graduate of Aylmer, C. I. After passing the Senior Leaving Examination, he taught very successfully for a year or two near his own home, Sparta, Ont., and at the beginning of this year came to Woodstock. While here he has given attention chiefly to the study of the ancient classics, but he has at the same time acquired a reputation for thorough scholarship, oratory and good fellowship.

CHARLES M. Clarke hails from Aylmer, where he studied for some time in the Collegiate Institute. His stay in Woodstock has been brief—only one year—but sufficient to gain for him a warm place in our affections. We wish him a prosperous course through McMaster University.

ORAN E. Kendall is a native of Quebec. After spending a number of years in the United States he made his home in New Westminster, B. C. Though not taking the regular matriculation work, he is a member of the third year class and intends to study theology in McMaster next year. Nothing truer could be said of him than the following remark made by one of his classmates a few days ago : "He is one of the truest men I ever met." During his three years in the College he has gained the respect and esteem of teachers and students alike. All wish him that success which his persevering energies deserve. Woodstock is proud of her 1895 presentation to McMaster.

D. E. WELCH is a Brantford boy. He started in the Preparatory Department and has each year made an advance step till now he leaves us to continue his studies in McMaster University. There are only two other students in the school who have been in attendance an equal length of time. We are sorry that the failure of his sight has hindered him in his work, and we hope that after the summer's rest he may be able to pursue the course he has mapped out. Where shall we find his successor in the sports of the College?

GEORGE R. WELCH was born in London, England, and is proud of his native land. Before coming to Canada he had been for a short time a pupil teacher in the London Public Schools. His first Canadian home was in London, Ontario, but he soon followed Greeley's advice and went West, and made his home in New Westminster, B. C. He has been three years in the College, and has proved himself a successful student pastor during two vacations. His earnestness of purpose and devotion to duty are sure to make his life a true success. We shall miss him, especially in the musical and literary exercises of the College.

J. T. JONES.—John T. Jones is a Toronto boy. John came to Woodstock three years ago, and since then has proved himself a worthy student. He has made thorough and rapid progress in his studies, nor is it too much to say that he has ever stood among the foremost in his work. We wish him good success in all his future work, and rest assured that he will acquit himself with honor.

A. K. SCOTT.—Albert was born away in Minnesota about twenty-five years ago. His has been a somewhat chequered career, but the ills of life have been unable to disturb the calmness and serenity of his bearing. In spite of his alien birth he is a very loyal Canadian, and a firm believer in Woodstock College. His cheery smile and sunny presence will long be remembered by his class-mates, and one and all will rejoice to know that " A. K." is meeting with success.

A. TARRIE.—Alexander Tarrie came to the College about three years ago. He brought with him a stock of good qualities to which he has steadily added during his stay here. Alec is a famous football player, and was ever noted for the dogged persistency of his playing. He brought the same hard working spirit into his classes, and indeed into all his work. At last success has crowned his efforts. We trust that in the sterner play of life the sterling good qualities of Alec may win him all the good fortune he deserves.

ELMA E. WOOD AND S. B. PINKHAM.—Elma comes from Onondaga, and has been at Woodstock. He wrote on the exam. for the provincial teachers' III class certificate last year, and this year intends trying for success. He and his room-mate and close companion, Spencer B. Pinkham, who also writes on the same exam., form a very happy pair. They are both jovial hearty fellows, full of life and good spirits, quite amenable to the rule requiring quiet after ten o'clock at night. We wish them success in their work, and are sure they will do famously, when writing.

THOMAS SURTEES.—Mr. Surtees is a late, but none the less welcome arrival at Woodstock. Mr. Surtees did not enter until Xmas, but since then has done good work, and carries away the esteem of all who know him. He hails from Liverpool, Eng., but from long residence in Canada has become loyal to the interest of his adopted country. We prophesy for Mr. Surtees a sphere of usefulness and many friends wherever he may go.

HARLEY C. NEWCOMBE.—Harley C. Newcombe is a much-travelled young man. He was born at Riverside, N. B., and at an early age went to sea, and spent some years aboard ship and in seeing many lands. He came to Woodstock College from the Pacific Coast. He graduates from the College with credit to all concerned. He will enter the Arts Department of our own University in October, and continue his course with a view to the Christian ministry. He is a young man of strong and noble purpose, and we doubt not he will fill a worthy place in the service he has chosen as his life work.

ARTHUR THOMSON.—Arthur Thomson is a Toronto boy who has spent three enjoyable and helpful years in Woodstock. He is one of the very youngest of his class, but in point of ability and scholarship, he is by no means the least. He possesses qualities that, if we are not mistaken, will in time place him in the front rank in life's race. We shall watch Arthur's future career with great interest.

JOHN C. MCFARLANE.—John C. McFarlane is a robust, good-natured Scotch laddie from the braes of Bruce Co. He has spent three or more years in Woodstock College, and during that time he has coped manfully and pluckily with all the difficulties incidental to the life of a self-supporting student. He spends the holiday months preaching on his old mission field at Sebringville, and in the autumn will enter McMaster University. He carries away with him from Woodstock the kindly regards of all, and our best wishes will follow him wherever he may be.

JAS. WEIR.—Jas. Weir is an Oxford boy. For about four years he has been a student in the College. For three years he walked in from the country, a considerable distance every morning, and during that time he made an enviable record for his punctuality. It was an inspiration to see "Jim" on the foot-ball field, where his punctuality came into fine play. He is altogether a young man of sterling worth, and possessed of qualities that are bound to make him a success.

Tom Scarlett.—Tom Scarlett is a stalwart of a stalwart class. It need only be mentioned that his birthplace was the now far-famed Muskoka. A man of action rather than of words, he ever exercised a strong influence over all his fellows. Tom loved his College, as the College loved him. He has abilities of a high order, and, rightly used, these will make Tom an honor to his *Alma Mater*, and to the name he bears. He will be followed by the affectionate interest of school-mates and Faculty.

Roy Simpson.—Roy Simpson is probably the junior member of the class of '95. His home is Drumbo, Oxford Co. He has spent three or four very happy years in Woodstock College, and during that time his scholastic progress has been steady and uninterrupted. At last he carries the coveted diploma, and carries it worthily. We are sure he will give a good account of himself in the Arts Department during the next four years. Ye McMaster boys, look to your laurels! We are glad to believe that Roy's place in Woodstock will before long be taken by a younger brother.

David Bovington.—David Bovington comes from the quaint old Kentish town of Tunbridge Wells, England. He landed in Canada six or seven years ago, and has spent the last four of that period as a student of Woodstock College. The subject of this sketch is a true Christian gentleman, distinguished for his manliness and courtesy toward all. Like so many Canadian youths Dave has had to fight an uphill battle while pursuing his educational course, but he has done it bravely and uncomplainingly. He is to be congratulated that he has passed the mile-post of graduation from Woodstock College. And it is greatly to the credit of friend B., that although on his back with a broken leg, he wrote on his Matriculation exam., and did it so well that, taken in conjunction with his record of the last two years of his course, he was adjudged to be most worthy of the fifty dollar Calvin scholarship. (What noble service Mr. Calvin is year by year doing for our denomination and the world!) Mr. B. is still the invalid, and may be so for the next two or three months, but his patience is equal to the strain. The students and teachers deeply sympathize with their companion and pupil, and hope that his restoration may be speedy and complete. Mr. B. seems to have a career of great usefulness before him.

Wm. B. Tighe.—Wm. B. Tighe is a native of Eastern Ontario, where he lived before coming West to Woodstock College, some two years ago. W. B. is the happy possessor of a combination of qualities that will make him useful and popular, in the best sense, wherever his lot may be cast. His work at College has been highly creditable, and his record was made through faithful, honest toil. His life's chosen work is the Christian ministry, and for his high calling, his purpose is to train by a long and thorough course in our schools. We all heartily wish W. B. Tighe every success in his future career.

THE

McMASTER UNIVERSITY MONTHLY

NOVEMBER, 1895.

CHANCELLOR WALLACE.

If, as some think, the life and destiny of men in the world are affected by the place and time of their birth, this is probably as true of Chancellor Wallace as of any other man. As to the place of his birth, its soil is one to which college presidents appear to be indigenous. In proof of this we have only to state that ex-Chancellor Rand, Chancellor Wallace's worthy predecessor, first saw the light only six or seven miles north from the latter's birthplace, while president DeBlois of Shurtleff, the youngest college president in America, was born only six or seven miles east therefrom. Moreover, it was only thirty miles west from the same spot, and on the same range of hills, that president Whitman, recently called from Colby to Columbian, stepped upon the sphere.

Nor should the time-factor be overlooked. God brings his agents into being, providentially and graciously trains them, and so has them ready at particular junctures for the special service he would have them perform. Chancellor Wallace was born thirty-eight years ago that he might come to the headship of McMaster University at "such a time as this." Unconsciously to himself, in the intervening years he was being trained and fitted for the position. In his preparatory studies at Worcester

(49)

he laid the foundation of the accurate scholarship and the severely critical and methodical habits of thinking which distinguished him in his Arts Course at Acadia.   These same habits
were strengthened during his Theological Course at Newton,
where, at the feet of Hovey, the learned and the strong, he traversed the fields of Biblical and Dogmatic Theology, learned the
art of careful and independent research, and acquired skill and
power for teaching and defending Christian truth.   From Newton he passed to his first pastorate in Lawrence, where he was
ordained in January, 1885, and spent six years in very successful ministerial and pastoral work.   In January, 1891, he became
pastor of the Bloor St. Baptist Church in this city, whence, after
four years, during which the membership of the church increased
from less than four hundred to over six hundred, he was called
to the honorable and responsible place he now fills.   On becoming the pastor of Bloor Street Church, nothing could have been
more foreign to his mind than the thought that he should ever
be asked to take the Chancellorship of McMaster; yet the first
was a fitting stepping stone to the second, and in the duties of
the first he was gaining valuable experience and discipline for
the somewhat similar duties of the second.   In the part taken
by him in the young people's movement, in the inductive study
of the Bible in which he led the young people of his church, and
in the organization of his church for various kinds of Christian
work—in all this he was familiarizing himself with the lesson
of administration and mastery of details which it would afterwards be necessary for him to put into practice in managing the
affairs of the University and in guiding and moulding the scores
and hundreds of young men and women who should from year
to year seek instruction within its walls.

On the first of May of the present year the denomination,
through its appointed representatives, called Mr. Wallace to the
Chancellorship, and after much thought and prayer, believing it
also to be the call of God, he felt that no course was left open to
him but to accept.   The educational knowledge and experience
of Dr. Rand had served a grand purpose in the launching of the
Arts Department of the University, and in the drafting of its
various curricula ; but now that his failing health made it necessary for him to throw off some of his burdens, it was the fitting

moment for Chancellor Wallace to step into his place. In this young Dominion, with its infinite possibilities of growth and development, we believe those of the University to be correspondingly great. Pursuing the lines laid down in his inaugural address, and giving to Christ the place in the University then indicated, Chancellor Wallace may fairly expect such growth and prosperity to mark his administration throughout.

NOVEMBER.

What ! here again, thou maid of sullen moods
And cloud-bound brow ! Across the meads of green
I see the brown track where thy feet have been ;
I hear thee raving in the songless woods !

Dear birds ! I almost envy them their wings
That bear them hence when skies are all agloom,—
When dead leaves whisper of the nearing tomb
And of the ruin of all earthly things :

Wings that can waft them to the sunny isles—
The ever fragrant and the ever green,
Where winter's icy heel hath never been ;
Where Nature's gifts are lavish as her smiles.

Yet Lord, my Lord, if I may stronger grow
In the true life beneath a sky austere
Mid airs inclement and surroundings drear,
Let rigid clime be mine ; let north winds blow !

M. A. MAITLAND.

LOVE.

The blooming flowers, the galaxies of space,
    Lie pictured in a sheeny drop of Even ;
And globed in one round word, on lips of grace,
    Shine out the best of earth and all of Heaven.

THEODORE H. RAND.

REV. JOHN KING.

No man is willing to toil in vain. We all like to see the fruit of our toil. The farmer who tills the soil is pleased to behold an abundant harvest. The capitalist is gratified when investments are profitable. The educator rejoices to witness the utility of his instructions in the improvement of his pupils. The physician is cheered when his skill is demonstrated in the recovery of his patients. Unproductive labour does not satisfy. This is an old and well established principle in temporal things, and is none the less true of things spiritual. It was predicted of Christ Jesus that " He should see of the travail of His soul and be satisfied." It was the mind and teaching of Christ that His people should not only bear fruit but much fruit, and that this fruit should remain, that their joy might be full. To this the great apostle alludes when he says : " That I may rejoice in the day of Christ, that I have not run in vain, neither laboured in vain." The same reward is in store for all who faithfully live for Christ, and who truly love His appearing. And as we are now writing of the long and eminently successful ministry of our late Father King, we can truly glorify God in him, and rejoice that he did not run in vain, nor labor in vain. We do not refer to his removal from the scenes of toil merely because he was an esteemed friend and patriot, who exerted an important influence in the religious world and ought not to be allowed to pass away without recognition of his character and services ; but because there were remarkable instances in his early history in which he and others saw the finger of God.

HIS BIRTH—John King was born of Presbyterian parents in Edinburgh, Scotland, in 1819. At the age of ten years he was sent to learn the lapidary trade with an uncle, who kept a shop in Prince's Street, Edinburgh. Then were the days in which the powerful and evangelical preaching and teaching of the Haldane brothers were permeating Scotland, especially its capital. Through the influence of John Terbot, a companion, young King was persuaded to attend the Baptist meeting on Niddery Street, where, according to his own words, his " mental eyes were opened, he saw himself in a new light," and was en-

John King.

quiring what he must do to be saved. In a few days he was led
to understand the new birth, and was trusting his hope of salvation on Christ alone. Through the teaching of John Terbot's
father, young King became interested in the subject of believer's
baptism as found in the Word of God, and was baptized by Pastor Robert Anderson at the age of 17, and united with the
church. He was gifted with a most retentive memory, read
much, especially his Bible, and thus stored up a large stock of
useful knowledge, which became of much practical value to him
in after life. He began to exercise his gifts in the church, and
made known to many in the byways and lanes of the city, the
way of salvation through Christ Jesus. Such humble efforts
were blest of God to the awakening and conversion of souls.
Thus in early life he had the cheering consciousness of God's
approval in giving himself diligently to his master's service.

About this time Rev. John Edwards, Sr., from Clarence,
Ont., paid a visit to Edinburgh, for the purpose of soliciting aid,
and persuading young men to engage in mission work in the
eastern part of Canada. While listening to an able address in
the Baptist church by Mr. Edwards, young King was induced to
offer himself as a missionary for Canada.

The first day of April, 1841, finds him under the care of
Mr. Edwards, on board the ship Mohawk, sailing for the shores
of Canada. After a seven weeks voyage he reached Montreal
about the 15th of May, and from there moved on to Fox's Point,
(Clarence, Russel Co.,) on the shores of the Ottawa. There he
preached his first sermon in Canada, in the house of Nicholas
Egar, from John III : 3. For several months he toiled through
the townships of Clarence and Lochaber, at times teaching school
in the day, and preaching at night ; having the encouragement
of God's blessing attending his labours. At this time he baptized a Miss Campbell, who was the first fruit of his preaching
in Canada.

His Ministry—After taking a short course in Montreal
Baptist College, Mr. King was induced to visit Chatham (Dalesville) church, Argenteuil Co., Que., where John Edwards, Jr., had
just closed a brief and faithful pastorate. There Mr. Edwards had
judiciously followed up the work of that great revival in 1835,
when under the preaching of Revs. Wm. Fraser, Jno. Gilmour and

young Daniel McPhail, over one hundred souls were converted to the Saviour, ninety of whom were baptized and united with the church in Chatham.

In 1844 Mr. King succeeded Mr. Edwards as pastor of Chatham church ; and at once entered upon a prosperous spiritual work. He preached his first sermon from the text, "Almost thou persuadest me to be a Christian," Acts 26 : 28.   A series of evening meetings were held for five weeks ; large numbers attended, many were converted, about fifty were baptized and added to the church.   The following winter Mr. King was married to Miss Elizabeth, eldest daughter of Deacon Peter McGibbon, who proved a most faithful, devoted and helpful partner during the many trials and successes of a forty-eight years pastorate. In his " Recollections of Early Days," Mr. King states, " of all the good temporal gifts of God to man, a good wife is the crowning one, and that gift God gave to me."   He was publicly ordained pastor of Chatham church in the year 1862, Revs. John Edwards, Jr , W. K. Anderson, and John Dempsey conducting the services.

The first ten years of this unusually long pastorate may be regarded as a series of evangelical meetings, under the faithful and united efforts of pastor and people, in which large numbers were yearly converted, some 450 in all, among whom were four young men who devoted themselves to the work of the ministry, Dr. R. S. MacArthur of Calvary Baptist Church, New York city, Rev. J. G. Calder, and the writer.   During those ten years Mr. King frequently assisted his friend W. K. Anderson of Breadalbane, where his faithful preaching was largely blessed, many being added to the Breadalbane church.   Such were times of great spiritual awakening in Dalesville, Breadalbane, Osgoode, and St. Andrews, under the veterans McPhail, Anderson, Dempsey and King.

1867-8 were years of immigration from Dalesville, through which the church became much depleted in membership.   Mr. King became convinced that the Lord had no more for him to do in those parts, and accepted a call from the united churches of Notfield, (Dominionville), Roxboro and Riceville.   His eight years of labor with these churches were not considered by Mr. King to be as fruitful or as happy as those spent in Dalesville.

Yet he had not run there in vain nor laboured in vain. A revival largely due to Mr. King's preaching began in the Presbyterian church with wonderous power. The Presbyterian minister requested Mr. King to preach in his church for seven weeks : it is believed that some 200 souls were converted to the Saviour, nineteen of these were baptized and united with the Notfield Baptist Church. In 1877 Mr. King returned to Dalesville, where he resumed the pastorate of Dalesville church, and continued faithfully ministering to church and people up to within three years of his death. In all he baptized about 1500 converts to Christ Jesus, his whole ministry covering a period of half a century.

QUALIFICATIONS—Physically Pastor King was tall, stout, robust, a strong looking man—for many years possessing a splendid constitution, well adapted to endure hard toil among the first settlers of Chatham Township. Though not having the advantage of much scholastic training, yet he was naturally gifted with more than average intelligence and powers of utterance. He was a calm, easy, fluent and effectual preacher. Nature and grace did much for him. It has been said by many that few of his age could excel him in plain, pungent and practical preaching, the proof of which is to be seen in the abundant fruits of his ministry.

While he held most tenaciously and boldly and fearlessly proclaimed Baptist principles, yet he was ready to unite with all who loved the Lord in efforts to do good. His pulpit efforts were always full of plain, earnest Gospel appeals to the hearts and consciences of his hearers; he did not shun to declare the whole counsel of God. Such is the preaching which this age requires. We live in an age when many are impatient of the Divine government. There is special need now of setting forth the office of the Divine Law in its relation to the Gospel. Shallow teaching from the pulpit, and shallow experiences from the pew, act and react to engender shallowness both of doctrine and life. For such evils the faithful and practical teaching of old Gospel doctrines is God's appointed remedy. The demands of the Divine Law in its relation to the Gospel were clearly and emphatically set forth by Pastor King, and the gracious results proved that they met with the Great Master's approval.

Indeed such qualifications for the Christian ministry are needed for all ages, because the human heart is the same. Men everywhere are to be saved in the same way, by repentance toward God and faith in our Lord Jesus Christ. We all enter upon our immortal career ruined by the fall. We commence life certain that we shall begin to sin as soon as we commence to act, and will sin forever in this world and the next unless redeemed by grace Divine, renewed and sanctified by the Holy Spirit. Through the Saviour's death their is hope for the chief of sinners ; and apart from Him their is no salvation. The necessity of regeneration by the Spirit of God, the Bible doctrine of believers baptism, the need of righteous living, the resurrection from the dead, the final judgment, and the eternal rewards of the righteous and the wicked are doctrines which from age to age, and from shore to shore are to be proclaimed, while there are sinners to be saved, and saints to be edified. Mr. King's one great aim was to make known these truths without fear or favor of man. Such gifts as he possessed were constantly used in advocating these doctrines before the world. We praise God that such doctrines remain, and that the church of God continues, though His people die. Our fathers are not, and the prophets do not live for ever, but as they silently pass away others step forward to take their place, and although messengers are silent the message is repeated ; new voices are taking up the truth as old ones grow faint.

His Death—Pastor King's illness was both protracted and severe, extending over three years ; most of that time he was confined not only to his home but to his bedroom. Much of that time he was not only unconscious but helpless. His was a most trying death. But however deep and varied may be the shadows which gather round the believer's death, he is never utterly desolate. As Father King once said to the writer during his last illness, " Christ never leaves me." How true, for has He not said, " I will not leave you comfortless, I will come unto you." All must be well for those who have lived for and served the Saviour. He never can revoke His promise or resign His charge. He has pledged Himself for the final safety of all His servants, and He will not withdraw His presence or withhold His hand in the most needful hour, and at length they will rejoice in the day of Christ that they have not run in vain neither laboured in vain.   Father King died Aug. 23rd, 1893, and his remains lie in Dalesville cemetery, a spot well known to himself, having officiated at the burials of a large number who lie there waiting the resurrection morning.

J. Higgins.

TO A CHILD SLEEPING IN SCHOOL.

How now, my boy ! thy books are tossed aside,
Thy rosy cheek is bowed, and thou'rt asleep—
Aye, sound asleep !—and dreaming, it may be,
Of pleasant pastimes in the open fields,—
Of murm'ring brooks, and bright-winged singing birds,
Or happier scenes at home !
     How sound he sleeps !
My fingers stray amid these golden curls,
Yet rouse him not from the serene repose
That folds his senses in the soothing spell
Of most untroubled rest.   One little stroke
Of this light twig on those small finger-tips—
How it would bring the hot blood rushing up
To these pure lily temples !   How the hands
Would grasp instinctively this fallen book ;—
And startled thought, half-consciously, would turn
To the neglected lesson, dreamily
Rememb'ring 'tis not learned.
     Dear little boy,
This shall not be !   'T were a rude hand, indeed,
Would dare profane such hallowed repose,
Or call a spirit from such blissful rest,
Sooner than Nature wills, to this sad world—
This world of many sorrows !
     Haply, he walks
With angels now—beware. beware, my hand !—
Shake not the dew-drops from the lily-bells
He may be culling now beside those streams

Whose dreamy music haunts me evermore—
Borne backward from the distant, dewy years
Of my own childhood !—

　　　　　　　Wonder, did he pause
In these dull studies, just to send a thought
Out on the glorious world ;—to call to mind
How pleasant is the music of the breeze
Up in the old elm-branches ;—how the bee
In the rich clover-blossoms nestling down
Murmurs its drowsy music ;—how mother-birds
Chirp to their tiny younglings in the nest
Down in the willow-boughs beside the brook,
While baby nestlings ope their ruby throats
To catch the dainty morsel she provides :—
How the young lambs, amid the fragrant grass,
Frolic and gambol all day long—while he,
Shut in by the dull walls of this close room,
Must con his weary lesson ! 'Mid such thoughts
It is not strange that sleep should hang a weight
On these soft, drooping eyelids, and bring down
This weary head with all its yellow curls
Upon his little desk.

　　　　　　　So, then, sleep on,
Thou tired little boy !—I shall not break
Thy peaceful rest ;—nor shall I thoughtlessly
Call thy young spirit from the path it treads
Back to this weary world.

　　　　　　　Oh ! far too soon
Thy day-dreams will be done ;—the dewy years
Of thy sweet childhood will be all gone by ;—
And thou, perchance, a weary-hearted man,
Wilt be a stranger, e'en like me to-day,
Willing to give a kingdom, were it thine,
For one blest hour of careless sleep like this !

　　　　　　　　　　　P. S. V. YULE.

WICLIF AND THE MENDICANT FRIARS.*

Nothing was more characteristic of the later middle ages than the multiplication of religious orders, and the prominence that these acquired in the body ecclesiastic. The terms " secular " and " religious " had since the sixth century been commonly employed to distinguished between the ordinary clergy and the monks. Monastic life from the time of Jerome onward was the ideal life. From the time of Gregory the Great it was a matter of principle as well as of policy with all the abler popes to bring the entire body of the clergy into conformity with monastic principles. Lay patronage offered the chief obstacle to the carrying out of this scheme. Kings and princes, having endowed the church with territorial possessions, expected tangible returns in the shape of military service, or wished to use the endowments in rewarding services already performed. Men who were not averse to taking part in secular pastimes, and who were noted for military prowess, were far more likely, under such circumstances, to be appointed to ecclesiastical positions, than monks who were supposed to live by rule, and who early developed a strong leaning towards ecclesiastical absolutism.

The monastic orders, especially the four orders of Mendicant Friars, the Augustinian, the Carmelite, the Franciscan and the Dominican, came forward to put into execution the hierarchical schemes of the popes. Trained to regard the papal supremacy as a matter of paramount importance ; placed under the weightiest obligations to the popes for privileges bestowed ; freed from the jurisdiction of metropolitans and bishops ; vastly superior to the secular clergy in learning, in knowledge of human nature, in enthusiasm, in every element of personal power ; recognized everywhere as representatives of papal principles ; they had free ingress into every diocese and parish in Europe, into the Universities, into the courts of Kings and Emperors, and they made their influence felt profoundly everywhere. Through them the popes became practically omnipresent and omniscient, so far as the state of ecclesiastical matters was con-

---

*From an address delivered on the occasion of the celebration of the Wycliffe Quin-centenary, in the St. James' School House, Toronto, Jan. 13, 1885.

cerned The secular clergy might cry out against them for invading their fields of labor uninvited, absorbing their revenues and assuming the offices of preaching, hearing confessions, administering the sacraments, and looking after charitable b quests. Armed with papal privileges, with personal superiority, and with a distinct purpose, they quietly pursued their way, their cause being promoted rather than hindered by the impotent denunciations of men who could not or would not give the people the instruction and guidance for which they were longing, and who could not but appear in the light of the dog in the manger. Possessed of the learning of the time, and watchful of opportunities, they could not possibly be kept out of the principal places in the Universities Having most of the preaching ability of the time, they readily secured the ear of the people ; " the dumb dogs " might growl and bark, they could by no means turn the tide of popular favor. Being reputed pious, while most of the secular clergy were sadly deficient even in the externals of piety, and being skilled in administering consolation to the sin-burdened, the sick and the dying, they gradually almost monopolized the work of hearing confessions. That they should have been charged with using their opportunities with the wealthy for the purpose of securing endowments for their institutions was most natural; if they sometimes used undue influence in this direction it is only what might have been expected.

What the order of Jesuits has been in modern times, this the Franciscans and the Dominicans were in the thirteenth, fourteenth and fifteenth centuries.

That these mighty and omnipresent orders should have become tyrannical and oppressive we can easily understand. Though founded on the principle of poverty—mendicancy being made obligatory on every member—their institutions became enormously wealthy and their greed insatiable, greed of wealth and greed of power. Was it not natural that their piety should come to be looked upon as hypocrisy, their humility as pride in disguise, their readiness to teach and to minister, as zeal for the advancement of their own power and influence ?

A prophecy of St. Hildegard, who lived long before the founding of these orders, precisely characterizes them as they were, or were regarded, in England in the thirteenth and fourteenth centuries. Were I disposed to adopt the maxims of modern Bible criticism, I should be very much inclined to the opinion that some zealous antagonist of the Mendicants during the fourteenth century fabricated this utterance and put it into the mouth of the good prophetess whose memory was fragrant and whose authority great. If it be prophecy indeed, no prophecy was ever more completely fulfilled. Here are her words : " In those days shall arise a senseless people, proud, greedy, without faith, and subtle, that shall eat the sins of the people ; holding a certain order of foolish devotion under the dissimulated cloak of beggary, preferring themselves above all others by their feigned devotion, arrogant in understanding, and pretending holiness, walking without blushing or the fear of God, in inventing new mischiefs strong and sturdy. But this order shall be accursed of all wise men and Christ's faithful. They shall cease from all labor, and give themselves over unto idleness, choosing rather to live through flattery and begging ; moreover they shall altogether study how they may perversely resist the teachers of the truth, and, with the mighty, kill them ; how to seduce and to deceive the nobility, for the necessity of their living, and pleasures of this world ; for the devil will graft in them four principal vices ; that is to say, flattery, envy, hypocrisy and back-biting. Flattery, that they may have large gifts given them. Envy, when they see gifts given to others, and not to them. Hypocrisy, that by false dissimulation they may please men. Back-biting, that they may extol and commend themselves, and dispraise others, for the praise of men and seducing of the simple. Also, they shall instantly preach, but without devotion or the example of the martyrs, and shall report evil of secular princes, taking away the sacraments of the church from the true pastors, receiving alms of the poor, diseased and miserable ; and also associating themselves with the common people, having familiarity with women and instructing them how they may deceive their husbands and friends by their flattery and deceitful words, and rob their husbands to give it unto them, for they will take all these stolen and evil gotten goods and say, ' give it unto us and we will pray for you,' so that they being curious to hide other men's faults do utterly forget their own. And alas, they will receive all things of rovers, pickers, spoilers, thieves and robbers, sacrilegious persons, usurers and adulterers, heretics, schismatics, apostates, harlots, panders, noblemen, perjurers, merchants, false judges, soldiers, tyrants, princes living contrary to the law, and of many perverse and wicked men, following the persuasion of the devil, the sweetness of sin, a delicate and transitory life, and satiety even unto eternal damnation." And so she goes on at considerable length piling invective upon invective and foretelling the utter ruin of the culprits.

Time would fail me to give extracts from the prose and the poetry of Chaucer, from " Piers, the Plowman," from Richard of Armagh, from Matthew Paris, from William of Occam, from Thomas Bradwardine, and from the great Italian poets Petrarch and Dante, describing the habits of the friars and showing how they were looked upon at about the time of Wiclif.

It was in the age of Wiclif that the friars attained to the summit of their power and their tyranny. Whatever could be said against them at any time from their rise to the sixteenth century, was true of them in the highest degree during the age of the Papal Captivity. In alliance with the Avignon papacy which had plunged itself into the very depths of iniquity, they could not escape contamination. Already immensely wealthy, they manifested an insatiable desire for accumulation, and under the pretext of carrying out the rules of their order in which begging was prescribed, they were enabled to extort gifts from rich and poor. Most assiduous were they in their attentions to wealthy people in declining health. They had invaded the halls of the Universities and were drawing to themselves by their skill, learning, wealth and power many of the most promising young men. It was ascribed to their zealous proselytism that parents became afraid to send their sons to Oxford, and that the number of students declined from 30,000 to 6,000. That they used every device within their power to win wealthy and promising young men to their orders is what might have been expected.

In the Universities they were content to hold no subordinate position, and their well directed and persistent efforts at control were generally in the end successful. Wiclif himself had bitter experience of their ambitious schemes, and of the underhand methods they were wont to employ in supplanting their rivals.

We may be sure that his love for them was not fanned into a
flame when he was deprived of the wardenship of his college, a
position for which he was eminently qualified and which he had
graced, and a friar put in his place. When these self same friars
diligently culled from his writings a long list of what they regarded as heretical propositions, got him arraigned before an
ecclesiastical tribunal and suspended from his teaching function
in the University, his opinion of the order was not likely to
change for the better. The fact is, he was so exasperated by the
determination of the friars to ruin him by fair means or by foul,
that he was led little by little into a position of the fiercest
antagonism to the whole body of mendicants, and to the very
principle of monastic orders.

The large collection of Wiclif's Latin Polemical Tracts
recently published for the first time, by Dr. Buddenseig, under
the auspices of the English·Wiclif Society, is made up in a large
measure of denunciations of the principles and practices of friars.
The pages of these tracts fairly bristle with "devils," "anti-
christs," "disciples of antichrist," "indurate hypocrites," "Pharisees," "evil beasts," "carcases that have gone forth from the
grave, wrapped in grave-clothes, driven hither and thither among
men by the devil," "Cretans—married with perpetual falsehood,"
"slow bellies, solicitous about feeding the stomach deliciously,
and too slow for working with their hands like the Apostles,"
"those putrid sects," "traitors to God and to men." He compares them with Mohammedans, by no means advantageously.
He accuses them of "spiritual fornication."

In his treatise on "The Foundation of Sects," Wiclif literally goes straight through the New Testament, book by book,
and applies every denunciation of existing evils and every prophecy of coming evils to the friars. He displays a wonderful
ingenuity in finding means of applying to the friars even the
most unpromising passages. When he writes a treatise on the
"Seven Gifts of the Spirit" he cannot forbear to emphasize each
gift and grace by contrasting it with the opposite diabolical
qualities of the friars. For example: one of the gifts of the
Spirit is the fear of the Lord. "And here believers mark how
those new orders and all those four sects have feared, where
there was no fear, because they love more their own snappish

order than the Christian sect or order, and are more afr id of the want of so-called temporal convenience than of the want of a good conscience. . . . And to this the devil himself seduces them by an argument of this kind : One's own order is better than any person in the same, but in proportion to the greater goodness must be the amplitude of the zeal, therefore one must be more zealous for the safety of his own order than for any person of the same, or any person of the church militant."

He cannot write about "The Twofold Chain of Love" without expatiating upon "that twofold chain of infamy invented by the father of lies, namely, the setting up of four sects upon the sect of the Lord Jesus Christ, and the setting up of their own traditions upon the law of the Lord Jesus Christ."

Wiclif's realism led him a long way in the direction of necessitarianism. But he felt constrained to deny any divine agency in connection with the friars and their doings. God does nothing superfluously or without cause. The friars are of no possible use. Therefore "they are worse than the priests of Baal, because they are priests of an evil, superfluous, non-causing God."

We might classify the elements of Wiclif's polemics against friars under the following heads :

1. *Economical and Political :* He represents that there were in England, in his time, at lea-t four thousand friars ; that these consume on an average each £10 annually, without producing anything whatever ; that they expend in building £40,000 a year. All this he regards as clear loss to the state, and so as oppressive to the poor. He accuses them, moreover, of political intrigue and bribery, of acting as agents for hostile kings, of selling the peace of the country as one would sell a sheep or an ox to a neighbor.

2. *Theological :* He accuses them of all sorts of false teaching. Not only do they teach error themselves, but they will not allow the true preachers of the Word to perform their functions. " A pseudo-friar," he writes, "preaching manifest heresy, is licensed by the bishop and defended by the secular arm, but a faithful priest wishing gratuitously to preach the Gospel of Jesus Christ will straightway be prohibited from preaching in that diocese."

3. *Ecclesiastical:* Wiclif would admit the lawfulness of only one sect, namely, that made up of all the faithful, whose Lord is Jesus Christ, and whose rule is the Catholic faith. Such a sect is sufficient for any Christian. He supposed that the tendency of sects was "to promote contentions, and preponderance in love for a thing that God cares less for, since it is necessarily at variance with the will of the Lord. What member of an order loves more a better man of another sect than a worse one of his own?" From the fact that in Galatians he finds sects mentioned among the many works of the flesh he infers that the sects are guilty of the whole list. Wiclif's soul abhorred the very principle of sects. Throughout all his writings church unity, based not on tradition but on Scripture, is advocated in season and out of season.

But fiercely as Wiclif opposed the friars, he was not without hope of their reformation. "I anticipate," he writes, "that some of the friars whom God shall be pleased to enlighten will return with all devotion to the original religion of Christ, will lay aside their unfaithfulness, and with the consent of antichrist, offered or solicited, will freely return to primitive truth, and then build up the church as Paul did before them." Martin Luther was an Augustinian friar.

This denunciation of sectarianism by the stern old theologian of the fourteenth century, comes with tremendous emphasis to Christians in the nineteenth century. Behold Christendom rent asunder into its hundreds of sects; instead of fighting against the common foe with might and main, consuming its energies and exhausting its resources in party contentions and in party enterprises; instead of occupying its intellect with ascertaining and teaching what the Lord has revealed, employing its ingenuity in upholding systems of doctrine and practice which, under the pressure of circumstances, ecclesiastical and political, happened at some time in the past to be stamped as orthodox, and which have come to be regarded as standards by which the word of God itself should be tried! Have we not all the same Bible? Have we not all similarly constructed intellects? Have we not all the same Holy Spirit to illuminate our intellects, and to lead us into the truth? Have we not all the same means of interpreting the Bible? Have we not all the same historical mate-

2

rials ? Have we not all the same facilities for understanding the teachings of these materials.

There are two ways and only two by which Christian union might be attained. A powerful hierarchy, with complete control of all the civil governments of Christendom, and using the civil arm for the forcible suppression of all dissent, might be thought a practicable way. It was tried in the middle ages under the most favorable circumstances. It will never be tried again with success. The only other method that has the slightest chance of success—the method that Wiclif advocated but which the time of Wiclif was not ripe for—is for all believers (true believers, I mean), really (not theoretically) to *accept the Scriptures as the only rule of faith and practice;* the Scriptures as they *are,* and interpreted according to scientific hermeneutical principles, not as they may chance to have been interpreted in some man-made creed. Christians will never unite on the Canons of the Council of Trent, on the Augsburg Confession, on the Heidelberg Catechism, on the Thirty-Nine Articles and the Prayer Book, on the Confession of the Westminster Assembly of Divines, on the Book of Discipline, or any other human statement of doctrine and practice that has been or ever will be made. I believe that scientific exegesis is little by little narrowing the range of disputed interpretations. I believe that Christians are coming little by little to see that the Bible and not party must have the first place. Yet the practical difficulties are of the most appalling kind, and we must not be too sanguine as to immediate results.

ALBERT H. NEWMAN.

Students' Quarter.

CLAUDIUS.

" In the murderer there must be raging some great storm . . . . . . which will create a hell within him."—*De Quincey.*

King Claudius was walking alone in his garden.

It still lacked almost an hour of sunrise. The sea, tumultuous from the storm of the past night, and overhung with sullen clouds, showed dark and angry in the grey dimness of early dawn. The gloomy fortress walls of Elsinore were as yet untouched by any tinge of the coming day, and their huge battlements, outlined darkly against the sky, watched grimly over the stretch of troubled waters.

Certainly there was little in this early morning scene of sombre sky, dreary sea, and sullen stone, to charm the eye of Denmark's monarch, that he should pace in solitude the paths of the royal park. But Claudius cared little for the cheerless view that met his eyes, dark-ringed with sleepless anxiety. Indeed, the fierce soul within half-consciously found a morbid satisfaction in the corresponding outer gloom.

Two months of kingship had brought small satisfaction to that ambition, which but a few weeks since knew no higher goal. Always present had been that maddening fear of his crime's discovery. Still, suspicion seemed to slumber. Indeed, sometimes, in secret, a mirthless laugh of contempt for his associates had raised its discords amid the hidden terrors of his soul—demoniacal glee, all scornful of their befogged perception. Yet as much as possible, he avoided all intimate companionship, dreading to meet in private even her whose guilty love first prompted him to kill a brother and usurp a throne. With tensest nervous energy he had striven to preserve before others an impassive and reserved demeanor. Political troubles enough he had, to account for any occasional show of harassed irritability.

But this morning a new fear filled his remorse-stricken soul.

What an awful dream it was! As he tossed in broken, restless sleep upon his couch, he seemed all at once to be standing in the royal garden upon the fatal spot, which, since that guilty day, his steps had shunned as they would the mouth of hell. Beside that rustic seat—what a death-bed for a king!—there stood a supernatural form with uplifted sword of flame. No interpreter was needed to read in the stern brightness of that awful face the sign of Heaven's Avenger. And as he stood defenceless in his guilty agony of fear, the sword descended. With a hoarse cry of terror the king awoke, but in the flickering light of his chamber-lamp could discover no one save the huge mastiff, which had for some weeks—such dreamers prefer mute watchers—been his nightly body guard. There was no more sleep that night for Denmark's unhappy lord.

Thus it was that the dawn found him treading rapidly the paths of his private garden.

"What must be the portent of that awful vision? O the horror of this threatening doom!"

II.

It was long past the midnight hour, but the shouts and revelry of the royal carousal continued in the banqueting hall of Elsinore. Claudius, with that strange, feverish inconsistency of despairing minds, had of late joined almost nightly in keeping wassail with his courtiers. The rude mirth and proverbial Danish excess served not to soothe, it is true, but to benumb with counter-irritation the fierce gnawings of remorse.

He was seated upon a raised dais, at one extremity of the long line of oak tables that extended from end to end of the low-browed room. Though, as behoved a Danish sovereign, he joined at every wassail in the shout that almost rent the sturdy hemlock rafters, he was more than ever sick at heart. The memory of his dream was upon him. By a nerveless fascination his eyes turned constantly toward the empty seat upon his right, which was reserved for Hamlet.

"Why has he not come? Why disobey his lord's expressed desire? Has filial sorrow alone to do with this, or can it be ——? O powers of hell!"

"Another bowl!" he called aloud. "Whose wassail this?"

"Prince Hamlet's"—shouted by a dozen throats, came from the farthest table where the younger courtiers were seated.

This health had been delayed in hopes of the prince's arrival, but was impatiently called for, now, by those of his own age. As master of the wassail, the king arose to give the toast. His hand, trembling with suppressed agitation, allowed a small quantity of the liquor to splash upon the table.

"An evil omen!" whispered those farthest from him.

He surmised the purport of their mutterings. With a suppressed oath he raised the huge silver tankard to his lips, but as they touched its embossed rim a dizzying dimness floated before his eyes, turned fixedly upon the seat beside him. Not empty to him — the face of his vision! Again it seemed before him, but now that fierce austerity was replaced by a wilder wrath. With a stupendous effort he drained the bowl—for a moment only did his features lose their accustomed mask—and the shouting crowd, the rattling drums, the braying trumpets, echoed the turmoil within his breast.

Abruptly he ended the rouse. As he stumbled weakly from the hall, the early dawn paled his attendants' flaming torches.

.   .   .   .

Alone, unheard, upon a distant battlement of the castle wall, a youth with eyes horror-wild, and features distorted by revengeful passion—a moment since his murdered father's spirit stood before him—has shrieked to his shuddering soul:

"'Remember me,'—I've sworn it."

STAMBURY R. TARR.

TEMPEST-TOST.

In a flash the rain roars down,
  Tearing a way to the ground
  With a splashing unmusical sound,
  With a quivering sharp rebound,—
Striking each dusty town
Into a gloom of the flood,
Into a chill of the blood,
  At the ravenous roar of the rain.

The thunder struggles for breath,
  Beaten with moanings of ire,
  Mad with a rebel desire,—
  Lightning, its heart of fire,
Goads it to desperate death,—
Fear follows everywhere
On the earth and the sea and the air,
  Forebodings of terror and pain !

Then the voice of the sea outcries :—
  " All my waves have in anger arisen,
  Scorning my bosom a prison,
  Lashing me while I listen
To the prayer as of one who dies :
' O Infinite Love, come thou,
 Save me and pilot me now ! '
  And straight there is silence again."

Low earth-murmurs kindle and loom,
  And its secrets have thickened the sky,
  Till it sweeps them before the fierce eye
  Of the hurricane hurrying by.
Clash all the fierce tones of doom,—
Storm ! and the world in collapse,—
Despair ! were it not that perhaps
  There's a whispering promise-refrain.

                              VIATOR.

THE INFLUENCE OF SPENSER UPON SUCCEEDING POETS.

As Spenser himself has optimistically observed (and* Longfellow after him) :—

> " After long stormes and tempests overblowne
> The sun at length his joyous face doth cleare :
> So whenas fortune all her spight hath showne,
> Some blissfull houres at last must needes appeare."

In such a manner was predetermined the inevitable reaction discovered in the Elizabethan Era,—a time of charm and glory for the nation, deft intermingling of poetical with practical, and of famous and unequalled literary activity and fruition. The reaction itself is less remarkable than the ready response of genius to the favouring conditions. A new and inspiring conviction filled and stirred men's minds, asserting itself in three distinct propositions,—historical, prophetic and personal :—England had triumphed! England should lead the world! England was theirs! Snatched from among the spoils of the Invincible Armada was the proud adjective itself, now exultantly adopted by the defenders of faith and country,—invincible!

One result of the crisis became marked and significant,—the great national progress in religious and economic life, which awakened a new spirit and provoked a more exalted notion of coming power and renown. England was free as never before,—free, by her stern resistance, from foreign molestation; free, by cautious and gradual undoing, from the grim ecclesiastical octopus; free, at last, to breathe, to think, and consciously to perform.

The Revival of Learning, however, though its bearing upon the external life of the nation was most important, occasioned at first but a faint response from the field of literature. Its indirect influence is noteworthy as quickening the popular love for letters, and as inspiring a brilliant and effective imagination. With great earnestness men attempted by the synthesis of expe-

---

*Hanging of the Crane.

> " After a day of cloud and wind and rain,
> Sometimes the setting sun breaks out again."

rience and speculation, to attack the problems which everywhere confronted them. The Copernican system was carefully elaborated; travel disclosed wonder upon wonder, abundant resources, and marvellous histories; men sought to know the truth about mankind; Science and Art rejoiced and prospered. The national truth-seekers, in a fervour of commendable curiosity, gathered around their learned ones, and went again to school.

What noble and illustrious teachers they had! Spenser and Bacon and Shakespeare and Hooker arose; Sidney and Raleigh, Milton and Cudworth; nor were the minor poets and dramatists to be contemned, who flocked forth to accomplish their abiding and distinctive works. Such large and original minds, so favourably conditioned for resolute activity and bright display, could not fail to bestow a lasting glory upon their age, perhaps unsurpassed in the history of literatures.

That this environment, these conditions, which have been but briefly indicated, were peculiarly favourable to the welfare of the Muses, is no less evident from their very nature than from the attesting productions of the poets themselves. " Never," declares Mrs. Browning, " since the first nightingale brake voice in Eden arose such a jubilee-concert; never before nor since has such a crowd of true poets uttered true poetic speech in one day. . . . Why, a common man, walking through the earth in those days, grew a poet by position."

Previous interests had been naturally economic and political for the most part; the new aspect of affairs just as naturally created the longing for poets. They arose, and found the work ready to their hands, the existing circumstances being the necessary outgrowth of preceding history and appropriate from every standpoint for the fostering of a great choir of singers. Memory of the past caprices and violent behaviour of Fortune, tempered by anxious hope and exultant aspirations demanded relief in poetry. Sidney, indeed, laments "now that an over-faint quietness should seem to strew the house for poets, they are almost in as good reputation as the mountebanks at Venice." But his own high standard is proof sufficient of the awakening; and while bestowing cautious praise upon Chaucer and Spenser, he desires rather to deprecate those wretched affectations whose authors "by their own disgracefulness disgrace the most graceful poesy."

The decade, from 1590 to 1600, was the turning-point. Spenser's great epic appeared, and the English drama was born. If Sidney's *Défense* had been written ten years later, it would have abounded in eulogy, for the noble grandeur and sweet cadences of the new poetry not only captivated the nation, but satisfied the most ardent poetical longings.

Curiously enough, Spenser endeavoured to justify his poem by asserting a definite moral purpose. This apology he offered out of deference to the opinion of certain sober judges who claimed that idle rhyming was not even respectable, which was true enough, and that most poets, if not all, were fools, to which notion, perhaps, we may be allowed to take exception. He felt bound to propitiate the Puritanic element, who considered all outsiders given over " to a reprobate mind, to do those things which are not convenient." But it was needless. He instinctively realized the behests of his genius. The moral is not the criterion of a poetical work. It is emphatically and essentially true that the poem exists in itself and for itself, else we look in vain for the poetry. *The Faerie Queene* is far more true to its author's genius than he probably supposed, nor is it the didactic narrative that his preface would proclaim.

The intrinsic nobleness and pervading merit of the poem amply justified its coming. It was readily received with delighted recognition and popular acclaim. It became "the delight of every accomplished gentleman, the model of every poet, the solace of every soldier," embodying to perfection the spirit of the age. Further than this indication, we reserve our final estimate of the great epic,—the inspiring cause of important effects; and proceed to deal more particularly with the effects themselves.

The product of Spenser's genius had been so earnestly craved and was so gladly, even enthusiastically, welcomed, that it immediately and directly influenced contemporary thought and literature. Nor is all the credit therefore due to Spenser, who himself in great measure simply transmitted the Platonic influence, and that of Ariosto and Tasso (not only in form, but in matter, as in Tasso's forest-scenes and Bower of Bliss ; and in absorption of Nature and passionate personification, as Ariosto) ; of Homer and Virgil, in their regard for character ; of

" That renowned poet   .   .   .   ..
Dan Chaucer, well of English undefyled,
On fames eternall beadroll worthie to be fyled ;"

of the *Morte d'Arthur;* the *Seven Champions of Christendom;*
and *Sir Bevis of Hampton.* Of these, named in the order of
subordination, the first five were the main sources.

Nor must we neglect mention of the strong personal influences exerted upon Spenser by Gabriel Harvey ; Edward Kirke ;
Sir Philip Sidney ; Lord Grey ; and Sir Walter Raleigh. The
effect of the poet's travels, likewise, especially in Ireland, is evident in the strong local colouring pervading *The Faerie Queene.*

It must be remembered, moreover, that most poets have
been directly affected by Classicism, Romanticism, or both. The
influence of Plato, for example, permeates English poetry in
Sidney, Herbert, Donne, Spenser and Milton. It is impossible at
any time to be dogmatic concerning the origin of a thought or
the beginning of a continuously transmitted influence. The
complete occasion never appears as distinct and inevitable, but
is interwoven into a complex. Much that might be traced to
Spenser can be traced as well to his contemporaries, and beyond
them both. There are fundamental world-thoughts common to
all generations and civilizations. The moods and revelations of
Nature ; faith, hope and love ; life, death and eternity ; all these
have been from the beginning ; and of these must all true poets
sing. None can lay final claim to originality. The poet, indeed,
is simply a reporter of the Universal Genius, granted a free
hand and an open heart.

" How sure it is,
That, if we say a true word, instantly
We feel 'tis God's, not ours, and pass it on,
Like bread at sacrament we taste and pass,
Nor handle for a moment, as indeed
We dared to set up any claim to such ! "

Nevertheless, there are always favourite fountain heads of
influence, whither men love to resort. We all praise our best-
beloved poets ; but they, whether openly or in secret, pay tribute
to Spenser, whose charm has ever gained for him the title of
" the poets' poet."

We have spoken of contemporary response to the Spenserian
stimulus, and now proceed to treat it broadly and briefly as far

as Milton, the last of the genuine Elizabethans, who, although
born ten years after Spenser's death, is yet directly connected
with him in various ways.

Readily enough in all truth, did the world receive Spenser
with relief and delight; even Webbe and Puttenham grew dis-
satisfied with their grotesque absurdities, and in restlessness and
bickering hoped for a change which they could not know how
to expect. Everyone read the poem so long awaited; rivalled
only by Chaucer, Spenser burned brightly in the firmament of
English Literature, more immediately conspicuous than ever
since, soon to beam in company with Shakespeare and Milton,
but with a sweet and benign influence forevermore. Lodge and
Drayton vied in their gracious praises. Poets, critics, and public
frankly applauded; and even great Shakespeare, master of all
men's minds, pays open homage :—

> "Spenser to me" is dear, "whose deep conceit is such
> As, passing all conceit, needs no defense . . ."
>
> "I in deep delight am chiefly drown'd
> Whenas himself to singing he betakes."

Anthony Wood has it that Warner gained no less contemporary
fame than Spenser; if this be true, posterity, at all events, soon
corrected the mistake. Samuel Daniel, however, received the
praise of Spenser; and returned it with interest; yet showed
but scant critical appreciation. He became Poet-Laureate at the
death of Spenser. Ben Jonson has recorded his respect. Michael
Drayton's *Polyolbion* evidences Spenser's influence, but, superior
as he is to his more immediate fellows, Warner and Daniel, his
verse is strained and tedious in comparison with that of " Colin
Clout." The "Amoretti" provoked much fellow-feeling. Court-
ing in verse, indeed, was a prevalent fashion; and, as Mr. Stopford Brooke has so admirably shown : Love, Patriotism, Philosophy of Life and a Conservative Religious Protest were necessary phases, distinct though intermingling, of poetic attraction
current in the period, till finally the first three were analyzed
and synthesized by the master of the Drama.

Of Shakespeare, then, we must now speak,—the mighty
poet who has comprehended at once the largeness of the world
and the most exquisite subtleties of variable human nature.

Spenser, indeed, transcended humanity, Shakespeare clung to it with what at times seems an almost painful tenacity. Both were related maternally to gentle stock, both had hard and early struggles, both boldly persevered and triumphed, of *that* John Bull propensity each has made an exhortation :

> " , . . . as she lookt about," says Spenser," she did behold
> How over that same dore was likewise writ,
> Be bolde, be bolde, and everywhere, Be bold."

And Shakespeare denounces doubts and craven spirits :—

> " Cowards die many times before their deaths,"—

therefore, be valiant! We have no record of his patient endurance and determined persistence, but we may surmise something of their degree and effect, in the development of his life and power. " Do not analyze," say his ardent admirers, including even Corson, who dissects and vivisects *all* his subjects, " ' Manifestum est poetam nasci, non fieri,' his was a genius that flashed a space, absorbed all, and vanished." They are largely right, Shakespeare's inspiration was direct and immediate, but patient study will discover *his* patient study, small, perhaps, but intense. The plays reveal some classical education and considerable attention, in common with Spenser and the times, to Italian literature. Genius, indeed, is greater than culture, in that while the latter can but smoothe and nicely adjust, the former translates all things into its own great world of light. Shakespeare would certainly have written had Spenser never existed, his genius could not have been repressed, and the helpful conditions of the age would still have ensured success. The differences of creed and character developed by the Reformation had ensured a free range, while change was balanced by the healthful conservatism evinced in regard to ancient religious and national foundations.

One Leonard Digges, indeed, resents the indebtedness of his master to external influence as stubbornly as some modern critics. Concerning the First Folio, he exclaims:

> " look thorough,
> This whole book, thou shalt find he doth not borrow
> One phrase from Greeks, nor Latins imitate,
> Nor once from vulgar languages translate :
> Nor plagiary-like from others glean ; "

But he is extravagantly jealous of Shakespeare's reputation; nor do we desire to institute any " odious comparison." Spenser and Shakespeare, indeed, are alike in many respects. We cannot hesitate to accord the former the admiration due to a classic. Both were for their age; but one was for all ages. Both wrote life, but the one as an idealist; the other, a realist. Even Shakespeare's sense of the Beauty John Keats made synonymous with Truth, did not exceed Spenser's; but his real and vivid reproductions of the race we run, mirror-reflected, perfected revelations of imperfection, have never been approached. As one weaves slender threads into a strong strand, so did he combine characteristics into character. Poet-philosopher and artist-poet ! all men call him master. ·

But even genius must read before it can write, and Shakespeare's praise of Spenser appears to justify the conclusion that he felt the latter's influence congenial and even grateful. It is not necessary to suppose that the great dramatist was ever directly swayed by the sweet-voiced Spenser. Both poets were masters of style, and the later necessarily received certain minor suggestions at least from the earlier. Shakespeare no doubt perceived Spenser's monosyllabic power. Both, indeed, present such phrases as " damned ghost," and " bold, bad man,"—an incidental likeness. Shakespeare also caught the trick of Spenser's favourite " respective construction," as in *Antony and Cleopatra* :—

" Hearts, tongues, figures, scribes, bards, poets, cannot think, speak, cast, write, sing, number, his love to Antony,"

the force of which arrangement is entirely misunderstood by Jevons in his *Logic*.

Decius in *Julius Cæsar* declares that his lord loves to hear

" That unicorns may be betrayed with trees,"

which fable is carefully elaborated by Spenser.

Shakespeare's *Venus and Adonis* is suggestive of Spenser's descriptions in the Third Book, cantos one and six. Both Hamlet and Sir Turpine " lack gall." The Saracen deity Termagaunt is common to both epic and plays. *King John* contains a reference to St. George and the Dragon, true to Spenser's picture. In conclusion we would notice the following curious and remarkable parallel :—

From *The Merchant of Venice,* of which we have the first mention in 1598, and which was not actually printed till 1600 :

> "The quality of mercy is not strained ;
> It droppeth as the gentle rain from heaven
> Upon the place beneath.   It is twice blessed ;
> It blesseth him that gives, and him that takes :
> 'Tis mightiest in the mightiest ;
>
> .   .   .   .
>
> It is enthroned in the hearts of kings,
> It is an attribute to God Himself ;
> And earthly power doth then show likest God's
> When mercy seasons justice.

The second part of *The Faerie Queene* appeared early in 1596.   In canto ten of the Fifth Book, Spenser writes :

> " Some clarkes doe doubt in their devicefull art,
> Whether this heavenly thing whereof I treat,
> To weeten mercie, be of justice part,
> Or drawne forth from her by divine extreate :
> This well I wote, that sure she is as great,
> And meriteth to have as high a place,
> Sith' in th' Almightie's everlasting seat
> She first was bred, and borne of heavenly race ;
> From thence poured down on men by influence of grace,"

followed by a stanza in explanation and justification.

This general similarity appears to grow more subtle upon examination.   Indeed, one becomes impressed at last with the conviction that even the universal genius would not produce such nice elaboration, like for like, in two different minds.   But the question of chronology is somewhat confused, so that we are fain to content ourselves with query and conjecture.

And now, with but a passing mention of George Wither, William Browne, and George Herbert ; the first of whom resembles Spenser in sincerity, but differs greatly in unaffected diction ; the second is like Spenser in facility of invention and felicity of expression ; the last in pure nobility ; we shall proceed to discuss the important part played by Spenser in the production of Milton's earlier poems.   The masque of *Comus* and the elegy of *Lycidas* are representative, and of these we shall treat.

Spenser and Milton are curiously enough connected in several ways, each of which has more or less significance as regards the question under discussion. Adam and Noah are not so far apart as is at first supposed, Methusaleh forming a connecting link contemporaneous with both. We generally regard Milton as comparatively modern beside Spenser, yet to Alice, the Dowager Lady Derby, both poets paid their homage, Spenser dedicating to her *The Tears of the Muses,* and Milton composing the *Arcades* primarily for her delectation. *Comus* was written for her son-in-law Lord Bridgewater. Both poets also, were Cambridge men, like many of their successors.

Milton could not fail to love Spenser, for both were like-moulded, similarly circumstanced and environed, and united in devotion to a God of intense reality, All-in-all, whose smile was heaven, whose frown was utter misery. Serious, high-hearted, beset and chastened through all their time, both were Puritans, but more than Puritans—both were poets. Spenser was no less congenial to Milton than Milton would have been to Spenser. But we can only indicate this harmony, and reluctantly omit its further illustration.

Dryden declares that Milton acknowledged " Spenser was his original," and he terms Milton " the poetical son of Spenser." *Comus* and *Lycidas* abound in testimony, some of which we shall now exhibit, reserving *Paradise Lost* for its chronological position.

A careful perusal of *The Faerie Queene* sheds a flood of light upon the spirit and development of *Comus.* Both poems, like Tennyson's *Idylls,* shadow sense at war with soul. The spirit of *Comus* is that animating the first two books of Spenser's epic, and many are the spoils from later books. Sir Guyon corresponds to the Lady ; the Greek σωφροσύνη, Spenser's " Temperance," to Milton's " Virtue ; " and so follow numerous minor equivalents.

The First Brother in *Comus* declares that

> " Wisdom's self
> Oft seeks to sweet retired solitude,
> Where, with her best nurse, Contemplation,
> She plumes her feathers, and lets grow her wings.
>
> He that hath light within his own clear breast,
> May sit i' the centre, and enjoy bright day ;
> But he that hides a dark soul and foul thoughts,
> Benighted walks under the mid-day sun ;
> Himself is his own dungeon "

With which compare from Spenser, first the hermit, whose

> " . . name was Heavenly Contemplation ;
> Of God and goodness, was his meditation,"

and secondly the words of Melibœus, in Book Six :—

> " It is the mynd, that maketh good or ill,
> That maketh wretch or happie, riche or poore,"

and again *Milton in *Paradise Lost :*—

> " The mind is its own place, and in itself
> Can make a heaven of hell, a hell of heaven."

Milton also transfers Melibœus into Comus, and thinking probably of Spenser, describes him as

> " The soothest shepherd that ere piped on plains,"

and proceeds to relate the story of Sabina, as given by Spenser in his Second Book.

The scene between the Lady and Comus is paralleled in Spenser's Sixth Book, where the chief of the thieves persecutes Pastorella. But the attitude of Milton's heroine is infinitely more noble. Here is an excellent opportunity for ethical pros and cons.

These are sufficient evidences of the general similarity of matter and spirit; the pastoral is also a strong common element. It remains to point out some examples of similar style. Just as Spenser contemned the common Elizabethan speech, and drew heavily upon his master, Chaucer, so did Milton, but in less degree, borrow words from Spenser. Spenser's object was to protest against prevailing euphuism, which drove him to an extreme; Milton's, to improve his poetry by following his artistic instinct, in which he admirably succeeded. Both poets use " decry " in these respective poems, meaning " to reveal "; Milton imitates " hall or bower" from Spenser; and uses " unblest " in the Spenserian sense. Other examples may readily be marked. The Spenserian " elongation," too, is introduced once, with good effect :

> " Come, let us haste, the stars grow high,
> But night sits monarch yet in the mid sky."

---

*Cf. Wordsworth : " The mind's internal heaven."

Now let us turn to *Lycidas* with its truth and righteousness, deep sorrow and sublime hope.   The poem itself is a Pastoral, not expressed as a spontaneous lyrical lament for the death of Edward King, but is representative of the Autumn swain, mourning the loss of his fellow.   The former, however, is the thought; the latter, the more soothing guise.

> " For Lycidas is dead, dead ere his prime,
> Young Lycidas, and hath not left his peer :
> Who would not sing for Lycidas ? "

A deft trick of style, caught from Spenser, as in

> "That iolly shepheard, which there piped, was
> Poore Colin Clout, (who knows not Colin Clout ?)"

The " three fatall sisters " of Spenser are often introduced by Milton, dominated, as both were, by classicism.   " The blind Fury " receives the emphasis in Lycidas.

We shall now adduce what we consider two excellent examples of Spenser's direct influence :—First, from *The Faerie Queene*, Book Three, Canto 3, stanza 4 :

> " Begin then, O my dearest sacred dame,
> Daughter of Phœbus and of Memorye,
> That dost ennoble with immortall name
> The warlike worthies, from antiquitye,
> In thy great volume of eternitye,
> Begin, O Clio, and recount . . . ,"

Milton, in *Lycidas*, following with

> " Begin then, sisters of the sacred well
> That from beneath the seat of Jove doth spring,
> Begin, and somewhat loudly sweep the string."

Secondly, from Book Three of *The Faerie Queene*, Canto 6, stanza 45 :

> " And all about grew every sort of flowre,
> To which sad lovers were transformde of yore :
> Fresh Hyacinthus, Phœbus paramoure
> And dearest love ;
> Foolish Narcisse, that likes the watry shore :
> Sad Amaranthus, made a flowre but late,
> Sad Amaranthus, in whose purple gore
> Meseemes I see Amintas wretched fate,
> To whom sweet poets verse hath given endless date,"

and in *Lycidas* thus ;

3

" Bring the rathe primrose that forsaken dies,
The tufted crow-toe, and pale jessamine,
The white pink, and the pansy freak'd with jet,
The glowing violet,
The musk-rose, and the well attired woodbine,
With cowslips wan that hang the pensive head,
And every flower that sad embroidery wears :
Bid amarantus all his beauty shed,
And daffodillies fill their cups with tears,
To strew the laureat hearse where Lycid lies."

Naming Cowley, whom Church describes as " made a poet by reading " Spenser, we pass on to Herrick, Lovelace and Vaughan.

Robert Herrick represents the School of Religious Poets, such as Quarles, Herbert and Crashaw. Like Lovelace, he wrote many amatory verses, besides religious pieces. He shows graceful fancy and fine taste, but has too evident a fondness for the lighter things of life (most reprehensible in a country parson) and for conceits of sound and sense. He has not been greatly influenced by Spenser, but his *Counsel to Girls*, at least, presents the " proof sufficient " of its origin : The Song of Temptation in the Bower of Bliss, at the end of Spenser's Second Book. The development is identical in both, and the expression exceedingly similar. We can but quote one line from each, though a detailed comparison will be found very interesting and fruitful. Spenser's Song exhorts the hearer to

" Gather therefore the rose whilest yet is prime,"

and Herrick's lyric :

" Gather ye rosebuds while ye may."

Lovelace and Vaughan show traces of influence, but to a slight extent only. Despite innate nobility of disposition, the artistic sense of these lyrists was comparatively feeble. There is too much awkward striving, subservience to effect, rather than free genius flowing naturally and securely, as did Spenser's, in its appointed course.

One school, during this period, threw aside all disguise and proudly avowed their poetical allegiance to Spenser. Phineas Fletcher, Giles Fletcher, Henry More (*Platonical Song of the Soul*), and Chalkhill, in *Thealma*, constitute the Spenserians.

A new departure began with Dryden, whose claims to posterity's appreciative recognition are not unfounded, though idealism only helped to make his work a palimpsest, the great bulk of which is quite unworthy.   In *Absalom and Achitophel* he excels Spenser in establishing the identity of allegory with fact.   The occasion and execution of this poem afford opportunity for comparison with *The Faerie Queene*, which, however, we cannot here undertake.   But Dryden's censure is more keen and bitter; his praise, more polished and insinuating; while he palpably sacrifices narrative to opinionated discourse.   We place him also in the warm stream of Spenser's influence, and offer the following in the relation of cause and effect :

In the third canto of his Fourth Book, Spenser has the following simile :—

> " Like an old oke, whose pith and sap is seare,
>   At puffe of every storme doth stagger here and theare,"

And Dryden, in his *Annus Mirabilis*, though owing most to Vergil, affords the following parallel to Spenser :—

> " All bare, like some old oak which tempests beat."

In canto six another simile is paralleled.

Dryden possessed abundant resources for his art, but altogether wanted the poetic necessity, the oneness and wholeness of Spenser or Milton.   But his pupil Pope was perhaps not too extravagant when he declared that

> " Waller was smooth ; but Dryden taught to join
> Tho varying verse, the full resounding line,
> The long majestic march, and energy divine."

We are now brought to contemplate *Paradise Lost* in its relation to our subject.

The two great epics of Spenser and Milton respectively are alike Puritan, without the bigotry.   Spenser's seeks, as he declares, " to fashion a gentleman or noble person in vertuous and gentle discipline," with King Arthur the ideal.   Milton's aim was to

> " assert eternal Providence,
> And justify the ways of God to men,"

with a noble anxiety to hush such moaning as Tennyson's Arthur embodied in the lines :

" I found Him in the shining of the stars,
I mark'd Him in the flowering of His fields,
But in His ways with men I find Him nct."

The source of this complaint is the more curious, when we consider Spenser's hero and Milton's early determination to write *his* epic upon King Arthur, and his confidential revelation of the scheme to Manso, the former protector of Tasso.

The Faerie Queene is first of all romantic, with clear classical elements and a pervading ethical tone ; *Paradise Lost* is too serious for romance or humour, but proceeds steadily to its work of Christian exposition and exhortation. Milton's epic had one great advantage: the poet believed what he wrote, and was thus enabled to secure the submission and subjection of all those poetic methods and requirements which too often succeeded in dominating the author of *The Faerie Queene.*

It is naturally to be expected that in *Paradise Lost* Milton should frequently show his obligations to Spenser, not only on account of the length of the epic, but also because of its character and its literary relation to the work of his illustrious predecessor. *Paradise Lost* and the first and second books of *The Faerie Queene* all contain the most vivid delineations of hell. Indeed, Spenser's second book and Milton's whole epic would fall to pieces without them. Milton's pictures show unmistakeable traces of the scenes described by Spenser; notably, the former's second book refers us to the latter's first and fourth. We have already introduced a specific instance of Spenser's general influence.

G. Herbert Clarke, '95·

(To be continued.)

EDITORIAL NOTES.

OUR new Chancellor, whose portrait accompanies the leading article of this number, has entered upon his duties in McMaster with the same earnest and genial spirit which won him so warm a place in the hearts of the people of Bloor St. Baptist Church. Students and professors alike already feel assured that under his wise and sympathetic management the year just begun will be a happy and successful one. Chancellor Wallace has high ideals of what McMaster's work and influence should be, as his fine inaugural address of Friday evening, Oct. 18th, clearly revealed. Let all endeavor to do their part that his and our highest expectations may be fully realized.

THE Senate and Board of Governors of McMaster University are to be congratulated that so able and acceptable a successor to Dr. Foster has been secured for the chair of Philosophy and Ethics. Dr. Ten Broeke has already won the esteem of his colleagues, and given evidence that his work in the University will fully realize what was expected of a Christian scholar of his wide experience and high attainments. His recent public address on the " Meaning of Philosophy and its Application to Education," proved his ability to handle the most difficult problems with the clearness of thought and force of presentation so essential to effective work in the lecture room.

ALL to whom the name of John King, of Dalesville, has long been familiar and dear will feel grateful to Mr. Higgins for his warmly appreciative review of a life so full of hard work and spiritual blessing. The portrait which we give with this sketch has been prepared from a small tin-type, the only likeness available for our purpose, and is, we are assured, the best that can be produced from it. If held at arm's length, and in a good light, it will prove a stronger and more interesting picture than the first glance might lead one to expect.

THE news of the death of Professor Boyesen, of Columbian College, on Oct. 4th, at the comparatively early age of 48, must have been a painful surprise to all. He had already acquired considerable distinction as a writer of popular tales of Norse life and manners, while his well-known essays on German and Scandinavian literature have established for him a high reputation as a scholar and literary critic.

KNOX COLLEGE deserves our gratitude for giving us the privilege of having such a distinguished and able defender of the faith as Professor Warfield, of Princeton. It was not our privilege, pressed as we are by our own work, to hear many of the lectures, but what we did hear were marked by broad scholarship, close reasoning, and sober judgment. Our readers will be glad to know that Dr. Warfield is a firm believer in the plenary inspiration of the Bible. Long may he be spared to his work and the world !

THOUGH more extended reference is made on another page to the Farewell Missionary Meeting held in College St. Church, on the 11th Oct., we cannot forbear a brief reference to it here. McMaster had a very deep interest in that gathering, since three of the number were last year in her class rooms. It is natural that this institution should send out missionaries. The Fyfe Missionary Society does much to foster the missionary spirit, and the whole purpose of the institution is to further the Kingdom of our Lord Jesus Christ. The quiet motive, the unaffected earnestness, and the great spiritual power that marked the Farewell meeting were something to be thankful for. These young men and women are seriously about their Master's business. The Stillwells, and the Priests, and Miss Smith go to their great task followed by our earnest prayers.

WE take great pleasure in reproducing the following communication from Prof. Farmer, which appeared in the *Canadian Baptist* of October 24th :

At the first meeting of the Faculty of McMaster University for the current season, a committee was appointed to draft resolutions expressive of the Faculty's appreciation of the work and worth of Dr. Rand and Professor Trotter. At our last meeting the committee reported. The report was adopted, and ordered to be published in the *Canadian Baptist* and *Messenger and Visitor.* The resolutions are as follows :

" *Resolved,*—That Dr. Rand, by his grasp of the principles underlying Christian education, his deep sense of their importance, the clearness and force with which he has enunciated them, and the energy with which he threw himself into the movement to give them effect in a fuller way among the Baptists of these Provinces, contributed very largely to the success of that movement which issued in the establishment of McMaster University.

"That, during the past five years, whether as head of the Arts Faculty, or as Chancellor of the University, Dr. Rand, by his alertness on its behalf, his fine administrative ability, his splendid hopefulness and flowing enthusiasm, as well as by his marked strength and popularity in the class-room, has done very much to win for this Institution its present honorable position.

" That, Dr. Rand, by his many fine personal qualities, has won the personal esteem and affection of his associates, so that the fact and prospect of the continuance of his association with us in work is to us a pleasure and a joy. And our hope and prayer is, that now, relieved of the heavy burden of the Chancellorship, he may, as Professor Emeritus and Lecturer, be spared for many years to do valuable service in his favorite subjects of Education and English, in which he has already achieved such distinguished success."

" *Resolved*,—That we place on record our personal esteem for Professor Trotter, and our appreciation of the excellent service he has rendered during the past five years. His genial manner and unfailing courtesy made him a very delightful companion ; whilst his clear views and sound judgment, his fine candor and genuine manliness, rendered him a most useful member of the Faculty. We admired the hearty and conscientious interest which he took in every depart- ment, and in the general life of the University. Of his work as Professor of Homiletics and Pastoral Theology we have heard only words of praise. It was marked by painstaking thoroughness and a contagious enthusiasm that made his lectures a delight as well as a profit to the students. He enjoyed in a large measure the esteem, confidence, and affection, not only of professors and students, but also of our people generally.

" Now that, in obedience, as he believes, to the will of God, he has re-entered the work for which his heart always yearned, our prayer is that the Holy Spirit may crown with a large blessing his pastorate in Wolfville—a pastorate for which he is so eminently fitted."

Trusting that you may be able to find a place in your columns for these resolutions, I remain,

On behalf of the Faculty,

J. H. FARMER, *Sec.*

Toronto, Oct. 19, 1895.

HERE AND THERE.

THE world of college journalism—what a world is that ! Dailies, weeklies, monthlies, quarterlies, annuals ! From the joke to the poem, discussion to dogma, cartoon to more pretentious sketch (*vide The Brunonian*). Herein are manifested the thoughts of all kinds of thinkers on all kinds of subjects. Not alone the warm glow of youth- ful enthusiasm,

". . . the wild joys of living ! . . ."

nor the delightful emotion experienced at the sound of the music of a new generation—not alone are these the perquisites of our exchange editor, but also the knowledge of mutual sympathy, fellowship and goodwill. More directly apparent does this become as our own learned graduates journey far abroad over the land, seeking what post curriculum they may devour.

To the forefront then again, O ye valiant corps of studentry ! Let valour prove your heraldry ! And may the resistless sweep of the editorial pen, comrades, arouse the slumbering nations to hitherto unconceived eras of discovery, prosperity and power ! We are the coming people.

At least, so one would judge from certain "eagle" editorials in *The Yale Record*, from whose bright pages we cull the following : "Yes, '99, thou art in our midst, and all we may now say is that 'you're better than '00.'"

VASSAR graduated one hundred last year.

AUTOCRAT of all the rushers : The football umpire.

AN excellent descriptive and critical article on Chicago University, written by Robert Herrick, and illustrated by Orson Lowell, occupies the position of honour in the October *Scribners'*.

"GIVE A THING AND TAKE A THING."

PATIENT :—" Oh, Dr. Pullem, you're giving me terrible pain ! "

DENTIST :—" On the contrary, my dear sir, I am particularly *painstaking.*"

We commend certain remarks upon the study of English embodied in the salutatory of *The McGill Fortnightly*, for Oct. 16th, to all students. This same issue contains valuable information regarding the new Principal, Dr. Peterson, whose portrait appears as a supplement.

THE income of the University of Chicago for the coming year is expected to reach $603,000. The faculty contains at present 157 members. The students in the graduate schools numbered last year 534, in the divinity schools 281, in the colleges 772, total, 1,587. Chicago has the largest graduate school in America.—*Ariel.*

THE poetry of most of our exchanges seems decidedly below par just now. But effort is needed every year afresh, and effort must precede effect. We quote, however, from *The Brunonian*, a little *Elizabethan* whose last stanza catches tune to the full :

I WAIT FOR THEE.

I wait for thee—dost thou yet know
Where anemones and lilies grow ?
And wilt thou come and meet me here
Where the wave of brook-song rises clear ?

I wait for thee—delay not so
To come where sweet-faced violets grow,
And lift their heads in sympathy
With a longing heart that waits for thee.

If all this sweetness thou didst know,
O thou wouldst never linger so,
But all thy grace would given be
To him who loves and waits for thee.

—*C. M. G.*

WILLIAM WYE SMITH has made an excellent translation in Scotch of the twelfth chapter of Luke. Here are some of its beauties reproduced :

" Fash-na muckle aboot the body, it is the clay-biggin we dwall in ; but be ye wyss and cannie wi' the tenant in't, the saul.

" 1. At a time whan the folk was sae mony an' that thick thegither that they war trampin' on ane anither, he begude to say till his disciples first o' a' : Be ye ware o' the barm o' the Pharisees, whilk is pretence ;

" 2. For naething is happit ower that sanna be brocht oot."

" 6. Arena five sparrows sell't for two bodles in a widdie ? and no' ane o' them but God keeps in mind.

"7. The verra hairs o' yer heid are a' coontit. Be na fear't : ye are better than a hantle o' sparrows."

.   .   .   .

" 23. For the life is mair than meat ; and the body than the cleedin.
" 24. Think o' the corbies that they naither saw nor shear ; for whilk thar is naither store nor barn—and God feeds them. Are ye no' a hantle better nor the fowls ?
" 25. And wha amang ye, though he be e'er sae fain, cud add till his measure ae span ?
" 26. Gif, than, ye canna do e'en a verra wee thing, why anent the lave o' the things sud ye be putten-tillt ?
" 27. Tent ye weel the lilies hoo they spring ; they naither toil nor spin ; and yet I say t' ye, no' e'en Solomon i' the heicht o' his glorie was brawlie buskit like ane o' these."

.   .   .   .

" 32. Be na fear't, wee flock, mickle lov'd, for weel-pleased was yer Faither to gift ye the Kingdom."

COLLEGE NEWS.

W. P. Cohoe,		R. D. George,
J. F. Vichert,		Miss E. Whiteside,
						Editors.

The University.

The skies are dark, the clouds hang gray,
   The summer days are over,
The winds blow chill from where they will,
   All nature's face is sober.
The sere leaf rustles to the ground,
   Our hearts are filled with yearning,
But ever is the freshie green,
   Within the halls of learning.

Freshie, in an awe-stricken whisper (gazing after bald and reverend senior) : " Say-y ! Is that man a professor? *He's got a gown on ! !*"

A new order of things prevails in the library this year. The magazines and periodicals have been removed to a separate room, and there has been a re-arrangement of the books. Mr. G. H. Clarke, '95, is librarian.

The Tennysonian Society began the term's work by an enthusiastic meeting, on Friday evening, Oct. 11th. The following officers were elected : Pres., Y. A. King, '98 ; Vice-Pres., H. Newcombe, '99 ; Sec.-Treas, A. B. Cohoe, '98 ; Counsellors, Messrs. Vining, '98, and McFarlane, '99 ; Editors, Messrs. Jones, '99, and Emerson, '99.

The Camelot Club, which proved itself so progressive a society last year, begins the new term with the following officers : President,

Mr. L. Brown, '96 ; Vice-Pres., Miss Burnette, '97 ; Sec.-Treas., Mr. Ben Oliel, '98· The club looks forward to future hours of profit and delight, as it brings itself in contact with the best genius of our literature.

AT the recent meeting of class '98 for re-organization, the following were elected to fill the offices for the ensuing year: Hon.-Pres., Rev. Dr. Thomas ; Pres., W. B. H. Teakles ; Vice-Pres., J. A. Ferguson ; Sec.-Treas., Miss E. Whiteside ; Orator, L. H. Thomas ; Poet., C. R Phelan ; Reporter, J. McIntosh.

THE regular annual meeting of the student body for the elections of officers was held in the chapel on Tuesday, Oct. 8th. The elections resulted as follows : Chairman, C. J. Cameron, '94 (acclamation) ; 1st Vice-Pres , E. J. Stobo ; 2nd Vice-Pres., W. P. Cohoe, '96 ; Sec.-Treas., E. P. Churchill, '97 ; other members of Executive Committee, W. S. McAlpine, '95 ; J. B. Paterson, '96 ; I. G. Matthews, '97 ; P. G. Mode, '97 ; A. Imrie, '96·

CLASS '96 met in the chapel on Wednesday, Oct 9th, and elected the following officers for the ensuing year : Hon.-Pres, Miss M. E. Dryden ; Pres., H. H. Newman ; Vice Pres., W Findlay ; Sec. Treas , G. N. Simmons ; Correspondent, L. Brown ; Poet, Miss M. E. Dryden ; Prophet, G. J. Menge ; Historian, A. G. Baker; Orator, J. C. Sycamore ; Minstrel, J. B. Paterson. Fitting reference was made by the retiring president, Mr. C. E. Scott, to the loss sustained by the class in the withdrawal of Mrs. H. E. Stillwell (formerly Miss Etta Timpany), and Rev. E. J. Bridgman, pastor of North Bay Baptist Church.

A FULL and enthusiastic meeting of Class '97 was held on Friday, Oct. 11th, for the purpose of electing officers for the present year. The election resulted as follows : Hon.-Pres., Prof. A. C. McKay ; Pres., Mr. H. N Mackechnie ; Vice-Pres., Mrs. J. Marshall ; Sec., Mr. W. R. Telford ; Bard, Miss M. E. Burnette ; Historian, Miss E. McDermid ; Orator, Mr. J. G. Matthews ; Correspondent, J. J. Patterson. A hearty vote of thanks was tendered the retiring officers for the able and satisfactory manner in which they had attended to the interests of the class.

THE Freshmen in Arts of the University held their first meeting on Friday, Oct. 11th, for the purpose of formally organizing themselves into " Class '99 " of McMaster. When duly organized they proceeded to the election of officers. Miss Cohoon was elected to the position of Honorary President. Mr. F. J. Scott will be the leader of the class throughout its first year of trial and conflict, and as President will, no doubt, do honor to his class. Contrary to precedent they elected a full staff of officers as follows : Vice-President, Miss Bush : Sec.-Treas., Mr. H. W. Newman ; Cor.-Sec , Mr. W. B. Tighe ; Poet, Mr. J. T. Jones ; Orator, Mr. J. C. McFarlane ; Minstrel, Mr. G. R. Welch ; Historian, Mr. C. S. Brown ; Counsellors, Miss Dubensky and Mr. H. Proctor.

WHEN the University re-opens in the Fall, the editors of the college news department find it difficult to prevent their column from being a mere list of appointments to office in the various societies : so promptly do all the slumbering activities awaken into life.   However, those interested in the Ladies' Literary League may be pleased to hear that it held its first regular meeting on Friday, Oct. 11th, when the following officers were appointed :—President, Miss M. E. Dryden ; Vice-Pres., Mrs. Bunt ; Sec.-Treas., Miss Bush ; Pianist, Miss Cohoon ; Critic, Miss Eby ; Correspondent to the MONTHLY, Miss E. Whiteside. Very deep regret was felt and expressed at the loss of the former efficient President, Miss Timpany, but the League hopes to continue the good work of the past.

IF the unfolding of mind be the good toward which we are to direct all striving, friends of the University will be glad to know that that apartment which was once given up to exercises for physical development, has now become the scene of mental gymnastics more intricate than any trapeze revolutions.   In short, the old gymnasium, little used in the past, and indeed almost half the basement, has been transformed into a science department with laboratories, lecture room, etc., complete.   The equipment for chemical and mineralogical work is specially thorough, and no student in natural science may henceforth be expected to take less than first class honors, in view of his superior advantages.

THE students of McMaster marched in a body to the College St. Baptist church on the evening of Friday, Oct. 11th, the occasion being the farewell meeting to our outgoing missionaries, three of whom, Mr. and Mrs. Stillwell, and Mr. Priest, go directly from McMaster.   The meeting was a noble one, the addresses being such as to awaken greater zeal for missionary enterprise, and the attention given by the large audience manifested a lively interest in our foreign work.   Needless to say, McMaster was proud of her representatives.   On Monday morning the student body was again present at the Union Station to witness, with many other friends, the final departure.   The time of waiting was occupied by the singing of hymns and the bidding of farewells, and the train pulled out amid waving of handkerchiefs, hearty cheering, and cries of " Boom on Mac ! "   McMaster was never interested in any missionaries more than these, and her earnest prayers will follow them on all their journeys.

THE Literary and Scientific Society met on the evening of Friday, Oct. 4th.   Mr. J. Russell, B.A , took the chair, and as retiring President, expressed his pleasure at the high degree of enthusiasm and interest which was displayed.   The officers for the ensuing year were nominated and on the following Monday at noon, they were legally elected by ballot as follows :—Pres., J. C. Sycamore, '96 ; 1st Vice-Pres., G. Sneyd, '97 ; 2nd Vice-Pres., J. B. Paterson ; Sec.-Treas., R. D. George, '97 ; Cor. Sec., J F. Vichert, '97 ; Councillors, Miss M. E. Dryden, '96, Miss M. E. Burnette, '97 and Mr. D. Nimmo, B.A.   The editors of the *Student* were elected on Monday evening : Mr. D. B. Harkness, '97, W. B. H. Teakles, '97, and A. W. Vining, '98, were elected. It is the intention of the Society's Executive to make the programmes this term so far as possible of an oratorical character. This intention carried out will make the meetings very interesting and at the same time develop the oratorical talents of the members of the Society.

On the evening of Friday, Oct. 14th, a reception was tendered the freshmen in Arts and Theology, by the students of other years. This was the second occasion of the kind which has taken place within the University. Receptions to freshmen will, in all probability, continue to be one of the most popular institutions of the University. After all had partaken of an excellent oyster supper, Mr. W. S. McAlpine, B.A., retiring chairman of the student body, made a brief introductory address which was well received. Mr. C. J. Cameron, B.A., was then called upon to speak on behalf of the students in Theology. As a patriarch in the Hall, he heartily welcomed all the new comers and relieved their minds by the assurance that in McMaster it is not the custom " to set the dogs on the freshmen," a custom very prevalent in some institutions. Mr. J. C. Sycamore, '96, was the next speaker. He represented the students in Arts, and his kindly words made every freshman feel that he spoke a welcome from the heart. Mr A. F. Baker, B.A., of Acadia, replied on behalf of the freshmen in Theology. He expressed his heart-felt thanks for the welcome which they as freshmen had received, and his relief at the discovery that there was no necessity to beware of the dogs. His speech was full of bright humor and touches of oratory. On behalf of the freshmen in Arts, Mr. J. C. McFarlane, one of the Woodstock boys, assured us all that his fellow classmates were fully appreciative of the kindness shown them, and that from thenceforth they would feel perfectly at home in the halls of McMaster.

The annual public exercises in connection with the opening of the University occurred in Bloor Street Baptist Church, on the the evening of Friday, Oct. 18th. The numbers present found a gratifying testimonial to the increased interest taken in the welfare of the University. After devotional exercises conducted by Rev. Elmore Harris, B.A., the chairman, Hon. John Dryden, delivered a brief address. The interest manifested, the progress of the University, the efficient and strong Faculty, the large number and excellent quality of the students in attendance, were all matters for which, on behalf of the Board of Governors he expressed thankfulness and gratification. He then introduced Chancellor Wallace, whose popularity was evidenced by the enthusiastic reception accorded him. His address was based upon the legend of McMaster University : " In Christ all things con-sist," and was a masterful setting forth of the truth of the legend. He spoke of the necessity and value of the most perfect spiritual training and development, together with intellectual discipline, in fitting young men and women for the duties of life. In McMaster, because of its ideals and principles, the conditions necessary for this education exists. If the past is a prophecy of the future, her work will be " both Christian in spirit and of such a quality as to commend universal respect and admiration."

In introducing Dr. Ten Broeke, as the new professor of Philosophy, Mr. Dryden expressed the great satisfaction it had been to the Board to secure a gentleman so eminently fitted for this position as was Dr. Ten Broeke ; and in his address the Dr. gave a practical demonstration of the very best kind of his fitness to occupy the chair to which he has been elected. He took as his subject, " The Meaning of Philosophy and its Application to Education." The address was of too intricate a nature for us to attempt to give a summary of it. Yet despite its metaphysical character the theme was treated with such clearness of thought and simplicity of style that for nearly an hour the speaker held the close attention of the promiscuous audience. We are sure we voice the wish of all who heard the address, when we express the hope that it will be given to the public in printed form.

MOULTON COLLEGE.

WE are glad to welcome again in our midst the posts who so cheered our dining-room last year, and we are also glad to see a number of new ones among them.

THE class of '96 organized the opening week, electing as officers :— Miss Dryden, President ; Miss Louie Matthews, Vice-President ; Miss Harris, Secretary ; Miss Mabel Wallace, Treasurer.

A MEETING of the Tennis players was called at the beginning of the term to form a club. The following officers were elected :—Honorary President, Miss McKay ; President, Miss Jessie Dryden ; Secretary Treasurer, Miss Sadie Rosser.

SHORTLY after the opening of the term we had the pleasure of again seeing Miss Fitch, before her leave-taking of Toronto. All the old girls received a call from her and very much enjoyed hearing her tell of her interesting experiences during her tour in the North-West, where she spent the summer.

THE " old girls' " annual reception to the new teachers and students was a decided success this year. During the evening Chancellor Wallace happened to drop in unexpectedly, and remained some time, adding much to the pleasure of all by his presence.

READERS of the MONTHLY will perhaps remember with what regret and sadness, Moulton, a few years ago, bade farewell to Major. It is, therefore, with great joy we announce that at last his place has been filled. We have another dog who answers to the name of Sefton and who is proving himself quite as interesting and amusing as his predecessor.

THE first regular meeting of the Heliconian was postponed to meet on the 25th of October, when the following programme was rendered :—

Instrumental, ... "Romance."
                    Miss Gilson.
Sketch, ... Origin of "Heliconian."
                    Miss J. E. Dryden.
Recitation, ... Selected.
                    Miss Orma Tait.
Vocal Solo, ...
                    Miss Boehmer.
Reading, ... Selected.
                    Miss Carmichael.
A Lilliputian Guest, ...
Instrumental, ... Nocturne by Scholtz.
                    Miss Cutler.

AT the beginning of October, members of our school had the opportunity of hearing Melba and her company of artists at the Massey Music Hall. Melba was, of course, the chief attraction. . Her singing is beyond description, and many of us will remember her wonderful voice for years to come. Mme. Scalchi's mellow notes were also duly appreciated, as well as the grand bass of Signor Campanari's, whose fine rendering of the numbers assigned to him called forth much applause.

WOODSTOCK COLLEGE.

DR. CADIEUX called upon us recently and gave a school address to the students, which was well appreciated.

WE were pleased to have a visit from our former teachers, Messrs. Robertson and George. Their genial faces will be always welcome, and the College heartily wishes them every success.

FOUR of our boys wrote on the Departmental Examinations last July ; two of them are now the happy possessors of Junior Leaving certificates, and one of a Primary. We are ready to congratulate James when word comes that his appeal has been sustained.

CHANCELLOR WALLACE paid us his first official visit on September 29th. Both Faculty and students were greatly pleased at the intense interest he displayed in our school affairs. He fairly captured the good wishes of all by the way he entered into our college life. We look forward with pleasant expectancy to his next visit.

WE were glad to see with us on the same day, Dr. Goodspeed, Superintendent McDiarmid and other members of the Ministerial Committee. We understand that they were busy until two o'clock in the morning, examining our young candidates for the ministry.

THE fears of us "old boys," that the attendance would be small this Term, owing to the large graduating class of 26 last year, have been pleasingly dispelled by the appearance of an unusually large number of new faces. The new fellows, too, seem to be good stuff, but, of course, not equal to the famous class of '95· There are now 109 names on the roll. At no time last year were there more than 110. We are expecting the usual increase after Christmas.

ON the 27th of September we held our annual games. Notwithstanding the cool weather the sports were well patronized by those invited ; and we were all pleased to see the faces of such old boys as Clarke, Jones, McFarlane, D. E. Welch, A. McDonald, Simpson, etc. The spectators expressed themselves as delighted with the emulous contests, and with the sportsmanlike spirit displayed by the contestants. After a hard struggle Emmet Scarlett won the championship cup. When we had assembled in the chapel, Mrs. Dadson and Mrs. Scott presented the badges ; Dr. Dadson, the cup, and Mayor Cole favored us with a speech. During these exercises Chancellor Wallace occupied the chair, and in his own inimitable way brought a pleasant day to a successful close.

GRANDE LIGNE.

THE school opens with bright prospects. All will be glad to learn that Principal Massé is in good health, and anticipates a profitable year.

JUDGING from the number of musical instruments in the school this year, we ought to be favored with plenty of music. No less than five students brought violins, another is skilled in playing the flute, and yet another the accordion, while we have heard the sweet strains of several mouth-organs in addition. We shall probably hear more of some of these later.

ON Sunday, October 20th, Rev. T. Lafleur paid us a very pleasing visit and preached an English sermon in the evening. He came to arrange for the celebration of the sixtieth anniversary of Madame Feller's arrival in Canada, which will take place in Feller Institute on November 1st. We expect to have a very pleasant and profitable time.

THIS year two of our old teachers are missing.   Miss C. Bullock, who has been with us for so many years, and who was so successful as Matron last year, has gone to Quebec City to conduct a day school in connection with our mission in St. Rochs.   Miss A. Bosworth, our Assistant Music teacher, is making an extended visit in England and France, to complete her education in music and French.   The places of these have been taken by Miss G. Laporte as Matron, and Miss Agnes Baker as Assistant in Music.   Miss Laporte comes to us with large experience in school work, and Miss Baker was formerly one of our own students.   Both have entered heartily into the work of the school, and have already endeared themselves to both teachers and students.

PROMPTLY on October 2nd we re-assembled, with a goodly number of pupils.   Among these are a large number of old pupils, but there are more new pupils than usual.   We miss a number of our best students of last year, who have finished their work here and have gone to higher colleges, or are otherwise engaged.   However, a number of others have stepped into their places and will graduate this year.   On the whole, we think our students are a younger class than we had last year, but there is no doubt that we have gained some good material among them.   There are a few empty rooms in the building yet, but we expect that these will be filled up within the next two weeks.

ABOUT two weeks ago it was a pleasure to the school and congregation to have Rev. L. Duteaud, our missionary at Quebec, give us an address on our mission work and workers in India.   The address was beautifully illustrated by magic lantern views, showing us some of the faces of our missionaries, and some of the peculiarities of the people and country where they are laboring.   Some few other views were shown.   One, a night view of Mount Vesuvius in eruption, was especially interesting.   Our interest and sympathy for the work in India will be increased by this address.   We are looking forward also to having Rev. H. F. Laflamme, of India, with us in a few days to speak again of the work there.   It is very seldom that we have an opportunity of listening to a missionary from India, so that their visits are long remembered when they do come.

96

THE

McMASTER UNIVERSITY MONTHLY.

DECEMBER, 1895.

GEORGE BURMAN FOSTER.

George Burman Foster was born in Monroe Co., West Virginia, April 2, 1857. His grandfather, John Foster, came from England in his boyhood, and served as a soldier in the war of 1812. His father Oliver Cromwell Foster is still living and is engaged in agricultural pursuits in the blue-grass region of West Virginia. At an early age young Foster was seized with a desire for mental culture and was able largely through his own exertions to secure in succession an academic, a collegiate, a university and a full theological course. He secured the diploma of Shelton College in 1879, after four years of study. Before entering upon his college course he had united with a Baptist church on a profession of faith and had consecrated his life to the gospel ministry. He was ordained in 1879 and the same year entered the University of West Virginia, where after four years of earnest application he was graduated with the honors of his class. On the completion of his university course he was united in marriage with Mary Lyon, daughter of Professor F. S. Lyon, and niece of Mary Lyon, the famous founder of Mt. Holyoke Seminary. In 1883 he entered upon a course of theological study in the Rochester Theological Seminary where he gained high distinction as a student and awakened among his teachers high expectations regarding his future career as a teacher.

After his graduation from the Seminary he served successfully for five years as pastor of the First Baptist church, Saratoga, N. Y. In June, 1891, he was appointed Professor of Philosophy in McMaster University, having been recommended to this position in the highest terms by President Strong, of the Rochester Theological Seminary, Professor Reynolds, of the University of West Virginia, and others. Having spent a year in special study in Germany he entered upon his work in McMaster, October, 1892. Denison University, of Granville, O., had shortly before conferred upon him the degree of Doctor of Philosophy.

Here he at once won the respect and affection of Faculty, students and governing bodies, by his enthusiastic devotion to his work, by his grasp of the subjects that had been committed to him, by his deeply sympathetic nature, and by his ability to make his work impressive and interesting. His ideals were high and he applied himself with the utmost severity to study. As preacher he was much in demand and many of our churches have pleasant memories of the earnest and thoughtful discourses with which he favored them.

When it was learned early this year that he was about to accept a theological chair in the University of Chicago, strenuous efforts were made by the Board of Governors, the Faculty and the students of our University, to retain his services; but he felt that duty lay in the new sphere, which seemed to him to have been providentially opened for him. He has carried with him to Chicago the good wishes and the high expectations of his Canadian friends. We shall watch his future career with deep interest and we shall be surprised if he do not speedily take his place in the front rank of theological teachers. His four years of special philosophical study have given him the best kind of preparation for teaching theology in a divinity school that forms part of a great modern university.

The following from President A. H. Strong, D.D., LL.D., under whom he studied theology and who has taken a deep interest in his subsequent career, may fittingly close our sketch :

"Dr. G. B. Foster is a man of native breadth and insight. He has the philosophical and theological bent. Training in the schools has given him a generous culture, and he knows the best that has been written both in English and in German. But Neander's motto especially applies to him : *Pectus est quad theologum ʾfacit.* He loves God and God's word, and a genuine Christian spirit pervades all his instruction. He is one of the few teachers who believe in, and who exhibit, the power of personal character to mould the minds and hearts of their pupils. He will always be an inspiring and elevating influence in any institution with which he is connected, simply because he regards his work as a sacred ministry to be conducted for God, and to be made the means of imparting to students something of the truth and the love of God. He has done noble work in McMaster University, but in the University of Chicago, with larger experience and greater maturity, he will do even a larger and better work ; while he will furnish to that great new institution precisely the element which it has needed—the element of deep religious and spiritual life."

ALBERT H. NEWMAN.

THE INCARNATION.

The Godhead shines in human face,
Heaven's pity weeps through human eyes,
And Mary's fragile arms embrace
The mighty God who built the skies.

Wonder of wonders ! David's Lord
Becomes his son ; and to atone
For human guilt, th' eternal Word
Stoops to the manger from the Throne.

Did ever such extremes unite,
Or natures join, apart so wide ?
He took our nature that He might
Be also God on our side.

D. M. W.

THE CHANCELLOR'S ADDRESS,

DELIVERED AT McMASTER UNIVERSITY OPENING, OCTOBER, 1895.

The legend of McMaster University, "In Christ all things consist," equally on account of its source and its ruling idea must excite more than a curious or fleeting interest. Embedded in the literatures of ancient Greece and Rome there are many clever apothegms which have been regarded as exactly fitted to be the mottoes of institutions of higher learning : it is significant that, in the selection of a motto for McMaster University, these were left and a text of Scripture taken. It is significant also that the motto of this university, almost alone of academic legends, contains no allusion to the gains and honours with which the world is accustomed to reward men who study laboriously and patiently. By the choice for the legend of our university of this divinely inspired sentence, which sets forth a basal principle of the Christian faith, the conviction is published that young men and women, while preparing for the great duties and responsibilities of life, need a clear vision of Christ rather than an alluring sight of the grandeurs and glories of this world.

As a text the meaning of this motto is sublimely comprehensive. In all literature there is not a statement concerning Christ greater or more daring. It is impossible for the human imagination to explore all that the thought involves : " In Christ all things hold together,"—all things in this world and in all worlds, whether they be minute atoms or boundless magnitudes, feeble insects or mighty angels, trembling dewdrops or majestic oceans, fretted pools or tranquil skies : thrones, dominions, principalities or powers ; " for in Him were all things created, in the heavens and upon the earth, things visible and things invisible." Christ, therefore, when presented to us as the " image of the invisible God," is seen to be the mightiest force, the fullest life and the supremest majesty of the universe.

This text, however, published as the legend of a university, has a meaning other than that which exegesis yields. It becomes then a creed, with wide horizons, profound depths and glorious heights, which imposes upon those who recite it the duty of absolute subjection to the example and lordship of Christ. If then he is to be our example, what is he ? And if we are to call him Lord, whither do his commands lead ? Let us know that he is more than a great Power : he is a great Man. He is more than a faraway Splendour distantly lighting up our present gloom : he is a Servant waiting to minister to the needs of our ignorant, weak, wayward humanity, " for the Son of Man came not to be ministered unto, but to minister, and to give his life a ransom for many." This legend, therefore, when changed into a creed, not only exalts to the place of lordship the Anointed of God, but declares that it is the Servant, the great, humble Minister of the human race, whom men ought most faithfully to imitate and obey.

McMaster University is not a Pharisee ; wears no broad phylactery ; is not inclined to mock God and mislead men by a pretentious use of texts from which her heart is far away. Our legend is our creed. We confess it reverently, and in the name of our Lord accept the responsibility which is involved in that confession. A service, a ministry, great in extent, exacting in nature, wearying in the ceaselessness of its recurring duties, is demanded of us, and we acknowledge fully the righteousness of that demand. This university does not come to this generation asking to be ministered unto, but offering to minister, and to give the fulness of her life for the help of many. Her professors are men who believe in God the Father, God the Son, and God the Holy Ghost ; confess themselves to be sinners saved by grace ; and realize, in some large measure, the sacredness of that ministry of teaching to which they have devoted their lives. Her students, with hardly an exception, are godly young men and women, who are eager to spend their lives in some noble service, and whether as ministers, teachers, physicians or leaders of affairs, to be still in some true and holy sense ambassadors for Christ. In prayer the academic year begins and ends ; each day of the year, almost each hour, is hallowed by prayer. If therefore there is any failure to realize the high ideals of service to which our legend summons us, this must be attributed to human infirmity and imperfection, and not to indifference or arrogance.

In undertaking to discharge the obligations of our sacred mission, it becomes our duty both to teach and to train the young men and women who look to us for guidance in their studies. This duty is a sacred trust. It is no light thing to be the teachers of those upon whom shall come the various trials and vast responsibilities of to-morrow. This is an intellectually expensive age, and he who makes the journey of life during the next fifty years will meet large demands upon his store of knowledge. As never before in the history of the world, the way of empty handed ignorance will be fraught with privation, distress and shame. It therefore must be the teacher's care that his students shall be abundantly furnished with the silver and gold and precious stones of knowledge, and that they do not start out upon their long journey burdened with mean coins or base counterfeits.

McMaster University exists for the teaching rather than the pursuit of truth. Much of the educational work of the present day is a menace to all that is holiest in faith and loftiest in morality because it is moulded in form and determined in spirit by the contrary of this principle. We are not now denying that there is truth to pursue; but we do most confidently and solemnly affirm that there is truth to teach. However vast may be the domain of the unexplored and unknown, it is yet true that something is known. Some truths are ours by the discoveries and attestation of the ages, and others by the unequivocal revelation of God. Such truths as have been abundantly proven or clearly revealed we dare to teach without apology or hesitation, while before such truths we dare not take the attitude of the denier, the doubter or the agnostic. Because it is our aim to send forth from this institution of learning, into the various spheres of responsibility and influence which educated men and women find, scholars whose opinions of truth and whose principles of conduct shall not be a fatiguing weight upon their own souls nor a source and occasion of irreligion in the communities in which they live, we seek earnestly and persistently to keep God in our thoughts and in all our teachings. Because truth is infinitely more than a mathematical formula, a scientific law or a philosophical statement, and that laws, principles, relations and revelations, come into the realm of truth only when those persons who discern and receive them are consciously subject to God in his relation to that which they have received, we hold that in all true teaching and learning God must be in all and over all, to incite and to restrain, to purify and to mould, to guide and to inspire ; and we maintain with an earnestness born of some knowledge of the perils of this age, that the lack of this conscious and confessed subjection to God in an institution of learning ought to be regarded as an inexcusable and fatal deficiency.

The mission of our university includes the work of training as well as teaching. Sometimes the question has been raised whether consecrated money ought to be used to furnish a literary education to our young people. This question can be proposed only when it is forgotten that the human mind is as much in need of development as of enrichment, and that a proper training can be given only where both tasks and environment are fit. If it is a religious act to give a man a sickle when the harvest waits the reaping, it cannot be an irreligious act to teach him how to reap and how to sustain his strength while reaping. If it is a part of religion to teach men true and noble ideas, it must also be a part of religion to teach them how to use these ideas nobly and effectively. Literary training has been given often with false aims and worldly motives. Culture has been sought for gain or pleasure or adornment. The arts college has been looked upon as tributary only to worldly success and power. But over against these false conceptions there stands a true conception, which we do well to honour. There is a pursuit of literary training which is as devout, unselfish and religiously earnest as any pursuit of theological furnishing can be. This is seen when young men, because they are eager for large service in the name of Christ, spend years in the fuller discipline of their mental powers, and in the acquisition of that knowledge which shall put them at an advantage in future Godly toils, having in all their tasks an eye single to God's glory, and realizing that the best offerings of a quickened intelligence and a carefully disciplined character are not too much to lay upon the altar of divine service.

For our children we have great and holy ambitions. We desire to see them equipped and anointed leaders in their day and generation. We are praying continually that God will accept them as His servants. If these hopes are to be realized our children must be well furnished intellectually, rich morally, and possessed of a faith at once intelligent, strong, simple and childlike. It therefore becomes necessary to create conditions which shall be favorable at the same time to the growth of both mind and character, conditions in which true ideas are imparted and intellect is quickened and moulded, while before the minds of the students, in all the stress and success of their daily life, its monotony or variety, its tasks or pastimes, there are kept constantly those great religious ideals of which we have been speaking to-night. Such conditions have been created in our university. Here high literary standards co-exist with high spiritual ideals, and the severest industry in study runs concurrently with the constant exercise of a simple piety. Thus to relate scholarship and godliness is essential to a proper development. Intellectual training, unaccompanied by the cultivation of the spiritual life, is both incomplete and dangerous, and he who thinks that literary development and the progress of the religious life in the soul are not compatible has reasoned carelessly. Not until the juice cannot fill the grape without injury to the vine, nor the blood flow vigorously through our veins without harming the body, need we look upon religion as an unmannerly intruder upon our busy, studious days. The religion of Christ is not the product of a chemist's experiment, the proper place of which is some ecclesiastical laboratory, but a life current which ought to be in full flow wherever man is, and most of all where man is young and growing; and therefore it should be abundant and strong in our colleges and universities. This is at once an explanation and a commendation of the distinguishing characteristic of our own university.

In years McMaster University is yet a child, but in achievement she already has shown herself possessed of mature and ample powers; and if the past may be read as a prophecy of the future, there is sufficient reason to believe that her ministry to this generation shall be both Christian in spirit and of an extent and quality which shall command universal respect and admiration.

Eleven years ago, as I went from the theological seminary to the responsibilities of the pastorate, a friend, whose eloquent lips have lately turned to dust, said to me, in earnest counsel,

"Give yourself in love to your people. This is essential to success in the ministry." To that advice I sought to give heed, and God did not withhold his blessing. Five years ago I was called to the pastorate of the Bloor Street Baptist Church in this city, and as I came to my duties here I remembered, and sought to heed, that former wise and Christian counsel; and again my work was not unfruitful. As I turn to my new duties this same advice, hallowed by years, and by the translation to heaven of him who gave it, comes to me once more, and I wish to obey its imperative injunction. To-night, without reserve or discrimination, I give myself in love to the professors and the students of McMaster University, to serve with them in this new ministry, this changed pastorate, praying that God will accept the service for the sake of his Son, in whom all things consist, and to whom we offer to-night our complete allegiance and most joyful adoration.

O. C. S. WALLACE.

THE DRAGONFLY.

I.

Winged wonder of motion
In splendor of sheen,
Cruising the shining blue
Waters all day,
Smit with hunger of heart
And seized of a quest
Which nor beauty of flower
Nor promise of rest
Has charm to appease
Or slacken or stay,—
    What is it you seek,
    Unopen, unseen?

II.

Are you blind to the sight
Of the heavens of blue,
Or the wind-fretted clouds
On their white, airy wings,
Or the emerald grass
That velvets the lawn,
Or glory of meadows
Aflame like the dawn ?
   Are you deaf to the note
   In the woodland that rings
   With the song of the White Throat,
   As crystal as dew ?

III.

Winged wonder of motion
In splendor of sheen,
Stay, stay a brief moment
Thy hither and thither
Quick-beating wings,
Thy flashes of flight ;
And tell me thy heart,
Is it sad, is it light,
Is it pulsing with fears
Which scorch it and wither,
   Or joys that up-well
   In a girdle of green ?

IV.

" O breather of words
And poet of life,
I tremble with joy,
I flutter with fear !
Ages it seemeth,
Yet only to-day

Into this world of
Gold sunbeams at play,
I came from the deeps.
   O crystalline sphere !
   O beauteous light !
   O glory of life !

V.

" On the watery floor
Of this sibilant lake,
I lived in the twilight dim ;
' There's a world of Day,'
Some pled, ' a world
Of ether and wings athrob
Close over our head.'
' It's a dream, it's a whim,
A whisper of reeds,' they said,—
   And anon the waters would sob.
And ever the going
Went on to the dead
Without the glint of a ray,
   And the watchers watched
   In their vanishing wake.

VI.

" The passing
Passed for aye,
And the waiting
Waited in vain !
Some power·seemed to enfold
The tremulous waters around,
Yet never in heat
Nor in shrivelling cold,
Nor darkness deep or gray,
Came token of sound or touch,—
A clear unquestioned ' Yea' !

And the scoffers scoffed,
In swelling refrain,
'Let us eat and drink,
For to-morrow we die.'

VII.

"But, O, in a trance of bliss,
With gauzy wings I awoke!
An ecstacy bore me away
O'er field and meadow and plain.
 I thought not of recent pain,
 But revelled, as splendors broke
From sun and cloud and air,
In the eye of golden Day.

VIII.

"I'm yearning to break
To my fellows below
The secret of ages hoar;
In the quick-flashing light
I dart up and down,
Forth and back, everywhere,
But the waters are sealed
Like a pavement of glass,—
Sealed that I may not pass.
 O for waters of air!
 Or the wing of an eagle's might
 To cleave a pathway below!"

IX.

And the Dragonfly in splendor
Cruises ever o'er the lake,
Holding in his heart a secret
Which in vain he seeks to break.

THEODORE H. RAND.

"LA REVEILLE."

'Tis a clear, frosty night in December. The starlight glistens on the snow. The ice crackles under the step, and the breath freezes on the air. 'Tis a night for the sleigh-bells to ring out their merriest jingle, and for a hearty greeting to fall on the ear with a more than usually cheerful sound.

The old-fashioned little church at Lichfield has put on its most hospitable appearance—an appearance at best certainly not imposing, for it is a rustic, dingy little place. However, it has done its best to be cheerful. Its huge stove glows with genial warmth, if not with polish, and through its four windows streams the brilliancy of its seven lamps.

You smile, reader, but still in this humble place the sovereign of the heavens deigns to meet with man, and listen to his poor petitions. Listen to the song of praise rising like precious incense from a rude censor. Softly, in low, quivering tones, it rises at first, then louder and louder it swells, as one and another join in the strain:

> " Come thou fount of every blessing,
> Tune my heart to sing thy praise."

Deep, solemn, touching old hymn! The little church rings with the melody, and the clear air bears its echo upwards towards the heavens—a sweet tribute of thanksgiving to the Omnipotent.

The hour of prayer and praise is ended. The honest farmers press around the minister to wish him good e'en, in their kindliest manner. For a few moments the air resounds with hearty greetings and the merry jingle of bells, but soon the old meeting house, notwithstanding its hospitable air, is left almost tenantless.

Three individuals still remain. One is the old man who has charge of the church, the others are deacon McDonald and deacon Smily. That is deacon Caleb McDonald who stands at the left side of the stove—a tall, fat old gentleman, in a large overcoat. He is about sixty years of age, a model picture of a sturdy Scotch·Canadian farmer. You would not call his face handsome, yet it is one of which the deacon need not be ashamed. A large, well-shaped mouth, with an expression made up of two parts Scotch caution and three parts American shrewdness, a long nose, and sharp, gray eyes, which have a faculty for looking in all directions at the same time, without giving their owner the disadvantage of a squint. These eyes have won for the deacon a notoriety among the small boys of the neighborhood, among whom he is known by the name of "Caleb the Faithful Spy;" and certainly very few things escape his observation. Many a fine lark has been entirely brought to naught by his quicksightedness.

Yes, Caleb McDonald is a clever, shrewd old gentleman, but he is not a general favorite. "The Faithful Spy" is the most complimentary of his numerous titles. He is also known as "Old Screw," "Stingy Caleb," and "Skin-flint," — names of whose uncomplimentary character there can be no doubt. The fact is, that when the deacon began life with the wide world as a potato garden and his hands as working capital, a dollar was a large sum ; and now that he has become the richest farmer in the township, a dollar is still a dollar, and is not to be lightly parted with.

Though mankind in general, and beggars and collectors for charitable purposes in particular, do not give the deacon a high name for liberality, still he does help to support his own church. When he sells his wheat, instead of putting all the proceeds into the bank, as we must confess he sometimes feels his evil genius prompting him to do, he silences the wicked one immediately, and with a comfortable sense of having gained a moral victory over the sins of the flesh, he lays aside the sum for the *cause.* Now if the gift is valued by the amount of sacrifice and moral effort required to give it, deacon McDonald's moderate donation must be exceedingly precious. In addition to this yearly amount, the deacon generally gives twenty-five cents towards a donation for the minister, and if potatoes are plentiful and the deacon finds it rather difficult to dispose of his, the minister is sent a bag or two. If a storm comes on and blows some plums off the deacon's trees, they are placed in the garret to ripen, and the minister is sent a share of them. In short, whenever a chance occurs of showing the minister's family a kindness of this description, the deacon always improves it.

Caleb McDonald is an honest man ; he never cheats anyone, though he understands how to drive a clever bargain. He is a deacon of Lichfield church, gives a sum in *hard cash* every year towards *the cause,* gives twenty-five cents now and then towards a donation for the pastor, and occasionally sends a present to the minister's family.   He owns the best two hundred acre farm in the neighborhood, has the best house, orchard and cattle in the county, and a good many thousands lying snugly in the bank. In fact he is an eminently respectable member of society.   Why do they call him " old skin-flint ?"

Well, we have given you an introduction to deacon McDonald, with an appendix ; and now it is time we took a look at his companion, deacon Smily—quite another person.   Small, wiry, with a smart, elastic step, and a face the perpetual picture of his name : a small mouth, the corners of which have a decided propensity to curve upward ; a pair of laughing black eyes, and a shock of curly brown hair, dashed here and there with silver. Everyone agrees with the boys that deacon Smily is a " regular brick."   We shall not praise him too much for his liberality— though his hand is as open as his heart—because it probably costs him less to hand over twenty-five dollars than it does deacon McDonald to unclasp his fingers from *twenty-five cents.* There is less *high moral effort* wanted.

The two old farmers were soon seated in deacon Smily's sleigh.   Deacon McDonald often takes a seat with his friend, as by this arrangement his horses are fresh for the morning's work. " Brother," said deacon Smily, when they had driven on quickly for a few moments, " I have a few calls to make if you do not object.   I promised to see poor Martha Monrow, and, by the way, you are a deacon, and might come along.   She'd be delighted to see you.´ Here we are at the place," and in a moment the lithe little man was standing at the door, with a basket on his arm, and his burly companion by his side.

The door was opened by a tidy Scotch woman, who heartily welcomed deacon Smily, and though she looked surprised at the sight of his companion, she gave them both a cordial invitation into a neat little room, at the one end of which was the sick girl's bed.   Poor Martha was indeed a sufferer.   For five long years had she been a prisoner to her couch, but she still was cheerful. Christianity was a power with her, which held firmly to her one bright hope after all other hopes had taken wing and fled.   Deacon Smily immediately crossed the room and spoke to the invalid : " Well, Martha, how do you feel to-day ? " At the first sound of the cheery voice, the sick girl's pale face lighted up, and she stretched out her hand eagerly to the visitor. " I have had one of my bad spells to-day, but I am better now, thank you." Her eyes fell on the second visitor, and deacon Smily said, " Martha, this is deacon McDonald ; you remember him, don't you ? " " O yes, very well," and with one of her brightest smiles, she held out her hand to the deacon. 'Twas a thin white hand, and some- how as his large hand closed upon it, a str nge feeling came over him. Deacon McDonald had a warm corner in his heart, and that pale-faced, gentle sufferer seemed to reach it by the shortest way. The last time he had seen her she was a rosy, romping girl, and now upon her pale face there was plainly written the sufferings of the years gone by. Something like remorse, too, mingled in his thoughts. He had done nothing during all these years to help her to bear her heavy burden. He stood quietly by while Deacon Smily spoke to her comforting and tender words. He saw her eyes brighten at the sight of the ripe golden pears which the deacon had brought her, and all this time feel- ings which long had slumbered in Caleb McDonald's heart awoke and swelled and surged in his breast. He had a sister once, who died long, long ago ; faded away day by day until she became too frail and beautiful for e rth, and took her flight for the regions of bliss. 'Twas long since he had thought of her, but now memory was fresh and vivid. As he followed deacon Smily from the sick girl's room, he brushed something like a tear from his cheek, a d inwardly determined that one of the boxes of peaches in his cellar should find its way to the invalid on the morrow.

The avenue, once opened to the deacon's heart, was not quickly closed. A visit to Widow Martin determined him to send her a load of wood. As he followed deacon Smily from one scene of suffering to another, and marked the glow of sunshine this good man's presence cast over the most dismal scenes, an enthusiasm began to kindle in his breast. The tiny spark of Christianity, which had been almost smothered by worldliness, now began to brighten into a ruddy blaze ; the slumberer was awakening.

'Twas late before Caleb McDonald went to bed that night. He sat in his large arm-chair, and the fire-light from the large wide hearth shone upon a ponderous volume on his knee. Over his countenance stole a softened expression as he read with a new interest the old, old story of Him who was rich yet for our sakes became poor.

Since that night many have been the blessings invoked upon Caleb McDonald's head, and "Old Skin-flint" is a title no longer used. The deacon's head is growing whiter, his step more un-certain; before many suns roll round, he will pass from this to the other side. But he is happy in the thought, and in that day many will rise up to call him blessed.

Tyro, 1876.   E. A. C.

TO A COMRADE.

Give me thy hand, for many years have fled
Since we as comrades wrought on India's strand,
And moons have waned, and friends have passed away ;
          Give me thy hand.

The world rolls on with its bright sister orbs,
That pass and repass in their paths of light ;
Great rivers flow, their drops return in rain,
          We meet to-night.

One will there is that guides those radiant spheres,
One love alone can reach the sons of men,
No joy is found in wanderings wild, until
               They turn again.

And so to thee, though many voices call
With Babel accents, in that Orient land ;
Friends may grow cold. yet when we meet again
          Give me thy hand.

                         R. Garside, '95 (Th)

2

THE PRELUDE.

The voice of the singer is silent now ;
His fingers pass over the keys ;
The notes of the organ are sweetly low,
Now dying away on the breeze.

The quaver, the swell, and the joyous tone,
In concord their music prolong ;
And twilight is sweetened amid the strain :
The singer commences his song.

O sweet was the prelude he played to-night ;
But sweeter the song that is heard ;
The sadness of mortals is hushed to rest,
Deep joy in each spirit is stirred.

The tones are all tenderly sweet, for now,
Not sounds that are carelessly wrong ;
But perfect the harmony sounding far   :
The prelude is heard through the song.

O Christian ! play well, play thy prelude now,
'Tis short, for it ceases with Time ;
The song will be sung through eternity,
Though endless, all perfect, divine.

Play carefully now, let no harshness mar
The music, the righteous may own,
For mortals so eagerly watch each day
To witness a harsh, ruffled tone.

O sweeten thy prelude with God's high praise,
And strengthen by might from above,
That mortals, while list'ning, may deeply long
To play the same music of love.

Harmonious then be the chords you strike,
All perfect in praise, though not long,
For oft in the music that floats thro' heaven,
The prelude is heard through the song.

The Tyro, 1876.   IDA.

THE DEACON'S SALOON.

[The following poem by the Professor of Latin in the Connecticut Literary Institution (Baptist), Suffield, was used with marked effect in the recent campaign against the Gothenburg liquor plan in that State.   Our thanks are due to our old friend the author for sending it to us. —Ed.]

" O .friends, you ought to come and see good temperance deacon
    Brown.
He runs a Gothenburg saloon, the only one in town.
He sells his whiskey, gin and rum in the new Norwegian way,
Which makes it just as pious to sell whiskey as to pray.

The deacon's shop is fitted up in a most uncommon style,
With Scripture mottoes on the walls—its enough to make you
    smile.
A Bible stands upon the bar—a hymn-book, too, they say,
With every bottle that he sells he gives a tract away.

The parson sometimes takes a hand to help the deacon out,
And oft the brethren, wandering in, stand solemnly about.
" You can't suppress this evil" they say with sweet accord;
" So we'll try to cheat the devil while we make him serve the
    Lord."

So they build their schools and churches with the profits of the
    " biz "
And they all rejoice to serve the Lord in such a way as this.
And they vote those churches all "dead slow " who work for
    " Kingdom come,"
With only "holy water" where they might have gin and rum.

And yet they say that Widow Smith, when her only son lay
    dead
With the deacon's tract beside him and a bottle near his head,
Could never see the difference—so very clear to some—
Between Pat Murphy's whiskey, and the pious deacon's rum.

ALFRED H. EVANS.

𝔖𝔱𝔲𝔡𝔢𝔫𝔱𝔰' 𝔔𝔲𝔞𝔯𝔱𝔢𝔯.

THE INFLUENCE OF SPENSER UPON SUCCEEDING POETS.

(Concluded.)

And now, lest our subject, however interesting, prove too enticing, we must be content to sketch rapidly the history of Spenser's influence down to modern times, beginning with the artificially-cut verse of Pope, in imitation and perfection of his leader, Dryden. Style, subject, sources were now all changing, and men read Spenser less. Yet Pope declares that he never lost enthusiasm for *The Faerie Queene*, and admired it greatly throughout his life. His criticism of Trevisan's demeanour after his escape from Despair shows acute appreciation. In his *Discourse on Pastoral Poetry*, he praises Spenser with discrimination ; and in many of his *Juvenile Poems* acknowledges his indebtedness. *The Dunciad* contains similar confessions, evincing considerable knowledge of the epic. Spenser declares in his very first stanza that

'Fierce warres and faithful loves shall moralize his song,'

and Pope borrows the concluding phrase in his *Epistle to Dr. Arbuthnot :*

"Not in fancy's maze he wandered long,
But stooped to truth, and moralized his song."

Such contemporaries as Ambrose Philips, Gay and Prior were also swayed by Spenser, especially as regards the pastoral.

Omitting mention of the poets that clustered within the dying school of Pope, we pass on to find not only a reviving interest in classics, but a conscious awakening in the field of criticism and knowledge of poet-lore. Enthusiasm spread and the past was eagerly ransacked. Many a forgotten poet found his long-delayed deserts at the hand of posterity, and it is not, therefore, remarkable that a second Spenserian school arose, animated by the master's grand old spirit. Warton produced a meritorious essay on *The Faerie Queene;* William Shenstone wrote his *School-mistress* in imitation ; James Thomson followed suit in his *Castle of Indolence*, 1784; and James Beattie also, in *The Minstrel* of twenty-three years later. This group also observed a rigid adherence to the Spenserian stanza, which has been favoured by many later poets, and of which a brief notice should here be given.

This peculiar stanzaic form is certainly entitled to its name, being Spenser's own invention. Doubtless the Italian 'ottava rima' proved grateful and suggestive to our poet as well as Chaucer's basal form, but Spenser's stanza is far the more noble and melodious. The concluding Alexandrine affords a perfect finishing touch, and is triumphantly adapted for climactic effect, whether of humour, pride or pathos. The form must invariably help, rather than retard, the expression of every good poet. As *Emerson says of Spenser, 'in his rhythm is no manufacture, but a vortex, or musical tornado, which, falling on words and the experience of a learned mind, whirls these materials into the same grand order as planets and moons obey, and seasons, and monsoons.'

The more modern throng is so large and representative of innumerable phases of personal and historical influence that trepidation characterizes our approach, and the conviction that adequate treatment is impossible within this limited scope deters us from too ambitious an attempt. We are content to select the three distinctive groups of Wordsworth and Coleridge; Byron, Shelley and Keats; and Tennyson and the Brownings. Even of these we must say but little.

Swinburne and Rossetti concur in praising Coleridge for high lyrical excellence, and in this field particularly may fruitful comparison with Spenser be achieved. Dean Church has shown, significantly enough, that Spenser's great and varying picture is the literal rendering of Coleridge's lines:

> " All thoughts, all passions, all delights,
> Whatever stirs this mortal frame,
> All are but ministers of Love,
>   And feed his sacred flame."

Wordsworth, the spiritual philosopher, the revealer of the holiness and glory of Nature, read Spenser with delight. Yet Spenser's Nature may be termed humanistic, and he made no

*On " Poetry and Imagination."

effort to interpret her moods and being, while Wordsworth's whole history of the soul is tinged with and interpreted by the philosophy of Nature. Wordsworth thus may be said to have inaugurated a new departure in English poetry; thoughtful observation, careless of expression, is sometimes noble, but often rude; and studied seclusion tended unduly to self-exaltation. Poets *need* an external world, real and vivid; and the recluse is sure to be one-sided. So much for Wordsworth's theory and method. There is a modern and fatal restriction, precluding the possibility of such keen, excited, and exultant vision as Spenser's.

At Cambridge, Wordsworth naturally dreamed of those great poets who had there been received and nurtured in youthful days. As his spirit felt the beauty of the place he thought that

> " Scarcely Spenser's self
> Could have more tranquil visions in his youth,
> Or could more bright appearances create
> Of human forms with superhuman powers,
> Then I beheld loitering on calm clear nights
> Alone, beneath this fairy work of earth,"

an early indication of his intelligent affection (if we may so speak) for Spenser, whom, indeed, in after years, he and Coleridge read together with as much enthusiasm as Homer inspired in the hearts of Keats and Cowden Clarke.

The stanzas written in his pocket-copy of Thomson's *Castle of Indolence* are noteworthy as both a self-revelation and a remarkably successful imitation of the Spenserian style and stanza. *Artegal and Elidure* shows similarity in subject, tone and treatment. But the preface to *The White Doe of Rylstone,* in point of feeling, appreciation and sympathetic imitation is Wordsworth's best recorded tribute to Spenser. We quote the first stanza :—

> " In trellised shed with clustering roses gay,
> And, Mary ! oft beside our blazing fire,
> When years of wedded life were as a day
> Whose current answers to the heart's desire,
> Did we together read in Spenser's lay,
> How Una, sad of soul—in sad attire,
> The gentle Una, born of heavenly birth,
> To seek her knight went wandering o'er the earth."

Many other examples could be cited,—let these suffice. Spenser affected Wordsworth, because both were high moral poets, revering the beautiful, worshipping the true, differing in method and perception, but united in honest and noble aims.

What an antithesis in Byron, the active, clever, passionate genius! We can find everything in him but a heartfelt satisfaction. Polished and satirical as Pope and Dryden, loyal as those of old to Nature, but reflecting himself upon his visions, and then again half-unconsciously, but altogether impetuously, following Wordsworth's spirit, however much he affected to despise it, he certainly presents a strange coalition of poetical instinct, intellectual influence, fateful circumstances, and a genius like a Fury, that drove him on forever. Byron cannot be called noble, but Spenser was. The one could be hypocritical, but not the other. Byron revelled in evil, Spenser related it fearlessly, as one to whom "all things were pure." Byron drummed experimental snatches upon the organ of the universe, merely to please himself; Spenser played from a brave poetic soul harmonies and melodies for all who would be charmed. The differences were wide, so that Byron heard but little from his fellow-poet.

Spenser, however, gave Byron his stanza for *Childe Harold's Pilgrimage*, in the preface to which he remarks that " the stanza of Spenser, according to one of our most successful poets, admits of every variety," and proceeds to quote Beattie's praise of the measure, concluding with the assertion of his own conviction that failure, if it comes, " must be in the execution rather than in the design, sanctioned by the practice of Ariosto, Thomson, and Beattie." But failure did not come.

Shelley, the supreme and swift dictator of the Imagination, rightly accorded it the first place in his being. He understood Wordsworth as Byron would not, and he too invested Nature with spirit. But methods again differed: Wordsworth saw all as the reflective philosopher, Shelley, in the image of Love. Anxious, sensitive, ecstatic soul! *Epipsychidion* is his involuntary autobiography. However carefully intellect served him, his utterance grew more passionate, quick, intense. His love was boundless, choking. He reached the point of over-satiation, of too keen joy,—

> " Woe is me !
> The winged words on which my soul would pierce
> Into the heights of Love's rare Universe,
> Are chains of lead around its flight of fire.
> I pant, I sink, I tremble, I expire ! "

The Spenserian stanza readily revealed his genius. *The Revolt of Islam* and *Adonais* have caught up the form and absorbed it to perfection, albeit some stateliness is curiously absent, though necessarily so. *Stanzas written in Dejection, near Naples* are in a measure adapted from the Spenserian, and exceedingly harmonious. Shelley was free and new and wonderful, and though he loved Spenser, his own flowing song was paramount. In *The Skylark*, however, where he has adopted the device of ending the stanza with an Alexandrine, (probably Spenser's stanza still rang in his ears), he has

> " And singing still dost soar, and soaring ever singest,"

while Spenser's Una

> " . . praying still did wake, and waking did lament."

Keats cries: I have known him ! Keats,—the large-eyed, melancholy Greek, full of love and reverence, vision, murmur, and melody. His life presents curious analogies with that of Spenser, of whom also he was a fervent, though not exclusive, disciple. Both were often dominated by sound and music, exquisitely sensitive as they were to sweetness of tone. Craik has it that the true poet alone can judge the essence of song, the musical element, such power over language belonging to only the "greatest poets—in Spenser especially, whose poetry is ever as rich with the charm of music as with that of picture, and who makes us feel in so many a victorious stanza that there is nothing his wonder-working mastery over words cannot make them do for him."

At sixteen, Keats obtained *The Faerie Queene,* and read it with immediate effect. Week after week he shouted over it in the ears of Cowden Clarke. " He ramped through the scenes of the romance, says his friend and tutor, "like a young horse turned into a spring meadow." With what keen relish the boy devoured the poem may well be judged by the extent of its influence upon his future work. He early employed the Spenserian stanza in some bantering verses about his comrade Charles Armitage Brown, in April, 1819, though his first experiment was made at the age of 19, *In Imitation of Spenser*, followed by the fragment of *Calidore*.   Spenser's impulse chiefly urged expression. In 1817 Keats produced his first volume, with the characteristic motto from Spenser on its title-page :—

> What more felicity can fall to creature
> Than to enjoy delight with liberty ?

His last long poem, *The Cap and Bells*, is written in Spenserians. His master's *Pastorella* appealed strongly to his poetic mind, so that he embodied her story in *Endymion*.   All through his poetry, indeed, *The Faerie Queene* appears by allusion and insertion.   He even undertook to write a new conclusion to Canto Five, of Spenser's Second Book.   Spenser's influence swayed Keats from first to last, though we would not claim persistent domination, nor, indeed, was it continually paramount.   *The Eve of St. Agnes*, in the Spenserian stanza, excellently exemplifies our opening remarks on Keats,—it is dreamy, picturesque, beautiful, and owes its all to sound.

Spenser's fierce lion, rushing towards Una, suddenly pauses, cowed and amazed by the Beauty of Truth.

> "O how can beautie maister the most strong,
> And simple truth subdue avenging wrong ! "

for indeed, as Keats has it

> " Beauty *is* truth, truth beauty."

Spenser describes the wiles of Phaedria over Guyon :

> " By this she had him lulléd fast asleepe,"

followed by Keats in *La Belle Dame sans Merci* :

> " And there she lulléd me asleep,"

his first manuscript reading :

> " And there we slumbered on the moss."

Certainly Spenser first gave Keats the key into the garden of fairy-land, music and enchantment, and proved ever after a choice companion.

We have spoken somewhat of Tennyson, with regard to his treatment of King Arthur. In 1872, Buxton Forman produced a criticism of "Our Living Poets," which *The Quarterly Review* at once proceeded to demolish. Tennyson's "Arthur" is declared to be artificial and non-existent. *The Idylls* are representative of modern thought and interests, while Arthur is ancient and improbable. To this we would reply that the poetic colouring and scenery are second only to the poetic occasion itself, while both are indispensable. It is claimed by others that 'Arthur is a modern gentleman,' and we do not demur. Human passions are world-lasting, and sense wars as fiercely against soul to-day as ever before. The action of the epic is an universal action. It is no mistake to resort to allegory where it has its own delights and can ensure the dual symmetry. If such objections should prevail, what of *Lycidas*, or of *The Faerie Queene* itself? Matthew Arnold terms poetry a "criticism of life," using the phrase in its broadest sense. This Tennyson accomplishes, and with the inestimable help of choice diction, clear-cut style, and artistic arrangement.

It is right that the Arthurian literature should have grown, and strange that its volume is not greater, for its hero is the ideal man, often naturally identified with Christ himself. Joseph of Exeter declared that "the old world knows not his peer, nor will the future show us his equal,—he alone towers over all other kings, better than the past ones, and greater than those that are to be;" Alberic :—

> "Hic jacet Arturus, flos regum, gloria regni,
> Quem probitas morum commendat laude perenni,"

and Sharon Turner: "all human perfection was collected in Arthur." Joyfully, then, Spenser and Tennyson turned to such an ideal, and realized their poetic purposes by realizing him.

There can be no good turn served by squabbling about *The Idylls;* 'hypocritical' and 'unreal' are words that show deplorable blindness or wilful perversity. Jacobs objects that Tennyson's epic is not an epic at all, or, at best, only a literary one. But his definition is designed to exclude all allegory, and appears trifling and arbitrary. An epic is an heroic narrative, which Sidney calls the best and most accomplished kind of poetry.

The introduction of a moral need not make it didactic. It is true, indeed, that the necessity of maintaining perfect proportion is an excellent opportunity for the exhibition of skill, and a distinct addition to poetic merit and achievement. Spenser's story has more sensuous charm; Tennyson's a more symmetrical balance.

The late poet-laureate, like Spenser and Milton, loved the classical; like Keats, he caught the antique spirit itself. His lyrics are unsurpassed. He is to the Victorians what Spenser was to the Elizabethans,—the singer of the tones that rule the times, the artist conscious of his work and subject. Tennyson is clearer and more brilliant, Spenser warmer and more spontaneous.

It is interesting to note how well Tennyson catches *Spenser's description of the sword Excalibur, and turns it to his own use. Jewellery abounds in both descriptions, but †Tennyson's is the more keen and gleaming. He is less enthusiastic about Arthur's accoutrements, making him ride

> . . . a simple knight among his knights,"

while Spenser devotes eight stanzas to Arthur's personal appearance. Both poets agree upon the legend of *The Holy Grail,* but Spenser grants it scanty space. The Merlin of *The Faerie Queene* is not at all mysterious, but launches forth into explicit narration of the lineage and race of Arthegall, son of Gorloïs. Both poets have disposed their material to excellent advantage.

Spenser often requires a whole stanza in which to tell the time of day, an easy grandeur quite in keeping with his broad, uplifting, transforming embrace of all the heterogeneous elements, commonplace or extraordinary, that go to make up *The Faerie Queene.* For example, (we quote part of a stanza only):—

> " By this the northerne wagoner had set
> His sevenfold teme behind the stedfast starre
> That was in ocean waves yet never wet,
> But firme is fixt, and sendeth light from farre
> To all that in the wide deepe wandring arre."

The Faerie Queene, Book One, Canto Seven.

†*Idylls of the King, The Coming* and *the Passing of Arthur.*

This no doubt suggested Tennyson's lines in *In Memoriam :*

> " The brook shall babble down the plain,
> At noon or when the lesser wain
> Is twisting round the polar star."

Little need here be said of Browning ; as the modern Christian poet he possesses many philosophical advantages over Spenser and Milton, but the three confound all comers with the faith defended.   Browning, however, in his genius and performance, is alone; influencing far more than influenced ; swimming across the Gulf-stream rather than carried down its current.   As to form, his *Misconceptions* appears to be a haphazard half-imitation of Spenser's stanza.   But his beautiful companion had loved old " Colin Clout," and of her we must speak a moment.

Mrs. Browning's classicism was more like Keats' than Milton's in its warm and kindred touch, but she is nevertheless a distinct modern, and knows how to make her aids subservient. With Spenser, she sat at the feet of Homer and Plato, and could not be satiated.   Her reading was wonderful in extent and sympathy.   Italy welcomed both the Brownings in her passionate embrace, and impelled their work as never before, not in Milton's life, still less in that of Spenser.   In the sixteenth century, however, Wyatt and Surrey came back from Italy and sang the first note of modern poetry, which inspiration is the lasting glory of the land of Petrarch.   They were the beginners of the amourist poetry in England, " sonnets mingled with lyrical pieces after the manner of Petrarch, and in accord with the love philosophy he built on Plato."   Sidney, Shakespeare, Spenser thus exulted, and of late the impulse appeared in the sonnets of Rossetti and Mrs. Browning.   The following fine characterization of Spenser appears in Mrs. Browning's *Vision of Poets*, for certainly Spenser was the greatest and noblest dreamer of England, and has led Mrs. Browning herself to sing in sleep :

> " And Spenser drooped his dreaming head
> (With languid sleep-smile, you had said,
> From his own verse engendered,)
>
> On Ariosto's, till they ran
> Their curls in one.   .   .   ."

What a chorus of testimony to the value of Spenser's work !

It is the poets' fairy-land,—but it is more. It is a philosophy
of life, depicting in a profuse harmony of colour and arrangement, mingled with the sound of exquisite music, the brave
endeavour of the soul to come and find new life in its pure
Source, and the evils that beset it by the way. As a hunter,
suddenly translated from the busy mart of commerce to the vast
and gorgeous jungle, so hail all poets with delight the glorious
scenery and open music of Spenser's epic. His high heart ex-
tolled all that was best in man, honoured true bravery, and
hoped for eternal happiness ; his good sense saved him from interminable sermonizing ; his artistic taste prescribed a charming
allegory, sweetness of melody, and superabundant decoration.
The discordant keys (and they are not few) are drowned in this
magnificent organ-recital of life and death, passion, humour,
hope, despair and triumph. God the Creator, the Saviour, the
Guide, breathes seriously throughout the poem ; and at His bidding hasten all His attributes, with individual intensity, to the
conflict with the idealized legions of evil. Each book recounts
special temptations, and deliverance in the crisis ; the actions of
the first two books, especially, are as skilfully elaborated as a
drama, and a painstaking analysis will reveal a handiwork that
would do no discredit to Shakespeare himself. The epic pro-
claims itself the product of a cultured poet and Christian philosopher,

> " Ay me, how many perils doe enfold
> The righteous man, to make him daily fall, .
> Were not that heavenly grace doth him uphold,
> And steadfast Truth acquite him out of all !
> Her love is firme, her care continuall,
> So oft as he, through his own foolish pride
> Or weaknes, is to sinfull bands made thrall."

Who could want a greater text ?

Let us glance for a moment at his summarized teachings,
many of which might well become mottoes of life-action :—

> " Sweete is the love that comes alone with willingnesse,"
> " Blisse may not abide in state of mortall men,"
> " The things, that day most minds, at night doe most appeare."
> " The vertue selfe, which her reward doth pay."
> " Who will not mercie unto others shew,
> How can he mercy ever hope to have ? "
> " Give salve to every sore, but counsell to the minde."

All these and many more are poetically wrought out, for the most part, in accordance with direct Christian teaching.

The reader will by this time have gained a fair idea of *The Faerie Queene*, since this whole essay may be viewed as a critique based upon results. We have attempted a summing-up, necessarily brief, and will offer in conclusion some specific appreciations.

Spenser has been charged with lack of humour, generally by those who have never read him, but who prefer buffoonery to serious progress, at all events. Yet *The Faerie Queene* contains a reasonable amount of humour, appropriately interspersed throughout the poem. The Renaissance spirit and Spenser's innate kindliness forbade hard Puritanism. What more could one desire than the laughable description of the " raskall rabble's " fear at the sight of the dead dragon ; or the demure gravity of the poet's address to the Queen at the beginning of Book Two ? The second and third cantos of this book have many such passages ; for example, such a picture as that of Trompart grovelling before Braggadocchio, is ludicrous enough :—

> " The seely man, seeing him ryde so ranck
> And ayme at him, fell flat to ground for feare,
> And crying, " Mercy," loud, his pitious hands gan reare."

In Canto Five, when Pyrochles is at last overcome by Sir Guyon, the poet humourously avouches that

> " Such homage till that instant never learned hee."

Book Four, Canto Five, contains much light English fun. In the Fifth Book, Radigund's death would have 'deprived her mother of a daughter.' In Canto Nine, Guile bears a 'great wyde net,'

> " With which he seldom fished at the brooke,
> But used to fish for fools on the dry shore,
> Of which he in faire weather wont to take great store."

For a final example, Canto Four of the last book shows us how Calepine

> " Catching up in hand a ragged stone
> Which lay thereby (so fortune him did ayde)
> Upon him ran, and thrust it all attone
> Into his gaping throte, that made him grone

> And gaspe for breath, that he nigh choked was,
> Being unable to digest that bone ;
> Ne could it upward come, nor downward passe,
> Ne could he brooke the coldnesse of the stony masse."

This is also a good example of Spenser's power of expression. The description of the fight between Arthur and the two Pagan brothers, Pyrochles and Cymochles, we have never seen equalled in vivid reproduction.

Spenser abounds in nice poetical devices. One of his most successful is parenthesis, as in :

> " So forth they goe together (God before),

and

> " But thine, my deare, (welfare thy heart, my deare !)

.

Another is his emphatic repetition, especially of monosyllables. A most artful contrivance is the following play upon words :

> " ' But dread of shame my doubtfull lips doth still restraine.'
> ' Ah ! my deare dread,' said then the fearefull mayd,
> ' Can dread of ought your dreadlesse heart withhold,
> That many hath with dread of death dismayd,
> And dare even deathes most dreadfull face behold ?' "

But Spenser's power in diction often made him careless, and exposed him to the charge of undue prolixity.

We leave *The Faerie Queene* with a sigh of regret, as we turn to the practical affairs of life, feeling that

> " This is the port of rest from troublous toyle,
> The world's sweet in from paine and wearisome turmoyle,"

full of such poetry as

> " With that the rolling sea, resounding soft,
> In his big base them fitly answered ;
> And on the rocke the waves breaking aloft
> A solemne meane unto them measured ;
> The whiles sweet Zephyrus lowd whisteled
> His treble, a straunge kinde of harmony ;
> Which Guyon's senses softly tickeled,
> That he the boteman bad row easily,
> And let him heare some part of their rare melody."

But we leave it also with increased faith and renewed devotion, remembering such assurances as this :—

" And is there care in heaven ?   And is there love
In heavenly spirits to these creatures bace,
That may compassion of their evils move ?
There is :—else much more wretched were the cace
Of men than beasts : but O ! th' exceeding grace
Of highest God, that loves his creatures so,
And all his works with mercy doth embrace,
That blessed angels he sends to and fro,
To serve to wicked man, to serve his wicked foe ! "

Indeed, the " heavenly grace " of "highest God" is the all-in-all
of the epic, whose throbbing scenes disappear before the higher
contemplation.

Still shall Spenser receive the homage of posterity.   What
is his art ?   What is all art ?   The adequate presentation of
truth, conceived of as synonymous with beauty and the good.
The performance of Spenser in large measure realizes this conscious ideal.

The Faerie Queene should therefore strongly attract the cultured mind.   Warwick has been justly called the " king-maker,"
but Spenser deserves a far greater title.   If the poet can be made
at all, *The Faerie Queene* will accomplish it, and this great epic
may yet inspire some lowly heart to flights as high as those to
which it lifted Milton and Keats.

Thy music, Spenser, swims the sea of sounds,
Whose surface trembles with the under-stream,
And evermore the distant shore surrounds,
Where truth abides within the Land of Dream,—
Strong singer ! whose full-ripened tones do teem
With rarest melody ; thy noble heart
Beats brave and true ; right stately dost thou seem,
Poet of poets,--master of all art,
Arthur delights our youth, maidens bless Britomart.

                    G. HERBERT CLARKE, '95.

THE LIFE AND WORK OF PASTEUR.*

"Suddenly this man goes.   His work will save more human lives than all the conquerors in the past and of the future did or will destroy."   So spoke Dr. Paul Gibier recently, of the Pasteur Institute in America, concerning Pasteur's death.   To some this may appear to be a very wide statement, but we think it is fully justified.   Few men in the course of history have done work which will influence human action and human destiny to such an extent as has Louis Pasteur.   His work has been among the infinitely little, but in this " little world " " the father of bacteriology " has discovered principles and laws which govern bodily ills, and which if rightly understood may be made available in the overthrow of disease and death—humanity's dread enemies.

But who is this Pasteur ?   What is his history ?   He is best known to-day as the inventor of a cure for hydrophobia.   We use the word inventor purposely.   This is the last and perhaps the most famous of his many achievements.   As a man the great scientist was patient, persevering, patriotic.   A remarkable characteristic of his work was its accuracy.   Pasteur made few mistakes.   This is doubtless the reason of the rapidity and wide extent of his work.   His life has been one triumphal march through the domains of disease and death.   France, the country he loved and in which he labored, recognized the true worth of this man, and heaped upon him every honor in her power to confer, and when he died mourned him as a nation.

One would expect that such a genius should come of remarkable parentage.   Louis Pasteur was the son of a tanner, yet in this father we recognize some of the characteristics which contributed to the success of the son.   Born in 1822 he received his earlier education at the schools of Arbois.   Here he displayed no special ability, but is described as shewing a fondness for sketching and drawing.   Afterward he entered Besançon College.   His course here was by no means brilliant, but the Professor of Chemistry, at the close of his pupil's course, declared that Pas-

*Read before the Natural Science Club of McMaster University.

3

teur knew more chemistry than himself. After this he entered the Ecole Normale, from which he graduated two years later with a degree. After holding several important positions, he finally settled down as the director of the scientific studies in the Ecole Normale, Paris.

Strange to say Pasteur began his work in the realm of molecular physics. "The weightiest events of life sometimes turn upon small hinges." While experimenting with the crystals of the tartrates and paratartrates, Pasteur unexpectedly landed amid the phenomena of fermentation. He found that ferments were in every case living things. This discovery was, no doubt, aided by the previous discovery of the yeast plant. In this same line Pasteur's investigations regarding putrefaction and acetic fermentation are invaluable.

But Pasteur was soon to come into conflict with the scientists of his day. As a result of his investigations he came to the conclusion that there was no such thing as spontaneous generation. Pouchet and Dr. Bastian were strong for this principle. All scientists were against Pasteur. But he did not stop to argue the matter. To prove his theory, Pasteur set up his laboratory upon a mountain-top where he had only pure air. He found that no fermentation took place there. Dumas was convinced, and Tyndal said of these experiments: "They have restored the conviction that life does not exist without antecedent life."

The work of Pasteur is noted for its practical character. This characteristic has been true of it from the beginning. Researches on the disorders of wines have saved much expense and trouble to the manufacturer. He has also been of much service to that class of citizens known as brewers. Five minutes work with the microscope now often reveals that which formerly meant heavy loss.

In 1868 the silk industry of France was well nigh ruined. Some plague had attacked the worms, and was rapidly destroying them. What was it? Dumas could not find out, and asked Pasteur to study the problem. "But I have never seen a silkworm," Pasteur objected. After much persuasion, however, he went to the scene of the difficulty. He soon discovered that certain parasitic corpuscles were the cause of the trouble. It was easy to tell the healthy moths from the diseased. "Healthy moths," reasoned Pasteur, " lay healthy eggs, healthy eggs hatch healthy worms." The problem was very simple. But all France called him a young fool, and the Academy publicly censured him. Pasteur by simple demonstration won the day. An Imperial villa was placed at his disposal, the net profits of which amounted to 26,000,000 francs. There was then no ground for doubt.

The later years of Pasteur's life have been devoted to a study of the germ theories of disease. In this department he proved that disease was due to the work of minute organisms. Having satisfied himself on this point he set about the problem, how to overcome these organisms. The secret he found in "virus attenuation." The principle is somewhat as follows : A tree or any other plant placed in the ground must find there the nutriment which it needs to sustain its life or it will die. 'So it is,' reasoned Pasteur, 'with the organisms causing disease. If they do not find those elements in the blood which they need to sustain them they will die and of course do no harm. How this can be done is the problem.' A quantity of parasites were obtained and after they had been reproduced a hundred times they were found to be as virulent as at first. If these, however, were exposed to the air for some time they became enfeebled. Animals inoculated with these were affected but slightly and were thereafter immune from the disease, the reason being that the attenuated virus so exhausts the soil that the virulent contagion when introduced has nothing to live upon and for that reason die harmless.

Perhaps Pasteur's boldest feat in this department was the famous Melun experiment. A number of cows and sheep were taken. Half of each were inoculated with attenuated virus. Fourteen days afterward, the whole of them were inoculated with extremely virulent virus. Three days afterward, over two hundred people assembled to witness the result, which, when seen, was the occasion of a "shout of admiration." Of the unvaccinated sheep all were either dying or dead and the unvaccinated cows were prostrated by an intense fever. The vaccinated animals, on the contrary, were alive and full of health.

Pasteur's last achievement has been his crowning glory. In

front of the Pasteur Institute in Paris stands a statue representing in bronze the life-and-death struggle between one of Pasteur's earliest patients and a mad dog. But hydrophobia has now lost some of its terrors. The hydrophobia virus has been discovered, the attenuated virus prepared, and now branch institutes are established in different parts of the world. People come to Paris from all over Europe to receive treatment. Some of the scenes in, and in front of the Institute, are described as very picturesque and amusing. Judging from the good nature and the happy faces of the crowd it has been said one would hardly suspect the purpose for which they come, such faith have they in the treatment.

The Pasteur Institute is a magnificent building beautifully situated in Paris. Here Pasteur resided, and here his followers will continue his work now that he is gone. The building was constructed and equipped by the subscriptions of grateful countrymen. In this very fitting and lasting way the name of Pasteur will be perpetuated in the history of the world. It was here that Pasteur labored, and here, according to his own request, he was buried, preferring this spot to a resting-place among the greatest of France.

WALLACE P. COHOE, '96.

ATTAINING.

Unwavering eyes on the end,
　Lips that are bidden to bleed,
　　When a man strives, depend,
Heart is the thing to heed.

" My beauty, I have you in hand,"
(Does he murmur?) " but hard was the price ! "
　　Not if he understand
Striving is sacrifice.

PLASHET.

RECOMPENSES.

There's rhythm in a heart throb
   And sunlight in a tear,
There's music in a smothered sigh
   And warning in a fear.

There's quiet in a shadow
   And peace in silent night,
There's silver in the morning cloud
   And guidance in the light.

There's pleasure in a cherished hope
   And solace in a dream ;
There's gladness in a home of care
   And glory in a gleam.

There's strength in every burden borne
   And added power in strife,
There's help in every tale of woe
   And death in every life.

There's beauty in a gathering mist,
   Sad tones in every bell,
There's doubt in every plighted troth,
   Release with every knell.

There's service in the humblest path
   That weary feet e'er trod,
There's rest beneath the sleeper's shroud
   And recompense with God.

O. G. LANGFORD, '95·

From Chicago Standard.

EDITORIAL NOTES.

THE fine copy in oils of Hoffman's great painting, "Christ in the Temple," by Mr. Herbert Clark, of Toronto Junction, which attracted favorable attention at the Toronto Industrial Exhibition last September, has been presented by the artist to McMaster University, and holds a place of honor in the Library Reading Room of the Hall.

AT the request of his numerous friends in McMaster University we publish with this number the portrait of the first occupant of the chair of Philosophy, whose departure, though to a position of far higher honor and influence, was deeply regretted alike by students and friends of our college. In bidding us farewell last spring the modest Doctor predicted that in the great institution in Chicago, he would probably be known simply by his number in the calendar. He has already developed into a pretty lively number, and the indications are that his public utterances are likely to contain something worthy of the attention and consideration of the best biblical scholars of the West.

TRAVELLERS who pass rapidly through foreign countries, keeping close to the regular tourists' routes and putting up at recommended hotels, and even students who live in hired rooms on upper flats in large cities usually see very little or nothing of the real home life of the people. To see this and learn to judge correctly of its attractions or privations, one must gain admission to the home and confidence of some well ordered families, and be one of them for a considerable length of time. In the November number of *The Leisure Hour* will be found a well written paper by an English lady, who enjoyed the privilege of living for many months with the family of a Protestant pastor in a humble village in Lower Silesia. The picture there drawn is one that all Canadians will appreciate and in spite of black bread and liver sausage, they will see much to admire in German home life.

A REMARKABLE BOOK has recently been published in Paris by M. Charles Letourneau, whose title in English is 'War Amongst the Various Human Races.' This work is the result of deep study and long and patient research into the origin and causes of war upon the earth in all ages and among the various races. In perfect accord with the sentiment once expressed by Voltaire that war is the epitome of all wickedness, the writer believes it is cruel and barbarous, the outcome of evil passions and ambitious designs. Cannibalism all the civilized world views with horror and disgust, but how much better is wholesale mutilation of bodies and destruction of life on the field of battle? How utterly inconsistent with civilization, not to say the spirit of Christianity, is the policy of the nations whose greatest ingenuity and a large portion of whose revenue is employed in the production of engines of death capable of destroying thousands of human beings in a few minutes ! The time has come in the history of human progress when wars should never more be resorted to. To realize this blessed consummation, the writer thinks republicanism must become the universal form of government, the prevalent but stupid admiration of military glory must be stamped out, and the sentiment of brotherhood so widely diffused among the nations that patriotism shall no longer be associated with ideas of conquest and military supremacy. If this good book should have a wide circulation and its principles be generally adopted in the author's own country, a long step would be taken towards the realization of his most Christian desire.

The following from a monastic chronicle of the thirteenth century should be of interest to some of our readers. The disturbers of the tranquillity of the ladies of the time was Cardinal Latinus :

" This man Pope Nicholas appointed Legates in Lombardy, in Tuscany, and in Romagnola. And he brought consternation upon all the women by a certain constitution that he promulgated, in which it was provided that the women should have their dresses short so as to reach the ground, and not more than a handbreadth further. For previously they were accustomed to trail the trains (lit. tails) of their dresses a yard and a half long over the ground. . . . And he caused this to be preached throughout the churches and he impressed it upon the women by precept, and [assured them] that no priest could absolve them unless they did as they were bidden ; which was more bitter to the women than any sort of death. For a certain woman said familiarly to one, that that train was dearer to her than the whole of the rest of the clothes that she wore. Moreover, the Cardinal Latinus enjoined in that constitution that all women, as well girls as young ladies, married women, and widows and matrons, should wear veils on their heads. Which was horribly grievous to them. But they discovered a remedy for that tribulation such as they could by no means find for the trains. For they had veils made of linen and silk woven with gold with which they appeared ten times better than before and attracted more successfully the eyes of beholders."

HERE AND THERE.

O. G. LANGFORD, EDITOR.

SOME of our exchanges print extracts from our magazine without giving due credit. Due courtesy is never misplaced.

TAKEN altogether, perhaps *The Brunonian* is our best exchange. The department " Alumni Brunenses," is always full of interest. When shall we have a column devoted to our own alumni?

THE *Yale Record* comes out with a fine cut of the British Lion with his head all bound up *apropos* of Yale's magnificent victory at the international football contest. It is a good hit.

THE *University of Michigan Daily* is almost entirely given up to the advocacy of sports, and advertisement. Nothing of interest about the *work* of the University seems worthy of publication.

THE *Ottawa Campus* in an editorial advises students to read much during their college course, pithily quoting from Bacon: " If a man read little he had need have much cunning to seem to know that he doth not."

THE College rush is not quite a thing of the past. The students of the University of Minnesota gave the freshmen quite a vigorous reception this year and the local papers undertook to criticize rushing in unsparing terms. *The Ariel* makes an effort at defence, but does not deny that the rush took place, nor that very unseemly greeting was tendered to the new men.

Tabor College Monthly is one of the most interesting of our smaller exchanges. The October number has a descriptive essay upon " Colorado and its Mines," by our old friend, T. P. Hall, M.A, Ph.D. It is racy and entertaining. Another article tells how five Tabor girls spent their vacation ministering to the physical and spiritual needs of the poor in the City of Omaha. It is a simple story of Christlike service which is very refreshing.

IT is rumored in college athletic circles that Amos Alonzo Stagg, the famous coach and athlete, is about to resign his position as director of physical training at the University of Chicago. Stagg has been falling from grace in the eyes of the Chicagoans for the past year, which has been greatly increased by the showing made by the football eleven in the recent games. Last summer during the disastrous baseball season for that university, Stagg was harshly criticised even by members of the faculty. It ended by his resignation being tendered, but President Harper refused to let the old Yale man go.

COLLEGE NEWS.

W. P. Cohoe, '96,   R. D. George, '97,
J. F. Vichert, '97,   Miss E. Whiteside, '98·
Editors.

The University.

The Muse of Science lately stepped out of her sphere and attempted to write poetry. The following was the result :—

ON THE WOODPECKER.

" He was of the order aves,
    He was wont to hunt for vermes,
Or if insecta he could find
They were quite suited to his mind.
    His eye was microscopic,
    His mandibles were choppic.
Avoidez bug ! ce fearful mal
Son alimentary canal."

A doubtful compliment : "That's a rattling good wheel you've got, old man."

Query : Is "Come into the kitchen, Ann," a parody on "Come into the garden, Maude"?

A senior reciting in Education recently informed the class on the authority of Mr. Spencer, that many children suffered from "under feeding and under clothing."

Told at the Chess Club—"Mate in five moves," muttered the weary tyro, as he tossed under the spell of Somnus, while fewer than that sufficed to check *him* with the hard, hard floor.

Thanksgiving Day, or rather the day before Thanksgiving, brought with it, as usual, our thanksgiving dinner, and the departure of many of the students to spend the short vacation elsewhere.

One of our foot-ball players, now a sedate theolog, inspired by his recent visit to Woodstock, recalled the following incident o student days there :
Professor in English (reading a metaphor)—"B—, what figure of speech is this?"
B—: "A conundrum."

It is not announced in the curriculum of our University, but it is nevertheless a fact, that every year the chairman of the dining-room delivers a course of two or three lectures on Etiquette and Deportment. Our worthy chairman, Mr. C. J. Cameron, B A., delivered the first of these for this year, on a recent occasion, to an interested and apprecia tive audience.

THE opening programme of the Ladies' Literary League given Friday, Nov. 8th, was a good augury for the year's work. Each of the Special Courses of the University was upheld in a five minute speech as follows:

Philosophy, ...	Miss Eby,
Moderns, ...	Miss Cohoon,
English, ...	Miss Whiteside,
Classics, ...	Miss Iler,
Mathematics, ...	Miss McDiarmid,
Science, ...	Miss Dryden.

The idea was unique and interesting; and the orations were all so eloquent that we feel sure even had the ambitious but undecided freshies been allowed to be present they would have been as undecided as ever.

THE statement: 'this is one that is really needed' may have become somewhat worn by frequent verbal use, but we introduce it now for the first time in print as the great *Defensio pro Societate Scaccorum,* —Plea for the Chess Club. It is indeed strange that the noble rage for this best of intellectual games should have reached both Toronto and McMaster Universities at the same time. Earnest enthusiasm prevails in both clubs, and each numbers over twenty members. We of McMaster meet on Saturday afternoons and are already developing some brilliant players—future Morphys and Anderssens. Prof. A. B. Willmott, M.A., B. Sc., is the worthy president, and Mr. G. H. Clarke, B.A., wields the secretary's quill.

ON the evening of the 15th inst., the Camelot Club of the University held its first meeting of the year. There was a large attendance and the meeting was of special interest to all. The Executive Committee of the Club were very happy in securing the services of Dr. Rand, who kindly consented to lecture to us. After the delivery of an excellent essay by Miss Whiteside, '98, on 'Swinburne's Genius,' and the reading of his "Forsaken Garden" by L. Thomas, '98, Dr. Rand was called upon for his address. In his opening remarks the Doctor took the opportunity of giving the club some strong advice respecting their study of Swinburne, and offered some suggestions which will doubtless be of profit in the future. His theme for the evening was "True Poetry, and the Proper Method of Studying it." This lecture, from beginning to end, was one of interest, and could not fail to inspire every lover of English song. We, as a club, are looking forward to a very pleasant and helpful winter's study.

THE athletes of the University have bestowed unusual attention upon foot-ball this fall. This is not to be wondered at when we consider the officers of the club. Enthusiasm reached a white heat when the name of Chancellor Wallace was proposed as Honorary President. Then followed the election of H. N. McKechnie, '97, President; F. T. Tapscott, '97, Vice-President; A. G. Baker, '96, Secretary-Treasurer; C. J. Cameron, B.A., Custodian, and Bert. W. Merrill, B.A., Captain. With such promptness as our forwards always display in a rush, the committee appointed secured for us a place in the Inter College League, and the rental of the athletic grounds adjacent to the college for our practices. Then practicing began in earnest. A second eleven was formed and challenged the first for a match, which resulted in a victory for the firsts, but gave them good team practice. Then excitement waged hot. Teams were formed in the different years and matches played resulting in good practices and any amount of fun. The playing of our first team in the League matches, while not winning them the first place, showed steady and rapid improvement until such a degree of efficiency was reached that the S. P. S. Club was beaten 6 to o. The last game played was the annual one with Woodstock. Enthusiasm was at its highest when preparing for this game, and the best wishes of the whole College followed the boys as they left for Woodstock the day before Thanksgiving. After a hard-fought game the club was able to return to Toronto winners by 2 goals to 1. If the interest is not allowed to lag we shall have a team hard to beat in the coming year. Boom on Mac !

AMONG the bewildering number and variety of our University societies none can boast so far-reaching an influence over the lives of our students, nor command such general interest and sympathy, as our Fyfe Missionary Society,—the oldest, most abiding, most unchanging of all. The first meeting was held on October 18th, when the following officers were elected : President, Prof. J. H. Farmer ; Vice-President, J. J. Reeve, B.A. ; Rec.-Sec., W. W. McMaster, B.A. ; Cor.-Sec., W. J. Pady, '97 ; Treasurer, Dr. Welton. These, together with Dr. Goodspeed (chairman of committee on voluntary work), Prof. P. S. Campbell, and Messrs. C. J. Cameron, B.A., H. Estabrook, B A., B. W. Merrill, B.A , J. C. Sycamore, '96, and Geo. Simmons, '96, constitute the Committee.

In addition to the election of officers, four addresses were given during the day, on their summer's work, by Mr. L. B. Crosby as representative of the Lower Provinces ; Mr. R. Scott as representing Western Quebec and Eastern Ontario ; Mr. Dougal Brown as representing the work in Western Ontario, and Mr. P. C. Cameron, B.A., who told of his work in Manitoba.

Each address contained many points of interest, but especially so that of Mr. Brown, who labored on Manitoulin Island. The work there savored somewhat of apostolic times and bore witness to the fact that persecution and the enduring of hardship as a good soldier of Christ were not altogether things of the past, even in fair Ontario.

At the close of the afternoon service the Rev. G. Dan, for many years missionary to the Bahamas Islands, addressed the Society for a few minutes, giving some idea of the extent and difficulty of his work.

The next meeting of the Society, which was held on Nov. 14th, was one of very great spiritual power and blessing, the thought for the day being " The Deepening of Spiritual Life." At the commencement of the morning session, Mr. A. Imrie gave a Bible-Reading setting forth the teaching of Scripture concerning the Holy Spirit. At the close of the Bible Reading, President Farmer called upon Vice-President Reeve to take the chair. Mr. Reeve having just returned from a three or four weeks' absence on account of ill health, was warmly greeted by the Society. The Rev. J. McP. Scott then gave an address on " Possibilities of the Christian Life." Referring to the craving of Christians for a deeper and truer spiritual life, Mr. Scott pointed out that the hindrance was in ourselves, since it was in the heart of God to give us what we so longed for. The address was beautiful in its simplicity, and went straight home to the hearts of all. The time allowed for the open conference which followed was all too short, and very many who were anxious to speak were unable to do so. The afternoon session was largely occupied by two very interesting and helpful addresses, the one by President Farmer, the other by Dr. Hooper, of the Beverley St. Church. After a few words from the Rev. P. A. McEwen, the meeting was brought to a close.

The annual public meeting of the Society will be held in the Beverley St. Church, on Tuesday evening, Dec. 10th, the Rev. Chas. Eaton, pastor of the Bloor St. Church being one of the speakers.

" How can I make the most of myself ?" was the subject of a most inspiring address to the students by Pastor Denovan on a recent date. We are sorry that space will allow only a few outline thoughts, but they contain gold.

" The world needs young manhood of the truest type. The ideal young man was Jesus Christ of Nazareth. He went about quietly, meekly, independent of social standing, or political party, without money, influential parentage or credentials ; and yet his life work of three years, in its far reaching power and influence is unparalleled in the world's history. Where are the great philosophers ? Where are the world's conquerors ? They are but names—names known to but few, while His works and words are an eternal living power which has emptied heathen temples of their worshippers, overthrown their vile priesthood and is now sapping the foundations of the ancient religions of India and China. Study and follow the life of Jesus. Do as He would have done in your place ; go nowhere He would not go ; do nothing He would not do. Christ was no sour ascetic, no sentimental young man, but a man strong and manly because pure and true. If there were no world beyond this, if death ended all, my best advice to you would still be, " Believe, confess, follow the young man Jesus Christ of Nazareth."

THAT worthy institution known as the Natural Science Club has begun its work for the year. The interest taken by the members in this most interesting department of research is sufficient to excite the admiration of a Herbert Spencer. The aim of this society is to foster a scientific spirit in the university and also to be of mutual good to its members. The President's gavel is held this year by Mr. A. Imrie,' 96, who is supported by a strong Executive. The first meeting of the year was very successful and prophesies good results to the enterprise. The scientific news for the month was gathered and given to the society by two of the members. A paper on " The Life and Work of Pasteur " was read. After this the Honorary President, Prof. Willmott, gave a talk on " Acetylene," illustrated by experiments. It was certainly strange to see a substance resembling an ordinary cinder turn into lime and a gas which burnt readily when water was poured on it. So strange indeed it seemed to a well-known professor of the institution on beholding it for the first time, that he said : " Oh, but its coal-oil you're putting on it." The moral is obvious. Attend the meeting of the N. S. C. and get enlightened on such subjects.

WHAT would McMaster do without its Glee Club and Quartette ? Indeed what is any student body without an organization for the development of the musical talent within it ? Without such an organization one of the pleasantest features of College life would be wanting. We are glad to say that we are not behind on this score, for besides vocal there is also instrumental talent and these are organized under the name of " The McMaster University Choral and Orchestral Union." Messrs J. B. Paterson, '96, and I. G. Matthews, '97, are respectively the President and Vice-President. Mr. E. S. Roy, '98, is responsible for the minutes and the cash. Mr. W. S. McAlpine, B. A., is Musical Director with Mr. W. J. Pady, '97, as his assistant, and Mr. A. G. Baker, '96, is Pianist. The Glee Club numbers about twenty voices which are capable of rendering very acceptable music. The Orchestra, which consists of ten pieces, is doing admirably. They expect to be at the service of the institution at an early date. The Quartette consists of Messrs. Wallace, '97, Th., McAlpine, B.A., Paterson, '96 and Cohoe, '96, who try to maintain the high reputation which McMaster Quartettes have won in the past. This Union courts no outside public attention It is organized solely for the purpose of rendering suitable music on Student and University occasions. Let us wish the Union success !

MOULTON COLLEGE.

EVERYONE who visited the Chrysanthemum show in the Pavilion this year, pronounced it the most successful exhibit that has ever been made by the florists of the city. The display of flowers was very beautiful Chrysanthemums, roses, carnation pinks and English violets were arranged in the most artistic manner, their rich and varied colors set off by the green of beautiful palms and delicate ferns. One could only go from one table and group to another, uttering exclamations of delight at each new beauty, and those of us who had never been there before, came away feeling well repaid for our visit.

THE Thanksgiving vacation was hailed with joy by those of our number who were fortunate enough to go home. Among the less happy ones who had to remain at the College, there were at first some with rather rueful faces. Under the influence of holiday privileges, however, and the usual bountiful and well-served Thanksgiving dinner, the clouds gradually dispersed, and some were even heard to say that ' Moulton was not such a bad place, after all, in which to spend a holiday,—if one could not go home.'

A VERY interesting meeting of the Mission Circle was held Friday evening, Nov. 15th, when the following programme was rendered :
Reading—' The Little Brown Towel '—Miss Needles.
Trio—' Saviour Lead me Lest I Stray '—Misses Dryden and Woolverton.
Map Talk—' Home Missions '—Miss Emma J. Dryden.
Vocal Solo—' Jesu, Jesu, Miserare '—Miss Boehmer.
Reading—' Try it again to-day '—Miss Brophy.
Special mention might be made of Miss Dryden's talk on Home Missions. We felt after listening to her clear and thoughtful presentation of the aims and needs of the work, that we knew much more about it than before, and that we should henceforth take a much deeper interest in it.

WOODSTOCK COLLEGE.

THE Literary Society intend to hold a concert in the near future for the purpose of defraying in part the expenses of making the rink.

A GLEE-CLUB of about 30 members has been organized, and twice a week sweet strains of music (?) are audible in the chapel-room, mingled with the discordant tones of the college piano.

HOCKEY—A Hockey-club has been organized for the coming season. Much enthusiasm is manifested among the boys, and under the captainship of " Huge " the team will be successfully led through the battles and dangers of next winter.

SUPERINTENDENT McEWEN was with us a few hours this week. He promises us a talk on Home Missions in the near future, and we know that on this subject so dear to his heart he will have something to say. He will find attentive listeners in Woodstock College.

ALL are looking forward in anticipation to the time when the keen frosts of winter will enable us to enjoy our large open-air skating-rink. It is 175 feet in length and 132 feet in breadth, and is furnished with hydrants for the purpose of flooding it when necessary. There will be ample room for all, hockey-players, experienced skaters, and novices.

OUR esteemed friend and former Mathematical Master, Mr. H. S. Robertson, B.A., now of Seaforth C. I., paid us a flying visit last week. His former colleagues on the staff, and his former students will always extend the heartiest welcome to Mr. Robertson. No doubt Seaforth is a very good place to live in, but ah ! the happy memories of Wood-stock ! Come again.

THE First Church has for three weeks been engaged in a series of special evangelistic services under the leadership of pastor Dadson, assisted by Rev. Bro. Judson Whyte, and his daughter. We believe the church has been quickened, and a spirit of inquiry has been awakened in many unsaved ones. We are glad the interest has extended to the college also, and that some among us are asking the all-important question, "What must I do to be saved?"

ON Friday evening, Nov. 1st, the College chapel was well filled with an audience of students and town friends, who assembled to hear an address on the subject, "Trust in God and Keep your Powder Dry," by Rev. Thos. Shields, Victoria. In the hands of Pastor Shields this historic saying has been made the text of a very excellent and enter-taining lecture. For over an hour he held the undivided attention of his hearers, as, with quaint illustration and solid argument, he unfolded his subject. The speaker showed that everyone is provided with a supply of amunition for life's conflicts ; that it is wise to preserve the amunition—the forces of our being, opportunities, etc.—in condition to be used effectively as occasion requires ; and that, with our trust in God, the victory shall be ours.

ONCE more the Football students of McMaster and Woodstock met in friendly combat on the spacious College campus. Two years have gone since the last game and owing to difficulties of expense, etc., it seemed for a time that another year must pass without bringing the rival teams together. Fortunately, the football team in McMaster, seconded by the zeal of some of the Woodstock students, overcame all difficulties and on Thanksgiving Eve. the McMaster boys arrived.

It is but fair to say that the effort to overcome these difficulties was amply rewarded by our pleasant associations with McMaster boys. For some of them, this was their first visit to Woodstock ; their impres-sions of the place, people and College were, we hope and believe, most favorable. Others were old students and were received by their *Alma Mater* in motherly fashion. All, we trust, were made to feel at home in their temporary surroundings. The McMaster boys are a hearty, genial, jovial lot. Some were called upon for speeches and responded right heartily and well ; some led Chapel service and there we saw and felt their deep-seated earnestness and spirituality.

Even in the game this manliness of spirit was shewn. Not a man on either team played roughly ; not a harsh nor improper word was spoken. The McMaster boys have improved of late ; they played a clever but straightforward game. Everything passed off smoothly with one sad exception, viz : The accident which befell Mr. Clarke. This, we are happy to say, was in no sense the result of rough playing, but purely a matter of accident, tinged perhaps with a slight confusion in the playing of McMaster's men. As to the game and its result we shall be pardoned for expressing the opinion that, on the whole, Woodstock had rather the better of the game. This, however, is in view of the fact that McMaster won by a score of two goals to one. In any case it was, we believe, the wish of the Chancellor that McMaster should beat and we felt in duty bound to pay deference to the express desire of the head of the University. Moreover it would have been unseemly that the visiting team should have had to return with their colors, (flaunted so freely and proudly on arrival), befouled with dirt and dragging in the dust. In conclusion, we would bid farewell to the McMaster team for only one year. If this commingling of the schools uplifts our ideals, makes us eager for McMaster and her halls, broadens our sympathies, widens our associations and advertises our schools, by all means let petty financial difficulties be overcome and let the meeting of the two teams be an annual event !

Grande Ligne.

The cold weather and snow of the last week have caused the boys to put away the foot-ball and base-ball, and now the demand is for skates and hockey-sticks. We have quite a number of new hockey players, and if the weather continues cold we hope soon to test their quality on the rink.

Literary Societies are good things in their place, but the boys of Feller Institute have decided that too many societies in one school are not for the public good. Consequently, the experiment of last year, in having only one literary society, with French and English meetings on alternate Friday evenings, is being persevered in with good results. The debates and the semi-weekly papers, " The Monitor " and " La Verité," show that wonderful improvement has been made since our societies were first organized two years ago.

Thanksgiving Day was enjoyed as usual, as a holiday, by the residents of Feller Institute. No roast turkey adorned our tables, but they were ladened with other good things that amply compensated for the disappointment some may have felt regarding the turkey. In the evening a lecture and supper were given in the church. The lecture, on " Hunting as Viewed by Women," given by Rev. M. B. Parent, was very instructive and elevating as well as amusing. By those who understood the French language it was thoroughly enjoyed. The lady who wears feathers, birds, or furs, and who heard this lecture, will henceforth be more careful of the way in which she denounces the cruelties of the huntsman. In order to enjoy the delicacies of the supper, however, it was entirely unnecessary to be French. No doubt some of the students would be still more thankful if Thanksgiving Day came twice a year instead of once.

THE

McMASTER UNIVERSITY MONTHLY.

JANUARY, 1896.

THOMAS S. SHENSTON.

" O good gray head which all men knew,
O iron nerve to true occasion true,
O fall'n at length that tower of strength
Which stood four-square to all the winds that blew !
The long self-sacrifice of life is o'er,
And we will see him, or his like, no more."

The subject of this sketch was born in Shoreditch, London, Eng., June 25th, 1822. "He was the son of Benjamin and Mary (Strahan) Shenston, and was remotely related to the poet Shenston." When nearly ten years old his father's family removed to Canada; the voyage from London to New York being, not six days, but six weeks. I do not know as to the roughness of the voyage, or the sickness of the young voyager; but that he was not meant for a sailor seems evident from the fact, that all his life he seemed to have as great a repugnance to the sea as did Mr. Spurgeon.

The family's first settlement was near Dundas, whence they removed to a farm near Guelph, and thence to near St. Catharines. But Thomas did not like the hard clay, and weary of unsuccessful farming, he betook him to St. Catharines, and to the harness-making trade. Here he evinced his loyalty and British pluck by enlisting under Mittleberger against the Fenian Raiders. Moving to Chatham he commenced business for himself, but the climate not agreeing with him, he removed to Woodstock, where his innate energy, diligence, and intelligence began to assert and manifest themselves. The ladder, though unseen, was before him, and he began to climb. On December 30th, 1843, he took, as he always thought, one of his most important upward steps, in marrying his loved and life-long companion, Mary Lazenby. Those who have known, as the writer has, for many years, this excellent woman, as wife, matron, and mother, will not wonder at her husband's ever increasing appreciation of her; or at his somewhat eccentric way of expressing it, by doubling his marriage fee to the minister who married them, on each promotion he received to public position. And such promotions came in quick succession, from 1849, when he was appointed magistrate, to 1853, when he came to Brantford and settled to his life work as County Registrar. How well and faithfully he filled that position is well known, and almost proverbial.

But a mind so sagacious and fertile as his could not be circumscribed to a Registrar's office. Business men soon learned to value his counsel, and almost every beneficent enterprise, material or moral, in the city, felt the influence of his farseeing interest and energy.

In the Y. M. C. A., Widows' Home, Children's Aid, and Bible Societies, he was among the foremost in sympathy and support, while the Orphan's Home was sustained by him for years. To the First Baptist Church, of which he was from 1856 to his death an honored member, he was a central, and perhaps the strongest pillar. As counsellor, supporter, friend, deacon, Sabbath-school superintendent for 29 years, and master and servant in one, few churches have had his equal, or risen more by the influence and energy of one man; while his intense interest in mission work, especially Foreign, gave both him and the church a enviable position in the denomination and in the land. "The liberal deviseth liberal things, and by liberal things shall he stand." And so Bro. Shenston, and the church he influenced so largely, experienced. In speaking thus, I would not depreciate other grand men, in some respects his superiors, who wrought so faithfully and nobly with him; but, as with David's thirty mighty men, he was among the first three, and in some respects, among them he was the first.

Perhaps the leading characteristic of Mr. Shenston's life was *faithfulness*. Like Hananiah, " he was a faithful man, and feared God above many." This was seen in all the departments of his manifold work. As Sabbath-school superintendent he was only absent from his place three times in twenty-five years. At preaching services and prayer-meetings he was almost always punctually at his post. And so in private and public, his duties were always strictly attended to. To the poor he was a judicious but generous friend. Instances of great interest have come to my knowledge that have helped to embalm his memory more deeply and lovingly in my heart. But from his method of doing, only eternity will reveal the treasures he thus laid up. Like self-made men generally, he carried with him throughout life idiosyncrasies which a liberal education and early friction with student life would have helped to eliminate or modify ; but all in all, he was a rare man, and considering his advantages, or disadvantages at the start, made great attainments in self-improvement and left a large legacy of good. If he did err in some respects, and who errs not ? his influence and efforts did very much to strengthen and extend the Baptist cause and the cause of Christ, not only in Brantford and Ontario, but in India and the world.

And now since he is gone,—
How many long in vain for that bowed form
Which all men knew so well upon our street ;
And fain would have again those greetings warm,
That halted now and then his hurrying feet,—
Not long, for public trusts pressed on his mind,
And schemes that needed brain to pave their way ;
While poor and sorrowing ones sought him to find
A heart whereon their heavy cares to lay.
And thus, like Job, the Christly friend of old,
" He made the widow's heart for joy to sing."
While woes and want that were not to him told,
He sought to find, and help and succor bring.
O love that lives in deeds, not words of air ;
That follows in the line, laid down of yore,
That does not end in bloom, however fair,

But yields the fruits of Christ's own life once more !
Each spot seems emptier now where he did come,
In office, street, or place of trade, or prayer ;
But O, how much more empty seems the home,
Where the lone widow sees his vacant chair !
The streams of life will still keep on their flow,
And summer songs will follow winter's psalm ;
But not again to her will come the glow
Since that " good night," and then the settled calm—
So sudden—" he was not, God took him ;"
And far up he heard the " welcome," and, " well done."
His doubts were over, light was no more dim,
His fight was fought, the *" victory "** was won.

                                        W. H. PORTER.

---

*The last word that in reading he had ever underscored, was Dr. Gordon's
last word, " *victory.*"

AŒDE.

(POESY,—loquitur.)

A body of beauty is mine.
    O poet, maker of me,
Withhold not the breath divine,
    The soul of truth that makes free.

Fair form in repose for a day
    (The body of beauty of me)
With the pulse beats of life all away,
    Is well, for beauty and thee.

Yet give to me life all aglow,—
    Not a devil of darkness to blight,
But a love-lit soul pure as snow,—
    Beckon me an angel of light.

A body of beauty is mine.
    O poet, maker of me,
Inbreathe with breathings divine,
    Or body alone let it be.

                                THEODORE H. RAND.

TOR ENGRAVING CO.

John Stuart Blackie

PROFESSOR JOHN STUART BLACKIE.

This rare old merry Greek Oracle, " Ultimus Scotorum," after far exceeding the ordinary age of mortals, has at long last gone over to the " silent majority." To him Greek was a divine tongue. His last thoughts were steeped in it. On his death-bed he ejaculated his favourite motto, ἀληθεύων ἐν ἀγάπῃ. He scribbled this on the corner of every envelope he used, and scrawled it on scraps of paper. " Work out my motto in daily life and earth will grow into heaven." It was his one cure for all life's ills. It was the great social and religious revolutionary force. He had another special motto that he loved to rub into the thought and soul of young men : χαλεπὰ τὰ καλά. Like Carlyle, Blackie scorned the easy road to noble things.

The Scottish Athens will evermore seem strangely wanting without its " Blackie." His students, and where are they not found, the wide world over, and in every vocation ? will all have a quiet tear to shed as they ponder auld lang syne and the big-souled, honest-breasted, eccentric and companionable old young man whom all young men loved right merrily and really. The memory of Blackie will always bring cheer to the heart and expansion and nobility to the soul. What a supreme and eloquent contempt he had for the critical book-worm, the common-place, and the modern Pharisee ! Nor was he one of your sedate, arm-chair, and orthodox professors. He would come into his class-room with a stately stride, hold up his hands, and gloriously repeat the Lord's Prayer in his pet Greek. He never frittered away a class-hour, and yet he would think nothing of dashing off a joke or a song in the midst of the lecture. But somehow or other anything that Blackie did seemed to be out of the common, had an invigorating moral tone to it. He would often give the class his opinions in English on some important question or event, and then demand of them the rendering of it in the Greek. He loved to pun on names, and even the colour of a fellow's hair. He once had an Irish student with a fiery head of hair and pointed him out in the distance on a public occasion as " yonder *beacon* on the back form." He cordially respected the principle of " give and take ; " he had sometimes the tables turned upon himself and none enjoyed the joke more heartily than himself.

He gloried in shocking the circumspect. He believed in soul-laughter, brain-laughter, and body-laughter. He dealt sledge-hammer blows at the severity of the old Scotch Sabbath, was perfection itself in the rendering of an old Celtic ballad, and could trip the light fantastic toe in the middle of a great public lecture. He was in his pew on Sunday morning, would play croquet of an afternoon, and turn in to the Salvation Army at night. His innocent jests, and right loud healthful laughter have been heard in many a spacious drawing-room. He had the knack of slapping, with impunity, a reverend Bishop on the back or the knee, and of joking the ponderous Oxford dons on their unnatural pronunciation of the immortal Greek. He once shook Carlyle in the midst of an interminable harangue and cried, "Let your wife speak, you monster!" He was vigorously conscious of his own picturesque figure, and paraded it with a comical and dashing audacity. "When I walk along Princes Street," said he to a lady, with a humorous and mischievous criticism twinkling in his eye, "I go with a kingly air, my head erect, my chest expanded, my hair flowing, my plaid flying, my stick swinging. Do you know what makes me do that? Well, I'll tell you—just CON-CEIT."

He attributed his longevity to a hearty soul in a hearty body. In his old age he has threshed every mountain in Scotland with his feet, and stood as a monarch on their heights. At eighty-two he took a run to Constantinople. He immensely enjoyed what he jocularly dubbed his two-week "One Shirt Expeditions" over his native heath. He loved Oban and Oban loved him. There was wonderful consistency and continuity in Blackie's make-up, from his cradle to his grave. At eight he didn't know his alphabet, and what is more he never "learned" it! He was born with a contempt for the grammar and for rudiments and for all preliminary drudgery. He maintained his independent and spontaneous eccentricities throughout his life. He was ever the incalculable quantity. I believe he was amusing to himself, and certainly he was to all who came within his range. For fifty years he was the most popular lecturer in Scotland. I remember one lecturing visit he made to Glasgow. It was a Sunday night. His subject—well, it was one of Blackie's subjects—"The Philosophy of Love." He launched out upon the love-songs of Scotland, burst forth in a Scotch ballad, and even danced a little. When the proceedings came out next morning in the papers, we religious people were shocked, and I think pardonably so too. But then, it was Blackie—it was just like Blackie, and so the storm died down. The following week, however, through some unknown source, he received a plain and faithful Scotch reproof, accompanied by an admirable caricature representing Mephistopheles carrying off triumphantly the sinning professor to other climes! What would Blackie do with the picture and the castigation? Lose sleep or appetite over them? Not he. They would be pasted in his scrap-album and exhibited to the first caller. So easily and sweetly could he take life with all its brunts and jars. He did'nt care a button for anybody, and yet he loved everybody, and this, perhaps, often led him into harmless sallies of unwisdom. His comments on public characters were thoroughly original and sincere. Of Carlyle, who was young Blackie's solid friend, he writes, " A notable monster, and to be respected for the many noble thoughts he has elaborated." " His work was to rouse the world, but I was wide awake and required no rousing. He was hard-hearted and hated sinners." Mrs. Blackie called on Mrs. Carlyle one day, and she was taken down some dark kitchen stairs, and lo ! there sat Carlyle, with trousers rolled up to the knees, and his feet in a tub of cold water. Blackie, on one of his annual pilgrimages to London, went to hear the late Charles Bradlaugh preach or lecture on a Sunday night. Here is his impression :—" A bull verily, a big Ajax, tall and broad. Having a fancy for looking closely at nature, I determined to go and hear him preach in his atheistic church at the East End. It was a notable exhibition. A terrible tearing assault against the Book of Exodus, and its anthropomorphic representations of the unseen God ; eloquence powerful and fervid of the first order. Really a remarkable man, and from his point of view triumphant over those who hold by the infallibility of the record, instead of the Divinity of the dispensation. He made incidentally a public profession of atheism, which caused me to write him a long letter. I imagine that in the Socratic way I may be able to do him some good. He is a manly, honest fellow, and quite worthy of gentlemanly treatment, which I am afraid he seldom receives."

I had a little visit with the old Professor once in his own Edinburgh home. Somehow or other it was impossible to feel shy or anything but at home in his presence. " Poor devils," he pleasantly and sympathetically exclaimed, when talking on the Irish question, which was hot at the time. Blackie didn't think the world would either fall or stand on Home Rule. It is needless to say that I saw a fine home. One little corner holds his own books, great and small, and amongst these might be noted his volumes on Homer, the Highlands, and Self-Culture. Few houses can boast the same number of distinguished photographs, all autographed: Cardinal Newman, Emperor of Germany, von Moltke, Gladstone, Morley, Sir John Millais, Henry Irving, Browning, Dr. Guthrie, Norman McLeod, Duke of Argyle, Shaftesbury, John Bright, Kingsley, Rosebery, Ruskin, and many more. I saw so many diverse walking-sticks in the hall that I thought the Old Oracle might have opened shop for the sale of sticks! He was in free-and-easy dress, and looked at peace with himself and all the world, in his blue dressing-gown and scarlet sash and the Panama straw hat, with his mighty white locks in glorious disorder over his shoulders. He loved a turn at backgammon with Mrs. Blackie at night, usually turned in for the night after eleven, and breakfasted at 7.30. Every hour had its specific duty, and Blackie, to the last, lived and preached the gospel of a busy and a cheerful and a clean life. On the streets he was distinguished from the multitude; and the literary world, at least, is familiar with the figure in the black frock coat, the ever-present plaid flung around him, the big broad-brimmed black felt hat, the small inquisitive neighbourly twinkling eyes, and the hair floating on the winds ! That figure now is " mouldering in the clay, but his soul goes marching on."

D. P. McPHERSON.

"THE MINISTRY OF THE SPIRIT."

A REVIEW.

The earthly ministry of the beloved Dr. Gordon came unexpectedly to a close less than a year ago. Almost the last work of that fruitful life was to send out into the world this book on "The Ministry of the Spirit." It may fitly be called his monument, setting forth the reflections and experiences of a life-time, and revealing the inner thoughts and life-impulses of the man. Those who knew and heard him will recognize in the book a sort of transcript of his character; the quiet calm dignity of his bearing, the steady assured march of his address, his self-unconsciousness, his deep earnestness, his reverent contemplative view of truth, his sincerity even when he seemed to err, his strong attachment to certain methods of scripture interpretation and forms of theological belief, are all reflected here. It need not be said that its teachings were to him no mere theories, but truths which he found to be a great practical force in the lives of many Christian people.

The *aim* of the work is principally to "dwell upon the time-ministry of the Holy Spirit," "emphasizing and magnifying the great truth that the Paraclete is now present in the church; that we are now living in the dispensation of the Spirit."

The *form* in which the doctrine is presented is determined mostly by two factors. The first of these is the belief that time can be divided, in the course of God's providence, into successive ages clearly defined and somewhat abruptly beginning and ending. Thus, an age ends with the first advent of Christ; a second, beginning thence, ends with His ascension; a third extends from that point to His second advent, with another or others to follow; and throughout these ages the divine economy is administered by the Father, the Son and the Spirit successively. The second factor which shapes the form of the book is his view of the relation between the work of Christ and the work of the Spirit in the world. By comparing the "time-ministry" of each a parallelism appears. This is indicated in the chapters of the book in about the following manner :—(1).

To the advent of Christ at a definite time corresponds that of the Spirit at Pentecost, "the birth-day of the Holy Spirit." (2). To the early infancy, growth, and baptism of Jesus correspond "the naming of the Spirit" (Paraclete), "the embodying of the Spirit," (His incorporation in the church), and "the enduement of the Spirit" (his impartation to the consecrated believer). (3). Corresponding somewhat loosely to the active ministry of Christ is the activity of the Spirit in "communion," "administration," "inspiration," and "conviction." (4). The "ascent of the Spirit" parallels the ascension of Christ. The historic career of Christ and the personal earthly activity of the Spirit are alike in their general features.

To some people this may seem a fanciful presentation of the subject adopted for the sake of simplicity. Not so to Dr. Gordon. He says, "the time-ministry of the Spirit is distinct from all that went before and introductory to all that is to come after —a ministry with a definite beginning and a definite termination." "For the fulfilment of a definite mission He came into the world at an appointed time; He is now carrying on His ministry on earth, and in due time He will complete it and return to heaven again."

In the treatment of his subject the author sometimes goes pretty far afield. It is quite clear that the object of the work is not only to describe the Spirit's work, but to promote as well the author's views on such other questions as Inspiration, Regeneration, the Church, the Second Coming of Christ, "Rapture of the Church." The whole book is adorned with a devout and humble (yet confident) spirit, a compactness of statement, felicity of expression and aptness of illustration truly admirable. Our principal concern is with its doctrines. An adequate discussion of these requires time and space, aided by studious reflection and a richer Christian experience than the reviewer can claim.

But to accept without hesitancy the book as a whole would be exceedingly unwise in any person. How often the careful reader will stop and reflect long over some of its far-reaching statements! Sometimes he will desire to repeat and emphasize sublime truths set forth; again, he will put a note of interrogation after some instance of doubtful exegesis; or again, he will write a marginal note correcting some minor but important error in quotations, these being taken sometimes from the A.V., some-times from the Revisers, and sometimes one of these amended by the author.   But here we can only touch the main features of the book.

First, consider the author's view of time as divided into dis-tinct ages indicated in prophecy and history, and the Spirit's relation thereto.   The belief that we are enabled by a study of the Scriptures to understand " the divine programme of the world's history," and the nature and, perhaps, the time of some events yet future, and also to set them in their proper relations to events past and present, has proved to be a very attractive belief to a large number of Christians, and is doubtless very comforting to minds which have been disturbed by their own attempts to unravel the mysteries of providence.   It may be granted that Dr. Gordon's application of this method of inter-preting revelation to the place and work of the Holy Spirit helps toward a clearer recognition of His personality and pre-sence.   But it may encourage mechanical conceptions of God's dealings with mankind and stimulate students of the Bible to further speculations, as has been too often the case.   Many de-vout students of God's words will shrink from going so far as Dr. Gordon.   They will feel that Christ himself is put too far away from us.   They will consider that Jesus' great promise, " Lo, I am with you alway," means something more than " His presence by the Holy Ghost."   They will fear that to represent the Holy Spirit as " Mediator between men and Christ " tends to a view of Christ as no longer Mediator between God and man; for the New Testament distinctly says that Christ is the " *one* Mediator," and never speaks of the Spirit as such.   To speak of the time when the Son of God was in the flesh as an age of grace, and the present age as in contrast, " a dispensation of elec-tion and outgathering" is to fail to see that *the present age is one of election just because it is an age of grace, because it is the age of the Mediatorial reign of Jesus Christ.*   Grace reigns now through Jesus Christ, who administers the kingdom.   And our fellowship is with the ascended Christ himself, because the Spirit in us is His own.   And it is because we have fellowship with Christ himself in the Spirit, and not because the Spirit is a sub-stitute for Christ, that He is our Comforter.   This does not hinder a fuller realization of the "presence" (Παρουσία) of Christ "when he shall be manifested."

The subject of the Spirit's work is a very difficult one, and, notwithstanding the clear light thrown upon it in many portions of Dr. Gordon's book, questions arise and mysteries appear almost as numerous as ever. What after all is meant by "the advent of the Spirit"? Is it the assumption of an official position among Christ's people, or is it a personal coming as truly as Christ's was? And if it is both of these, as seems the author's view, what sort of coming or presence or office is described in accounts of His operations before the advent of Christ, when heroes wrought and prophets wrote, "being moved by the Holy Ghost"? Zachariah was as truly "filled with the Holy Ghost" previously to the birth of Jesus as were the apostles at Pentecost. What sort of coming was it when He fell upon the baptized believers in Samaria, or the unbaptized believers in Cornelius's household, or the twelve disciples at Ephesus? Then, what is meant by the extra-scriptural phrase, "the ascent of the Spirit"? Is it the ascent ("rapture") of the church? To discuss this would lead us far into the question of Christ's second coming; but it may not be out of the way to remark that the passages of Scripture quoted in the last chapter of the book do not seem to teach what its caption suggests.

Second, consider some currents of thought and belief traceable in the book.

(1) *Pre-millenarianism.* This is reflected in the division of time into distinct and contrasted ages and dispensations; in the representation of the present age as one of outgathering to be followed by the fulfilment of Joel's prophecy (but see Acts 2: 14-21,) in a coming age of ingathering; in the view of prophecy as literal and mainly predictive, that is—a fore-view of events in chronological order, instead of being a setting forth of principles and the manner of their operation in the world; and it appears in the reliance placed upon ceremonial ordinances of the law of Moses as mathematically accurate anticipations of history even in regard to the order and degree of separation of events in time.

(2) *Mysticism.* There is a false mysticism and there is a true, and it is not always easy to say where the one begins and

the other ends. The false mysticism treats the "inward voice" as the voice of God, and it shades off on the one hand towards rationalism, and on the other hand towards fanaticism; but the true mysticism, while acknowledging the value of inner experiences and "intuitions," subordinates them to a revelation coming from without, and recognizes the source of truth and duty as external to the personal consciousness. A strong current of mysticism runs through the book under review. For instance, speaking of the meaning of the term Paraclete, it is said, "The heart of the church is the best dictionary of the Spirit,"—an admirable utterance, but how many questions and difficulties spring out of it. The testimonies and experiences of certain Christians are regarded as supplying an argument for a special conscious enduement of the Spirit (pp. 74, 85, 93, 95). An understanding of the meaning of Scripture is held to be the special possession of Spirit-taught men. The church is exhorted to " a prayerful waiting upon Him, the Spirit, for guidance,"—with the expectation that "the signs of the divine choice may be clearly manifest," as much so "as in the beginning." Whether this mysticism is sufficiently guarded may be left to the reader's judgment.

(3) *Confidence in the Scriptures*. The worth of the book is principally in its wealth of Scripture. It swarms with Bible-quotations. Everywhere is manifest a prayerful attempt to ascertain their meaning. Equal reverence is paid to Old and New Testaments. Both are treated as possessing infallible authority. Their language is " a language of the Holy Ghost." Their very words are inspired. No middle view between verbal inspiration and no inspiration is admissible. This is the doctrine taught, and the book lives up to it. The chapter devoted to this doctrine carries us back to a work of the Spirit anterior to the "age" to which the "time-ministry of the Spirit " properly belongs; it is therefore not a necessary part of the book, nor is the doctrine vital to a reverent and adequate view of His ministry. It is a little unfortunate that in the defence of this view of inspiration such passages as 2 Tim. 3 : 16 and 1 Pet. 1 : 10, 11 should have been quoted from the A.V. without due attention to the important changes in the Revised Version.

Third, a few words may be said in reference to some promi-

nent doctrines. ' Of these take first, " The Enduement of the
Spirit." By this is meant the baptism of the Spirit *given* once
for all at Pentecost, but not actually *received* by every believer.
It is an experience distinct from regeneration and subsequent to
it; as consciously enjoyed; as marked in its fruits; obtained
through a distinct act of faith directed toward the Holy Spirit,
as the other is obtained by an act of faith directed toward Christ.
" It is still the duty and privilege of believers to receive the Holy
Spirit by a conscious definite act of appropriating faith, just as
they received Jesus Christ," (p. 68. See also pp. 70,74, 92, 94).
This is called an act of consecration, and a prayer is set forth
suited to such an act : " O Holy Spirit, I yield to thee now in
humble surrender. I receive thee as my Teacher, my Comforter,
my Sanctifier and my Guide." But where in the New Testament is there anything like this ? On the contrary it may be
pointed out that the expression, " faith toward the Holy Ghost "
is entirely without parallel in the Scriptures ; for there God in
Christ is presented as the object of faith. Neither is there a
single instance of prayer addressed to the Holy Spirit.

The result of a Christian teacher's views on this point may
be serious. The subject is a difficult one. Men swing to extremes
about it. Confusion is common as to the real teaching of passages supposed to bear upon it, and it must be pointed out, though
reluctantly, that this confusion pervades much of the chapter on
" The Enduement of the Spirit," despite its many lucid statements
and its noble and exalted thought. Whether a man may receive
Jesus as his Saviour without receiving the Holy Spirit, whether
a man may be a full Christian and yet lack the Spirit, whether
the Spirit, if received in regeneration, ought afterwards to be
received in another sense, is not made perfectly clear; but the
book bears toward an affirmative answer. For instance, the
sealing of the Spirit, (which the N. T. never speaks of as pertaining only to *a class* of believers), the filling and the anointing
are regarded as three aspects of the one spiritual fact, namely,
the enduement which is experienced by some believers, but not
all. What the author would have done with such passages as,
" If any man hath not the Spirit of Christ, he is none of His,"
" As many as are led by the Spirit of God, these are sons of God,"
" Know ye not that ye are the temple of God, and the Spirit of

God dwelleth in you?" and the many others of like import, which are spoken of Christians without distinction, does not appear.

Two general criticisms may be given of the chapter under discussion :—1st. The import of its teaching is misleading. It seems implied that a regenerate man may be an unconsecrated man,—a most dangerous conclusion, obscuring the character of true conversion. [Note—The term "consecration" so often heard is not to be found in the N. T., Rev. Vers. Its nearest equivalent is "sanctification"; but every Christian is represented as sanctified]. The author would undoubtedly admit that every man regenerate through faith in Christ is a proper subject for baptism; but the baptism implies a union already with the Spirit, since it is a baptism "into the name of the Father and of the Son *and of the Holy Spirit.*" Or again, baptism sets forth a union with Christ in death, burial and resurrection life, (Rom. 6 : 3-5). Can one conceive of a consecration more thorough than that?

2nd. The passages urged in support of the doctrines do not yield it. One class of these refer to the coming of the Spirit upon believers (as Acts 2 : 1-7; 8 : 14-17; 10 : 44-46; 19; 1-7). The special circumstances of the time required (Acts 2 : 2-4) these miraculous displays appealing to the senses. If we are justified in expecting a baptism of the Spirit now, are we not also justified in expecting the gift of tongues and miraculous powers and in resorting to the laying on of hands for it?

Another class of these passages is represented in the teachings of the Epistles. As an instance take Gal. 3 : 2, 14. These are said to represent the Galatians as receiving the Spirit "by faith toward the Holy Ghost," not the same as faith toward Christ. But the context shows that it is just this saving faith in Christ, in opposition to works of the law, Paul is speaking of. To enforce his argument that men are saved simply through faith in Christ, he recalls their own experience of receiving the Spirit. If this had been by an act of faith different from that of accepting Christ as Saviour, his argument would lose its force. And so far from regarding that gift of the Spirit as subsequent to conversion, he dates it at the very beginning of their new life : "Having *begun* in the Spirit, are ye now perfected in the flesh?"

The other passages brought forward will be found under examination to yield a not dissimilar result.

However, let not our inability to accept Dr. Gordon's view
lead us into making the sad mistake of overlooking the great
truths which, no doubt, he was aiming to express : God wills
that His saints should live lives of power and glorious victory
over sin, and do great works of ministry to men through the in-
dwelling of the Spirit bestowed upon the believer by the ascended
Christ.

Our space is already gone before we have been able to touch
the most important chapters of the book, those setting forth the
" communion " and the " administration " of the Spirit. The
former speaks of what the Spirit works *in* us as individuals, the
latter of His work accomplished *through* us as members of the
body of Christ. These chapters ought to be read again and
again. With the exception of a stray sentence here and there,
they may be safely commended to the earnest attention of every
man.

In " the Communion of the Spirit," His work is described
as making " true *in* us that which is already true *for* us in our
glorified Lord." As the Spirit of Life He accomplishes our regeneration, which is not a development of a life naturally possessed,
but the impartation of a new life whose source is from the beginning," " from above," even from God himself. " The lost
image of God is not restamped upon us, but renewed within us."
Notice here one striking sentence : " The sonship on which the
New Testament dwells so constantly is based absolutely and
solely on the new birth, while the doctrine of universal sonship
rests either upon a daring denial or a daring assumption—the
denial of the universal fall of man through sin, or the assumption of a universal regeneration of man through the Spirit." As
the Spirit of Holiness he accomplishes our sanctification, which
"consists in the double process of mortification and vivification,
the deadening and subduing of the old [nature] and the quickening and developing of the new." Thus the dying and quickening
of Christ is re-wrought in us, the former by means of the latter,
and not the reverse as asceticism teaches.

Finally as the Spirit of Glory he accomplishes our transfigu-
ration at the coming of Christ.

In "The Administration of the Spirit" the sovereign authority of the Holy Spirit is set forth in three particulars: 1st. In His ministry and government of the church—His choice of its officers, and His direction of its work; 2nd. In the worship and service of the church—its preaching, its praying, its service of song; 3rd. In the missions of the church. How the reading of this chapter sets a man's heart yearning to see it fulfilled in the churches. Their need is a deeper spirituality, which can be enjoyed only by a humble and obedient recognition of the presence and authority of the Spirit. We forbear to quote from the chapter under consideration, because if we quote any of it, we must quote it all. Objection has been taken to many statements in the book, but when we read this part of it, we can forgive them.

In conclusion: An examination of the book has compelled adverse criticism of many portions. This is regrettable, because the purpose of the work is lofty and its underlying thought is true and abiding. The frame-work of the book may not endure, but the spirit of it will live; and one result will be the quickening of many individuals and churches that were once half-dead. May it be so!

GEORGE CROSS.

ON THE DEATH OF FREDERICK HALLARD.

Oh, name him not, nor all the shadowy host
Of lovely dead, whose memory haunts my soul!
Be they as bright now as the starry pole,
For me they are not, and to me is lost
The presence of their beauty evermore!
He was a youth whom to behold was joy,
Dowered with all grace of the fresh-hearted boy,
Pure as white light, and on his face he wore
A wealth of smiles to greet all kindred life.
Erect he grew, and light-plumed, like a flower,
More blushing fair from fragrant hour to hour,
Till when there came a cruel, cruel knife
And lopped his pride. I turn my face away:
Tears bring no help: I can but work and pray.

JOHN STUART BLACKIE.

2

Students' Quarter.

THE ESSENTIALS OF ORATORY.

"Is oratory a lost art?" is a question frequently asked and variously answered. The question itself suggests one of two things: either oratory is a lost art, or it comes so little into prominence that its existence is uncertain enough to occasion the question. The latter suggestion seems to me a truth.

Oratory is not a lost art; it has only stepped into the background. The art of arts has become the least prominent and this is a misfortune. Any loss of power is a misfortune to the loser.

Oratory is a great power, and there are to-day marvellous opportunities for the exercise of it. In the pulpit, at the bar, on the political platform, what opportunities for the man who can stand before his fellows and thrill them with his thought, fire them with his enthusiasm, and animate them with his will!

Surely if power is desirable the oratorical art should be assiduously cultivated. Yet its cultivation is persistently neglected by the majority, even of those who expect to occupy positions where its power would be of inestimable value to them.

This neglect is in part due to the great prominence given to training along particular lines. Intellectual training is the object of almost all our educational work. We are content to spend years in patient labour that we may be able to think; caring little, however, about the expression of thought, with the result that very often the attempted expression is the burial of that which intellect has brought forth. Yet all this vigour of intellect and wealth of thought is valuable only in so far as expressed. The sweetest harmonies may be ringing through a man's soul, but they do not benefit the world until with skilled fingers he sweeps the keys and pours forth those harmonies in sweet soul-thrilling music. An artist may have conceptions of beauty transcending anything that men have ever seen, but they are valueless until they live upon the canvas. So with a man's thought. It is useful and valuable only when communicated to his fellow men. How important then that he learn to express thought as well as conceive it.

This neglect of the study of oratory is due in part also to the opinion entertained by many that orators are born, not made. This may be true, but oratory is certainly no ready-made gift handed down to men from heaven. Those whom nature has endowed most richly with musical talents require years of hard work and training before they become accomplished musicians. Much more will he who pursues that most subtle and difficult of arts, oratory, require earnest toil and thorough discipline before he can hope for success. Most men are born with a certain amount of oratorical talent. Indeed, has not every man, who is neither idiotic nor mute, abilities of an oratorical character ? He has a physical exterior and a voice, both of which he constantly uses in conversation. He has a mind and an emotional nature of more or less sensitiveness. He is capable of feeling, thinking and of expressing more or less perfectly his emotions and thoughts. These powers, which are his by nature, well developed and wisely used, give oratorical power. Some men by reason of a stronger personality, and superior abilities, will be greater orators than others, but every man who can think, feel and talk has oratorical gifts.

In possession of these abilities what training does he need, in order that he may use them effectively ? He requires every possible kind of training. The whole man is to be developed, and there is no education, no form of healthful discipline which will not be of service to him. Everything that will tend to perfect voice and body will be of value to him. Every thing that will increase his knowledge, quicken his observation, sharpen his intellect, render more sensitive his emotional nature, wing his imagination, strengthen his will, develop his individuality, will be of service to him. So where I argue in favour of a study of and training for oratory I am simply arguing for the best training and most perfect development of every power that man possesses.

We gain some conception of the training required and of the powers needed for oratory when we consider what an audience is. It is composed of individuals of every character and disposition. No two of them can be impressed in exactly the same way. The orator may have a single truth to present. How shall he express it so that every individual in his audience will grasp it ?   A logical presentation of it will reach the intellectual man, but his emotional neighbor will not be affected by it until the orator makes it glow with feeling.   The imaginative man is reached by neither logic nor emotion.   Something bold and brilliant impresses the truth upon him.   Now the orator, to be successful, must have power to reach and influence all kinds of temperaments.   But manifestly he cannot influence intellectual men unless he be intellectual himself ; he cannot move emotional men unless he have emotion within himself.   He cannot inspire imaginative men unless he be imaginative himself.   He is the supremest orator who by reason of his diversity of developed powers and his wise use of them can most powerfully influence the greatest number and variety of men.

The reader may think that if this be true there is no occasion for the regret expressed in the beginning of this article, that so little attention is paid to training for oratory.   I am ready to admit that all the education and discipline so earnestly and patiently striven for is helpful and essential, but while these things which ought to be done are done, my regret is that other things which ought also to be done are left undone.   To some of the things left undone I wish now to call attention.

The study of elocution is much neglected.   Elocution is not oratory, nor will the study of elocution make one an orator.   In fact it is possible for a man to be an accomplished elocutionist and not understand the first principles of oratory.   Elocution is valuable because of the development and control of voice and body which a faithful study of it gives.   It certainly is of importance that both voice and body be brought to the highest degree of perfection, and for this end elocution is of incalculable value.

The voice is a wonderful instrument and its possibilities of development almost unlimited.   When well developed its services to the orator are of inestimable worth.   But an organ so delicate and capable of so many variations will require a vast amount of careful exercise and training to bring it to perfection.   The body also should receive attention.   The testimony of two witnesses is stronger than that of one, and a sentiment will be immeasurably more effective when expressed by both voice and body at the same time than when expressed by the voice alone.   The position and movements of the body are often eloquent; on the other hand it frequently happens that a speaker's wretched voice, ungainly postures and awkward gestures detract the attention of his audience from his subject. True elocutionary training will remove these defects and by perfecting voice and body make them instruments of power.

But the development of voice and body is far from being the most important thing to which the would-be orator must attend. The most perfect organ is useless unless there be a master to touch the keys, and the most splendidly trained voice and body are of little value unless there be behind them a master power to direct and control. This power, I believe, lies in psychic activity. In true oratory every faculty is actively working. Intellect, imagination, the emotional nature, are all in a condition of the greatest alertness and activity. The personality too is aroused and is flashing out in every tone and look and gesture. Voice and body if well disciplined respond readily and submit themselves to the direction of these forces.

But how may these forces be called into operation? What will induce the highest activity of these faculties? Inspiration from the subject may contribute to this end; perhaps also inspiration from the audience. Indeed it frequently happens that these two influences stimulate a man's faculties and lift him to that condition in which he speaks with greatest power. But, and this is the point which I wish to emphasize most strongly, a man can and ought to do by the exercise of his will, just what the influences from his subject and his audience have done for him. For physical earnestness, for proper mental and emotional conditions, let him depend upon his will. He may be susceptible to all the inspiring influences which come from the audience and from the subject, but he must not be dependent upon them. If he is dependent upon them, he will utterly fail where they are lacking. He must be self-reliant. He must have his will so developed that it will marshal all his powers and make them do their best under any circumstances. And this perfect mastery of his powers will but the better enable him to profit by all the helpful influences which may come from his subject and his audience.

Further, there is needed an overmastering purpose. It may

be possible for an orator to delight and thrill an audience, without having any very strong purpose. But before he can greatly move them and influence their wills he himself must be actuated by a mighty purpose. An earnest purpose and an unyielding will, together, will do more than anything else towards enabling a man to achieve the highest success in the oratorical art; and this success is surely desirable because of the power which it gives. For its attainment then I would say let voice and body be carefully trained. Let intellect, the emotional nature and the imagination be brought to the highest perfection. Place the will in supreme authority over them and then let there be behind all some mighty purpose connected with human life in time and in eternity. These all combine to give to their possessor in a superlative degree that mysterious but all-powerful influence over the minds and wills of men which true oratory exerts.

JNO. F. VICHERT, '97·

THE PALACE OF SONG.

In an hour of despondence and gloom
    He shewed me the Palace of Song,
Where the bending trees in the murmuring breeze
    Make music all day long.

Suffused with a rapturous joy,
    I heard the Seraphim raise
To the hautboys clear in that ringing sphere
    One loud hallelujah of praise.

Majestic crescendoes of joy!
    Sweet diminuendoes of love!
And the lyric wine of those songs divine
    Transported my spirit above.

Those thrilling and jubilant chords,
    That music that never shall cease,
By the crystal flood in the Palace of God,
    Had spoken me Infinite Peace.

O. G. LANGFORD, '95.

—Christian Herald.

HOME AND CHARACTER.

The subject carries us back at once to the home of our infancy, and what words fall upon the ear with so much of music
in their cadence, as those which recall the scenes of happy
childhood now numbered with those of the past ? But while
only memory can trace the past, fond recollection delights to
dwell upon the events which marked our early pathway, when
the unbroken home circle presented a scene of peace and enjoyment, found only in the bosom of a happy family. Happy the
life whose roots have penetrated deep into such a soil, and have
drawn from it the elements that form a strong character.

Tennyson, in "The Bugle Song," gives simple but beautiful
expression to an important truth which he makes the climax of
this little poem. The scene is an English landscape as it appears
in the evening to the spectator. The day now is almost past
The sun grows broader as he travels toward the western horizon.
His long rays "shake across the lake," lighting up old ruins
with splendor. Nature assumes an air of soberness and silence.
It is an hour which the thoughtful welcome, as bringing senti-
ments and affections, which if not so practical from an earthly
view-point, are yet more fruitful in deep experiences of soul,
searchings of heart, questionings of spirit, height and sublimity
of aspiration, than the busy toilsome day. The turbulence of
activity, or thought, or passion is stilled : we listen to the dying
sounds of labor and toil, and when all is still about us we feel a
kindred quiet of soul to possess us and calm the agitation of the
day. Without distraction we can listen, and there are borne in
upon us, voices which before were too faint to be heard. The
"Horns of Elfland" make nature vocal, with sounds and songs
sweet as music from an angel's lyre. We catch the sounds, store
them in memory, and not too soon, for "thinner, clearer, farther
going," they die. They die, but

"Our echoes roll from soul to soul
And grow forever and forever,"

so lasting and far reaching is the influence of man upon his
fellows.

The meshes of a net are not more surely knit together than is man to man. Every human life is a centre of influence for ·good or for ill, and while we may be forgetful or unconscious of this secret force ; by our deeds, by our words, by our very thoughts, we are exerting it. We ask ourselves why we have grown into this character rather than into another, why we are what we are while others who entered the race of life when we did, are better or worse than we ? The answer is not far to seek. The soul is a sensitive plate receiving and retaining impressions from almost every source, and we are what we are, because the rays of influence fell upon it from minds true, pure, and good, or perhaps because rays from a darkened mind came upon it, and produced the image that now appears. " I am a part of all that I have met." This conclusion is inevitable ; we cannot escape it. A ring of light dilates around a pebble thrown into water. The little silvery ripple expands, from its inch of radius farther and farther, until its circumference touches the most distant bound of the lake, until every bay and tiny inlet has responded to its influence. There is not one individual, however humble, who may not, rather who does not cause a ripple upon the sea of humanity, and exercise some influence, however small, upon the world. Nor can the individual be found who has not been thus influenced.

If individual influence be so great, and is so important a factor in the formation of character, how much more then is it true that home associations are largely responsible for the characters of those who come within the circle of their influence ! It is the prerogative of home, to make the first impressions upon our natures, and according to its own character to give the first bent to our lives in one direction or another. Through life we bear the image and superscription of the homes that have reared us. The home makes the first indelible stamp, and sets the first ineradicable seal on the plastic nature of the child. Every stratum of our being must be removed, before home impressions can be banished from our characters. A pound of gold may be drawn into a wire that will girdle the globe. The influence of every true and worthy home is a golden cord, binding the hearts of each member of the household to every ennobling virtue, and a gentle but effective rein restraining from an evil course of conduct. The individual who has had the advantage of being nurtured in a home of piety, of character, perhaps of somewhat stern principle and of strong attachment to religious sentiment, where supreme regard is had to laying deep and lasting the foundation of earnest, reverent character, has already strong assurance of success in life ; and whoever has brought from such a home the convictions which form the basis of a vigorous moral life will not speedily fall a prey to the temptations that surround men in every station of life. The recorded experiences are at our disposal, of many who have left virtuous homes, and coming under the power of strong temptation have experienced the supporting influences of home life. Even when heart and will had given way, the remembrance of a father's patient care, a mother's tender sympathy, the cherished love of brothers and sisters, and the thought of the shame and grief that would come to all from the exposure that *might* follow have almost invariably had a restraining power.

It is true that occasionally an individual rises superior to, or falls below, the moral influence of the home, but such instances are comparatively rare. The majority of those who have become noted in all vocations of life—the most illustrious statesmen, distinguished warriors, eloquent preachers, and the greatest benefactors of human kind, owe in large measure their greatness to the fostering influence of homes, often poor and humble but virtuous. In these days, much attention is paid to legislative reform and rightly so; schools, colleges and universities are preparing men for engagement in the varied callings of life. Machinery in every department of church and state, is being set in operation for the defeat of vice and for the amelioration of unfortunate conditions. But each and all these agencies are proving themselves inadequate to their self-appointed tasks. The responsibility has been placed by the highest authority, upon another institution older than universities, older than human governments, older even than the church. In that comprehensive command: "Train up a child in the way he should go, and when he is old he will not depart from it," the responsibility is directly placed upon the home. Prevention is ever much better than cure. The place to reform men is not the reformatories, prisons and penitentiaries of our land, but in the homes. Let but the homes be centres where the grand principles of industry, economy, sobriety, and veracity are taught and exemplified—where the twig is bent in the direction in which the tree should incline, and the problems which are racking the brains of benevolent toilers for man's betterment, will be of comparatively easy solution. Parents are not responsible for bestowing upon their children this world's goods in abundance, nor are they always responsible for furnishing them with a college education ; either might prove ruinous. But every parent is responsible for sending the son or daughter into life with the principles of moral right and wrong, deeply implanted with.n his or her nature. No parent is guiltless who neglects in the home training of the child this first requisite to an honorable upright character.

> " Each creature holds an insular point in space ;
> Yet what man stirs a finger, breathes a sound,
> But all the multitudinous beings round
> In all the countless worlds, with time and place
> For their conditions, down to the central base,
> Thrill, haply, in vibration and rebound,
> Life answering life, across the vast profound,
> In full antiphony by a common grace ? "

M. C. McLean, '98 (Th.)

THIRTEENTH ANNUAL REPORT OF THE FYFE MISSIONARY SOCIETY.*

It is our privilege to present to you to-night the thirteenth annual report of the Fyfe Missionary Society. Our desire in so doing is not to gain applause for work done, nor yet that we may be entertaining, but that we may be eloquent, for "true eloquence," says Broadus, "is so speaking as not merely to convince the judgment, kindle the imagination and move the feelings, but to give a powerful impulse to the will." We believe that feeling will be aroused, that imagination will be kindled and judgment convinced, but how to give a powerful impulse to your wills is the problem. Yet even here we believe the difficulty may in a great measure be removed if we can awaken in

---

*Read at the annual public meeting of the society, 1895.

you a true sense of the relation, which as members of the Baptist denomination, you bear towards this society. Ownership ever brings with it responsibility. McMaster University is the heritage of Canadian Baptists, whereby their sons and daughters, through all time, may receive a Christian education. It is theirs to rejoice in, theirs to care for, and they and they only are responsible for the influence of its various departments of activity. Then how careful, how watchful, how solicitous should they be concerning that department which strikes the very keynote of its spiritual life! Now while we are very grateful for the many friends, who rejoicing in our society, have watched over its interests and cherished its aims, we nevertheless feel that there are others who have scarcely begun to realize what a mighty influence for good exists in our midst. In presenting this report therefore, it shall be our aim to give such information as shall be most likely to deepen your appreciation of the importance of the society to the University, to the Denomination, to Home and Foreign Missions.

But before proceeding to portray its influence in these various directions we would say a few words regarding one or two of our officers.

You know that great artists sometimes resort to the doubtful practice of announcing their appearance in any place as positively their last. President Farmer more than once gave us to understand that as President of this society he had positively made his last appearance. Yet he is with us to-night in that same capacity, and we are glad that he is. It is, however, only due to our president to say that his acceptance of this office for the third time, was, as he expressed it, "against his very best judgment." It is needless to point out that even the "the very best judgment" of our professors is, at times, liable to go seriously astray. But in regard to the office of Corresponding Secretary we are not able to report so favorably. We cannot but feel that in Mr. Priest's departure for India we have sustained a great loss. Mr. Priest, who occupied this position for several years, was a wise counsellor and a very able secretary. Indeed so diligent and efficient did he prove himself as a correspondent that we find him, only a few weeks after the close of the term, with all arrangements made to sail with a Mrs. Priest for India.

But coming now to the influence of the society.   Influence, what a subtle thing it is!   Who can measure it?   One moment in full view, the next completely hidden, but only to appear again in a form and manner least expected.   Let us watch it as it works embodied in the Fyfe Missionary Society.

If we would estimate a man's true influence we must know him in his home.   The Fyfe Society has a home—McMaster University—and a wonderful influence in that home.   We have always felt its power over the traditions of our University, but each passing year makes this more evident.   We believe its establishment in our midst was providential, and that so long as it is faithfully preserved it will do much to maintain the Christian character of the University.   It is true we have a grand motto—" Τὰ πάντα ἐν Χριστῷ συνέστηκεν" "In Christ all things hold together," but these words, however noble they may be, will avail but little unless embodied in a life.   We believe the spirit breathed in our motto has crystallized in the Fyfe Missionary Society.   Meeting as it does but once a month, you may be doubtful of its great influence, yet, like the leaven of our Lord's parable, it permeates and transforms the whole University life. To us this meeting one day in each month, the setting aside of all studies to engage in religious thought is in danger of becoming an old story.   We are like a man who, in ignorance hangs a valuable picture in his attic, where it remains almost forgotten till some stranger begins to expiate on its many beauties.   It does us good occasionally to see ourselves as others see us.   A few weeks ago we were speaking of the society to a prominent Presbyterian minister.   He was at once intensely interested; the thought of its value struck him with great force.   It seemed as if for the first time a ray of light had pierced a black cloud of perplexity, for in it he saw a means of keeping alive the spirituality of University students.

Let us hear also the testimony of Chancellor Wallace, our Honorary President.   Addressing the society at its first meeting in October, he said, "Occasionally during the past few years, it has been my privilege to meet with you at chapel service.   It was always a matter of surprise to note the deep spirituality that seemed to pervade those services.   I wondered if it were charac-teristic of the University life.   I did not think it could be.

Since coming among you I have changed my opinion. I find this deep spiritual life pervading every department of our work, and I believe we have the secret of it in these monthly missionary days."

One other testimony, from a student pursuing advanced work among us—"I have been in many colleges and in some have noted more activity in actual Christian work than at McMaster; but in no other University or Christian school have I found the deep earnest spirituality characterizing the students in their daily life as I find here."

Now our object in repeating these testimonies, is by no means the glorification of the student-body, but rather to give credit where credit is due, and to impress upon our own minds, and upon your minds, and upon the minds of the whole Baptist denomination, the fact that, while we have a glorious heritage in our University, its value to the denomination is many times enhanced by the existence of the Fyfe Missionary Society. In proof of this let me quote freely some words of Dr. Rand's, addressed to the society in January last. He said, ' It was a remarkable fact that, the history of Baptist institutions of learning showed that not one had been founded without having for its chief end the promotion of the cause of Jesus Christ, yet it was sad to notice that with but few exceptions, institutions founded with such noble thought were fast becoming secularized.' We hope, nay, we have reason to believe, that in the Fyfe Missionary Society we have a power that shall forever remove the day when such shall be true of McMaster University.

But if such is the influence of the Society over the University life, does it not stand to reason that its influence over the denominational thought in succeeding years must also be great? Some have laughed at the very idea of a Christian University, and mockingly asked how Christianity, much less Baptist doctrine, was to be imparted through the study of Latin, Mathematics, Philosophy, or other of the sciences. And the objection might very largely hold good were it not for the existence in our midst of some such society as the Fyfe, for by no means all of the students are pursuing *theological* studies. Whence then are *they* to get their training in Baptist, or, as we believe, New Testament principles and thought? Not by the study of a

Cæsar or a Juvenal, not by following the subtle mind of an Aristotle or a Plato, not by tracing the locus of some imaginary point, nor yet from some fossil of by-gone ages, no matter how well preserved, but, as we believe, by attending the various meetings of our society.

And what of this society in its relations to Home Missions? You are well aware that a large proportion of its members spend the summer months as missionaries, using this word in its large sense of gospel preachers. We shall not attempt to estimate all the good resulting to Home Missions from this work. The most we can do is to present a few facts and figures, thus giving you some knowledge of the power expended, from which you must form your own judgment as to its importance.

So far as we have been able to ascertain there have been added to the denomination through the labors of our members during the five months of summer some four hundred and seventy-seven persons, an advance over last year of nearly one hundred, of whom over three hundred were received by baptism. It is, of course, true that these same students would, in all probability, have been preaching had there been no such society as the Fyfe, yet judging from the testimony of theological institutions at large, there can be little room for doubt that the success of our members as soul-winners is largely traceable to the influence of the society which keeps them spiritually alive in the midst of the too often withering influences of merely intellectual pursuits. So that, instead of leaving the University in the spring cold and unproductive as winter, they go out with souls burning for Christian service.

Examining more closely the details of the past summer's work, we find that nearly three thousand, one hundred and fifty sermons were preached, being divided among one hundred preaching stations; about one thousand, five hundred prayer-meetings conducted; seven hun lred Sunday School lessons taught, three thousand tracts distributed, and nearly twelve thousand pastoral visits made. The total number of students engaged in this work was the same as last year, about sixty. It is hard to realize the amount of work, worry and anxiety that these figures represent.

The lights and shadows of a student's missionary life are

many and various.   His youth and inexperience, each a serious
disadvantage in some respects, are in other respects his only
hope.   If we might change the words of a well-known quotation,
we would say "that youth leaps in where age would fear to
tread."   It is frequently the student's lot to enter fields that
would entirely overwhelm an older man with discouragements,
meuts, but youth and buoyancy of spirit seem to carry him
successfully over the hard places.   Still, even in an ordinary
field his work is by no means light.   He must preach twice and
often three times each Sunday, and conduct one or more Bible
classes.   During the week he must, as a general thing, shoulder
the responsibility of the Young People's Meeting and the prayer
meetings, one or two or three as the case may be, and feels, if
he has any voice, he must by no means neglect the choir practice.   He must visit each afternoon, study each morning, and
what is often still harder, he must at all times and under all
circumstances be pleasant and interested in everybody and
everything about which anybody and nobody may choose to
converse with him.   But then, of course, he gets well paid; most
certainly !   He is guaranteed the munificent sum of about one
dollar a day, or the wage of an ordinary street-car driver, who
has little to do but to·sit and turn a crank, while the student-
pastor has often to turn not one but many cranks.

But of all the discouragements that meet a student none are
more perplexing and disheartening than the petty jealousies and
quarrels, for they are not worthy a more dignified name.   You
have little idea how prevalent they are, and what trifling things
lead up to them.   The following conversation between two
returned students will furnish a sample.   " Well, what kind of
summer did you have ? "   " Just fair."   " Why, what was the
matter ? "   " Split in the church."   " Is that so, what was it
about ? "   " Oh, two of the leading members quarrelling over a
dead sheep, they have been at it for a year or so."   Followers of
the Lord Jesus, just think of this : quarrelling for one whole year
over a dead sheep !   When persecution raged, the heathen world
admiring cried, "Behold how these Christians love one another!"
When in these days liberty of conscience prevails, the world
derisively points and repeats sarcastically, " Behold how these
Christians love one another ! "

But there are lights as well as shadows. A very interesting as well as encouraging feature of the past summer's work is
the large number of " special meetings " that have been held, all
of which were greatly blessed by God. The following are the
places at which these services were conducted: Acton, Belfountain, Canaan, Georgetown, Goodwood, Minesing, McNab,
Pinkhand, Renfrew, St. Eugene and Whitby. As a result of
these meetings, some two hundred professed conversion. Up to
October 15th, however, only seventy-one had united with any
church ; some have been received into fellowship since that date,
and doubtless others will follow during the winter. From this
you will see that the number of baptisms reported during the
summer would, in all probability, have been very greatly
increased, had the students been able to remain on their fields
another month or six weeks.

While remembering the Home field and the influence of the
society there, we must not forget the Foreign, for the two
supplement and condition each other. What then is the Fyfe
Missionary Society doing for Foreign Missions ? Dr. Strong, of
Rochester, referring to the fact that their society for twenty-
five years has not failed to send one of its members to the
Foreign field, says: " I would feel as if the spirit of the Lord
had departed from us if this were not the case." Thank God
that we too can point to a rapidly increasing number of those
who have gone out from our midst. It is not many weeks since
we bade farewell to three of our members, Mr. and Mrs. Stillwell and Mr. Priest. But having thus wished them God-speed,
shall we forget them and their fellow-workers in the distant
land ? Surely not ! In their strange and lonely life, burdened
with crushing responsibilities, they will often crave our sympathy
and prayers. They will miss the touch of a kindly hand, and
the sound of a familiar voice, and it will gladden their hearts to
know, as they do know, that away off in the home land the
members of the Fyfe Society call their names, and bear their
wants to the Throne of Grace, where they have the ear of the
King. And thus it is that the influence of our society reaches
out and beyond, and touches the lives in far-off India.

Returning once more to our own city, we would speak a
word concerning the society's work among the poor. You will

remember that last year we had three missions, River Street, Carlton Street and Rose Avenue. The last two have been amalgamated, the work being continued on Amelia Street. We have also taken up work in a much neglected district, to the northwest of the city; the outlook for each of these missions is very encouraging.

Of course we desire to do good wherever possible, yet one of our chief aims in establishing these city missions is to provide a field of labour for those students who are without preaching stations, during the winter. For it is keenly felt that if the society is to do its work in regard to keeping up the spiritual life of its members, it must provide some outlet for practical work.

In conclusion permit a word about our finances. While we raise, annually among ourselves, fifty dollars for the support of a native preacher in India, and another fifty dollars for the work in the North-West, still the chief expense is in connection with our city missions, some three hundred dollars being required for these alone. Of this last amount about one hundred dollars is also raised among the members of the Society, leaving a balance of two hundred dollars to be raised by its friends. It is true this leaves you but little opportunity to show your interest and generosity, yet we trust you will be considerate of one another, and that none will give more than his due proportion of the needful amount.

With this little word of caution we commend to you the Fyfe Missionary Society; and ask that by your prayers, sympathy and gifts you will stand nobly by us. Then shall the work prosper in our hands; then shall go forth from our midst those ever loyal to the Master's cause, thus bringing the highest honor to the name of Baptists.

" He that overcometh I will make him a pillar in the temple of my God and he shall go out thence no more: and I will write upon him the name of my God, and the name of the city of my God,......and my own new name."

Signed on behalf of the Society,

WM. W. McMASTER, '94,

Recording Secretary.

3

TYPES.*

I.

" Largesse ! largesse ! " cried the rabble ;—
　　On them the proud prince looked
　　With nod indifferent, nor brooked
Their loud acclaiming babble,
Yet he threw them coins, as one
That tosses stones, in fun.

II.

This wealth of mine, this fortune,
　　How it flashes, gleams,
　　And joys me !   O meseems
Should any one impórtune
A jot of it, I 'd turn and hiss
In sudden anger, " Fool, this ? this ? "

III.

He generous bounty did impart
　　With unobtrusive grace,
　　His noble, kindly face.
Finds home in every loyal heart.
His touch the flame of truth renewed,
Ah, Heaven grant us gratitude !

G. Herbert Clarke, '95.

---

*Written for Founder's Day, 1895.

EDITORIAL NOTES.

Many of our readers will be pleased to see the familiar name of their old friend D. P. McPherson at the close of our second article, which he has kindly contributed in response to a request from the Editor. Our genial Canadian brother is standing stoutly for the Baptist cause in Old England and under circumstances, we doubt not, which call for as much of Blackie's "good Scotch rummlegumption" as he can command. Mr. McPherson writes that he is at present deep in the anxieties of church-building, and hints that there are old friends of his in Ontario who might lend him a helping hand if they knew his address. It is 4 St. James' Place, Exeter, England.

We hope every student who reads Mr. McPherson's racy article on Professor Blackie will wish to know something more of this wonderful Scotchman, so pure, so earnest and so inspiring in all he said and did. They will find delightful reading in Anna M. Stoddart's Life of John Stuart Blackie, 2 vols., Blackwood & Sons, Edinburgh. This work, published at about 16s., has already run into a third edition. Our specimens of Prof. Blackie's poetry will be found in Vol. II.

The portrait of Professor Blackie, which accompanies our second article, is from a photo by Moffat, Edinburgh, kindly sent us by Mr. McPherson and certified by him as one of the Professor's latest photographs.

PROFESSOR BLACKIE'S CONFESSION OF FAITH.

Creeds and confessions ! High Church or the Low ?
   I cannot say ; but you would vastly please us
If with some pointed Scripture you could show
   To which of these belonged the Saviour Jesus.
I think to all or none ; not curious creeds
   Or ordered forms of churchly rule He taught,
But soul of love that blossomed into deeds,
   With human good and human blessing fraught.

On me nor Priest, nor Presbyter, nor Pope,
   Bishop, or Dean may stamp a party name ;
But Jesus, with His largely human scope,
   The service of my human life may claim.
Let prideful priests do battle about creeds,
The church is mine that does most Christ-like deeds.

JOHNSON'S UNIVERSAL ENCYCLOPEDIA, New Edition; Charles Kendall Adams, LL.D., President of the University of Wisconsin, Editor. 8 volumes, published by A. J. Johnson Company, New York. This appears to be in all respects a new work, and fully up to date. In general plan it is a good deal like Chambers, but contains many articles of special interest to Canadian students which they will look for in vain in any other Cyclopedia. Such are descriptions of all our towns and cities, articles on Canadian history and literature, and brief biographical notices of distinguished Canadian authors and statesmen of our own and past days. This alone should secure for Johnson's Cyclopedia a large sale throughout the Dominion. It is worth six dollars a volume, cloth. A copy has recently been placed in the Yorkville Public Library. Mr. Bain says its the best Encyclopedia (of the size) he knows of.

THE readers of the MONTHLY will be interested to learn the latest conclusions of Dr. Sayce, the leading orientalist scholar of England, in reference to the "higher criticism" of the Old Testament. In an article in the October *Contemporary Review*, he deals some hard blows against this view. Fifteen years ago, he was favorably disposed to this criticism; but now he says "those of us who have devoted our lives to the archæology of the ancient Oriental world have been forced back into the traditional position, though doubtless with a broader basis to stand upon, and clearer views of the real significance of the Biblical text," and he adds, "Year by year, almost month by month, fresh discoveries are breaking upon us, each more marvellous than the last, but all, as regards the Pentateuch, in favor of the old, rather than of the new." He declares that he sees "no reason for denying that the Pentateuch is substantially the work of Moses." This is significant testimony, coming from such a distinguished and representative source. Even Dr. Cheyne, the most pronounced higher critic of England, has been compelled to concede that his theory and that of his compeers must be modified in view of archæological discoveries. It is also reported that Prof. Buhl, the successor of Dr. Delitzsch, of Leipsic, declares that "the drift of German Biblical criticism is decidedly towards more positive and more orthodox opinions."

HERE AND THERE.

O. G. LANGFORD, EDITOR.

HOMER.

ILIAD BOOK II. ll. 453-473.

From Professor Blackie's Translation.

" And now the war was sweeter far to each well-greaved Achæan,
Than to seek his home across the foam of the billowy broad Ægean.
As when destroying fire hath caught a stretch of dry old pines
High on a hill-top, and afar the blazing forest shines ;
So shone the copper-coated host, as rank on rank advances,
While flash quick brands in a thousand hands, and gleam the eager lances.
And as the uncounted tribes that scour the sky with mighty vans
Of geese or vagrant-banded cranes, or the long-necked race of swans,
Where far the Asian lowland spreads, and by Cayster's flow,
Freely on joyful pinions sail, and wander to and fro,
And with their clanging wings loud rings the mead where they alight ;
Thus swarmed the Greeks from ship and tent, to find the fateful fight
Far o'er Scamander's plain : and earth rebellowed to the sound,
As the mail-clad men and the four-hoofed horse tramped o'er the hollow
        ground,
Till on the broad grass mead they stood, a marshalled multitude,
Countless as flowers in flowery spring, or leaves in a leafy wood.
And even as swarms of busy flies on buzzing wings are spread,
Drifting in clusters through the air, close by some shepherd's shed,
In the spring-time, when in the pail the creaming milk doth flow ;
Not fewer then the Argive men in many a glittering row
Stood ; while each long-haired warrior pants to pierce some Trojan foe."

Many of our most valuable exchanges have made very favorable comments upon Mr. G. H. Clarke's article entitled "Spenser's Influence upon Succeeding Poets," which appeared in our November and December issues.

The *Varsity* clips the following from the sporting column of the *Globe* of November 11th :

"The girls of Vassar College held their athletic sports in the rain at Poughkeepsie, N.Y., on Saturday. Miss Leslie Baker won the running broad jump, with a leap of 11 ft. 5 in. Miss Brownell won the running high jump, 4 ft. The girls wore divided skirts and sweaters." Can it be possible that the ladies at Vassar thus disport themselves in masculine attire ?

ACCORDING to *The Ariel*, President Harper, of Chicago University, has thoroughly vindicated himself in the Prof. Bemis controversy. The following sentence, which was supposed to have come from President Harper, he flatly denies :   " It is all very well to sympathize with the workingmen, but we must get our money from those on the other side, and we cannot afford to offend them." We are glad for the sake of the university that the matter can be put right.

The McGill Fortnightly is always full of interesting matter.   The November 27th number has a readable article on Gray, giving special attention to the various amended editions of the Elegy ; another writer discriminates well in an article upon the old theme, Prose and Poetry. A later issue has some gems of musical poetry from which we clip the following :

WITH THE DEAD LEAVES.

IN MEMORIAM.

Watching the dead leaves drift along,
  Urged by the keen wind's restless feet,
Tossed here and there in a shuddering throng,
  Through the lanes of the well-swept street ;
Wanders my memory back to the time
When I wooed my love with sigh and rhyme.

Then it was spring, and the sun rays shone
  On fresh young tints from a cloudless sky ;
And I with my sweetheart strolled alone
  To tell her my soul's deep ecstacy ;
I kissed her smiles, and my thoughts love-mad
Ne'er dreamed that the future could be so sad.

But winter came and the green leaves fell,
  My Love's soul went to the Dreamland shore ;
And the winter with dead leaves sang the knell
  Of the good true heart I should woo no more ;
So when I hear the leaves and the rain
  I think of my love, and live again.

Stat Nominis Umbra.

Trinity University Review gives up nearly three columns to a poem (?) "The Dying Pugilist."   It is the last groan of a regular old bruiser whose highest ambition had been to break the head of anyone who was foolish enough to face him.   Sometimes we wonder what lesson is to be learned from such a recital as this and what kind of taste is cultivated by giving it publicity,

THE following clipping is from the editorial columns of the *Boston Transcript* for October 30 : "Chinese women are beginning to make their little footsteps patter down the corridors of time and rouse the echoes !   The appointment of a Chinese girl as secretary of the medical class in the University of Michigan brings forth the liberality of co-education in that institution with dramatic effect.   The University at Ann Arbor ranks high in the estimation of the European scientific world, and in its halls have been, at one time or another, some of the strongest men and women who have adorned American scholarship. The young lady from China, whom her classmates have chosen their secretary, proves, by the very fact of her position as a medical student there, her force of character and her humane and beneficent purpose of life.   The Chinese woman is evidently done with the universal implication that she is a nonentity."

THE *'Varsity* administers a severe scolding to those who write essays for the literary societies : " Concerning the charge laid against the essayists, it must be admitted by all who have attended the regular sessions of any of the different societies, that they have heard read more than one contribution to the polemical literature of the day, dignified by the name of essay, but with very little in the subject matter to warrant the assumption by the author of such a title for his hastily-written, carelessly-constructed and entirely plagiaristic production. It is needless to say that these are the grand exception ; for most men and women, when they are asked to take part in the programme and give the result of some of their thought and reading to the public, for the benefit of all those who wish to increase in knowledge, feel that they are under a responsibility, that they are in duty bound to do their very best, and that they have no right to waste the time and impose upon the patience of those who come to hear them." It is thought the new *Quarterly* will do much to raise the standard of quality in these productions.

THE following clipped from *Harper's Weekly* contains some good common sense comments : " The claim of the daily press that it sets forth the news in the order of its importance does not seem to be sustained by its method of treating the news from the colleges. Overmuch prominence, perhaps, is given to the news of a game of football between two colleges, which is an event of importance, but not of the highest importance. But no attention whatever is paid to the collegiate year, to the conditions under which the vast collegiate system of this country resumes its serious work of education and progress.

" It would be no exaggeration to say that the opening of the collegiate year is a more important event than the opening of a session of Congress. The growth of the American colleges in numbers and wealth during the past thirty years has been one of the great facts in our history. It has been accompanied by a corresponding increase in the influence of a collegiate life on politics and society. No other institution—religious, political or social—has grown as the college has ; it is fortunate to reflect that its influence has been wholly beneficial.

" The annual game of football or the athletic meeting is not the important event in the college record. It is perhaps of less importance than the story of any other day in the year. The real life of the college, the real meaning and value of the vast and magnificent array of learned endowments in this country, the small ones as well as the great ones, can be understood only by those who look more deeply into the subject than do some of the editors of the daily papers."

DR. JOHN STUART, B.D., Ph.D., late of Hartford and Owen Sound, Ont., has retired from the Presidency of Iowa State University. His place has been filled by A. B. Chaffee, D.D., of whom *The Central Ray* gives a most excellent portrait. The esteem in which Dr. Stuart was held is shown in the following : " Our late president, Dr. John Stuart, in the mastery of Greek and Moral Science stood, we believe, near the topmost rung in his profession. Bravely and gallantly he shouldered the work of an institution and carried it along by the assistance of his loyal faculty.   Not only was Dr. Stuart a scholar and teacher, but he also had an insatiable longing for the souls of men.   None knew better than he the spiritual condition of each student."   From a perusal of Dr. Chaffee's inaugural address it would seem that the ideal of the incoming President does not differ very widely from the well-known ideal of McMaster.   Let the following paragraph speak for itself : "In this 'constant' of method by which souls are brought into profitable contact, there remains one other quality.   This is in my estimation a spiritual quality.   It subordinates man's other considerations to his spiritual.   It makes character more than learning.   It regards faith, hope and love as of greater value than the principal parts of a verb or the re-action of acids and bases.   It lays as a fundamental axiom that a man without cultivation of spirit is a trained brute, not a disciplined and developed man.   It places greater emphasis upon kindness of heart and benevolence of disposition than upon technique in knowledge and skill in manipulation.   It places God above His creatures, and man supreme in creation."

COLLEGE NEWS.

W. P. COHOE, '96,   R. D. GEORGE, '97,
J. F. VICHERT, '97,   MISS E. WHITESIDE, '98·
                                                    Editors.

THE UNIVERSITY.

O Founder's night ! O Founder's night !
Erat much optimus delight,
Fresh homo cheering Alma Mater,
Sed* soror a few hours later.

*Latin for remorse, grief, sorrow.

Two warm rooms :—Where the Bakers hang out.

OVERHEARD in the corridor :—" Tighe, Tighe, bring down my Human Body !"

THE McMaster Choral and Orchestral Union recently gave a successful entertainment under the auspices of the W. C. T. U. in Dovercourt Road Hall.

AN enterprising Toronto pastor recently advertised his Sunday evening service in the following suggestive way :—" Evening Service : subject : 'Woman.'   Come and worship."

PROFESSOR in English :—" It is a question whether we should consider Satan or Adam the hero of Paradise Lost.   Our sympathies go out to Satan in spite of ourselves, and at any rate we are more like Satan than we are like Adam."

WE are very glad to note the successful ordination service held at Bridgewater, N.S , whence our old friend Harry A. Porter, '94, emerged a full-grown Reverend.   Bridgewater will hereafter prove the source of stirring and cheering news.

OUR Literary Society meets the Literary Society of Victoria University in an inter-collegiate debate on the evening of Friday, Jan. 24th, Messrs. W. W. McMaster, B.A., and E. J. Stobo, will represent Mc. Master.

DR. WANLESS, travelling secretary of the Students' Volunteer Missionary Alliance, visited the Hall and addressed the prayer-meeting on the evening of Dec. 17th.   He spoke chiefly of the work and needs in India, where he himself laboured for some years.   We have among our students several members of the Alliance.

THE auction sale of the Reading-room papers was more successful from a financial standpoint than usual this year.   This we may say was due, not to any material improvement in the financial condition of the students, but to the energy and enthusiasm which Mr. A. N. Marshall manifested in wielding the hammer.

FRIDAY evening, November 29th, the Ladies' Literary League held their fourth annual open meeting in the University Chapel.   Quite a number of friends were present in spite of the unfavorable weather. The president, Miss M. E. Dryden, '96, opened the meeting with a few words of welcome and briefly stated the aims of the League and the way in which these aims were furthered.   The programme was as follows :—

Instrumental Solo	Miss Burke.
Reading—" In the Children's Hospital " (Tennyson) , . .	Miss A. G. Iler, '98.
Vocal Solo	. Miss Boehmer.
Address	Prof. Alexander. University of Toronto.
Instrumental Solo . . .	Miss Burke.

" The Maple Leaf."

Professor Alexander's address was most interesting and impressed itself deeply on all those present.   It was the first time McMaster had had the pleasure of welcoming Prof. Alexander, but after such an intellec- tual treat we trust it is but the delightful foretaste of future visits.

THE regular meeting of the Literary Society on Dec. 13th was one of special interest, and will be remembered as one which placed another gem in the circlet of McMaster's honors.   At the request of the Thir- teen Club of the city, arrangements were made for a friendly debate on the subject : " Resolved,—That the present system of Party Govern- ment is not in the best interests of the Nation."   The affirmative was ably presented by Messrs. J. H. Hathaway and J. E. Maybee, C. E., Solicitor of Patents, representing the Thirteen Club, while Messrs. C. J. Cameron, B.A., and B. W. Merrill, B.A., representing McMaster

Literary Society, upheld the present system of party government. At
the close of the debate, Mr. Rowell, Barrister, in his excellent summa-
tion of the arguments advanced by the opposing speakers found that
more conclusive points had been made by the speakers on the negative.
Our boys therefore sang " Boom on Mac," with considerable vigor.
Two solos by Mr. Fred. W. Lee were heartily appreciated.

> Some hae meat and canna eat,
> And some wad eat that want it,
> But we have meat and we can eat
> And so the Lord be thankit.

These lines are what those who were privileged in attending McMaster's
annual Christmas dinner saw printed across the top of the *menu* card.
It was clearly demonstrated on that day, in spite of previous doubt,
that given meat, McMaster men could eat. Such a bill of fare as there
was ! For the first time too we had the pleasure of entertaining the
Senate and Board of Governors. In addition to these Dr. Geikie
represented the medical profession, and representatives were present
from the University of Toronto, Queen's, Western University, School
of Pedagogy, Wycliffe, Knox, the Dental School, and Woodstock College. The dinner proved a perfect success and was enjoyed by all.
Then came the toast list. Among the speakers on that occasion were
the Chancellor, Hon. John Dryden, Dr. Geikie, D. E. Thomson, Esq.,
Q.C., J. Short McMaster, Esq., Dr. Sykes, and others. The success of
the dinner is largely due to the efforts of the High Kakiac, C. J. Cameron, B.A., assisted by Messrs. Stobo, Cohoe, Sycamore and McMaster.

Two of the years have already held their rallies. Class '97 held a
very successful and enthusiastic one on the evening of Thursday, Dec.
5th, at the home of Mrs. Menzies, 89 Jamieson Avenue. At the beginning of the evening, President McKechnie, in a short address, welcomed the guests and on behalf of the class thanked Mr. and Mrs.
Menzies for so kindly placing their residence at the service of the class
of '97. Mr. J. J. Reeve, B.A., responded happily to the address of welcome, after which the evening was spent in social intercourse interspersed with musical selections and an art exhibition. On the evening
of Dec. 12th, the Freshmen held their rally. Dr. and Mrs. Newman
kindly opened their residence to the class for the occasion. After short
addresses by the president, Mr. F. J. Scott, Chancellor Wallace, and
Mr. P. G. Mode, '97, a programme was rendered consisting of a vocal
solo by Mr. G. R. Welch, '99 ; oration, by Mr. J. C. McFarlane, class
orator ; recitation, Miss Bailey, '98 ; class history by Mr. C. L. Brown,
historian ; and an instrumental solo by Miss Cohoon, '99. A " Quiz
Match " in the latter part of the evening proved very interesting and
amusing. Both classes are to be congratulated upon the success and
pleasure which attended their rallies.

THERE is no feature of University life at McMaster more pleasing
and at the same time more profitable than the open meetings of the
Literary Society. From the first suggestion of an open meeting until
the last number of the programme is heard all are interested and ready

to lend a helping hand. The enthusiasm of President Sycamore not only took hold of his staff of officers, but spread to the youngest member of the freshmen, and considering the excellence of the regular meetings we were not surprised at the success of the open meeting. Realizing the difficulty of accommodating the many friends who attend our open meetings, the committee of arrangements seated the dining-room for the occasion. The platform was beautifully decorated with palms, ferns and flowers, and festoons and wreaths of evergreens made the room like a summer bower. The Orchestra and Glee Club were in their best musical spirit, and showed what good material, under good leadership, can do. McAlpine's "Auld Scotch Sangs" are always encored. Miss Hart has many warm friends in every department of the University, and we are always delighted when she steps upon the platform. The hearty and persistent encores show the delight which Miss James always gives her audiences. Miss Woolverton's instrumental solo speaks much for the musical talent among our lady students. The editorial staff of "The Student" are to be congratulated on :

> "This folio of four (?) pages : Happy work !
> What is it but a map of busy life ?
> Here rills of oily eloquence in soft
> Meanders lubricate the course they take.
> Cataracts of declamation thunder here,
> While fields of pleasantry amuse us there,
> With merry discants on a nation's woes."

No one who heard the earnest eloquence of our debaters could doubt for a moment that the future welfare of the nation depended upon the question under discussion. They gave us four *good* speeches. We were honored by having with us as judge of the debate the Hon. J. A. Boyd, Chancellor of Ontario, and we would have been delighted to have listened to a longer address from so eloquent a speaker.

THE exercises in celebration of Founder's Day were held on the evening of Friday, Dec. 20th, and were attended by larger numbers than those of any previous year. Our halls, usually very sober in appearance, assumed for the occasion a festive and variegated dress. Bunting, flags and lanterns tastefully arranged made the interior bright and pleasing to the eye. A varied programme furnished something interesting, amusing and instructive for mind and heart. In the dining-room at 8 p.m., Rev. P. K. Dayfoot, M.A., of Port Hope, delivered an oration on "The True Ideal in Education." After showing the imperfections of the educational ideals of the Greeks, Romans, and Chinese, he described what he conceived to be one true ideal. In Christ and His teaching are found this ideal. To the attainment of this ideal all branches of secular study, inasmuch as they contain truth, contribute, and in this ideal is found the answer to the questions of the philosophers, "Whence ? How ? Whither ? " The frequent applause during the delivery of the address manifested the appreciation and pleasure which the audience felt. At the conclusion of the exercises in the chapel the audience adjourned to the halls, where a variety of programme and entertainment was presented. Guests were at perfect liberty to roam where they pleased and listen to what they preferred.   Two students' rooms, one a model of order and neatness, the other quite the reverse, attracted much attention and were thronged with visitors. Those who came into the vicinity of the chapel heard issuing from it sweet strains from the orchestra. In one end of the hall views were projected upon the screen, among them many mirth-provoking local hits. On the stairs a programme of music, oratory and elocution was presented, and such music, such oratory, such elocution! The members of the quartette in their heroic effort drew to themselves the sympathies of their hearers; the orators covered themselves with glory, and the elocutionist presented so vividly Campbell's picture of the battle of Hohenlinden that it can surely never fade from the memories of those who heard it. When all the parts of the programme had been rendered and refreshments served in the dining-room, the playing of "The Maple Leaf Forever" by the orchestra brought the evening's proceedings to a close. The form of entertainment was a decided innovation and was apparently much appreciated and enjoyed by the very large number present.

THE following are some of the books recently presented to the Library:

From the University funds:—Tiffany: A History of the Protestant Episcopal Church in the U. S. A.; Mac Coun: Historical Geography Charts of Europe (Mediaéval and Modern); Brooke Foss Westcott: The Gospel of Life; A. H. Sayce: The Hittites, and The "Higher Criticism" and the Verdict of the Monuments; J. D. Davis: Genesis and Semitic Tradition; Robert Flint: Historical Philosophy in France, French Belgium and Switzerland; S. R. Driver: Isaiah, His Life and Times, an Introduction to the Literature of the Old Testament; A.B. Bruce: St. Paul's Conception of Christianity. From Dr. Newman:— W. P. Strickland: History of the American Bible Society; Alonzo King: Memoir of George Dana Boardman; Westminster Abbey Sermons; Alessandro Gavazzi: My Recollections of the Last Four Popes; G. F. Wilkin: The Prophesying of Women. From Prof. M. S. Clark:—F. Weidner: An Introduction to Dogmatic Theology; Chiniquy: Le Prêtre, La Femme et Le Confessionnal; J. Snodgrass: Heine's Wit, Wisdom and Pathos; Richardson: Wacousta; Vandam: An Englishman in Paris; Masterpieces of Foreign Literature. From Mr. W. S. W. McLay, B. A.:—Shakespeare's Works, and Peile: Primer of Philology. From Mr. G. H. Clarke, B.A.:—Stevens: Usages of the Best Society; The McMaster Muse.

We must also acknowledge the receipt of important records, reports etc., from both the Ontario and Dominion Governments.

MOULTON COLLEGE.

Some of our number had the pleasure of attending the open meeting of the Ladies' Literary League, and enjoyed the occasion exceedingly. All the numbers on the programme were excellent, and the main feature of the evening,—Prof. Alexander's scholarly and extremely interesting lecture on "The Function of Poetry," was fully appreciated. The lady-students of McMaster are certainly to be congratulated on the success of the evening, as well as on the earnest manner in which they are striving to advance the high literary aim they have placed before them as a society.

WE are in hopes that on our return after the holidays we shall have the pleasure of spending some pleasant afternoons on our rink. Its size has one thing in its favor, namely, that those who practice on it have a very fair chance of becoming experts in the art of turning the corners gracefully.

MOST of us have enjoyed the privilege of attending sociables held in our respective churches during the past month. On December 3rd the Baptist girls attended the reception to the Rev. Mr. Eaton, held in Bloor Street church. On the 5th the Presbyterians were present at a sociable given in their church, and those who attend the Methodist church, in their turn, enjoyed a social evening there on the 11th. Such evenings are always welcome, and afford us pleasant recreation.

THE following is the programme rendered at the open meeting of the Heliconian Society, which took place on the 19th of December :—

PIANO DUET,	.	.	" Radieuse,"	.	.	*Gottschalk.*
			Misses Tilson and Kirk.			
RECITATION,	.	.	"The Student's Story."	.	.	*Longfellow.*
			Miss Edith Taylor.			
" THE HELICONIAN,"	.	.	.	.	.	.
			Editors, Misses Wallace and Brophy.			
PIANO SOLO,	.	.	"Mazurka, No. 4."	.	.	*Godard.*
			Miss Violet Kirk.			
RECITATION,	.	.	"The Starless Crown."	.	.	.
			Miss Edith Carmichael.			
VOCAL SOLO,	.	.	"Good-bye, Sweet Day."	.	.	*Varmah.*
			Miss Boehmer.			
Recitation,	.	.	.	.	.	Selected.
			Miss Mabel Wallace.			

DEBATE.—*Resolved :* " That written examinations should be abolished." Miss Jessie Dryden. . . . Miss Jennie Cutler.

RECITATION,	.	.	" The Knight and the Page."	.	.	*M. C. Howe.*
			Miss Orma Tait.			
PIANO SOLO,	.	.	.	.	.	*Arabesque Lack.*
			Miss Nina Tilson.			

WOODSTOCK COLLEGE.

DIGESTION v. INDIGESTION.—*First Student*—(in dining-room after a story)—" Gentlemen, I read in Physiology that stories and jokes aid digestion." *Second Student*—(combatively)—" I don't think so, for Tommy Jimmie told a story and it stuck in my throat for a week, and even then I didn't swallow it."

A POST-CARD from Paris, France, addressed to Woodstock College, Woodstock, Md., reached our college a few days ago, after having received the following amusing endorsement : " Not for Woodstock, Eng., Try Canada, U.S.A."

"SLEEPING IN."—One of our teachers has not escaped the contagious disease known as "sleeping in," which at times is so rampant among the members of the school. One morning at the breakfast table, as his chair was vacant, one of the boys, obeying the kindly impulse of the golden rule rather than the sterner mandate forbidding eatables to be carried up from the dining-room, procured a tray of viands, and followed by two other students bearing "res frumentaria" of corn-beef and brown bread sandwiches, proceeded to the room of the missing member of the Faculty. It is said that they expect the compliment to be returned at some future date.

WE are exceedingly glad to welcome a new accession to the ranks of the "Old Boys of the College," in the person of the Minister of Agriculture, who, having now gone through our class-rooms, taken three meals in the dining-room, and slept one night in the College, claims to be one of the boys—a claim we are very proud to admit. His strong and inspiring words will not soon be forgotten. He proposed "Pluck and Plod" as the motto of a successful life,—pluck to do the right and to do as well as any one else. Chances come to every one, but it is pluck that seizes them, and plodding that develops them.

THURSDAY, Dec. 12th, was one of the gala days of last term, when we had the honor of entertaining the delegates of the Ontario Fruit Growers' Association, assembled in Woodstock for their annual session. About forty most intelligent-looking gentlemen arrived at the College about eleven o'clock, and spent one hour or so in visiting the various departments. The Manual Training, as one of the most novel features of the school, appeared to be an object of especial interest. All then repaired to the dining-hall, where an excellent dinner was enjoyed, and brief addresses were delivered by Principal Bates, Mr. T. H. Parker, resident of the local Association, Mr. G. R. Pattullo, Hon. John Dryden, the president and vice-president of the Association, and Prof. Saunders. A half-holiday completed the day's pleasure.

ON the occasion of the Laurier demonstration the boys were invited by Mr. Sutherland, M.P. for North Oxford, to attend the meeting *en masse.* They assembled in full force in the Opera House, in the upper gallery, which was reserved for them that they might enjoy the fellowship of the "dei." Having to go early to avoid the rush, they had a full hour to wait before the arrival of the speakers, but the time did not drag heavily. The audience enjoyed a fine concert, furnished by the combined talent of the College and Woodstock Collegiate Conspicuous among the numbers was a song written by the College bards and sung to the tune of "Vive la Compagnie." Before Mr. Laurier's entrance many interesting and instructive speeches had been delivered by the aid of the megaphone, and College songs as well as voices were almost exhausted. The appearance of Mr. Laurier and his colleagues was the signal for loud and tumultuous cheering and for the conclusion of the concert. Everyone was charmed by the silver-tongued orator except our concert-leader, who expresses the suspicion that the "silver tongue" was merely nickel-plated.

GRANDE LIGNE.

WE are glad to see Mr. Pelletier with us again after a severe illness of two weeks. A few days ago, however, Mr. Wadleigh fell from the trapeze in the gymnasium and now takes his place with a broken collarbone. He is doing well though, and we hope to see him in his usual place among us in a short time.

OUR skating-rink is in fine condition now, and the students are making the best use of it, as well as of the numerous ponds in the neighborhood. The teachers also are sometimes so enticed as to spend part of their evenings gliding over its glassy surface. Even the gymnasium is deserted, now that this chief of winter sports lends itself to our enjoyment.

On Dec. 10th our Principal made an announcement that was very pleasing to the students ; viz : that in honor of the birth of his son he would close the school for the Christmas vacation on the evening of Dec. 20th, instead of the 23rd, on condition that the students would promise to return promptly on January 2nd, 1896. Of course this promise was eagerly made, and just as eagerly kept.

ON December 9th the residents of Feller Institute and Grande Ligne were delighted to learn of the arrival of another Protestant, who has come to make his dwelling among us. At present he intends boarding at the house of Mr. and Mrs. G. N. Massé for a number of years. We have not as yet had the pleasure of seeing very much of this visitor, nor do we know his name, or the color of his eyes or hair. We have learned, however, that he weighs about nine pounds, that he has excellent lungs, and will be twenty years old in A.D. 1916. Mr. Massé informs us that he is a thorough Protestant, his father being a staunch Baptist, that he is a firm believer in equal rights, and that he declaims loudly against any interference with his own individual liberty. In fact, he is the autocrat of the house.

THE celebration of the sixtieth anniversary of the arrival of Madam Feller and Mr. Roussy in Canada was a day to be remembered at Feller Institute. This should have taken place on Oct. 31st, but for various reasons was postponed one day. On the morning of November 1st a few friends came from Montreal to join in the celebration. The afternoon was spent in listening to interesting addresses, given by Revs. T. Lafleur, A. L. Therrien, G. N. Massé and M. B. Parent, on the life and work of Madame Feller, Messrs. Roussy, Riendeau, Côte, Normandeau, Cyr, Rossier, and Miss Jonte. We were shown how the work had grown, through much self-sacrifice and trial, from such a small and insignificant beginning, to its present importance and influence. After the addresses, the graves of the missionaries buried in our little cemetery were decorated with flowers provided for the purpose by Miss Chapman of Brooklyn, N.Y. Thus passed a pleasant, and we believe, very profitable day devoted to the memory of our pioneer missionaries.

ON Oct. 30th, Rev. H. F. Laflamme paid us his promised visit, and gave us an address on the work of the Canadian Baptist Mission in India. Rev. L. R. Dutaud had, on a previous occasion, given us a magic-lantern talk illustrating the habits and customs of India's people; Mr. Laflamme told us of their religious beliefs. The evils of caste, polytheism, pantheism, etc., were set before us in such a way as to show us the awful religious need of the people. The duty of giving the gospel to them, and to the world, was earnestly pressed home, and the hope was expressed that some of our students might some day find themselves giving the gospel to India as well as to Quebec. It did us all good to have Mr. Laflamme with us, to encourage us in our work here by making us feel that we are working for the same Master, encountering the same difficulties and discouragements, and shall one day share in the same rewards of the same glorious conquest as our missionaries in India, China, or Africa.

Mrs. A. E. Massé's annual concert took place as usual this year on Friday, Dec. 13th. Quite a number of invited guests attended. From Mrs. Massé's previous record in giving concerts, we all expected an enjoyable evening, and though the style of music was not the same as usual, our expectations were fully realized. In contrast with previous years, when the selections have been taken from the old masters, sometimes devoting a whole evening to a single author, the selections this year were all taken from the best modern compositors. The following programme was well rendered :

PIANO,	"Spanish Dances,"		*Moszkowski.*
	Mme. Massé et Mlle Baker.		
PIANO,	"Valsette,"		*Sauer.*
	Mlle. Pearl de la Ronde.		
CHANT,	"Cherette,"		*Rœckel.*
	Mlle. Ruby de la Ronde.		
PIANO,	"A la Valse,"		*Bohm.*
	Mlle. Antoinette Lachance.		
FLUTE,	"Heimweh."		*Jungmann.*
	M. Stewart de la Ronde.		
PIANO,	"Berceuse,"		*Beaumont.*
	Mlle. Hannah Dutand.		
PIANO,	"Redowa,"		*Mason.*
	Mlles. Schutt et Vadnais.		
CHANT,	"A Winter Lullaby,"		*De Koven.*
	Mme. Massé.		
PIANO,	"Cabaletta."		*Lack.*
	Mlle. Ruby de la Ronde.		
PIANO,	{ (a) "Deuxième Mazurka,"		*Godard.*
	{ (b) "Polish Dance,"		*Scharwenka.*
	Mlle. Baker.		
QUATUOR VOCAL,	"Parting and Meeting,"		*Leslie.*
	MM. Therrien et Rossier,		
	Mlles. Piché et Gendreau.		

A Bartch

THE

McMASTER UNIVERSITY MONTHLY,

FEBRUARY, 1896.

DEACON ARCHIBALD BURTCH.

In this age of newspaper enterprise, few men of prominence among their fellows escape the efforts of the irrepressible interviewer—whose object is to "write them up," either for the immediate use of his paper, or to pigeon-hole the manuscript till the subject's decease, when it will be published and sent broadcast over the land. Those who have been passed over by the discriminating interviewer, may, and many do, write their own autobiography, and, for the modest sum of twenty-five dollars, preserve the shadow of their person, and a short statement of their own merits, in the pages of one of the many popular "pictorial encyclopedias" of this printers' age.

In either of the methods mentioned, it becomes an easy task for biographers of an imaginative turn of mind to elaborate an extremely interesting biography. But at the end of the last century, when the subject of this sketch was a youthful emigrant to the wilderness of Upper Canada, interviewers were unknown, and newspaper facilities for recording the passing events of this new country did not exist. Schools were not yet established, and he who wished to be conversant with the "three R's"—reading, 'riting and 'rithmetic—had to teach himself on wet days and Sundays; or, which was the commoner practice, by the light of a log fire in the evenings, often with no other text-book than a copy of the Bible; with a shingle, or the inner side of a piece of bark for a slate and copy book, and a charred stick for a pencil.

That Archibald Burtch was one of the ambitious youths of his day who aspired to "book-learning" under such circumstances as we have described, is evident from the fact, that he subsequently occupied nearly all the public offices in the gift of the people, many of which required a good degree of education. Very little documentary evidence is available, and all the cotemporaries of his early youth are dead, except his second wife, "Grandma Burtch"—whose name, for over sixty years, has been a household word in nearly every home in this district, and in every other land where the teachers and early students of the Canadian Literary Institute have gone and carried kindly remembrances of her Christian zeal and abundant hospitality, to themselves and all others who came within her motherly influence. She still lives at the great age of ninety-two, and is well cared for by her step-son—the present "Deacon Burtch"; but the feeble state of both her body and mind precludes the possibility of her now giving interesting events with which her mind was stored three or four years ago. "Grandma Burtch" has passed away since the above was written.

We learn from the Bible record that Archibald Burtch first saw the light at Cooperstown, New York State, May 13th, 1786; his father's name being Zechariah, who himself was the son of a U. E. Loyalist.

In the year 1792, the first Governor-General, Simcoe, issued an invitation to U. E. Loyalists, and others who preferred to reside under the British flag, to come to Upper Canada and possess the land. Among those who responded was a friend of Governor Simcoe's, a Mr. Watson, and his cousin, Thomas Horner, a man of considerable means. They selected the township of Blenheim, which the Governor granted verbally, but the promise was never carried out by his successors. They returned to York State; but Mr. Horner returned to Canada in 1793, and settled on what he named Horner's Creek, near what is now the Governor's Road, at the south edge of Blenheim, and there erected the first saw mill—carting all the materials therefor from his native state. This was the first white settlement west of Brantford, except a small one where Chatham now stands, and it is supposed that Mr. Horner was the cause of the Burtch family following in the year 1799.

We are informed that the family remained some time at the small settlement on the Grand River, where Brantford now stands, and where they provided themselves with a yoke of oxen and a home-made sled, wherewith to convey themselves and their goods to their destination. At the Horner settlement they again halted a short time and, probably, laid in a stock of provisions, before undertaking the last stage of twelve miles. This proved to be their most tedious and perilous journey, on account of the many miry swamps, and the thick timber which had to be chopped before they could proceed. Frequently the oxen had to be unyoked and driven through singly, then yoked up and hitched to the sled on the other side of the swamp, by means of a connection of long poles tied together and reaching across the whole swamp. Thus it took three days to reach the brow of the hill overlooking the valley westward, where the town of Woodstock now stands. Here, on lot No. 18, in the first concession of East Oxford—at that time called " Oxford on the Thames," and embracing what now constitutes three townships—they 'squatted,' claiming the 200 acres under the rights of first settlers. Young Archibald, a youth of thirteen, assisted his family to erect a log shanty for a residence and a shed for the oxen.

The reader, like the writer, can only fill in from imagination the hardships, privations, and fears that this single family must have endured in the heart of this great wilderness; exposed to wild beasts, Indians, and a short supply of food. No roads, no bridges over the rivers, no mills to grind their corn when grown, and no place within reach to purchase supplies for food and clothing, even if they had money. True, in the winter, when the swamps were frozen, they could go to Hamilton or Toronto, but it was little better there, even if in existence at all.

The first assessment roll of which we have knowledge was in 1812, and from it we learn that there were then 60 persons assessed, and, among them, " Zechariah Burtch, lot 18, concession 1 — 200 acres, 30 cleared—1 horse, 2 oxen, 4 cows." " Archibald Burtch, north half lot No. 19—100 acres, 6 cleared, 1 horse, 1 cow." He subsequently purchased the south half, whereon stands Woodstock College, and of which thirty-six acres are now owned and occupied by the college.

In the year 1812, Mr. Burtch married the daughter of Peter Teeple, J.P., who, during his residence here, married between 400 and 500 persons under the then existing laws, which authorised magistrates to marry persons, if not within 18 miles of the residence of an Anglican clergyman. A story is told in Shenston's Gazetteer that a couple applied to Squire Horner to be married, who, on figuring out the distance to the nearest clergyman's, found it to be only 15½ miles. The bridegroom suggested that they walk 2½ miles in an opposite direction; this the squire agreed to, and there, standing on a fallen tree, made them one.

The issue of the marriage with Susan Teeple—Mr. Burtch's first wife—was two daughters and three sons; born in his own home on lot number 18, near where the present homestead stands. Belinda married the Rev. W. H. Landon, but died in 1837. Henrietta married John Blow, and, also, died in 1837. William married, but both he and his wife died many years before the father. Reuben Hamilton married twice, and both wives are dead. Henry Teeple Burtch married Mary Galloway, in 1843; and both live near Woodstock College.

On the 5th of June, 1824, Mrs. Archibald Burtch died, and on the 28th of October of the same year he married Jane Blow, who, at the age of 92, now lives with her step-son, "Deacon Burtch," in the old homestead, as before stated. "Grandma" proved not only a faithful wife and mother to his motherless children, but a "mother in Israel" in the truest sense, and one whose energy, zeal and hospitality were co-ordinate with her husband's in every good work and Christian enterprise. So great was their hospitality that their house became the stopping place of all new settlers and travellers, on what had become a public road through the Province—the Governor's road—and it became a serious drain on the resources of the household. To remedy this latter feature, they were induced to open a tavern and general boarding-house; and this is said to have been the first and only hotel in the settlement for some years thereafter.

In those days whiskey was the general beverage, and the price being but twelve to fifteen cents per gallon, few people refrained from using it, and no one questioned the propriety of so doing, as it had not then produced the evil results which it gradually manifested later. Mr. Burtch, however, abandoned its sale; and from the strong stand he took in church discipline— especially in the use of this article—we may presume that he dropped it from conscientious convictions. They continued, however, to keep a boarding-house; for, during the erection of the old St. Paul's brick church in 1833, they boarded fourteen of the workmen, besides others.

I have been informed by those who remember him well that in his prime, no man in the settlement could accomplish more work than he, and that at all gatherings he was champion in the many athletic feats of the time.

As the country became more settled, municipal institutions were introduced. In 1839 the large and, at that time, handsome, Woodstock Court-house was erected, (only recently demolished to make room for the present graceful structure). The courts for the "District of Brock" were held there. The first County Council was held in the court-house the 8th of February, 1842. Archibald Burtch represented East Oxford as councillor, and continued three years in succession. We find that as early as 1811 and 1812, he occupied for two years in succession, the position of Town Clerk, Assessor and Collector, for "Oxford on the Thames," and it is possible even earlier; for a minute has been found in an old township book dated in 1800, that "a town meeting was held," but no particulars are given as to the work done. I have not learned whether he occupied the position of Village Councillor or School Trustee in Woodstock, after its incorporation, but believe it quite probable. In 1851 he was appointed a Justice of the Peace, but was seldom called upon to act in that capacity: either in performing the marriage ceremony or in the matter of justice, as there were other magistrates more ambitious for prominence in that respect.

Mr. Burtch was a life-long reformer, and specially attached to the Hon. Francis Hincks, who made Mr. Burtch's house his home during his many campaigns in the County of Oxford. He was also a progressive and public-spirited citizen, giving of his means and labors abundantly to every commendable enterprise. To the G. W. R. Company he gave ten acres of land running across his whole farm. To the old Woodstock and Lake Erie

Railway Co. he gave a right of way, from south to north, nearly a mile long, besides part of the station grounds.

The matter of higher education, in connection with the Canadian Literary Institute, is where his sterling qualities were so fully developed and manifested. Knowing the value of an education, from the lack of opportunities in his own experience, he was a persistent advocate of bonusing the school named; and it was largely through his influence that the sum of $16,000 was pledged towards the erection of suitable buildings here; besides giving the site of six acres, then valued at $4,000, he also headed the subscription list with $1,000, besides frequent subscriptions thereafter. The subscriptions for this object were taken in the flush times, caused by the Crimean war, but the collecting was done largely " after the war," when the reaction had come, and, as a consequence, a large shrinkage and serious loss.

The contract for the building was let to Messrs. Scofield & Bent, for the sum of $20,000, and the payments were made from the subscriptions; but, when they began to fail, the Building Committee gave their personal notes to the contractors, who discounted them at the branch of the Montreal Bank here. At length the bank refused to renew the paper, and sued the committee and contractors for over $1,400. At this time the floating debt amounted to about $3,000, and, to protect the committee and save the Institution from collapse, Deacon Burtch mortgaged his lands and homestead for the sum required to save the property from entire ruin. The money was obtained from a farmer, and, it is said, the ruinous interest of twenty per cent. per annum paid.

In a later period in its history, the Executive Committee gave their personal notes for $10,000 at one time, but no one had to mortgage his home to furnish security, nor did the interest often exceed the rate of six per cent. per annum.

Mr. Burtch was the treasurer of the building fund till the election of the permanent Board of Trustees on the 18th March, 1857, and no one can enumerate the sacrifices he made to meet the emergencies of the hard times referred to, or mention all his labors of love on behalf of this, to him, beloved institution. The lack of space at my disposal overrides the desire to attempt it on this occasion. At the meeting above referred to he was the first one nominated as trustee, which office he held till his death, and once at least he was President.

We come now to the most important and the best beloved of all his labors : those in his connection with the people of God in church life. In the year 1817 the population of the whole county (which also included at that time West Nissouri, Oakland and Burford) was only 530, with but 78 dwellings, such as they were. The only church was a strict communion Baptist church in West Oxford, under the charge of Elder Mabee. This was a long distance from where Woodstock now stands, but it is known that some of the settlers attended service there. In the year 1822, on the 22nd of April, Elder Thomas Tallman of New York State visited the settlement ; and, after preaching to the people, was requested to organise a church—the name given being the " First Free Communion Church of Oxford." There were nineteen organic members, from families of old settlers whose names are quite familiar yet, but none of the name of Burtch. In the month of October, the same year, another church was organised at Horner's Creek ; and, on the 13th day of the same month, a council was called to ordain James Harris and Darius Cross to the work of the ministry—both having united with the First Church. In 1823 the Springford church was organised, and others later on.

We learn from the church record that, on the 28th day of August, 1824, Archibald Burtch was among the number baptised and added to the church ; and that in the following December he was appointed deacon. It is evident, from the minutes of the church, that he at once entered fully into the spirit and labors of the church ; for we find his name on almost every committee, council, and delegation ; and almost all meetings held quarterly and some annual conferences were held in his barn, when the log school-house was too small for the number assembled ; and such was his hospitality that he kept open house for all God's people who came—invited or not.

In 1826 he was appointed church clerk. In every case of discipline—and they were frequent in the early history of the church—he always took a firm stand for personal purity, and consistent walk and conversation in every day life. I am informed by an aged brother of the Woodstock church who lived, as a hired man, with Deacon Burtch for the first three years of his residence in Canada, about the time of the rebellion, that never did he know a more upright and Godly-living man. While fond of listening to or telling a good story, he never would allow any man to tell an obscene story or use an oath without rebuke. No matter how many boarders or hired people he had around him, or how busy the season, he never failed to assemble them all at the morning and evening worship conducted by himself. In all his dealings with his fellow man, he was the soul of honor. Such is the testimony of those who still remember him.

His seat at all meetings of the church was occupied; rain or shine, week-days or Sundays. For forty years the covenant meetings of the church were held monthly, on a week-day, and however rough the weather or busy the season, Deacon Burtch was present, and his prayer exhortation, which was given in a sort of singing intonation peculiar to old men of his day, was indeed music to our ears. For forty-one years he filled the office of deacon well, and was ever a true and faithful friend to his pastor —in fact he was a " pillar of the church." He was ever anxious to preserve the purity of the church in the doctrines " once delivered to the saints," and was always found on the side of those who contended for the restriction of the communion to baptized believers; and, when the question was finally settled in 1842, he seconded the resolution moved by deacon Blake : " That the communion be restricted to baptized believers."

As before stated, he was instinctively a reformer; hence in the matter of Church and State and all its attendant evils, he took strong grounds, believing that no man's conscience should be trammelled by any man-made creed ; nor should he be taxed to uphold one church above another, and that too whose manner of worship might be distasteful to him.

The First Baptist Church worshipped in the old log schoolhouse on Deacon Burtch's farm—where it was organized—till 1836, when a nice frame edifice was erected on a lot on Chapel Street, given by Deacon Burtch, and was opened by a week's meetings conducted by the then pastor, Rev. W. H. Landon.

In the year 1855, a handsome brick building was erected where the present one now stands on Beale St. Deacon Burtch was active in labors and money in its erection ; and well we remember the earnest though pleased expression of his features as he moved, sprightly as a young man, up the long aisles, distributing the bread and wine, or taking up the collection.

In June, 1857, he was one of the delegates to the association, held at Harris Street Church, when the Woodstock Church was unanimously admitted into the Association of Churches.

Mr. Burtch never seemed weary of working in a good cause. As late as January, 1864, the faithful old Deacon took an active part in all Church and Institute work.

I cannot better close this brief and imperfect sketch than by quoting a paragraph taken from the published history of the First Church—of which he was so long an honored member :

"January 5th, 1866 : Dear old Deacon Burtch has passed over to the 'Great Majority' and 'the place that has known him so long shall know him no more for ever.' It may be truly said : 'This day a prince has fallen in Israel.' From the day of his 'new birth,' and entrance into the church—August 28th, 1824—to the day of his death (nearly 42 years) never had a church a more faithful member, or a more zealous and watchful deacon—always at his post, always liberal in support, and hospitable to all—strangers as well as friends. The latch-string of his door was always out to every weary traveller or benighted footsore pilgrim in the wilderness. The Canadian Literary Institute, as well as the church, owes its continued existence largely to his self-sacrificing love ; for when the former was in the deep waters of financial distress, he mortgaged his own house to rescue it from bankruptcy. What more need be said ? An interesting volume might be written in commemoration of the life of this faithful servant of the Lord and friend of humanity ; but this is not the time or place to do more than record these facts. His memory is enshrined in our hearts, and his 'works do follow him.'"

R. W. SAWTELL.

THE EPISTLE TO THE GALATIANS OR PAULINISM
POLEMICALLY STATED.

The term "Paulinism" is one which has obtained much favour in Germany and France and the British Isles, as a convenient word to denote the type of doctrine for the establishing and proclaiming of which the great apostle gave all the strength he had from the time of his conversion to the day of his death. There are objections to its use, the most serious of which is that it might tend to foster the idea that Paul alone was the author of this doctrine, or that he had a special monopoly of it. An impression such as this would be very unfortunate, as it would lead ultimately to the extreme "Tendency-Theory" of the Tübingen school—a theory, the fallacy of which, in its fully developed form, is more and more being recognized. But if we guard ourselves against this error, the term has obvious advantages to recommend it, for it shoots through a system of doctrine all the romance which is added to it by the devotion of a man possessed of great heroism and sincerity combined with remarkable mental balance.

The key to this system is the conception of *sin* and *grace* which the ardent Jewish scholar gained in his intense struggles after righteousness—for that was his consuming passion. These new conceptions, which came to him with his spiritual experience on the way to Damascus, became the starting point for an entire reconstruction of his system of theological thought; for he now proceeded with wonderful care to apply to all spheres of his mental life the new principles of thought which he had faith to believe were able to bear all the strain that could be put upon them. He spent many years in quiet meditation testing and trying his new system under the Holy Spirit's influence until he had mastered not only its general principles but also its details. His own sad experiences with law in the past, would make him all the more clear in his view of grace, so that when the time arrived for him to step out as a public champion of this type of Christian Theology, he was a soldier that needed not to be ashamed. Step by step he was drawn onward until he became the most conspicuous figure in the early churches. His preach-

ing in his missionary journeys left no doubt as to what he believed, and it soon brought upon him the storm of opposition
which was sure to arise from those who hated his preaching because it seemed so disrespectful to Moses and the Mosaic system.
These men (to whom the name "Judaizers" is generally given)
held that it was necessary to go through the door of Jewish ceremonial in order to be eligible for the blessings of the gospel.
This, in their view, was the only position that gave due prominence at once to Moses and to Christ. They regarded Paul as
their personal enemy. It was they who precipitated the action
which led to the Jerusalem Council, (Acts xv.); and with fiery
missionary zeal they busied themselves with the churches where
Paul had preached, in the hope of uprooting the doctrines of
grace which he had planted there. Amongst the Galatian
churches—where the apostle had already laboured—they even
succeeded in inducing many, if not the majority of the members,
to accept a theological position which the eagle eye of Paul saw
was in its last analysis inevitably that of justification by works.
This brought matters to an acute stage, and in the epistle to the
Galatians we see the defence which Paul makes of his own
teaching. We may, indeed, call *Galatians,* "The polemical statement of Paulinism," and it has all the advantages of a spirited
debate in the presence of actual opponents where every word is
directed to the winning over of those who are addressed.

It has usually been thought that these Galatian churches
were in the north, but Prof. Ramsay has recently* with a great
deal of persistence and acumen sought to prove that the churches
intended are those in the south of Galatia which Paul visited in
the first and second missionary journeys related in the Acts. For
our present purpose, however, the precise destination of the letter is not so important as the argument and doctrines of the
letter itself. Nor is it of chief importance for us to enquire in
what town Paul himself was when he wrote.

When the first preachers of the gospel undertook to press
the supreme claims of Christ upon the life and thought of men,
they did not find the minds of their hearers unoccupied, for there

---

*"The church in the Roman Empire before A.D. 170," pp. 102 fol. ; "St.
Paul the Traveller and the Roman Citizen," pp. 178 fol., and articles in "The
Expositor," 1894, and 1895.

were claimants that were clamouring for supremacy jealous of
the story and the doctrines which the Christians proclaimed.
Amongst these the most formidable at first was the orthodox
Judaism of the times. For towards the Mosaic Law the Gospel
preachers had to take some position, since this was a living issue
to which they were certain, sooner or later, to be driven. Dr.
Harnack* has in the following propositions stated the four possible ways in which the Old Testament and the Gospel could be
brought into relation :

" 1. The Gospel has value for the people of Israel ; and for
the Gentiles only on condition that they individually unite themselves with the people of Israel. The careful observance of the
law is also necessary, and is the condition under which the
Messiah's salvation is imparted.

" 2. The Gospel has value for Jews and Gentiles; the former
are, upon profession of faith in Christ, under obligation as formerly, to observe the law, the latter are not : but for this very
reason they cannot upon earth unite with the Jews in church
fellowship.

" 3· The Gospel has value for Jews and Gentiles ; and no
one, whether Jew or Gentile, is any longer under obligation to
keep the law. For the law is set aside (or rather fulfilled) and
salvation, (secured in the death of Christ upon the cross) is appropriated by faith. The law, in its literal sense, is of divine
origin, but it was from the beginning intended only for a definite period of history.

" 4. The Gospel has value for Jews and Gentiles. No one
is bound to keep the ceremonial law and to offer sacrifices, because these commands themselves are only the outward shells
for the moral and spiritual commands which the Gospel has
brought to completion in a fully developed form."

It was the third of these positions which Paul felt to be the
true one, and for the defence of which he set himself ; and nowhere do we find his position more clearly and concisely defined
than in the Galatians.

The theme and the spirit of the epistle cannot be better indicated than in Paul's own words—" As many as desire to make

---

*" Dogmengeschichte",—Band i, SS 79, 80.

a fair show in the flesh, they compel you to be circumcised; only that they may not be persecuted for the cross of Christ. For not even they who receive circumcision do themselves keep the law; but they desire to have you circumcised, that they may glory in your flesh. But far be it from me to glory, save in the cross of our Lord Jesus Christ, through which the world hath been crucified unto me and I unto the world. For neither is circumcision anything, nor uncircumcision, but a new creature."—(vi : 12-15).

After the inscription in which the assertion of the writer's standing as an apostle divinely appointed, is, contrary to his usual custom, emphatically made, Paul hastens to express his surprise and pain that the people who had treated himself and his message with such unusual heartiness, should so soon have changed their whole theological position in order to adopt a different gospel. For the teaching they now accepted was not "another gospel," but "a different gospel," as far removed in kind from what Paul had taught as a rock is different from an eagle. Since these two doctrines cannot both be true, if the apostle can prove that his came from God he will have succeeded in establishing his case. This he proceeds to do, taking for his thesis the following statement—" For I make known to you, brethren, as touching the gospel which was preached by me, that it is not after man. For neither did I receive it from man, nor was I taught it, but it came to me through revelation of Jesus Christ."—(i: 11, 12). By the providential events that had guided his steps he had been kept away from the other leaders amongst the early churches, so that whatever he knew of the gospel had come to him directly from the Lord. Indeed so far was he from being dependent upon the others, that he was able on one occasion to take issue, and that publicly, with so influential a man as Peter, at a time when the essential error of the position taken by him at Antioch was so hard to detect that even Barnabas was carried away by the arguments used. Events had proved that, although he stood alone, he was right.

Nor is the Old Testament against the doctrine of justification by faith. It was by faith that Abraham was justified, the opinions of the Judaizers to the contrary notwithstanding. And the covenant of God with Abraham was not one of law but of promise. This covenant, since it has priority in time, could not be disannulled by the Mosaic system, which was not introduced till four hundred and thirty years afterwards. We must, then, seek some other explanation of the function of the law than that it was God's ultimate intention to save men by it. The only satisfactory account that we can find of it is that it was to do for us what the slaves in charge of school-boys did for them, who when they had conducted the boys safely to school had done their duty. For the law's function was simply to lead us to Christ. To go back to the law is, then, to go to school to the slave who escorts to school, instead of going to school to the teacher, and this is to lose ground. Nor is the error of the Judaizers any less evident from the fact that it leaves little position for Christ. " I do not make void the grace of God, for if righteousness is through the law, then Christ died for nought." (ii : 21). Further, justification by faith, contrary to the opinions of those who do not know its practical working, makes us sons of God, and heirs to His glory, and elevates conduct in a way that nothing else can, and on this side also it is unimpeachable.

Of these three courts of appeal—the relation to the Jewish law ; the place left for Christ ; and the effect upon human conduct—the first is the most difficult in which to win a favourable verdict. For there seems to be no answer to the argument, " If righteousness is through the law, then Christ died for nought,' provided one takes the search after righteousness as seriously as Paul did—for to him the presentation of a mere example of righteousness would only leave one as helpless as before, and would make the death of Christ a waste of divine force that would be quite incomprehensible. And as for the effect upon the standing and character of the believer, the proof was not very difficult, since it could be made clear by applying the test to those who were around them.

The most difficult line of proof to lead was that from the Old Testament. Here the courage, skill, and Scripture knowledge of the apostle are most conspicuous. For in the construction of his system of doctrine he had no more difficult adjustment to make than that in which his task was to give due place to Christ, and at the same time pay no disrespect to the Mosaic law which all Jews—himself included—believed to have come by divine appointment. The use made of the covenant with Abraham and its basis shews remarkable dialectic skill and the argument must have carried great weight with a candid seeker after truth. For to one who accepted Paul's premises there could be no escape from his conclusion that he had Abraham with him and not against him. From this position, captured so unexpectedly, he proceeds to storm the chief citadel of his opponents— their doctrine of salvation by the Mosaic law, a position which was powerfully entrenched in Jewish patriotism. Reminding the reader that the covenant of God with Abraham (which was not one of law but of promise) cannot be superseded by the law, the apostle carries his position with one brilliant rush—" For if the inheritance is of the law, it is no more of promise : but God hath granted it to Abraham by promise." " Is the law then against the promises of God ? God forbid : for if there had been a law given which could make alive, verily righteousness would have been of the law. Howbeit the Scripture hath shut up all things under sin, that the promise by faith in Jesus Christ might be given to them that believe." (iii : **18, 21, 22**).

This makes it clear at one stroke that, whatever the law does, it does not bring righteousness. It remains, then, only to show what purpose the law served—for he agreed with his opponents that it had some purpose to serve. For this side of the question he has also an answer. He assumes that it is quite orthodox to recognise a development in the plans of God with man, and he boldly asserts that the law had served its purpose in preparing the way for Christ, or, as it is put in another epistle, that " God, having of old time spoken unto the fathers in the prophets by divers portions and in divers manners, hath, at the end of these days, spoken unto us in his Son, whom he appointed heir of all things, through whom also he made the worlds."— (Heb. i : **1, 2**). When therefore the Christ has come, the Mosaic system can be allowed to drop away, not indeed as men eject a traitor and deceiver, but as they treat in love and respect an old and faithful servant who has done his work well, but whose occupation is now gone. In selecting an illustration to make this clear, the apostle falls back upon the wealth of knowledge of life brought to him by his keenly observant eye. He remembers how certain slaves in wealthy families were employed, not to teach the children, but to escort them in safety to school. And here he rests his case—" The law was our boy-leader to lead us to Christ." It is impossible not to believe that in a mind of such instinctive reverence as that of Paul there would remain a deep-seated affection for the " customs of his fathers." But this affection would lead him only to see to the respectful and honorable burial of a horse that had fallen dead after having brought its rider safely to his destination over a rough and stormy road. And so Abraham's real heirs are his spiritual descendants—"And if ye are Christ's, then are ye Abraham's seed, heirs according to promise."—(iii : 29).

There is much in the epistle that still invites attention—the standing and character brought by the new life ; the further statement of the place of the cross, and other matters ; but that would lead us too far afield for our present purpose. Here we have had to content ourselves with a statement of the general drift of the Epistle.

In his method Paul combines keen logic, with either stern severity or earnest entreaty according as the case demands the one or the other ; and all through the Epistle there breathes the spirit of one who is swayed by human feelings and is conscious of human weaknesses ; of a man who knows what heart-breaking there is in the dreary path of error, and what joy there is in the way of truth with Christ to walk beside him. He is conscious that as the servant of Christ it is his duty to please, not men, but God, and in the light of this responsibility he writes all he has to write. He was capable, as we know from the *Acts*, of making concessions for the sake of peace, when no principle was violated by it ; but in this Epistle he makes it quite clear that when truth was in danger he could make no compromise. He could never believe that error was truth for any man who only believed that it was truth. This widely spread philosophy of error found no sympathy in his heart. And above all, the Epistle proves itself to be the utterance of a man who was not only a theologian but a Christian, who knew not only how to " contend earnestly for the faith which was once for all delivered unto the saints," (Jude 3) ; but also to " live by the faith of the Son of God."

The Epistle is strong, because the writer knew what it was

to thrill with the spiritual electricity that came from Christ; because living and thinking and working were for him dominated by one principle; because a power higher than himself was now the source of his being; and because his own personal religious experience could be described in these exalted words—" I have been crucified with Christ; yet I live; and yet no longer I, but Christ liveth in me; and that life which I now live in the flesh I live in faith, the faith which is in the Son of God, who loved me and gave Himself up for me."—(ii : 20).

J. L. Gilmour.

Students' Quarter.

THE SCHOLAR'S MATE.

Felix Gifford should have been studying hard. It was impossible, however, in his present frame of mind to concentrate his attention upon higher mathematics. He ran his fingers nervously through his thick, waving hair; he irritably wheeled around on his chair into several different positions, all to no avail. Two " A's," two " D's," two " E's," an " L " and an " I " seemed to chase one another in mad pursuit across the paper; he could make neither head nor tail of the page before him. He flung the book on the table, arose and walked the room.

Finally he decided to try his luck in preparing the morning's German lecture. Perhaps Adelaide would rest content with monopolizing the pages of higher mathematics without attempting to dispute Margaret's prerogative as heroine of Goethe's Faust. If not, Mephistopheles must be called into action.

Felix ran his eye along his book-shelf. " Faust—let's see—Faust." And this time to-morrow he would be playing chess with the sweetest, most bewitching—fortunately, or unfortunately, the speedy discovery of the book of which he was in search checked his wandering thoughts. It was not Adelaide with whom he had to deal at present, but Margaret. Let him remember it !

2

Before settling down to work, Felix, having a faint suspicion of headache, went to his washstand, and dampening a
towel tied it around his forehead. A handkerchief, no doubt,
would have served the purpose a trifle better, but to-night he
was not responsible for his actions. A moment or two after this
performance he was apparently deeply engrossed in the translation before him. Five minutes later and he was staring vacantly
into space.

"Could he checkmate her?"   All his hopes were staked on
a game of chess. "If you win," Adelaide had said when he had
urged his suit, and she had set the evening for the game, "I will
be your queen." "And," she had added mischievously, "it won't
matter, you know, if you allow me to take your queen."   Certainly an original way of putting off her lover, but a terribly
trifling incident on which to base the whole course of a lifetime.

How Felix would have smiled and have been reassured had
he known that Adelaide, dear Adelaide, was at that moment
pulling cruelly at the golden heart of a Marguerite, flinging the
petals to the ground, metamorphosing it in fact into Fortune's
Wheel :—

"Er liebt mich,"   .   .   .   (He loves me)
"Von Herzen,"   . . . . (From his heart)
"Mit Schmerzen,"   . . (Painfully)
"Über alle Massen,"   . . (Above all things)
"Zum Razen,"   . . . (To madness)
"Kann's gar nicht lassen," (Because he cannot help it)
"Klein wenig,"   . . . . (A little)
"Fast gar nicht," . . . (Hardly at all).

She had a pretty German accent, and presented a quaint
little figure standing there under the chandelier all alone. Her
grey eyes grew larger and more intense as she neared the last
fainting petal :

"Fast gar nicht,"
"Er liebt mich,"
"Von Herzen,"
"Mit Schmerzen."

Painfully ! How painfully at that moment she could not
realize.

For the second time Felix flung down his book ; then

quickly went out into the night. The sky mocked him in the shape of a huge chess-board where King Sun had already been checkmated in his bright career by Queen Moon. What hope was there for him? Of what use were the stars or minor pieces after the game was done?

.   .   .   .

When Felix at last found himself really seated at the board opposite Adelaide in all her characteristic beauty, he felt himself checkmated before the game began by those wonderful speaking eyes. He made the ordinary opening move, however, of the King's pawn.

Adelaide followed suit with a mental " Er liebt mich," making use of the chessmen in something the same manner as she had of the petals of the Marguerite.

Black played again—King's bishop to Queen's bishop's fourth.

White, happening to have no original ideas at the moment, simply did the same on her side, with, of course, the exception of " Von Herzen," under her breath.

The black Queen, perceiving that her road to glory lay by way of King's bishop's third, immediately took advantage of it.

" Mit Schmerzen!" What was the matter with white? Instead of moving her King's bishop's knight to King's bishop's third, or bishop's pawn a square ahead, thus keeping black's Queen at bay, out jumped the Queen's officious young knight to Queen's bishop's third. A simple mistake for a little maid in love to be sure. She had touched the wrong knight, but as Felix brought up his Queen with a trembling hand, Adelaide did not realize that she was checkmated—and that, by the scholar's mate —until he leaned over and kissed her. Then it was that Adelaide thought, " Gewiss, ' Über alle Massen.' "

DIE KÖNIGIN.

SILENT MUSIC.

" *All* thy works praise thee."

" Not a flower
But shows some touch in freckle, streak or stain
Of his unrivall'd pencil.   He inspires
Their balmy odours, and imparts their hues,
And bathes their eyes with nectar, and includes
In grains as countless as the seaside sands
The forms with which he sprinkles all the earth."

All nature sings a song of praise :

" There's music in the brooklet
   As it swiftly glides along,
I love to stand on its pebbly shore
   And list to its passing song.

There's music in the rushing wind,
   As it shakes the forest trees,
There's music in the milder tones
   Of the soft and gentle breeze.

There's music in the thunder,
   As it rolls along the sky,
It is the grand, the deep-toned bass
   Of nature's harmony.

There's music in the insect's hum
   As it sports the sunny bower,
And spreads its gauzy wings and sips
   The nectar from the flower.

When evening over hill and vale
   Her deepening shadow flings ;
The nightingale in clear, soft tones
   A treble solo sings.

And when the morn expands the flowers
   And the leaves with dew are wet,
The thrush and blackbird then unite
   And warble their duet.

The little songsters of the wood
   To swell the choir attend,
And in one grand harmonious song
   Their tuneful voices blend.

The wide world is the orchestra
   Of nature's music hall,
The azure sky its lofty dome
   And the atmosphere its wall.

> Here the music nature gives,
>   Her notes so wild and free,
> To me are sweeter, dearer far
>   Than all earth's minstrelsy."

Earth's minstrelsy is stiff, precise, accurate, measured, labored. There is a glorious freedom, a delicious unexpectedness, a divine spirituality about the music of nature. The rippling tremolo of the wavelets on the evening lake lapping the smooth sand, the soft swell of the summer breeze as it sifts through the fibrous birch and plays around the mountain glen, the dulcet notes of the feathered choir, the low cremona of the sighing pines, these all sing to God. True, some of this music we have never heard. The swaying of the mighty rock is too measured, the vibrations of the maiden-hair that nestles at its base are too rapid to make music that mortals can hear, but He made them, and He tuned for each of them an invisible lyre. He hears their music and to Him its harmony is exquisite, perfect. Bye-and-bye, when the microphone shall have lent its aid to our dull sense, we shall glory in music which has been included for centuries among the secrets of nature, but there will always be depths which the great Creator has reserved for His own joy. "All thy works praise thee." I alone would not be silent. But I cannot sing with the birds, my voice is dissonant. The soul vibrations are so much swifter than those of the voice that they are inconsonant, and silence is better music than sound. I feel a shrill delight too high for the dull sense of hearing to gratify, a sense of sound too deep for human interpretation ; the range of soul music is too great for expression, so in silence rapt and sacred I murmur below a whisper:

> " Sing, my soul, sing hallelujah,
>   Raise a song to God above !"

Doth my soul make music which Thou canst hear but which is all silence to me ?

O. G. Langford, '95·

MATHEMATICS AS A FACTOR IN LIBERAL EDUCATION.*

As modern education advances there seems to be a tendency in men to narrow down to some one branch of learning, and to pursue it as a life-long task. The reason is plain : if any man wishes to be an authority on any one subject, he must give that course of study his almost undivided attention, the more so since new material is necessarily accumulating in any branch of learning.

What I have affirmed applies more properly no doubt to higher or post-graduate work, but however it may apply, we must admit that there is a striking tendency along this line in our Canadian undergraduate schools, as a glance at any of their curricula will show.

Let us then consider some of the reasons why a liberal education should be acquired along with a special branch of work,— say mathematics—in an undergraduate course.

We may first consider what Tyndall has to say on the subject : "The circle of human nature is not complete without the arc of feeling and emotion. And here the dead languages, which are sure to be beaten by science in a purely intellectual fight, have an irresistible charm. They supplement the work of mathematics by exalting and refining the æsthetic faculty and must be cherished by all who desire to see human culture complete."

If a man would be truly cultured, all his faculties must receive their appropriate share of training. In order that a man may understand better the time in which he is placed it seems important that he should know what has taken place in past decades—hence the necessity of history. If a man would appreciate the beautiful around him, the æsthetic side of his nature must be cultivated, hence the necessity of a thorough knowledge of his own language and literature, and of the fine arts. If a man would know what is going on in the world he must study the great political issues and economical questions of his nation. However useful then and however valuable the science of mathematics becomes to its students, we are not therefore to study it to the exclusion of other subjects of equal importance.

---

*Read before the Mathematical Society of McMaster University.

People who do not care for attainment in mathematics are very apt to consider it one of the most narrowing of studies, and my first purpose herein is to show that the study of mathematics in itself is a subject well fitted to give a liberal education in a large degree. I shall deal with my subject from three standpoints : the utilitarian, the æsthetic, and the purely poetical aspects of mathematics.

The science of mathematics is based on the fact that one theorem depends for its proof on a more elementary theorem, and this in turn on a still more elementary theorem, until we are really driven back to the foundation principles, the axioms of the subject. Hence, since these elementary theorems may be applied in so many different forms, the powers of the reasoning faculties are strengthened.

Early in a study of mathematics, moreover, and in mathematics more than in any other branch of learning, the habit of concentration—a habit so necessary in all work—is formed. Bacon has said : " If a man's mind be wandering, let him study geometry." Once the chain of reasoning is lost, a fresh beginning must be made if an adequate conception be desired. In such a manner, almost unconsciously, the habit of concentration is formed. No science is so systematic in its methods of procedure. He who studies mathematics becomes systematic in *all* his work, and this means the occupying of time and energy to the best advantage.

A man may be successful in business without a knowledge of the classics, but he must know something about mathematics, —arithmetic at least. Thus we see how closely our science is connected with the great business world around us. It is the keen eye of the mathematician in the business man that must watch the shifting conditions of the banks, clearing houses and insurance companies ; his calculating brain must devise the answering plans and events of his commercial career. But the real uses of mathematics lie in its application to the sciences of mechanics, optics, heat, acoustics, astronomy, electricity, chemistry, geology, architecture, painting, music, navigation, etc. Here surely is a liberal education in the application of mathematics to these several branches of learning. The last fifty years of mathematical research in connection with electricity alone have

accomplished more for humanity than three centuries of philosophical thought. In concluding this part of my subject, let me
quote from a prominent writer : " Applied to engineering it has
enabled men to bridge rivers and tunnel mountains ; under the
head of electricity it has enabled him to flash his words from the
far land and girdle the earth with a spell; and under the head
of that sublime subject astronomy, its power is so great that the
astronomers by observation and calculation write out the history of a star with perfect accuracy for a million years."

Let us pass to the æsthetic element in mathematics.
Beauty in all architecture lies for the most part in its symmetry,
and is not this symmetry an outgrowth of the mathematical
genius of the architect ?

The subject of conic sections should be especially interesting to its readers, since the curves with which it is concerned
are the paths that the sun and the planets describe in their
march through space. Certainly, by studying conics we are
finding out the great laws of the universe which God Himself
set in motion at a word.

In painting, the laws of perspective must be thoroughly
understood. In music the theory of sound has a mathematical
basis. "A Division of the Scale," and "An Introduction to
Harmony," were two of Euclid's famous books. Gœthe considered that the beautiful was nothing more than a manifestation of the great laws of nature. Then, when we consider
mathematics in its definite relation to the fine arts, and the
eternal, fixed and immutable laws of nature,

" Beauty chased he everywhere."

But can there be poetry in a science often regarded as the
most prosaic ? People are ever ready to admit that mathematics cures mind-wandering, that it is a great auxiliary to science,
but they consider the mathematician as a " cold logical engine,"
devoid of any imagination whatever. In brief, they fail to see
that mathematics contains poetry.

Poetry is not fine phrases nor polished diction, but the
feeling within us of truth and beauty. Euclid writing his
" Elements," and Newton his " Principia," heard far more noble
harmonies than many a petty word-juggler of to-day. Let the

student then, as he studies his geometry and calculus, observe their essential truth and beauty, and let him bring it down to his every-day life, and to the minds and comprehension of his fellow-men.

The discovery of the laws of gravitation, the discovery of the Asteroids and of Neptune, make the imagination stagger, and fix a mighty gulf between man and his God. The great mathematicians have wonderful imaginations. This fact has proved itself a significant and striking episode in the marvellous discoveries recorded by the historians of mathematics.

Mathematics, we conclude, is useful; there is beauty in its study; there is poetry in its laws. It is, therefore, of great and lasting service as a factor in liberal education.

ARTHUR M. OVERHOLT, '97·

FAME.

Fame: what a lofty word that is! What a large place it has held and holds to-day in the history of humanity! Who is there that has not felt its impulse? It plays a unique part in the life of every man, society and nation. The rudest cannibal inhabiting the islands of the sea finds it in his breast, and the wisest philosopher who treads the halls of learning, with all his refinement and culture, discovers too a something in his heart which calls forth the best effort of his life. Fame's content in these two instances is doubtless greatly different, but in the inner nature of the desires of both, there is much that is common between them.

Almost any man, of whatever creed or condition in life, has an ideal—a goal which he is ever striving to attain. There are few really shiftless mariners on life's great sea—few men who are content aimlessly to drift with the current of circumstances; most men, on the contrary, endeavor to stem the tide, and trimming their sail, direct their bark to some desired haven.

The fixing of an ideal in life seems to be a universal tendency. It stands out as one of the essential marks of humanity. As Robert Browning sings, we should

> " Rejoice we are allied
> To that which doth provide
> And not partake, effect and not receive !
> A spark disturbs our clod ;
> Nearer we hold of God
> Who gives, than of his tribes that take, I must believe."

The character of the ideal cherished, the object after which the whole man strives, the centre about which his life revolves, is doubtless not precisely the same in any two instances. But the desire to obtain is there nevertheless and the effort put forth, however feeble. We are firmly convinced that there can be nothing more helpful in the upbuilding of strong character, than the cherishing of a noble purpose. Ralph Waldo Emerson's pen gave to the world more than a mere rhetorical flourish when he advised young men :

> " Hitch your wagon to a star."

Here, indeed, he enunciated the first essential element to success. Most men who fail in life, fail not from the lack of energy, nor yet from the lack of ability, but rather because they have chosen a wrong ideal. They build on the shifting sand foundation of some earthly selfish hope instead of on the solid granite rock of established truth, unselfish purpose, and the desire for the general welfare of mankind. Then, in an hour of storm, their fine superstructure goes down with a crash, and they come off from the great battlefield of life worsted in the fray. Desiring to save their lives by selfish misery they lost them, and found themselves paupers in the extreme.

Hence we see plainly that it should be the aim of every wise father, the burning purpose of every truly devoted mother, the first duty of every true teacher, both to place before the aspiring youth a truly noble ideal and to aid in its resolute attainment.

Strange to say, this prime duty, this most grave responsibility, this standard by which every man's life shall finally be judged, receives but scant attention in the home, in the classroom, and in the public life. How many a zealous father and devoted mother allow the son and the daughter to step out from home into the awful responsibilities of life with no such strong advice and counsel ? How many teachers both in public schools and colleges, who meet the youth in his ideal-making time, who come into contact with him when the purposes of his life are just being formed, whose influence on his future destiny is incalculable,—how many allow the student to pass out from under their tuition into the "hot fords of life" without a single hour's conversation concerning their first necessary purpose? For do not all desire to set before the young aspiring student a true ideal to follow after in life? And thus they fail to discharge their first duty before their Creator God, and their brother man. When a man launches out into the high seas of commercial and public life, he has little time for ideal-making then. He is pressed by his business and seldom seriously reflects. Besides, he is much the man he is ever to be. There are, indeed, instances of marked revolutions in men's later lives, but we must declare these the exceptions. How many men, when the sun of their life is all but set, and the evening shadows have already begun to gather about them, feeling now that they must soon set sail on eternity's ocean, wake up to the fact that they have been following a false leader, cherishing a worthless purpose, worshipping a dumb idol, and bartering their soul for naught? We can never tell of the unspeakable pain of men and women who go out into the eternal blackness of darkness and wake up too late to the sad and awful fact that they spent their whole lives unavailingly, that they chose the wrong master, that they cherished a false purpose.

Fame is but the choosing of an ideal and the effort to reach it. John Milton, in his immortal elegy, sings concerning it:

> " Fame is the spur that the dear spirit doth raise
> (That last infirmity of noble minds)
> To scorn delights and live laborious days."

Many illustrious men, both of the past and present, men of mighty deeds and mighty words, stand bound together by that one strong word "fame!" In its pursuit has been invested the best which muscle, brain and life could offer in all ages and in all climes. The undying works of the great groups of poets tell a marvellous story of self-denial, of diligent mental discipline, and often of painful and lonely experience.

The progress of the race, as a whole, is always slow. Of the individual it must likewise be gradual. Self-denial, solitude and loneliness are the necessary antecedents of any high standard of excellence in any sphere. Only through the attainment of the highest excellence can come true and enduring fame. Few men, as Lord Byron, "awake and find themselves famous." The history of their slow attainment to that high position is full of much that tells of hard toil and dogged perseverance. The history of the world's greatest warriors, of those "who climb to eminence over men's graves," is a record of efforts almost superhuman, of discipline strict and tedious, and of privation and suffering hardly thinkable. Yet these must be endured before he is entitled to have his name linked with the "Immortals." And how often from the life blood of his heart, whose every throb bespoke his patriotic loyalty, has the flower of immortal fame sprung forth never to die !

> " There's many a crown for who can reach.
> Ten lines a statesman's life in each !
> The flag stuck on a heap of bones,
> A soldier's doing ! what atones ?
> They scratch his name on the Abbey stones."

The greatest thinkers and students of the ages, whose works and discoveries have proved an inestimable heritage to mankind, did their seed-sowing in a study-chamber where solitude and loneliness found their continual abode ; but the reaping brought them fame.

To us now, after this discussion, the question naturally suggests itself,—Is fame a worthy end ? The solution of this problem does not occur to every seeker after worldly applause. Many rush on in their consuming desire for fame and fail to pave with the truest motives and the most just deeds that road which leads to her high citadel. Fired by their ambition, they trample down forever the hopes of many an aspiring fellow mortal, and heedlessly, with no true purpose dominating their lives, seek only self-gratification. Such a course of conduct as this we must surely denounce in unsparing terms. But again we ask,—is the desire for fame, in the inner and truer nature, good, just and noble ? Does it tend to increase the true, the beautiful, the good in society and in the world about us ? We answer that it may play a very helpful part in the life of every man, society, and nation. It is true that he who pursues after fame as the goal in itself can never be virtuous and noble in the highest sense of virtue and nobility. Fame that comes unconscious born is best. The good and lasting name, "of greater value than much riches," is the sweetest and best heritage of man. With such to crown our lives we never can be poor.

L. BROWN, '96·

EDITORIAL NOTES.

No other name could more fittingly be associated with that of the late Dr. Fyfe in the story of the founding and subsequent success of the Canadian Literary Institute of Woodstock, than that of the grand old deacon, the record of whose long Christian life and ardent devotion to the work of ministerial education in its early and critical days is placed in attractive and permanent form in this month's issue. Bro. Sawtell, so long associated with Deacon Burtch on the Executive Committee and in general church work, is probably the only writer who could so well recall these events of former days which have contributed so largely to the gratifying condition of our educational work of to-day. We are greatly indebted to Mr. Sawtell for the time and care he has given to the preparation of this paper, which will help to keep alive and sacred the memory of another of God's honored servants to whom Woodstock Church and College owe so much. Since the biography of Deacon Burtch was put in type, his aged widow, "Grandma Burtch," so touchingly referred to by Mr. Sawtell, has been called away to join the ranks of those who have gone before. She died at the residence of her son, Deacon R. H. Burtch, of Woodstock, on Friday, 7th inst., at the great age of 91. May her good deeds through many long years, and especially her kindness to the students of Woodstock College never be forgotten by any of them who knew her !

ABOUT 45 years ago, there was living in the village of Norval, Peel Co., a remarkable old Highland Scotchman, named Hugh Black, one of the best land surveyors of his day, a clever mathematician, a profound Gaelic scholar, a man of great intellectual activity and of wide general information. Many stories are still current among the old settlers of Halton, Peel and Wellington, of the old surveyor's sturdy liberalism, his ready and incisive repartees, his ingenious and curious etymologies, and of his remarkable memory of the exact location of any corner post he had ever planted or used in his measurements far and wide.   In a recent afternoon's conversation with his daughter, whom the writer has known for many years, as well as other members of the family, he learned that to this rare old Highlandman's mental vision, coming events frequently seemed to cast their shadows before, and that time and again, when many miles away from the scene of the occurrence, he had remarkably distinct intimations of the fact that death or a serious accident had happened to some member of his family or to one of his intimate friends.   On one occasion he suddenly dropped his work sometime before tea, and started to walk a long distance to his home, giving as the reason for his strange conduct that one of his boys was dead.   When he reached Norval late in the night, he found that one of his boys had been drowned about 4 o'clock in the afternoon. On another occasion at Norval, he had spent the whole of the evening in the solution of a number of intricate mathematical problems proposed in a certain American paper he was receiving.   About half past eleven, having solved the last one, he turned his chair towards the fireplace, and sat for some moments gazing upon the burning coals. Suddenly he started up, and calling to his wife, asked whether she had certain articles of clothing clean and ironed, adding that old G. (a surveyor in Mulmer) was dead, and he would have to go up there.   On her asking when old G. died and how he knew, he replied that it was just now, and that he had told him so himself.   Miss Black remembers dintinctly being awake at that moment, and hearing this remarkable conversation.   On being asked whether she was not startled by hearing her father talk in this way, she replied that they were too much accustomed to hearing him say curious things to be at all surprised.   The following day, a messenger came from Mulmer with a request for Mr. Black to go up to that Township and finish a piece of surveying that Mr. G. had tried to work out from Hugh Black's notes of a former survey.   The old man had been obliged by bodily weakness to give it up, and had died the night before at 11.30 p.m.   Almost his last words were a request that Mr. Black should be sent for to finish the job himself.   It appears, therefore, from the narrative of our informant that, at the very moment of its occurrence many miles up the country, Mr. Black became as fully aware of the death of his old brother craftsman as if he had been verbally informed of the fact.   How are such communications to be accounted for?

ONE of the latest additions to the Library is "The Bampton Lectures for 1893," or "Eight Lectures on the Early History and Origin of the Doctrine of Biblical Inspiration," by Dr. Sanday of Oxford.

Dr. Sanday accepts the main premises of the Higher Criticism—the untrustworthy character of Jewish tradition as to the authorship of the O. T. books and the composite character of many of these — with the particular conclusions that a considerable element in the Pentateuch is not earlier than the captivity, and that Deuteronomy first saw the light not long before 621 B.C. Yet he thinks that the O. T. loses none of its value. " On the contrary," he maintains, (to quote his own words), " stumbling-blocks have been removed ; a far more vivid and real apprehension of the O. T. both as history and religion has been obtained ; and the old conviction that we have in it a revelation from God to man is not only unimpaired but placed upon firmer founda_tions." In the first two chapters we are shown the historical position of the Canon in the early Christian centuries, and the conception of inspiration which then obtained. That conception, in so far as the New Testament is concerned, is that the scriptures are inspired by the Holy Spirit and bear the authority of Christ, and this inspiration is even "verbal " and extends to the facts as well as doctrines ; whilst the O. T. has a perfection which implies, at least in the case of Philo, an inspiration which might be called "verbal." The next five chapters sketch consecutively the process by which that conception was reached. These chapters reveal a wealth of learning and form exceedingly interesting reading. The difficulties of the problem are brought out into clear relief, and one cannot but be impressed with the fact that the world of scholarship has very little exact knowledge of the actual composition of the books and their formation into a Canon. It is these difficulties and this ignorance apparently which constrain Dr. Sanday to accept a lower view of inspiration than most of us hold. His view he regards as one drawn inductively from the facts. And in the closing chapter he compares this 'inductive' with the common 'traditional' view, maintaining that the former is quite as real and quite as fundamental as the latter. This is the most interesting chapter in the book, and in the course of it the author deals with the real *crux* of the view he has adopted, i. e., the bearing on it of Christ's references to the Old Testament. We recognize the candor and moderation of Dr. Sanday's discussion here ; and yet we could not accept his position without feeling that some violence was being done to our conception of our Lord. When all allowance is made for the doctrine of the κένωσις, still we must believe that *whatever Jesus positively taught is true.* Even granting that there were some things He did not know, yet surely as a peerless Teacher He would deal not in His ignorance but in His knowledge. " We speak that we do know, and testify that we have seen " is

His own emphatic declaration. To us there is less difficulty in accepting the plenary inspiration of the Old Testament on the authority of Jesus than in accepting the 'inductive' view of Dr. Sanday in the face of Jesus' testimony. And we are the more content with the traditional view—the view of those who were nearest the sources of evidence—as we see how, from time to time, confident assertions of the critics are being disproved by archæological research.

F.

HERE AND THERE.

O. G. LANGFORD, EDITOR.

King's College Record, an excellent journal otherwise, devotes only an inch or two to exchanges. A recent number contained a warm tribute to Oliver Wendell Holmes from the pen of C.G. D. Roberts. We have space for only two stanzas :—

"But, Humour's mild aristocrat,
　He wandered through these busy days,
Half wondering what the world was at,
　And shrewdly smoothing it with praise.

And now he lives but in his page,
　Where wit and wisdom are comprised,—
The gentlest breeding of the age
　Most graciously epitomized."

A pretty girl,
A College man,
A Summer eve
You understand.

A sad farewell
The Summer past,
He to his books,
She home at last.

Same pretty girl
His photo near ;
A perfumed note,
A tiny tear.

Same College man,
Same perfumed note,
A hurried glance
At what she wrote.

A careless laugh,
A passing jest,
The note in shreds,—
You know the rest.

　　　—MABEL CORNELIA DAGGETT, '96. In the *Sibyl*.

THE war scare has passed, but it has left its impress upon the thinking world in both hemispheres. The dignity and honor of the British nation has been fully sustained. "Common sense will settle it" said the greatest of living statesmen, and it has settled it. But it has left an influence which will not pass away in an hour. The expressions of loyalty from all parts of the British dominions must have been most gratifying to the mother land.

Many little verses, perhaps ephemeral in their character but containing the true ring of national pride, have appeared in the current literature. These, if gathered together, would tell the real sentiment of the people better than many of the inflamed and retaliatory editorials that have appeared. The following, clipped from *The Week*, are well worth preserving :—

CANADA TO ENGLAND.

—1896—

If England's golden noon to-day should wane,
   Though England's summer drew into a close,
We crown her mistress of the world again,
   And twine our maple leaves around her rose !

Canadian hill and long Canadian plain
   Shall deck her autumn wreaths with younger flowers,
And by her side we norland sons remain,
   Remembering her liberty means ours.

For their old homes can English hearts forget?
   O island home, across Canadian snows,
And cleaving seas, we crown thee mistress yet :
   Our maple leaf shall redden to your rose !

Oxford, 1896.   ARTHUR J. STRINGER.

Whispering woods and sorrowing sea,
   And wind that ruffles her bending wheat,
Are full of the voices of destiny,
   Which over and over repeat :

"Canada ! white-browed queen of the north,
   Whose aurora crowneth thy snow-bright hair,
From the pole-star's burning thou goest forth
   To the lakes that thy commerce bear.

"Thy left hand holdeth the twisted clue
   Of a hundred strands, that under the sea
Bindeth the old world fast to the new,
   Thy mother England to thee.

"Thy right hand beckons the swift-winged ships
   Out of the ocean where sinks the sun,
Cooling at even his burning lips
   Where the western currents run.

"Who are thy children ? The careful Scot,
   The ready Irish, the Briton strong,
And the French of a France which was and is not,—
   All these to thy house belong.

" Like a Damask blade, where the twisted steel
　　Makes the mottled scimitar tough and true,
The blended strains in thy face reveal
　　A power possessed of few.

" Their's thou art ever, and they of thee ;
　　So shall ye together be strong and great ;
For thou art the daughter of destiny,
　　The child of a favouring fate."

JOHN EDMUND BARSS.

Of a more permanent value is the poem of Rudyard Kipling in the London *Times*, now well known on both sides of the Atlantic. Having been reviewed in many of our literary periodicals, and believing that the poem is its own best commendation, we present it to our readers in full, without criticism :—

THE NATIVE BORN.

We've drunk to the Queen.　God bless her !
　　We've drunk to our mothers' land,
We've drunk to our English brother
　　(But he does not understand) :
We've drunk to the wide creation.
　　And the Cross swings low to the dawn—
Last toast, and of obligation—
　　A health to the Native-born !

They change their skies above them
　　But not their hearts that roam !
We learned from our wistful mothers
　　To call old England " home."
We read of the English skylark,
　　Of the spring in the English lanes,
But we screamed with the painted lories
　　As we rode on the dusty plains !

They passed with their old-world legends—
　　Their tales of wrong and dearth—
Our fathers held by purchase
　　But we by the right of birth :
Our heart's where they rocked our cradle.
　　Our love where we spent our toil,
And our faith and our hope and our honour
　　We pledge to our native soil !

I charge you charge your glasses—
　　I charge you drink with me
To the men of the Four New Peoples,
　　And the Islands of the Sea—
To the last least lump of coral
　　That none may stand outside.
And our own good pride shall teach us
　　To praise our comrade's pride.

To the hush of the breathless morning
　　On the thin, tin crackling roofs,
To the haze of the burned back-ranges
　　And the drum of the shoeless hoofs—
To the risk of a death by drowning,
　　To the risk of a death by drouth—
To the men of a million acres,
　　To the Sons of the Golden South.

To the Sons of the Golden South (Stand up !)
  And the life we live and know
Let a fellow sing o' the little things he cares about
If a fellow fights for the little things he cares about
  With the weight of a single blow !

To the smoke of a hundred coasters,
  To the sheep on a thousand hills,
To the sun that never blisters,
  To the rain that never chills—
To the land of the waiting springtime,
  To our five-meal meat-fed men,
To the tall, deep-bosomed women,
  And the children nine and ten !

And the children nine and ten (Stand up !)
  And the life we live and know.
Let a fellow sing o' the little things he cares about
If a fellow fights for the little things he cares about
  With the weight of a two-fold blow !

To the far-flung fenceless prairie,
  Where the quick-cloud shadows trail,
To our neighbors' barn—in the offing
  And the line of the new-cut rail.
To the plough in her league-long furrow,
  With the grey lake gulls behind,
To the weight of a half-year's winter
  And the warm wet western wind !

To the home of floods and thunder,
  To her pale, dry, healing blue—
To the lift of great Cape combers,
  And the smell of the baked Karoo,
To the growl of the sluicing stamhead
  To the reef and the water-gold,
To the last and the largest Empire,
  To the map that is half unrolled !

To our dear dark foster mothers,
  To the heathen songs they sung—
To the heathen speech we babbled,
  Ere we came to the white man's tongue,
To the cool of our deep verandahs—
  To the blaze of our jewelled main,
To the night, to the palms in the moonlight,
  And the fire-fly in the cane !

To the hearth of our people's people—
  To her well ploughed, windy sea,
To the hush of our dread high-altars
  Where the Abbey makes us We,
To the grist of the slow-ground ages.
  To the gain that is yours and mine
To the Bank of the Open Credit,
  To the Power-House of the Line !

We've drunk to the Queen—God bless her !—
  We've drunk to our mother's land ;
We've drunk to our English brother
  (And we hope he'll understand).
We've drunk as much as we're able

And the Cross swings low to the dawn :
Last toast—and your foot on the table--
A health to the Native-born !

A health to the Native-born (Stand up !)
We're six white men arow,
All bound to sing o' the little things we care about,
All bound to fight for the little things we care about,
With the weight of a six-fold blow !

By the might of our cable tow (Take hands !)
From the Orkneys to the Horn,
All round the world (and a little loop to pull it by)
All round the world (and a little strap to buckle it)
A health to the Native-born !

RUDYARD KIPLING in the *Times.*

YALE College offers a new course this fall. It is a unique one.
It is a course in modern novels ! One novel a week will be undertaken
and mastered. It is needless to say that already the class numbers
250 ; and that, too, in spite of the fact that only Seniors and Juniors
are admitted. Dr. W. S. Phelps is the instructor. His aim, it is set
forth, is to train young men to read novels as mental food, and not as
time-killers.

THERE is a peculiar little periodical comes to our sanctum called
Praeco Latinus. This paper, published at Philadelphia, is said to be the
only one in the United States of its kind. It is what might be called
a kicker and vigorously does it protest against the method pursued in
the teaching of Latin in most of our colleges. It claims that Latin is
not a dead language but that it has been almost *murdered* by the present method of teaching. It advocates *spoken* Latin claiming that no
person ought to profess to know a language he cannot *speak.* Whatever may be the cause it is plain that the four to six years usually spent
upon Latin in our colleges gives but poor results. It would be no
more than fair that professors of Latin should examine this journal and
see if it contains any truth.—*The Athenæum.*

ACCORDING to the statistics in the New York World Almanac
there are 243 college men in the present Congress, the Senate having 48
and the house of representatives 195. The following is a summary of
the colleges represented and the number of men from each :—
University of Virginia, 15 ; Harvard, 14 . University of Michigan,
13 ; Yale, 10 ; Princeton, 7 ; Dartmouth, 7 ; Centre (Ky), 5 ; Western Reserve, 4 ; Washington and Lee, 4 ; Columbia, 4 ; Iowa State, 4 ;
Hamilton, 4 ; Amherst, 3 ; Kentucky University, 3 ; University of
Georgia, 3 ; Cumberland, 3 ; Georgetown, 3 ; Union, 3 ; Mercer, 3 ;
Virginia Military Institute, 3 ; De Peauw, 3 ; Jefferson, 3.
Nineteen other colleges have two each, and eighty-eight more
have one representative each.—*U. of M. Daily.*

King's College Record has a short review of a recent book : Balfour's " Foundation of Belief." A taste is not enough of such a book

as this.   It is good, wholesome, and well seasoned ; but it requires to be taken slowly and well masticated.   Truly, there are giants amongst the leaders of English politics.   In *Richelieu* the wonder is expressed that

> " So great a statesman should
> Be so sublime a poet " ;

but our modern Cato Major, the G. O. M., is equally an authority in statesmanship, theology and Homer, and is employing his latter days upon an edition of Butler's *Analogy.*   And here is his comparatively youthful opponent, now First Lord of the Treasury, and leader of the House of Commons, giving evidence that something more serious than golf employs his leisure moments, by the production of a theologico-philosophical treatise, which in the opinion of some critics is the strongest apologetic work which has appeared since the aforementioned Butler's *Analogy.*   Its importance is shown from the attention which it has received from such men as Huxley, Spencer, Dr. Martineau and Dr. Fairbairn.

Some have complained that its results are merely negative, and therefore that its tendency is to general skepticism.   It is negative and destructive in the sense of showing the unsoundness of the assumptions of " Naturalism," (under which general term is comprehended the various anti-Christian systems which teach that there is nothing know-able outside the range of natural science) ; but the object of the book is only to remove objections, hence the modest sub-title, " Notes Introductory to the study of Theology."   It is a beautifully written book, though very closely reasoned.   There are some cleverly chosen illustrations.   Here is one : " As chalk consists of little else but the remains of dead animalculæ, so the history of thought consists of little else but an accumulation of abandoned explanations."   (New York : Longmans & Co., $2.oo.)

ALTHOUGH the *Brunonian* is one of our best exchanges, we doubt if it is much improved by the cartoons that have lately been introduced. The paper and typography are of the best.   The verse has not been as good as last year but the following is worthy of quotation :

THE MANGER BED.

Again, above the hills of Bethlehem,
The round, white, winter moon climbs up the sky,
In its cold light, asleep the lambkins lie
Close huddled, and the dull swain watches them
With heavy eyes.   He sees not by the hem
Of wood and wold the road run windingly
To north, nor does he see the passer-by
Slow journeying onward to Jerusalem.

Past midnight, and the shepherd slumbers deep,
No seraph voices in his simple dream
Open his eyes to gaze on heaven.   No train
Of comet leads, where sages kneel and weep
And God smiles up from baby eyes.   No gleam
Lights the lone cave, the stalls, the broken wain.

No ! in the souls of men the Christ is born,
  Now while the stars look down with earnest eyes,
And night is list'ning for the breath of morn.
  Within the human heart the God-child lies.

The world awakes. The angels sing again
And clearer, " Peace on Earth, Good will to Men."
  —F. SEVERANCE JOHNSON.

LISTEN TO DE CHIPMUNK.

I heerd de chipmunk talkin' to de peacock t' other day
About his bright tail feathas, an' his highfalutin' way ;
De peacock wuz a struttin' an' a floppin' of 'is wing,
An' de chipmunk tumbled flip-flops when de peacock tried ta' sing.

" Yi ! yi ! mistah Peacock, what dat howlin', got a fit ?
Doan you know, yo' poah ole fellah, you kaint sing a littl' bit ?
Bettah strut an' show yo' feathers, you makes a pooty show,
Be satisfied with what de Lawd gibes on dey irth down heah below.

" You'se proud an' mouty stuck up in yo' feathas bright an' fine,
But you show your common raisin' in you singin' ebry time.
So you bettah keep yo' mouth shut, an' de world will nebber know
But you wuz made to look at—yas only made fo' show.

" Den de chipmunk growled an' capered, turned a flip-flop on de groun',
And de peacock heerd a sermon dat had a splendid soun',
De sermon ob de chipmunk could be took by some I know
Ob de people in de world heah dat wuz only made fo' show."

—WILLIAM EMMET WELCH, in the *Southern Collegian*

EDWARD A. BOK, writing of football in the *Ladies' Journal,* characterized it as a brutal sport. This has called forth a whole volley of replies in our exchanges, vigorous and telling. Advocates of the old game defend it in strong language. Prof. Richmond of Yale says that in 30 years he has not known of a football player of that college sustaining any serious injury. Another professor from the West says the game has not been detrimental to scholarships but rather a benefit, an aid to discipline and of general physical advantage.

IN *The 'Varsity,* Miss E. M. Graham, in writing very sensibly upon popular music, advocates encouragingly a better class of music in parlor and opera as well as in the church and Sunday school. Miss Helliwell's poem in the same number is worthy of warm commendation. Another number has a good critical article on Duncan C. Scott, one of our young contemporary Canadian poets, by Frank B. Proctor. It is appreciative, judicious, and evinces good discrimination.

THE universities of Wales present many curious features to the American college men, says the *Yale News.* Conducted as they are, on an entirely different system from the colleges of this country, they afford many opportunities of noting the different methods used to obtain essentially the same ends. The three universities of Bangor, Aberystroth and Cardiff are the chief centres of education in Wales. These are situated in North Wales, Central Wales and South Wales in the order named. There is no dormitory life in any of them, and the students live in registered boarding houses, in which they must be by ten o'clock each night. In June last, the first examination preparatory to a degree was held. Before then the universities did not grant degrees. Now, however, a student may take the degree of B. A., after at least three years study and passing satisfactorily in three examinations.

Co-education has been adopted, but the rules are so strict that representatives of opposite sexes cannot even speak to each other in recitations. The recitations are carried on in English, although Welsh is the language of the students. The dialects differ in different localities, the purest Welsh being found in the north.

THE *Trinity University Review* has an article on " borrowing," particularly applicable to students in the residence :—

" For the resident man the term borrowing has completely lost its meaning ; in fact, in residence we have returned to the state described in the early chapters of the Acts ; in short, we are unconscious communists. The motto engraved in invisible letters over each door reads, " All mine is thine, take it when you will." For instance, you lay in a stock of note paper, not for yourself but for your corridor ; the same corridor has a common ink bottle, a common mucilage pot, a common match-box, common cups and saucers, a common kettle, common eatables and drinkables, tobacco, clothes, and what not ; truly a veritable nest of Communists—an ideal state of Socialism ! Generally speaking, our borrowing is reciprocal in its character, i. e., we seldom return the article itself, but expect the lender sooner or later to borrow an equivalent. Good faith and good nature flow beneath all, and to abuse one's privileges in this respect is to be promptly frowned upon, and earns for the offender a 'spungy' name and reputation."

This hardly represents an ideal state of things. Every man has a personality, which includes his possessions, that every man is bound to respect. Do McMaster men need the suggestion here contained ?

THE following clipped from *The Ariel* of Minnesota tells its own story. We may be glad that a more conservative view prevails of the value of degrees in Canada than in the United States :

The small college has become a nuisance. Mushroom " universities " spring up in a night, entice one or two hundred students inside their walls on some pretext, fill the various chairs with half a dozen superannuated ministers and set about raising a howl over " educating the youth." At commencement time they confer degrees with a hilarious liberality. A B.A. is stuck on every half educated youngster who has been in the vicinity long enough to acquire a legal residence ; numerous merchants and pork packers whose generosity has made the " college " possible are adorned with LL.D., and if some professor's salary is in arrears he is staved off with a Ph.D. or D.D. and as a result degrees have been so cheapened in America that they are rarely used by their possessors. The small college has become a positive injury to education. Young people who have enjoyed small facilities for independent investigation or of coming in touch with the latest discoveries, and with men of the most advanced ideas, go out into life with the impression that they are educated. This is no fanciful picture. It is what is going on in half a dozen schools in every state in the West. If these denominations would sell out their present plants and put the money into dormitories near the University, they would attain the object for which their present institutions are maintained at a far less expenditure, their young people would receive a better education than they can now obtain, and the taxpaying parent would receive a return from their own expenditure. In addition, the dormitories would be a great conservative moral force in the life of the University. The stand they might take on a popular question would affect the entire student body, and if they should become the social centers for the men and women of the various church affiliations they would fill a great need. It is to be hoped that some such thing may be done in the University of Minnesota during the next ten years.

THE Yale *Alumni Weekly* says the following of the Olympic games : Prof. William M. Sloane, of Princeton, the American representative on the International Committee in charge of the Olympic games, to be held at Athens next spring, reports such great interest in this country that it bids fair that a team from the different athletic clubs and colleges will be sent to compete in the different events. Some very prominent men have been appointed to the honorary committee from the United States. Among those who have promised to serve are President Cleveland, who will act as chairman ; Joseph H. Choate; Provost C. C. Harrison of the University of Pennsylvania, Albert Shaw, editor of the *Review of Reviews* ; S. B. G. Laste, editor of the *Ephemeris* ; and the following college presidents : Dwight, Eliot, Gilman, Low and Patton. It is expected that the large colleges will be represented in most of the events. The games will continue for ten days and on the entire programme there is nothing that would be new to American college men. According to Prof. Sloane the large athletic clubs are seriously considering the invitations received from the Hellenic committee. Nearly every event is limited to amateurs. These games next spring are designed to be the first of a series of such meetings ; consequently the success of this attempt would mean a great deal to international athletics of the future. The next meeting will be held at Paris on the occasion of the World's Exposition in 1900, and the third meeting, according to the present plans, in New York in 1904. An executive committee for America is being chosen by Prof. Sloane.

THERE is a Persian proverb, with a quaint Oriental ceremonialness about it, which says that mankind is of four classes : First,' he who knows not; and knows not he knows not : he is a fool, shun him! Second, he who knows not, and knows he knows not : he is ignorant, teach him ! Third, he who knows, and knows not he knows : he is asleep, awake him !   Fourth, he who knows, and knows he knows : he is wise, follow him !

˙ COLLEGE NEWS.

W. P. COHOE, '96,   R. D. GEORGE, 97

J. F. VICHERT, '97,   MISS E. WHITESIDE, '98·

Editors.

THE UNIVERSITY.

A wise senior's sage remark : " Half the lies you hear ain't true.'

THIRD year English specialist looking into Spenser's " Faerie Queene " :—The man who wrote this was a mighty bad speller."

JUDGING by his recent pranks, the German Emperor, we beg to opine, is anything but a remedial Bill.

EXCITED candidate in the recent elections for Literary and Scientific Society, laying down his platform : " McMaster expects every man to do her duty."

SEVERAL visitors have honored us with their presence at chapel recently. Among those have been Rev. C. A. Eaton of Bloor St. Church, Evangelist Palmer and returned missionary La Flamme.

THE graduates were invited by the Faculty of Moulton College to attend the At Home given by them on Friday the 14th inst. The afternoon was a perfect success, all who were present enjoying themselves very much.

A would-be-polite young sophomore recently went out to tea. Observing that one of the ladies present bore a strong resemblance to his hostess, he hastened to forestall introduction by bowing sweetly and murmuring : " Mrs. C.'s sister, I prefer." Who knows what he meant to say ?

Dr. F. L. Anderson, pastor of the second Baptist Church, Rochester, and son of Dr. Gelusha Anderson, Chicago University, led our devotional exercises Feb. 7. At the close of the service, in a brief address, he said that the world wants honest men ; men honest in the shop ; honest in the study ; honest in the class ; honest with themselves. His words touched life in its practical aspect and were much appreciated by all.

AN enthusiastic meeting of the Tennysonian Society was held on Friday evening, Jan. 17th, for the purpose of electing officers for the ensuing term, the ballot resulted as follows : President, A. W. Vining, '98 ; Vice-Pres., C. L. Brown, '99 ; Sec.-Treas., J. P. Schutt, '98 ; Councillors H. A. Ben Oliel, '98 ; J. A. Ferguson, '98 ; Editors of the Argosy, W. B. H. Teakles, '98, and H. W. Newman, '99·

The Rev. Geo. C. Lorimer, D.D., the famous pastor of the Tremont Temple Baptist Church, Boston, Massachusetts, has accepted the invitation extended to him in behalf of the University to preach the Baccalaureate sermon in May. Not only the members of the graduating classes, but also all friends of the University are to be congratulated that it has been possible to secure the services of a preacher of such eminence for this occasion.

THE Philosophical club of McMaster University was organized Jan. 9th. A large number have from the beginning manifested an interest in its purpose. One of the chief objects of the society is to make clear what some of the problems of philosophy are. It is desired that the students consider this organization as their own, then, it will prove the means of making the study of philosophy, not only less burdensome, but more attractive and beneficial. Meetings are held every other Thursday evening from seven to eight o'clock. The papers already presented, together with the discussions following, have been excellent. All success to the Philosophical Club !

A meeting of the Ladies' Literary League was held January the 20th in Moulton Chapel. The morning was devoted to Hawthorne. Mrs. Holman gave a most interesting talk on Hawthorne, his life, personal character, family and business relations, and his works. His writings were taken up and interpreted with such a sympathetic appreciation of the author's thought and comprehension of his genius that new light was thrown on many passages, obscure to the ordinary reader. The talk was supplemented by readings from Mrs. Hawthorne's letters by Miss Cohoon, '99, and a selection from *The Scarlet Letter* by Miss Eby, '97. Instrumentals were given by Miss Woolverton, '97 and Miss Whiteside, '98.

ON January 10th a meeting was held in the chapel for the nominations to office in the Literary and Scientific society for the spring term. Throughout the following week excitement ran high, culminating when the elections took place, resulting in the following ballot :—Pres., Mr. J. J. McNeill, '96 ; 1st Vice Pres., Mr. P. G. Mode, '97 ; 2nd Vice Pres., Miss M. E. Woolverton, '97 ; Sec.-Treas., Mr. A. M. Overholt, '97 ; Cor.-Sec., Mr. J. F. Vichert, '97. Councillors, Miss M. E. Burnette, '97, Miss N. Cohoon, '99, Mr. Welch, '99. Editors of "Student": Mr. I. G. Matthews, '97 ; assistant editors, Miss M. E. Dryden, '96, Mr. J. C. Sycamore, '96.

THE Theological Society of McMaster University recently elected the following officers for the ensuing term :—Pres., B. W. Merrill, B.A.; Vice-Pres., M. C. McLean ; Sec.-Treas., C. J. Cameron, B. A. Members of the executive, J. J. Reeve, B. A, and W. S. McAlpine, B. A. With this new staff of officers the society has taken on a fresh lease of life and the executive committee is determined to make this one of the most aggressive and important societies in connection with the University. Subjects connected with Homiletics, Pastoral Theology and all the different phases of pastoral life will be brought forward for discussion by the members of the society, and addresses will be delivered by distinguished speakers from the different city churches. Two very successful meetings have already been held which augur well for the future.

THE NATURAL SCIENCE CLUB:—An even more than usually interesting programme was presented at the February meeting of the Natural Science Club   Mr. A.G. Campbell,'97, in his summary of current scientific news drew attention to the recent investigations of underground temperatures, made by Prof. Agassiz, showing an increase of 1° of temperature for every 22° feet descent. The result of late studies of vegetable physiology and of malaria were also noted. Of most interest, in Mr. J. Schutt's resume of inorganic news, was the announcement of the discovery by Prof. Roetgen of Vienna, of a method of photographing through ordinarily opaque substances. Prof. Willmott made additional comments on several of these items. Mr. W. S. McAlpine, B. A. read a collection of articles on visible music, on the effects of various musical sounds on animals as proved experimentally, and on the phenomena of musical visions. Mr. H. H. Newman, '96, gave an instructive talk on Coleoptera, illustrated by specimens of his own collection. He discussed their characteristics, habits and habitats, and the best methods of securing and preserving the various species.

ON the afternoon of Monday, Feb. 10th, the Faculty and students of our University had the pleasure of listening to an address from Dr. J. M. Stifler, Professor of New Testament Exegesis in Crozier Theological Seminary. The Professor chose as the subject of his address : " You can't eat your cake and have it." During the course of what the Dr. was pleased to term "a few whimsical remarks," he called attention to the fact that if young men and young women expect to reap any reward in the future of this life they must toil and labor in the present. At the conclusion of his address Chancellor Wallace, in a few words, thanked Dr. Stifler for his visit and expressed the hope that this would not be the last time that McMaster University would have the privilege of welcoming him within her walls.

FRIDAY, January 24th, was a day looked forward to by *certain* McMaster men with feelings somewhat :—" I wish it were over, but I'm not afraid of them." That day is now looked back upon by *all* McMaster men with feelings such as "we are glad it is over and over as it is." But why all these feelings? Because that was the night of the inter-collegiate debate with Victoria. It is a well known fact, the knowledge of which is derived from- experience, that a snow storm on such an occasion is a good omen. So it proved this year. The snow storm came and with it victory for the second year to McMaster. Through our limited accommodation we are indebted to our Victoria friends for the use of their commodious chapel. The programme was, we think, a credit to McMaster. The orchestra was present, rendering several selections in its usual pleasing style. Mr. W. S. McAlpine,

B. A., sang " Castles in the Air," in such a manner that he had to respond to an encore.   Miss Hart, a well known friend of our college, entertained us with a recitation.   Miss R. Boehmer from the Moulton college delighted us with her songs.   After another recitation by Mr. Vichert, '97, the Glee Club sang a " Sailors Chorus."   Then came the battle.   The question was :   Resolved that " Municipal ownership and working of monopolistic services is practicable for the city of Toronto and would be in the interests of said city."   Victoria had the affirmative.   It was held by Messrs. W. H. Graham, '96, and J. W. Baird, '97. The negative side was argued by Messrs. W. W. McMaster, B. A. and and E. J. Stobo '96 Th.   After both sides had consluded the Hon. R. Harcourt M. A., in a very happy and pleasing style summed up the debate, declaring amid applause the victory in favor of old McMaster.

CHANCELLOR Wallace presided at the afternoon meeting on the Day of Prayer for Colleges.   All present knew that on the evening before in the prayer meetings of the Baptist churches of the city, and during the week in many churches and homes in various parts of Ontario and Quebec, prayer was offered on behalf of the University. This gave to the meeting a peculiar tenderness and solemnity.   Many prayed, fort he different departments of the University, Feller Institute and Samulcotta Seminary being remembered in earnest supplications. The fact that within a few days a number of the students of Moulton College had been converted was reported, and occasioned thanksgiving. Former students of the University, Woodstock College and Moulton College, who are now engaged in Foreign Missionary service, were named, and the blessing of God was asked upon them and their work. Letters were read from parents of students, graduates and others closely related in sympathy to the University, and their expressions of goodwill and appreciation of the work being done in the Hall were cheering and helpful.   A telegram sent by the Rev. Thomas Trotter, B. A., from Wolfville, Nova Scotia, was greeted with hearty applause.   The Rev. J. P. McEwen, on being called upon, responded in a brief address of sympathetic, earnest counsel.   The meeting, from beginning to end, was one of gracious fellowship and spiritual uplifting.

FRIENDS of McMaster will be glad to learn that the interest in the meetings of the Fyfe Missionary Society continues unabated.   In spite of the temptation, which the suspension of lectures for a whole day affords, to snatch a few free hours to oneself, the attendance at each and all of the meetings of the society has been very gratifying.   The December meeting was full of interest.   Mr. Churchill read a paper giving an excellent digest of the Missionary news of the world during the current year.   Following this was an address by Mr. McAlpine on " The Holy Spirit's Presence and Power in the Lives of Believers," which was well calculated to open up the subject for the discussion which followed.   During the progress of the meeting the Chancellor introduced a native of India, who after some years spent in study was about to return to India as an evangelist.   In the course of his remarks he gave it as his conviction that no great progress could be made by missionaries in

India till the higher classes had been won for Christ. On Dec 12th, the annual public meeting of the Society was held in the Beverley St. Church, President Farmer occupying the chair. After the reading of the Secretary's Annual Report, addresses were given by Rev. Chas. Eaton and Superintendent McEwen. Mr. Eaton's words were stirring and full of enthusiasm. Mr. McEwen's address was very timely. He pointed out the great need for care and caution in receiving candidates for baptism ; and deplored the tendency of the times to make large additions to chuch membership regardless of spiritual qualification. Our last Missionary day was spent in reviewing the christian activity and spiritual life in American colleges. To this end Mr. E. J. Stobo had prepared a very exhaustive report which he read before the Society. The report showed that Canadian colleges compared favorably with those in the States, nor could one help feeling that of all Canadian colleges, we had reason to rejoice that in regard to the spirituality of professors and students alike McMaster University stood second to none. Dr. O. P. Gifford, of Delaware Ave. Baptist Church, Buffalo, will preach our annual sermon on April 12th.

The Librarian acknowledges with thanks the receipt of the following new books for the library :—

From the Mathematical Society :—Joseph Edwards : Elementary Treatise on the Differential Calculus ; from Harvard University : Catalogue for 1895-96 ; from Mr. Frank Sanderson, M.A. : Mortality Experience of Canada Life Assurance Co., 1847-1893 ; and Life Assurance in Canada. From the American Government : Report of the Commissioner of Education, 1892-93.

The following additions have been made by the University :—

W. Sanday : Inspiration ; McMaster University Examination Papers, 1891-95 ; Henry Sweet : A New English Grammar ; An Anglo-Saxon Reader ; J. H. Muirhead : The Elements of Ethics ; Edward Hall : Volcanoes, Past and Present ; George G. Findlay : The Epistles of Paul the Apostle ; J. B. Mozley : Eight Lectures on Miracles ; R. G. Moulton : Shakespeare as a Dramatic Artist ; Edward Caird : The Evolution of Religion, 2 vols. ; George A. Smith : The Book of Isaiah, 2 vols. ; Cunningham Geikie : New Testament Hours (the Gospels) ; A. W. Verrall : The 'Agamemnon' of Æschylus ; W. Y. Sellar : The Roman Poets of the Republic ; the Roman Poets of the Augustan Age (Virgil) ; Horace and the Elegiac Poets ; Stopford A. Brooke : The History of Early English Literature ; Edward Dowden : Shakespeare, a Critical Study of his Mind and Art ; J. J. Lias : Principles of Biblical Criticism ; F. J. A. Hart : Prolegomena to Romans and Ephesians ; W. St. Chad. Boscawen : The Bible and the Monuments ; Christoph Sigwart's Logic, trans. by Helen Dendy, 2 vols. ; A. W. Pollard : Chaucer ; T. R. Lounsbury : Studies in Chaucer, 3 vols. ; S. Leathes : The Law in the Prophets ; J. B. Lightfoot : Notes on Epistles of St. Paul ; Muir and Morley : Watts' Dictionary of Chemistry ; J. A. Symonds : Studies of the Greek Poets, 2 vols. ; Willibald Beyschlag : New Testament Theology, 2 vols. ; Ernst Von Meyer : A History of Chemistry.

MOULTON COLLEGE.

We have been greatly disappointed in the progress our rink has made this winter, although as partial compensation for its non-appearance we had a very pleasant afternoon's skating at one of our city rinks.

Miss Buchan entertained a number of her friends at an Afternoon Tea on Saturday, January 25th. Several of the students attended and spent a very pleasant afternoon, meeting a number of the young people of Bloor Street Church.

The musically inclined members of our school enjoyed hearing two excellent concerts lately, the Mendelssohn Choir and the Albani Concert. We had been looking forward to these entertainments for some time and our expectations were fully realized.

On the Day of Prayer for Colleges we had the privilege of hearing two excellent addresses. Mr. Weeks of Walmer Road led our morning meeting and Mr. Eaton of Bloor St. Church the evening. At the Chapel service Miss Dicklow read us a very kind message from our former principal Miss Fitch, showing us that she still remembers us and has the interests of the College at heart.

On Friday evening, Feb. 21st, a very interesting meeting of the Mission Circle was held. Miss Rogers, who returned from the foreign field last June, spoke to us on the manners and customs of the people of India, and gave very clear and impressive pictures of real life in that country, as she herself has seen it. At this same meeting a very interesting letter from Mrs. Stillwell was read, giving some of her first impressions of India.

The young ladies of M. L. C. all enjoyed the break in the general routine of every day life in the form of the At Home given by the Faculty on Friday, Feb. 14th. The spacious parlors were thrown open to a large number of guests. D'Alesandro's orchestra played at the rear of the main hall, and mingled their music pleasantly with the busy hum in the reception room. The decorations, which were much admired, were due to the efforts of Miss Hart and Mrs. Dignam.

One of the brightest and most pleasant evenings that we have spent this year, was on Saturday, Jan. 25th, when the boarders were given a sleighing party by Mr. Wright and his daughter Miss Josephine. The sleigh started at seven and for two hours we enjoyed the drive in the clear air, while we had ample opportunity to appreciate to the fullest extent the wonderful beauty of the frost work on the trees, which appeared in the electric light to sparkle with millions of diamonds. After this delightful drive, we returned to Mr. Wright's residence where we were entertained in the kindest manner by Mrs. Wright. This evening will long be remembered by our students as one of the pleasant events in their life at Moulton.

Woodstock College.

A slight variation.

In the spring a young man's fancy lightly turns to thoughts of exams ;
Then beneath his midnight taper, he crams and crams and crams and crams.

(with apologies to Lord Tennyson)—B.

WE are sorry to announce the death of the only brother of our fellow student Mr. J. Atkins. We sincerely sympathize with him in his bereavement, and trust that what now seems so hard to bear, may in the end prove to be for the best.

THE same sympathy is extended to Mr. Hurlburt, who a few days ago lost his father. But a year ago his mother died, which casts a deeper shade over this last bereavement.

ONE of the teachers was enrolling a new boy. " Of what denomination are you ?" said the man with the pen. " Well, our folks 'tends meetin' in the smoky hollow school house, three miles an' a half down the Cordroy road."

REV. Mr. Bone made his annual visit to the College on Feb. 13th. His intimate knowledge of men enables him to do a work that few others could perform, and renders his addresses exceedingly interesting. Mr. Bone has a style peculiar to himself but one highly appreciated by the College boys.

PROF. M. S. Clark's lecture on the celebrated French Novelist, Daudet, was both entertaining and edifying. Although most of us were unacquainted with the subject of the lecture we enjoyed this introduction and felt a desire for a better acquaintance with " the Dickens of France."

LA GRIPPE.—The students have had their yearly visitation of " La Grippe," and judging from the prevalence of coughs and colds, and the number of trays sent up to sick rooms its visit was not without effect. However, all have succeeded in weathering the gale, and the fourth year students are back at Latin prose again with their wonted vigor.

THE following officers were elected this month by the Philomathic Society. President, Mr. W. F. Spidell ; Vice President, Mr. F. E. Brophey ; Secretary, Mr. L. C. Stone ; Curator, Mr. F. J. Wellwood ; Marshall, Mr. J. P. McLennan ; Critic, Mr. A. L. McCrimmon, M.A.

ON Thursday, Feb. 6th, a missionary meeting was held in the chapel room. Addresses were delivered on Foreign Missionary Work by Revs. A. P. McDiarmid and La Flamme. The result was a noticeable strengthening of the missionary vitality at the College.

A deep spiritual feeling characterized the gatherings at the College on the day of prayer. Rev. Joshua Roberts of Woodstock gave an address in the forenoon on "The need of a day of prayer for Colleges." In the afternoon Rev. Mr. Hutchinson of Brantford spoke, taking as his subject : "The Holy Spirit." Both addresses were good, and we believe had a permanent effect. Mr. John M. Whyte was also present and by his sweet songs cheered the hearts of the listeners. After tea, the regular College prayer meeting was held, which proved, indeed, to be one of special blessing and consecration.

WE have a good rink here, thanks to the faculty. Some of the ladies' men in the College, for we have a *few* of this genius here, are in a state of discontent at the absence of the fair sex from our rink. They have called a meeting, and have appointed a committee to wait on the Faculty for permission to invite the ladies to our rink. The committee are :—Messrs. LaKais, Phipps and Whittaker. It is said that Mr. Mc-Neill, representing the Faculty, is in *hearty* support of the movement.

OUR hockey-team has more than sustained its reputation this season, and has, up to the present, borne the palm of victory over all opposing teams. The last match, a very interesting one, was with a London team which visited the College on Feb. 1st. Owing to soft weather, the match could not be played on our open-air rink, but took place in the town rink. The game was in every respect a friendly one, and was enjoyed by all the spectators, the score being 3 to 1 in favor of the college. The only accident was a cut from the puck received by one of the visitors.

CHANCELLOR O. C. S. WALLACE visited the College on Feb. 3rd. The students met in the chapel room in the afternoon, for the purpose of listening to the genial head of the University. The address of this gentleman held the attention of even the youngest boys. This we ascribe to the Chancellor's easy and sympathetic manner. There was one remark particularly, a student's axiom, which all that heard it are sure to remember. Never take for granted that you know anything, always prove to yourself that you really do know it. The Chancellor urged upon the students thoroughness in their work.

THE

McMASTER UNIVERSITY MONTHLY.

MARCH, 1896.

DANIEL ARTHUR McGREGOR.

At the mention of the name of D. A. McGregor, what memories come crowding to the mind! And all of them are sweet and inspiring. I have yet to meet the man who knew him well who did not honor and love him. It is indeed fitting that his face and memory should be kept fresh in our minds.

Up and down through our land, in the pulpits and other spheres of life, there are many who were fellow-students of McGregor, and all speak of him with sincerest admiration. When he came to Woodstock College (then the C. L. I.), many at first wondered at the sturdy, ruddy young man from the country. He had a strong and expressive face which bespoke a noble soul within, but he was so exceedingly and really modest that he could scarcely trust himself to express his opinions with any freedom. But shortly he began to feel more at home in his new surroundings, and then his native strength of mind, and solid and accurate information, the result of careful reading in the Osgoode home, gained for him first the respect, and then the admiration, of all. And as the real spirit of the man became more fully known, he was greatly beloved.

As a student his life was of the choicest character. In his studies he was painstaking and accurate. In the literary societies he easily led the van, especially excelling as a brilliant

essayist and logical debater.   In the religious life of the College
he was always a positive and elevating force.   His every day
conduct, so pure and truthful, gave him a vantage ground from
which to exhort, to warn, and to encourage.

As a companion he was especially sought after.   Many an
old student can recall walks and talks most delightful and
profitable which they were privileged at times to have with
Mr. McGregor.   During the hours of freedom from study—from
four to six—he was as light-hearted and merry as a boy.   He
was more than a match for any with his keen but always kindly
mirth and quick repartee; or, if his companion had any sorrow
or perplexity, he was instantly in the fullest sympathy with
him, and ready to comfort, encourage, advise, or, if he thought
the circumstances demanded it, wisely and tenderly to admonish.
Few indeed have been the students who have so completely
won the esteem alike of teachers and fellow-students.

It was not my privilege to be with him in Toronto University; but he was the same there as in Woodstock, only more
fully developed.   All his powers of mind and heart were still
reaching upward.   While attending the University he assumed
the duties of a pastor.   His ideals as to preaching were so high,
and he was so conscientious in endeavoring to attain to them,
that he had not the time to give to society the attention that
he otherwise would. His entire strength was consumed in faithful preparation for the class-room and the pulpit, and in pastoral
duties.   For although he was carrying a heavy course of study,
D. A. McGregor was not the man to enter the pulpit without the
most careful preparation of heart and mind for its sacred duties.
The people of Whitby and Brooklin, of which churches he had
the oversight at that time, bear testimony to his thorough personal work as an under shepherd.

There are those who feel that Mr. McGregor allowed his
regular work so completely to monopolize his time that he did
not take the relaxation and vigorous exercise necessary to sustain and develop his physical powers.   Endowed by nature with
a sturdy frame, his muscles strengthened by the exhilerating
out door toil on the home farm, he did not seem to realize that
any intellectual strain could do him bodily injury.   But after
years seemed to prove that he had drawn during his student

life too heavily and unceasingly upon his physical resources.
At the time, however, neither himself nor his most intimate
friends seemed to have any realization of this. He was so
bright and cheerful; so eager for work; so free to give to others
the sympathy and help which he never sought for himself.

At length the long literary and theological courses were
completed, and he was at liberty to devote his whole time and
strength to the gospel ministry. With high ideals he entered
upon what he supposed would be his lifework. And he had
large hopes too. For although he was the most unassuming
of men, yet he had some just estimate of his own abilities,
accompanied with unbounded faith in the power of the gospel,
and confidence in the Divine promises. He had but two pastorates. The one above mentioned, at Whitby and Brooklin,
where he was ordained in 1878; the other, in the town of Stratford, from 1881 to 1886. With what earnestness of purpose he
threw himself into the work, those who knew the man may well
imagine. His pulpit efforts were of the very best quality. He
had a logical mind, a keen intellect, a well furnished memory,
an exceptional literary taste, an intimate acquaintance with
God's word; his own faith was rooted and grounded in the
truth, and back of all was a man permeated with the Spirit of
Christ and a great heart moved by Divine love. As a pastor,
too, he was faithful and tireless. None were overlooked. Strong
men found in him a wise counsellor, children a tender guide,
and every one a sympathetic friend. He soon became known
in the town as a man of power and of pure life, and his influence
reached far out into the surrounding country, whither he made
frequent excursions with the gospel message. Many instances
might be given of his rare wisdom, power, and tact while pastor.

And Mr. McGregor, unlike too many, did not cease to be a
diligent student after he had obtained his parchment and left the
College halls. His truthful nature sought eagerly the truth.
While he might read papers and magazines, he believed that the
best and most abiding thoughts were to be found in books.
He supplied himself with as many of these as he could procure, and not simply read but mastered them. For years it was
his custom to keep steadily at work till one o'clock in the morning, his overstrained eyes aided by two pairs of glasses. To

what good purpose he toiled, those well know who listened as he spoke from pulpit and platform, and. afterwards in the class-rooms of Toronto Baptist College. For he was not left long in the pastorate, but long enough to prove that he was a master workman in that department of Christian service. A vacancy occurring at this time in the Faculty of Toronto Baptist College, with great unanimity the mind of the denomination turned to the young pastor at Stratford. While, as he himself said, not weary of his first chosen work, yet he was conscious of tastes and talents which made the professoriate attractive to him. Years before, his old teacher, Dr. Fyfe, with that keen insight which always characterized that noble man, had seen in Mr. McGregor possibilities which gave promise of signal service as an educationalist.

As his many friends and the friends of the College saw him begin his work in Toronto, there was a general feeling of satisfaction that one so highly gifted and qualified, a Canadian born, who had constantly breathed the atmosphere and so fully caught the spirit of our Canadian Baptist Church and College life, was to aid in moulding our coming ministry. No one had misgivings as to the quality of the work he would do. He soon proved himself a master in the various departments in which, on account of changes in the Faculty, he was called upon to teach. Successively he lectured in Homiletics and Pastoral Theology, Rhetoric and Oratory, and Mental Science, until, finally, he filled the chair of Systematic Theology, a subject to him most conge-nial. There was only one higher position in the College. The possibility of its being reached came all too soon through the illness and resignation of Dr. Castle, the esteemed Principal. When the time arrived for the appointment of a successor, with not only entire unanimity but with enthusiasm, the minds of the governing bodies, of the Faculty, of the students and of the de-nomination at large, turned to McGregor. So quickly had he proved his right to lead our educational work, not only on account of his great mental power, but equally on account of his nobility of nature.

But he was never permitted to perform the active duties of Principal. Divine grace was to shine forth through him in con-ditions how different! In the fall of 1889 he was stricken down with paralysis, apparently the result of an injury received months previous while handling a heavy piano. Oh, those long and weary autumn and winter days, alternating between hope and despair! Oh, those hallowed and consecrated days! The lessons that were learned at his bedside are an inspiration and a benediction still. The desire for life was strong within him for the sake of his work and his loved ones; but he was as submissive and trustful as a child. Well does the writer remember him saying one day, " I had far rather lie here as I am and know that God is dealing with me than to be well and strong and not be conscious of His presence." How brave he was! And how he hoped against hope. Never was he more the Christian nobleman than during those last months. Like another Samson he manifested even more strength in his death than in his life. I may not dwell upon the closing scenes. Suffice it to say that everything possible was done to restore health or prolong life. The Board of Governors brought a specialist from New York to see him. Then he went to New York hospital. But it was not to be, and on April 25th, 1890, he went from us. His body was brought to the chapel of the College which he loved so well. There tender and appreciative words were spoken over his coffin before it was laid away in Mount Pleasant cemetery.

It would seem fitting that brief mention should be made of other relationships in which Mr. McGregor stood, and of other services which he rendered. In 1881 he was married to Miss Augusta Hull, of Princeton. As might well be imagined he was a most thoughtful, tender, and devoted husband. What a happy home was that of the Stratford pastor and his wife! Many friends and strangers too were blessed with its delightful hospitality. It was indeed a treat to meet Mr. McGregor at his own table, and to listen to the most entertaining, sparkling, or profound table-talk. He was a model host. And when children brightened that home, new qualities, as eminent and captivating as any seen before, shone forth in the father. With what tenderness he loved his children was shown in a special manner when his bright and only boy died. It was a considerable time before he could trust himself to speak at all calmly of his great loss. And it is impossible to read without tears those deeply tender and chaste expressions of affection for his wife and children, which are contained in his letters published in his memoir. And as he loved so he was beloved. His children's happiest hours were those spent in their father's company, and his broken-hearted widow had no desire to live after he was gone, and soon followed him into the presence of that King all glorious of whom he loved so well to think and to speak, and of whom he sang with such rare poetic genius.

I must not delay to speak of the signal service he rendered the denomination while Home Mission Secretary. During his pastorate in Stratford and for two years while teaching in the College, he filled this position. With great wisdom, faithfulness, and patience, he gave himself unstintingly to this important work. No church was too small, no pastor too obscure, to demand the best that was in him. And many an hour when he should have been renewing his exhausted energies in much needed sleep he spent in writing letters or in taking journeys to advise, encourage or admonish. Nor may I tell of his influence in our associations and conventions and through the *Canadian Baptist.*

McGregor was a large man indeed. How rapidly he grew, and how earnestly and wisely he wrought, may be inferred when we remember that it was only nine years from his graduation from the University till his death, and in this time, with the full consent of all, he had gained the position of head of the denomination.

But I feel that I am not presenting as I would the worth and work of this truly noble man. In every relationship of life he seems to me to have reached almost, if not altogether, the ideal. As husband, father, brother, friend, as companion and counsellor, as pastor, preacher, or professor; in logical argument or in playful humor, in force and beauty of expression, whether by speech or pen, he was surpassed by none. Had he an equal ? It is disparaging none, and doing him mere justice, to say that among us all, his contemporaries, in every position and relationship he was *first.*

"Beyond my praise to-day,
  He spurs me yet with his remembered name.
" Captain and Saviour of the host
    Of Christian Chivalry !

We bless Thee for our comrade true,
  Now summoned up to Thee.
We bless Thee for his every step
  In faithful following Thee
And for his good fight fought so well,
  And crowned with victory."

S. S. BATES.

COMPENSATION.

I.

I had a blossom that I lov'd
  More than all flow'rs beside;
It bloom'd at morning, but at noon
      It died.

I sorrow'd for my blossom lost;
  But, while I wept, the earth,
Made rich by dead leaves of my flow'r,
To choicer ones, in that same hour,
      Gave birth.

II.

I had a hope so sweet, so sweet,
  Amid the noise and strife,—
A hope of earth.   Its fleeting breath
Fann'd virtues, panting in their death,
      To life.

EVA ROSE YORK.

GRAND LIGNE EDUCATIONAL WORK.

The Grande Ligne Mission has regularly comprised in its educational work three schools, one in Quebec, another in Coaticook, and the other Feller Institute at Grande Ligne. Besides these schools, the Grande Ligne Board sometimes sends a teacher to such places as Sorel or Maskinongé for the summer months to teach the children of the converts, who are not able to support a school of their own, and who object to having their children brought up in the superstitions from which they themselves have just been delivered, or being subjected to the persecutions that they would certainly receive in the Catholic schools.

The Quebec school, doing primary work, was first opened up in September, 1895, to be a sort of auxiliary to our mission work there. This school is in charge of Miss Carrie Bullock, formerly a teacher at Feller Institute. Up to Christmas, 1895, the attendance was 41 pupils, of whom 20 were either Jews or Roman Catholics.

The school at Coaticook is only partially supported by the Grande Ligne Mission, the remaining support being given by the Eastern Baptist Association. This school was organized a few years ago by Miss Rue Parker, for the purpose of giving better educational advantages to the French and Catholic children of the district. It is now in charge of Miss Kate Stobo, daughter of Rev. E. J. Stobo, known and honored for his services in Quebec. Last year the number enrolled in this school was 88, of whom 26 were Roman Catholics. This year up to Christmas, 1895, the attendance was 60, of whom 22 were Catholics, 14 being French and 8 Irish. This school is becoming well known among the Catholics, and is very highly spoken of by those who send their children to it. That it has a positive religious influence is shown by the fact that the priest has preached against it, and forbidden his people to send their children to it. The only effect his preaching has had, however, so far, has been to take away one French boy, whom he promised to send to Ottawa to be educated for the priesthood, if he would attend the French school for another year. Miss Stobo writes that a good many of the parents have spoken to her about the hymns and the texts of Scripture which she has taught the children. They say they are very beautiful, and they like to hear the children repeat them at home.

The most important of our schools, however, is Feller Institute. The purpose of this school is, (1) to give an education to the children of our French Protestant converts, who have no other means of getting it in Protestant schools; (2) to evangelize both Protestant and Catholic children, young men and women who come to the school ; (3) to seek out and train as far as we can young men suitable and capable for mission work. Nearly all our present missionaries and mission workers have come from the students of this school, and unless unexpected outside help arrives, we believe that most of our future workers will come from the same place.

At Feller Institute there are to be found yearly from 125 to 135 pupils, who come from all parts of Quebec, a few coming from the New England States and Eastern Ontario. From ten to fifteen per cent. of these students are Catholics ; about an equal number are of English origin, and the remainder are French Protestants. Thus it will be seen that the Grande Ligne Mission has under the direct, personal and daily supervision and influence of its teachers from 250 to 275 pupils per year, of whom nearly twenty-four per cent. are Roman Catholics. This influence we believe is of the best Christian character, and who can tell what splendid fruitage it may produce in the coming years ?

At Feller Institute, which is our only residential school, the English students all pay the full fee of twelve dollars per month for tuition and board. The French are required to give all that we believe, upon investigation, they or their parents are able to pay. Some few pay the full fee. In age the pupils vary from thirteen to thirty years. They are drawn from all classes of society, but the same requirements are made of all, and no privilege is granted to one that is not under similar circumstances granted to all.

In intellectual training our pupils range all the way from the alphabet to the entrance into the university. Some young men of twenty or twenty-five years of age are just beginning to learn to read in their own language, having never been to school until they came here.   This year in fact we have sixteen pupils between thirteen and twenty-eight years old, who would be classed in the lowest reading class in Ontario public schools. Five of these would average twenty-three years of age.   Some of them can speak passably well both English and French, but cannot read except the very smallest words in either language. On the other hand, there are annually about twenty-five pupils here studying Latin, and about ten in Greek, which number we think will compare very favorably with that of the pupils in these subjects in many of the Ontario High Schools.   This year we have five students who are preparing to write on the university entrance examinations next June.   There are six others preparing for teacher's certificates, or to enter some theological college next year.   These will compare very favorably as a whole with the Ontario High School pupils.

In the higher classes in English, French, and Mathematics, the number of students is much larger than those above given, for the reason that all pupils are required to take these subjects, while only those who intend to take a more extended liberal education, or are preparing for some examination, study Latin or Greek.

As most of our students go to McGill University, the amount of work done in English, Classics, and Mathematics is largely determined by the requirements for entrance there.   At the same time we do not confine ourselves to the limits set by Mc- Gill.   In English we add to its required work the critical study of at least two standard poetical works.   In Mathematics, three books of Euclid, and Trigonometry are added.   In Latin extra work is done in Bradley's Latin Prose, and sometimes a book of Cicero.   In Greek we add one book of Homer's Iliad, and Arnold's Greek Prose, while in French nearly three times the required amount of work is done.   We do this extra work in these subjects in order to give our students who may enter Mc- Master University, where the entrance standard is higher, a better chance to compete with those who enter there from Woodstock and Moulton Colleges.

Instruction in the Bible is not neglected.   There is one class a week in Bible Controversy, on subjects on which the students are likely to come into conflict with their Roman Catholic neighbors.   Another class a week takes up the New Testament doctrines.   Another meets three times a week to study New Testament History in French, and there are three more classes, two French and one English, meeting three times a week each, in Old Testament History.   Besides this daily class-room work, the religious life of the school is still further developed by the chapel service every morning before classes begin, prayers every night at the close of study hours, the general prayer-meeting every Wednesday evening, the boys' and girls' separate prayer-meetings every Saturday evening, Bible-classes studying the International S. S. lessons every Sunday afternoon, and morning and evening services in the church every Sunday.   Regular attendance upon these services is required of all pupils, both Catholic and Protestant.

The teaching in some of the primary subjects, such as geography, dictation, reading, and the lower classes in arithmetic, grammar and history, is done in both French and English. This makes the work in these subjects double what it is in most schools.   British and Canadian history and hygiene are taught altogether in French, while Latin, Greek, Geometry, Algebra, and the higher classes in arithmetic are taught entirely from English text-books.

There is provided also a good course in music that takes the entire time of one teacher and an assistant.   There are, however, two subjects usually taught to some extent in High Schools that are altogether left out of our course, viz : German and the Sciences.   There has been as yet, on the part of our students, no call for these subjects.   If they were required of us, we should be compelled to engage another teacher, for our present staff is already heavily overloaded.   Painting and drawing also find no place in our school.

Feller Institute differs very much from other schools in the amount of manual labor required of the pupils.   All boys and girls have to take the entire care of their own rooms.   They have in turn also to sweep and dust their respective buildings, dormitories, halls and class-rooms every morning.   The chores at the barn, maintainence of fires in the furnaces, cleanliness and order of the grounds, shovelling of snow and many other odd jobs are the work of the boys.   The girls are kept from posing as mere fine ladies of society, too nice to work, which (neuter gender) we hope none of our girls may ever become, by being required in different bands to wash the dishes, and do the ironing for the whole school every week. In the case of some students this kind of work is taken in partial payment for their tuition and board here.

The total annual expense of Feller Institute is about $7,000, of which over $4,000 is covered by the receipts from the students. Our endowment fund furnishes $1,000, and about $800 is provided in the shape of scholarships. This leaves about $1,200 to be taken from the general funds of the mission.

To the successful work of our mission schools there are many hindrances. One is the natural carelessness and indifference of the parents, many of whom do not know the value of even a common–school education. They have managed to get a scanty living without an education, and they think their children can do the same. Consequently, they will keep their children at home in the spring and fall on the least excuse, while they will not think of sending them to school if there is any work for them to do on the farm. Many parents also fear that their children will be estranged from the life of the farm by sending them away from home to school. This fear is not altogether groundless, for students, after spending a few years here, are often not content to settle down to the monotonous and unprogressive life of farming, as it is carried on in this province. Many of our young men, therefore, have had to fight their own way, sometimes against their parents' will, to earn a little money in advance every summer in order that they might get a little education during the winter. There are others who would gladly do the same, but they are kept at home doing chores all winter, without pay and without schooling, until they are twenty-one years old, victims very often to the selfishness rather than to the poverty of unenlightened parents. These we are glad to have come to us, for they make our best students, and there are many bright examples among them, that have done honor to our school, and to French Protestantism. French Catholics also, besides fearing for their religion, are afraid that their children will lose their national character and become Anglicized. This fear, however, we overcome by giving them a better training in the French language than they can get in most of their own schools.

Our English friends sometimes criticise us for receiving students for so little money, or for less than the cost of their education. In other words they say that our fees are sometimes so low that it amounts to paying the pupils to come to the school. In some cases this is true. But do not our missionaries do the same thing among the Telugus ? And what is their excuse for so doing ? Again, why is it that we have a large endowment for McMaster University, Moulton and Woodstock Colleges, and that students can there get an education at less than its actual cost ? Is it not that more of our Baptist young people than could otherwise do so may become enlightened, intelligent, Baptist Christian citizens, and a means of enlightening others ? A worthy object, surely. Very well then ! Can we afford that the children, young women and young men who come here, many of whom have to strive a good deal harder to earn the means to come to school at all, than young men in similar circumstances in Ontario, can we afford that these shall always remain the same agricultural and commercial, social and political, religious and moral incubus to our country that their ancestors have unfortunately been ? Can we allow them always through ignorance to endanger the freedom and progress of all Canada, as their fellow-countrymen are doing at the present time ? The very asking of these questions should be their sufficient answer.

But let it be remembered that we are not pauperizing our students. So soon as it becomes evident that any pupil is not taking advantage of the opportunities here offered, or that he expects help without any effort on his own part, so soon are our doors closed to that pupil. We try only to help pupils to help themselves, and if they will not, our help ceases too.

But little more need be said. Our work will stand on its merits. If any one is still incredulous, let him visit the school, and examine closely into its work, and we are confident he will be both surprised and delighted with the result of his investigation.

E. NORMAN.

Grand Ligne.

A TRUE IDEAL OF EDUCATION.*

Mr. Chairman, Members of the Faculty, Fellow-Students and Friends,—I am to speak to you to-night on a true ideal of education. Does this topic seem threadbare and worn with age? Then let the great importance of the subject be the plea that will justify its choice.

Looking back along the line of history, I find that in every nation that has attained to any prominence in civilization, there has been an educational system of some sort. Even in Egypt, which was one of the oldest if not the very oldest of the ancient empires, there was an educational system so thoroughly organized that it could be said of Moses, 1,500 years before Christ, that he was trained in all the learning of the Egyptians; and when God wanted a statesman to give laws to His people, it was not some wandering and unlettered shepherd but this Egyptian-trained lawyer, whom He appointed, ordained and commissioned to assume the office and perform the task.

I find also that those educational systems were centered about certain ideals to which the systems themselves were conformed, and for the securing of which the educational methods were directed. A few examples will illustrate :

In the Confucian system, which prevails to-day in China, the whole aim of education is the Civil Service. There is no country where students are more diligent or painstaking, or where a larger number present themselves at the tri-annual examinations, but the one thought of each and every candidate is that the obtaining of a degree will be the passport to one of the many offices in the gift of the government.

The system of which Buddha was the founder had in view not the uplifting but the annihilation of the individual. Life, according to his teaching, is only evil continually ; and the supreme purpose of all effort should be the blotting out of personality and the sinking of existence in undisturbed Nirvana, absolute quietude, and self-effacement.

The Grecian idea was more material and more practical. There the State was everything and the citizen existed only for

---

*Founder's Day Address at McMaster University, 1895.

the State. For the State he was born, for the State he lived, for the State he died. Living or dying he belonged to the State.

The Roman thought was military. Rome went forth conquering and to conquer. One by one the countries surrendered to Roman arms until the city of the Tiber ruled the world. It was natural then that to the Roman the one object of life should be conquest, and the ideal man should be the soldier. To this end was Roman education. To march and countermarch, to stand in the cohorts and handle the pilum and the sword, this was the ambition of every Roman lad.

These ideals, so far as they went, were praiseworthy. The Civil Service needs trained officials. The repression of the individual is wise and safe. Citizenship in any state is important. Conquest is worth striving for in any department of life. But the weakness of all these systems is their one-sidedness. They are all of them partial in their application, and all of them together would not produce anything more than a man entirely earthly in aim and method of life. There is in them nothing of aspiration or up-reaching. There is in them no recognition of anything higher or nobler than the powers of this world, and in the case of Buddhism there is a shrinking from even these, and a desire to find refuge in complete forgetfulness. But any system of education that is to be world-wide in its application, that is to make for the highest good of the state and for the truest development of the individual, must include all that these systems included and more. What then is a true ideal of education? It is the cultivation of the whole being of the student so as to develop the very best of which every student is capable bodily, mentally and spiritually. Nothing less than this will be a true ideal of cultivation, and this ideal if realized will satisfy all the demands of society, the state and the individual.

Have we any pattern or model to which we may conform in our pursuit of this ideal? Certainly. Long ago there lived in Palestine a man who was the embodiment of human nature in its highest form. Physically he was perfect, being free from all taint of disease and all bodily weakness. Mentally he was marvellously keen, intuitively perceiving the truth of all questions however shrouded in the fogs of casuistry, without going through the slow process of argumentation. Spiritually he was so highly developed that he lived and moved and had his being in a region to which the saintliest of all ages have never reached even by the most arduous toil. Here then is an example of the very best of which human nature is capable, and here is the incarnate ideal to which every true system of education will strive to attain.

It will be evident then that the education for which I plead is Christian education. We hear much in those days of a rallying cry " back to Christ." Whatever this may mean in theology it certainly is true in education, and the truest system will be that which produces the most Christ-like character.

If this definition is valid, it will bear the test of being applied to details. Can we teach Mathematics in this spirit? Why not? What are the Binomial Theorem and the Differential Calculus and the Laws of Kepler but the methods by which Christ wrought when he made the worlds? Can Science be so taught? Assuredly. What are we doing when we study Geology but, as Hugh Miller expressed it, walking in the " footprints of the Creator?" and what is the science of Astronomy but as one said as he sat at his telescope, the " thinking of God's thoughts after him?" Can we teach Philosophy thus? Yes verily: and only as it is thus taught, will Philosophy have any profit. Vinet, the Swiss theologian and philosopher, declares that Philosophy is concerned about three questions—Whence? How? Whither? Has philosophy by searching found an answer to these? Let the speculations, the theorizings, the disputings of the various schools of philosophers from Thales to Hegel and from Hegel to Herbert Spencer, bear witness to their failure. But back to Christ let us go, as did one who sat at the feet of the philosophers of his day, and who turning from them found in the Teacher of Nazareth the answer which he penned in Romans 11 : 36—" For of Him (Whence), and through Him (How) and to Him (Whither) are all things," and in that brief sentence we have the answer to the profoundest problems of philosophy.

In view of the fact that philosophy is being taught in our own land in such a manner as to undermine the very foundations of evangelical truth, we have reason to congratulate ourselves that the chair of Philosophy in this institution has been and is now occupied by a Christian teacher who is loyal to the

truth as it is in Christ.   Here then we have an educational pro
cess that will lift men to the highest development of which they
are capable, and enable them to respond to all the demands that
may be made upon them in society and in the state.   Here we
have an educational system including all that other systems
have contained, and adding to them an attachment of our life to
the source of all being.   Here we have an educational ideal that
will not have finished its work in us until we are all brought
from step to step to the fulness of the stature of Christian manhood and womanhood.

P K. Dayfoot.

Students' Quarter.

PAUL'S CONCEPTION OF THE GOSPEL MINISTER.

The interest of the New Testament centres, for the most
part, about two characters—one, the despised and rejected Nazarene, the other, a young man who, when the new teaching
entered the synagogue of Cilicia, opposed it with all the bitter-
ness of a Pharisee of the Pharisees.   A murderer of Stephen, a
persecutor of the Christians, he is met by the Lord Jesus Christ,
his opposition crushed to the ground, his heart filled with a high
and holy purpose, and his talents employed in preaching " the
faith of which he once made havoc."   It is hardly possible to
exaggerate the extent, the importance, the permanence of the
services which were rendered to Christianity by Paul of Tarsus.
He is the great example of a true minister of the gospel.   In the
Acts of the Apostles and in his own Epistles we get glimpses of
his heart and are able to comprehend something of the idealof
a gospel minister which found a place there.   Lofty it was in
very truth, but as we consider the man may we not say that he
attained it ?

The purpose of this paper is to examine the life and writings of the Apostle to the Gentiles, and, by an inductive study

2

to re-construct, imperfectly it may be, Paul's general conception
of the ministry. There is no figure in any age which so deserves
to be set up as a model for Christian ministers, and there is no
pastor who so clearly apprehended God's thought of the ministry
which he had "received of the Lord Jesus Christ." Let us examine then Paul's idea of

I. *The Minister as a Man.*—On two different occasions
Paul specified at considerable length the qualifications of a minister of Jesus Christ. The first passage is I Tim. 3: 2-7—" A
bishop then must be blameless, the husband of one wife, vigilant,
sober, of good behaviour, given to hospitality, apt to teach ; not
given to wine, no striker, not greedy of filthy lucre ; but patient,
not a brawler, not covetous ; one that ruleth well his own house,
having his children in subjection with all gravity ; (for if a man
know not how to rule his own house, how shall he take care of
the church of God ?) ; not a novice, lest being lifted up with
pride he fall into the condemnation of the devil. Moreover, he
must have a good report of them which are without, lest he fall
into reproach and the snare of the devil." So when Paul directs
Titus to ordain elders, he gives the same directions almost to a
word—" If any be blameless, the husband of one wife, having
faithful children, not accused of riot or unruly. For a bishop
must be blameless as the steward of God ; not self-willed, not
soon angry, not given to wine, no striker, not given to filthy
lucre ; but a lover of hospitality, a lover of good men, sober, just,
holy, temperate ; holding fast the faithful word as he hath been
taught, that he may be able by sound doctrine both to exhort
and to convince the gainsayers." Titus 1 : 6-9. He urges Timothy
to be " an ensample to them that believe, in word, in manner of
life, in love, in faith, in purity ; and he himself is so conscious of
being without reproach that he exhorts the Philippians as follows :—" The things which ye both learned and received and
heard and saw in me, these things do, and the God of peace shall
be with you." It would seem from these passages that any disciple of Christ, of blameless manners and pure character, meek,
forbearing, temperate, sober, just, holy, thoroughly attached to
the doctrines of the gospel, having a natural gift for teaching
and having some experience in the Christian life—not a novice

—has the qualifications for the ministry according to the Pauline standard. So much for personal character and gifts. The apostle requires more than this. He regards

II. *The Minister as an Apostle.*—We use the word in its primary sense, "a sent one." He is a "minister of Jesus Christ." How came he to "minister unto the Lord?" Did he thrust himself into this sacred calling, was he constrained by others, or is he "a chosen vessel?" There seem to be two marks by which the candidate for the ministry may know that preaching the gospel is his life work. The first of these is

a. *The subjective call*—Paul speaks of himself as "a called apostle," "separated unto the gospel of God." In Damascus Ananias had said: "Brother Saul . . . . The God of our fathers hath appointed thee to know his will, and to see the Righteous One and to hear a voice from his mouth, for thou shalt be a witness unto all men of what thou hast seen and heard." Before Agrippa Paul represents Christ as declaring that he had appeared to him "to appoint him a minister"; and therefore in writing to the Galatians he tells them that he has been "called through His grace" . . . . to preach Him among the Gentiles. He speaks of Archippus as receiving the ministry in the Lord, and warns the elders at Ephesus to take heed to the flock over which the Holy Ghost had made them overseers. So conscious is he that the minister is a "called" man that he cries "How shall they preach except they be sent?" and so intense is his conviction that he is "separated unto the gospel of God" that he pours out his heart to the Corinthians in the burning declaration :— "Though I preach the gospel I have nothing to glory of ; for necessity is laid upon me ; yea, woe is unto me, if I preach not the gospel !"

But may not the preacher be mistaken as to his call ? May he not be in error regarding his motives and overrate his capacity ? There is another evidence by which a man may be assured that he has not mistaken the voice of God, viz:

b. *The call of his brethren*—Whether Paul was ever ordained as a minister of the gospel, during the early years of his preaching career, is uncertain. To the Galatians he writes as "an apostle not from men, neither through man but through

Jesus Christ and God the Father." It *is* certain that he was designated as a missionary. "Now there were at Antioch, in the church that was there, prophets and teachers, Barnabas and Symeon that was called Niger, and Lucius of Cyrene, and Manaen the foster-brother of Herod the tetrarch, and Saul. And as they ministered unto the Lord and fasted, the Holy Ghost said, ' Separate me Barnabas and Saul for the work whereunto I have called them.' Then when they had fasted and prayed, and laid their hands on them they sent them away. So they being sent forth by the Holy Ghost went down to Seleucia and from thence they sailed to Cyprus." Here then we have the church, under the direction of the Holy Spirit, setting men apart for a special work. As we follow the history of the gospel among the Gentiles, we find Paul on the return trip of the first missionary journey appointing " elders in every church," and in the closing years of his life exhorting Titus to appoint elders in every city of Crete. He warns Timothy : " Neglect not the gift that is in thee, which was given thee by prophecy, with the laying on of the hands of the presbytery," from which we gather that ordination was by the eldership. So important did Paul consider the work, and so many were the dangers of unworthy men entering the ministry that we find him advising his son in the faith to "lay hands hastily on no man." To sum up—Paul holds to a personal divine call to the work, in the necessity of the ministry to the life of the church, in publicly accrediting the minister of Christ by the laying on of hands, and in exercising great care as to those who are thus accredited.

We now proceed to consider

III. *The Minister as a Preacher.*—In the letters to Timothy Paul speaks of " the gospel whereunto I was appointed a preacher and an apostle and a teacher," or as the words may read, " a herald, a sent one and a teacher." As an apostle he occupied a peculiar relation to the Lord Jesus Christ, standing side by side, though " born out of due time," with the fishermen of Galilee whom Christ chose " to be with him, and that he might send them forth to preach, and that they might have authority to cast out devils." For the sake of convenience we shall consider heralding and teaching as two aspects of the same work, and shall characterize them as what is commonly called preaching, and to this work we believe Paul thought every minister of the gospel is called.   What then is

1. *The preacher's theme?*—In Damascus Paul preached that Jesus is the Christ, the long-looked-for Messiah; in Antioch of Pisidia his first sermon centered around the resurrection; in Ephesus he calls the elders to witness: " I shrank not from declaring unto you anything that is profitable, and teaching you publicly and from house to house, testifying both to Jews and to Greeks repentance toward God and faith toward our Lord Jesus Christ." Before Felix he reasons of " righteousness, temperance and the judgment to come," and tells Agrippa, " I stand unto this day testifying both to small and great, saying nothing but what the prophets and Moses did say should come ; how that Christ must suffer, and how that He first, by the resurrection of the dead, should proclaim light both to the people and to the Gentiles." In the Roman prison the old man preaches " the kingdom of God and teaches the things concerning the Lord Jesus Christ," and in view of the headsman's axe charges his own son Timothy to " preach the word." He writes to the Corinthians: " I delivered unto you first of all that which also I received, how that Christ died for our sins according to the scriptures ; and that he was buried ; and that he hath been raised on the third day according to the scriptures; and that he appeared to Cephas"; furthermore, he proclaimed "Christ Jesus as Lord." So earnest is he in defending this gospel that he cries out, " If any man preacheth unto you any gospel other than that which ye received, let him be anathema " (Gal. 1 : 9). In one word the preacher's message is "the things concerning the Lord Jesus Christ."

So much for the message.   What then should be

2. *The preacher's purpose?*—Paul appears to regard it as two-fold :

a. *The salvation of sinners*—His message to both Jews and Greeks was " repentance toward God and faith toward our Lord Jesus Christ," and in Iconium he " so spake that a great multitude of both Jews and Greeks believed." He tells the Corinthians: " To the weak I became weak that I might gain the weak ; I am become all things to all men that I may by all means *save some.'*

His " heart's desire and prayer to God for Israel is that they may be saved;" and concerning the Galatians he writes: " We also thank God without ceasing, that, when ye received from us the word of the message, even the word of God, ye accepted it not as the word of men, but as it is in truth the word of God," and deplores the fact that Judaizing teachers " forbid us to speak to the Gentiles that they may be saved." His thought of the world is, " All have sinned and come short of the glory of God"; his thought of atonement, " While we were yet sinners Christ died for us"; his conception of the medium of salvation, " Believe on the Lord Jesus Christ and thou shalt be saved "; his purpose in heralding the message, to "save some." But the gospel preacher is not content with merely heralding Christ as a Saviour who frees from the penalty of sin; he labors that he "may present every man perfect in Christ." Col. 1: 28. This leads us to consider Paul's view of

b. *The edification of the saints.*—To the Apostle the newly regenerated soul is a " babe in Christ " for whom milk and not strong meat is the appropriate food; but to " the full-grown " (1 Cor. 2: 6) he teaches "God's wisdom in a mystery." It will thus appear that to " feed the flock of God," to " rightly divide the word of truth," is a work requiring superior knowledge and skill. The gifts of the ascended Christ to the Church were for the " perfecting of the saints, unto the work of ministering unto the building up of the body of Christ," and one of the essentials in a bishop Paul declares to be aptness to teach. He exhorts Timothy to " give heed to reading, to exhortation, to teaching," and tells him that " every scripture inspired of God is also profitable for teaching, for reproof, for correction, for instruction in righteousness, that the man of God may be complete, furnished completely unto every good work." He believed that " great is the mystery of godliness," and his letters to the churches are occupied with the profoundest problems of human life. He is " a debtor both to Greeks and Barbarians, both to the wise and to the unwise," and in his letters does not neglect the " deep things of God," but dwells upon them so that Peter is obliged to confess that in the writings of his beloved brother Paul there " are some things hard to be understood." Though " not many wise after the flesh are called " into the Kingdom, though slaves compose the principal element in the early church, when Paul would write to the Romans, his letter is characterized by strict logic and lofty ideas; and when he would warn the churches against· false teaching, he sends out a circular letter, generally known as the Epistle to the Ephesians, marked by involved sentences and profound mysticism. What a commentary upon the modern clamor for simplicity in preaching! The Epistle to the Romans is not simple; the letter to the Galatians is not simple, nor is that to the Ephesians; yet these letters were read to the assembled churches composed, though they were, of the poor and ignorant and despised of this world. "We speak wisdom among the full-grown, yet a wisdom not of this world....but we speak God's wisdom in a mystery.... which things we also speak not in words which man's wisdom teacheth, but which the spirit teacheth, comparing spiritual things with spiritual" (1 Cor. 2: 6-13), "admonishing every man and teaching every man in all wisdom that we may present every man perfect in Christ" (Col. 1 : 29). It is thus very evident that gospel preaching must l e marked by profundity as well as simplicity; that the flock must have not milk only but strong meat also; that the whole counsel of God must be declared if the hearers are to be "filled with the knowledge of his will in all spiritual wisdom and understanding." It is very interesting, therefore, to note the relation of theological to moral teaching in Paul's epistles. The first half of his letters is generally occupied with doctrinal statements, the second with moral exhortations. To Paul Christian morality was emphatically a morality of motives. The whole history of Christ, in the great features of his journey from heaven to earth, and from earth back to heaven again, is a series of examples to be copied by Christians in their daily conduct. The commonest acts of humility are to be imitations of his condescension, and the ruling motive of love in their relations to others to be the recollection of their common connection with him. The doctrines thus become living fountains of motives for well-doing. After such teaching no wonder Paul can write to the Colossians: "As therefore ye received Christ Jesus the Lord, so walk in him, having in him your root, and in him the foundation on which ye are continually built up; persevering steadfastly in your

faith as ye were taught, and abounding in thanksgiving."
Col. 2 : 7.

And now a most delightful phase of our study is presented:—

IV. *The Minister as a Student.*—The materials, however,
are very fragmentary. Before we proceed to examine them let
us think of the age in which the great apostle lived. Never
was the cultivation of the intellect and taste carried to higher
perfection. The poets and orators, the historians, sculptors and
architects of this heathen world, are, to the present day, our
acknowledged masters. And this tremendous force was all
arrayed against the Church of Christ. Yet God chose "the
weak things of the world to confound the mighty." In Corinth
the man of "much learning" (Acts 26 : 24) spoke "not with
excellency of speech or of wisdom proclaiming the mystery of
God." His was the simple story of a crucified Messiah, with no
"persuasive words of wisdom" to embellish it. Nevertheless,
here and there in his Epistles we catch glimpses of his thought
of the preacher as a student. To Timothy he writes : "Until I
come apply thyself to public reading, exhortation and teaching.
Neglect not the gift that is in thee, which was given thee by
prophecy with the laying on of the hands of the presbytery.
Let these things be thy care; give thyself wholly to them; that
thy improvement may be manifest unto all men." 1 Tim. 4 :
13-15. It is very evident that faithful preparation for the
public services of the church is counted by Paul a prime essential to success in the ministry. Timothy is again exhorted:
"Be diligent to present thyself unto God as one proved trust-
worthy by trial, a workman not to be ashamed, declaring the
word of truth without distortion." II Tim. 2 : 15. The scriptures are "profitable for teaching, for confutation, for correction,
for righteous discipline; that the man of God may be fully
prepared and thoroughly furnished for every good work."
II Tim. 3 : 17. Here it is clear that the minister of the gospel
must be acquainted with the Word of God in its multiplied
applications to the needs of men, and such knowledge involves
hard study. No man can declare the Word of God without dis-
torting it unless he has entered into its spirit and understands
the relation of part to part.

It would not be difficult to found a presumptive proof of
Paul's own practice in this matter from the wonderful acquaint-

ance with the Old Testament which he shows in his writings, and from his ability to combat the errors of Gnosticism when they appeared in the churches. His epistles are always marked by intellectual vigor and acuteness. Nothing weak ever came from his pen, and the presumption is that, all his life, he was a student in every sense of the word. A most pathetic picture is presented in his last letter. He has been sentenced to death, and the old man shivers in a gloomy cell in the Roman prison. He writes Timothy: "The cloak that I left at Troas with Carpus bring with thee; and the books, but especially the parchments." The cloak to warm him, but why ask for the books? Do we not see here a flash of student enthusiasm in "the prisoner of Jesus Christ"? We prefer to think so. Both presumptive evidence and actual statements show that Paul believed that the minister of Jesus Christ should be a diligent student.

But it is as a pastor that Paul reveals to us his heart. The good old man almost seems to talk with us as we read his letters to the Corinthians, the Galatians and the Philippians. What tenderness and fidelity and zeal we see in the apostle of Jesus Christ! Let us gather up the passages which reveal his conception of

V. *The Minister as a Pastor.*—In the outset we must draw attention to the fact that, what, in our day, is popularly called pastoral work, was almost unknown in the apostolic age. It is true that at Ephesus Paul taught publicly and "from house to house" but pastoral visitation, as we have it, is a product of the ages. If, therefore, we should appear to neglect this side of the pastor's work, it will be remembered that an inductive study of the Epistles does not yield materials for such a treatment.

What is Paul's thought of a Christian pastor? He is appointed to "take care of the church of God." How shall he perform his work so as to win His praise? (I Cor. 4 : 5). It seems to me that Paul based the outer life upon the inner, and that it is beyond question he thought that the pastor's private life should be characterized by

1. *Prayer.*—Let us see his own fidelity in this matter. "God is my witness, whom I serve in my spirit in the gospel of His Son, how unceasingly I make mention of you always in my prayers, making request, if by any means now at length I may

be prospered by the will of God to come to you." (Rom. 1: 9).
" I . . . . . cease not to give thanks for you, making mention of
you in my prayers." (Eph. 1: 16).   " Always in every supplication of mine on *behalf of you all* making my supplication with
joy." (Phil. 1: 4.)   How much is involved in these statements
we can only guess, but it does appear that the Apostle to the
Gentiles laid the case of each church before the Lord, yea more
than that—every member found a place in his desire and prayer
to God.   He exhorts the Ephesians to " supplication for all the
saints," and we cannot believe that he would ask others to do
what he himself failed to do.   The great heart of Paul beat with
the warmest solicitude and love for every member of his flock,
e. g. : the incestuous person at Corinth, Euodia and Syntyche at
Philippi, Archippus of Colosse, Onesiphorus at Ephesus and the
multitude of persons at Rome to whom he sends greeting.   He
lived in the atmosphere of prayer—prayer for himself, prayer
for the churches, " prayer for all the saints."   The prayer life is
of necessity secret, and the glimpses which we get in the Epistles give only the faintest clues to the tender persistence of the
Apostle in his supplications before the throne.   We can well believe that those whom he admonished " night and day with
tears " were the subjects of many an earnest petition in the prophet's chamber.   May we not say that the tearful admonition
was likely preceded by tearful petition, and that the tenderness
of soul with which he approached his people was an outcome of
his secret communion with the Father.   We cannot enter into
the secret chamber and discover what transpired there ; we
know not " the strong crying and tears " which its walls witnessed ; we are unacquainted with the language in which the
overburdened heart of Paul carried its care and sorrow to Him
who put him into the ministry ; but this we do know that no
one ever became a prince with men unless he first was a prince
with God.   The Apostle of the Gentiles was, beyond doubt, a
princely workman.   We believe, therefore, that he won his coro-
net in the secret chamber ; and there too must every minister of
our own day win his most glorious victories.

Another distinguishing trait of character found in the gospel minister claims our notice.   Paul believes that he should be

2. *Earnest and faithful*—Here again we can examine only

the merest fragment of the evidence. In his farewell address at Ephesus he says: " wherefore I testify unto you this day that I am pure from the blood of all men. For I shrank not from declaring unto you the whole counsel of God. Take heed unto yourselves and to all the flock, in the which the Holy Ghost hath made you bishops, to feed the church of God, which He purchased with his own blood. . . . . Wherefore watch ye, remembering that by the space of three years I ceased not to admonish every one night and day with tears." Consider the affirmations made here: Every man has been admonished with all tenderness; the work has been continuous, " night and day"; the whole counsel of God has been declared, whether it is pleasing or not; and therefore Paul is free from the blood of all men. What pastor can say as much with a clear conscience? Too often our language is, " Oh that I had been more faithful !"

An elder or bishop, Paul believed, is a ruler of the flock. He is placed over it "in the Lord," (II Thess. 5: 12); he has the right to "reprove, rebuke and exhort," (II Tim. 4: 2), and to do so "with all authority," (Titus 2: 15), because of the divine message he bears; he is to "command and teach," (I Tim. 4: 12), and "the elders that rule well" are to be "counted worthy of double honor," (I Tim. 5: 17), As a consequence we have Paul rebuking incest, faction and profanation of the supper at Corinth, heresy in Galatia, strife at Philippi and idleness and gossip at Thessalonica. Yet while all this is so, the tone of Paul's letters is always that of loving appeal. Listen to some scattered sentences from the letters to the Corinthians : " I write not these things to shame you, but to admonish you as my beloved children. For though you should have ten thousand tutors in Christ, yet have ye not many fathers; for in Christ Jesus I begat you through the gospel. I beseech you, therefore, be ye imitators of me." " Are we beginning again to commend ourselves ? or need we, as do some, epistles of commendation to you or from you ? Ye are our epistle, written in our hearts, known and read of all men." " We are ambassadors, therefore on behalf of Christ, as though God were entreating by us : we beseech you on behalf of Christ be ye reconciled to God." Or hear this touching appeal to the Galatians: " My little children, of whom I am again in travail until Christ be formed in you, yea, I could wish to be present with you now, and to change my voice; for I am perplexed about you." When we remember that these words proceed from a soul bursting with a sense of wrong, and recall the difference between the greeting in this Epistle as compared with those to other churches, we can feel the wondrous tenderness of the Apostle's heart. He begins with a brief, plain address, " To the churches of Galàtia," and then breaks at once into the subject of which his mind is so indignantly full : " I am amazed that you are so quickly shifting from Him who called you into the grace of Christ into a different gospel, which is not merely another, only there are some who are troubling you and wanting to reverse the gospel of Christ. But even though we or an angel from heaven should preach contrary to what we preached unto you let him be accursed." Yet the soul that can be stirred to its very depths with indignation on account of disloyalty to Christ, can also at the same time fathom the deeps of tender solicitude and love for the erring ones. In Paul's ministry we behold a blending of authority and gentleness, and the balance is always true. He labored to present every man "perfect in Christ "; in season, out of season, publicly and from house to house, rebuking sin and beseeching in Christ's stead, he carried on his work. He loved Christ, he loved the truth, he loved souls, he was true to his mission, and free from the blood of all men. God make us such pastors !

Our study of the minister as a pastor has been very imperfect indeed. We cannot leave the subject, however, without considering the pastor's claims upon his flock. He has

3. *The right to the loyal support of his people.* He is to be esteemed " very highly for his work's sake." As the pastor he is the director of the church's activities and has a right to expect his people to rally round him in his endeavor to carry forward the banner of our Lord. Paul says : From Thessalonica the word of the Lord sounded forth " not only in Macedonia and Achaia, but in every place their faith to Godward is gone forth." In his letter to the Philippians he speaks of his " fellow-workers " in that city, and in writing to Colosse he requests the Christians to pray that God " may open unto him a door for the word." The spirit of the Pauline teaching is that the people are to be imitators of the pastor, that they are to copy his

enthusiasm and zeal in pushing forward the cause of Christ; that the things they have learned and received and heard and seen in him are their model (Phil. 4 : 9), even as Christ is his; that they are to pray not only that opportunities of advancing the interests of the Kingdom may be multiplied, but also to respond to the apostolic appeal for a personal interest in their petitions, because the preacher's success is measured by the faith of the people (1 Cor. 11 : 15-16). In his work the people are to relieve the pastor of financial burdens, for "the Lord hath ordained that they which preach the gospel should live of the gospel. They are to consecrate themselves and their substance to the promotion of the Kingdom of Christ, and complete on earth the work which He came from heaven to accomplish.

We have reproduced but the merest outline of the wondrous picture of a Christian pastor drawn by the master hand of the greatest minister that ever carried the message of glad-tidings to sinful men. The real beauty of the picture is found in those delicate strokes of the brush which only he who has the artist-soul can give. We feel that our sketch is poor and feeble and faulty as we place it alongside of the original; yet, we trust, it has been drawn with some appreciation of the conception which filled the heart of the master-painter. Our next subject is of a vastly different nature :—

VI. *The Minister as a Hero.*—The ministry of the gospel appeals very strongly to the heroic in human nature. The great Apostle to the Gentiles is one of the most striking examples, on the page of history, of fidelity to duty in the face of certain death. His intrepidity manifests itself

1. *In pulpit fearlessness.*—Perhaps the most remarkable example of this trait of character is seen in Paul's conduct before Felix. His audience consisted of a Roman libertine and a profligate Jewish princess, yet he was faithful in delivering his message. He discoursed of "righteousness, temperance and judgment to come," and with such power did he present the truth that the vile wretch, whose career in Palestine had been marked by treachery, savagery, avarice, private murder and public massacre, "trembled" before "the prisoner of Jesus Christ." When he spoke before Agrippa, he did not shun to tell the story of Him who was crucified on the charge of laying

claim to the Jewish crown. So anxious was he that he should be faithful in heralding the gospel that he requests the Ephesians to pray on his behalf that utterance may be given him in opening his mouth to make known with boldness the mystery of the gospel, for which he is an ambassador in chains, that in it he may speak boldly as he ought to speak. Eph. 6 : 20. Even in Rome where we might expect him to cease from his labors, he discourses with the rough soldiers until the glad-tidings are known through " the whole prætorian guard." To rebuke the sin of his jailers might involve increased suffering, yet the old man concerned himself not with that but with the message. It is not surprising, when we remember that his life was spent in proclaiming the gospel amongst those who were bitterly opposed to it, to find him writing to Timothy : " I charge. thee in the sight of God, and of Christ Jesus, who shall judge the quick and the dead, and by his appearing and his kingdom, preach the word; be instant in season, out of season; reprove, rebuke exhort, with all long-suffering and teaching." As a trustee he is to give to his fellow-men what God has committed to his charge (1 Thess. 2 : 4) ; as a steward he is to set the Living Bread before them, and urge the starving multitudes to eat and live ; as an ambassador he, in Christ's stead, is to beseech the rebellious sons of men to be reconciled to God. In fulfilling his mission he must of necessity speak plainly, he must needs give offence, but his judgment is with the Lord. For Christ's sake he must dare to be faithful even at the cost of ease and popularity.

But the heroic spirit of the gospel minister manifests itself at another point.

2. *In controversy* he shows whether or not he has backbone. In our day we hear a great deal about Christian charity, and we cannot have too much of it, but charity does not involve striking hands with errorists. Paul " resisted Peter to the face because he stood condemned," and his language is rugged and fearless. He was not particularly careful about hurting the feelings of the Judaizing teachers in Galatia when he wrote : " If any man preacheth unto you any gospel other than that which ye received, let him be anathema." He left Timothy at Ephesus to combat heresy in the church there (II Tim. 1 : 3), and he tells

us that heretics are to be excluded from fellowship (Titus 3 : 10). All this involves heroism on the part of the minister. His own feelings are not to be taken into consideration. He may believe in the sincerity of the erring brother and in the genuineness of his piety, he may be attached to him by the tenderest ties of friendship, it may mean the tearing of his very heart-strings to condemn his friend's course, but the minister of Christ is "set for the defence of the gospel." The cause of truth demands that error shall be exposed and attacked, and in doing this the Christian preacher may suffer the keenest pain, for it often involves misjudgment, severed friendships, persecution and mental distress. To face such consequences the man of God must have the heroic spirit, or he will falter in the performance of his duty.

Once more we behold Paul's heroic spirit manifesting itself.

3. *In readiness to undergo privation and suffering.* In writing to the Corinthians he recounts his trials : " Of the Jews five times received I forty stripes save one. Thrice was I beaten with rods, once was I stoned, thrice I suffered shipwreck, a night and a day have I been in the deep ; in journeyings often, in perils of rivers, in perils of robbers, in perils from my countrymen, in perils from the Gentiles, in perils in the city, in perils in the wilderness, in perils in the sea, in perils among false brethren ; in labor and travail, in watchings often, in hunger and thirst, in fastings often, in cold and nakedness. Besides those things that are without, there is that which presseth upon me daily, anxiety for all the churches." What a catalogue of suffering ! What a life of incessant adventure and peril is here disclosed to us ! How full of heroism must the great apostle have been to face such hardships, hampered as he was by a feeble physical constitution (II Cor. 4 : 7-12) ! We are reminded of his words to the Galatians : " From henceforth let no man trouble me ; for I bear branded on my body the marks of Jesus." As Hausrath remarks, " These words suggest the picture of an old general who bares his breast before his rebellious legions. and shows them the wound-prints which prove that he is not unworthy to be called their commander." The grand old general urges Timothy to suffer hardship with him as " a good soldier of Jesus Christ." This exhortation

applies with equal force to every minister of the gospel.   Paul's suerings were endured in preaching the glad tidings in what was, in his day, the foreign field.   At the present time, home and foreign mission work calls for self-denial on the part of the minister ; but the tendency of many a workman is to seek ease and gratify ambition.   There are, however, not a few who emulate the Apostle in suering hardship, and will, with him, receive the reward of fidelity.

We have striven to copy in its main outlines Paul's portrait of the Christian minister.   As we view the original from various standpoints another characteristic is revealed.   We shall endeavor to reproduce it :

VII.   *The Minister as a Victor.*—During his ministry Paul seems to have been oppressed with the fear lest after he had preached to others he himself should be rejected (I Cor. 9 : 27). We cannot tell whether or not this thought caused him much serious discomfort, but we know that many a gleam of sunshine stole into the Apostle's life.   He has great comfort in the converts whom he has led to Christ ; they are his " epistles known and read of all men " (II Cor. 3 : 1) ; they often manifest this love to him by acts of kindness (Phil. 2 : 26) ; and he has the conviction that when Christ comes they shall be his glory and his joy (I Thess. 2 : 19).   The work which he has done is to be tested by fire (I Cor. 3 : 10-15), yet he has no doubt as to the issue.

And now the thirty years of wandering are over, the sentence of death has been passed and the good old man is pouring out his heart to his son in the gospel : " I am now ready to be oered, and the time of my departure is come.   I have fought the good fight, I have finished the course, I have kept the faith ; henceforth there is laid up for me the crown of righteousness which the Lord, the righteous judge, shall give to me at that day ; and not only to me but also to all them that have loved his appearing."   What a glorious picture !   Paul the triumphant warrior, Paul the victorious athlete, Paul the successful defender of the faith !   The crown of righteousness in full view !!   Fidelity about to receive its reward !!!   The scriptures reveal no more. The curtain falls upon one of the noblest of lives.   Yet as Stalker says : " Wherever the feet of them who publish the glad tidings go forth beautiful upon the mountains, Paul walks by their side as an inspirer and guide ; in ten thousand churches every Sabbath and on a thousand thousand hearths every day his eloquent lips still teach that gospel of which he was never ashamed ; and wherever there are human souls searching for the white flower of holiness or climbing the difficult heights of self-denial, there he whose life was so pure, whose devotion to Christ was so entire, and whose pursuit of a single purpose was so unceasing is welcomed as the best of friends." May we, who have been called into the ministry, be animated by the same spirit, achieve like victories, live again in lives which we have inspired with love for the gospel, and be, at the last, like "the prisoner of Christ," crowned as victors.

EDWARD J. STOBO, '96 (Th.)

THE STUDENT VOLUNTEER MOVEMENT.

The command of our Lord, " Go ye into all the world and preach the Gospel to every creature," has been ringing down the years, inspiring the Christian people to give their all for the spread of the gospel. Individuals have been moved by it, and have gone forth and sacrificed their lives for their fellow men. Societies have been organized, the church has partly recognized her true attitude towards the command, and the church and society working conjointly have accomplished much towards the obeying of the command.

But it was not till the year 1886, at Mt. Hermon, Mass., that the Student Volunteer Movement was organized. And from that day dates the commencement of a new epoch in Christian missions. The students were confronted with the question of missions ; and it was impossible for them to study God's word, draw near to Him in prayer, and come into close touch with needy souls, without having passion for world-wide missions awakened. And hence the inter-collegiate work unconsciously took on a missionary department. Since then over seven hundred consecrated, Spirit-filled students have gone forth to mission lands.

3

This missionary spirit was not confined to America alone; for in the summer of 1889 the students, meeting at Northfield, Mass., were startled by a cablegram from the Sunrise Kingdom, in which the Christian students of Japan cabled this sublime message : "*Make Jesus King.*" This message found its way to Sweden, where it constrained Scandinavian disciples to call a conference of students in 1890, representing Norway, Sweden, and Denmark. It also seized the students of the British Isles, and they have united the university forces of this Western Island Empire, and the missionary volunteers already number hundreds there, of whom 90% are in the foreign field.

The organization has not been without its difficulties. It was regarded with suspicion even by its friends. But it has outlived much unfavorable criticism, survived many perils, overcome many difficulties and much opposition, and continues to increase in numbers and effectiveness; as illustrated by the Detroit Convention in 1894, a Convention which stands unique among missionary gatherings, and indicates a firmly established and undeniably successful enterprise. Now, in its tenth year, this is probably the most effective agency for spreading, fostering, and utilizing the missionary spirit that anywhere exists.

Questions may arise like these : What is the purpose of this organization? and how is its purpose to be accomplished? Its purpose is to lead students to a thorough consideration of the claims of foreign missions upon them, to foster this purpose, to unite volunteers in an aggressive movement, to maintain an intelligent interest at home, but especially to secure a sufficient number of qualified men and women for the work of evangelization of the world in this generation. The declaration card, reading, "It is my purpose, if God permit, to become a foreign missionary," forms a simple basis for membership and organization.

Its purpose is to be accomplished in being true to the Master, the Lord Jesus, who gave the command to go and preach the gospel to every creature. And the volunteer who is Christ-like in mind, in character, in service, will be used of God in accomplishing this purpose. The believer is the only Bible that the world ever reads. He is so taken up by the Spirit of God and possessed, that he has become a living epistle, known and read of all men.   When this divine and glorious service is fulfilled, the kingdom of God will come, and not till then.   Then we shall enter upon the final and fruitful harvest age of the earth and the world, " when all shall know the Lord," and His sceptre shall sway the earth in righteousness and peace through the millennial age and forever more.

ANDREW IMRIE, '96·

PETRI INTERROGATIO.

Diligis Me, Simon Joannis ?
> Diligis Me ?
Immo vero, Tu scis quia
> Amo Te.

Pasce agnos,
> Pasce, dicit,
Agnos Meos !

Diligis Me, Simon Joannis ?
> Etiam, Domine,
Petrus ait : Tu scis quia
> Amo Te.

Pasce agnos,
> Pasce, dicit,
Agnos Meos !

Amas Me, Simon Joannis ?
> Amas Me ?
Contristatione Petrus :
> O Domine,
Omnia Tu nosti, quidem
> Amo Te.

Pasce oves,
> Pasce, dicit,
Pecudes !

G. HERBERT CLARKE, '95.

EDITORIAL NOTES.

"EDEN LOST AND WON " is the title of a new book by Dr. Dawson. It is made up chiefly of articles which appeared in the *Expositor.* Those who have read them in this periodical will be glad to secure them in this more permanent form. Dr. Dawson's object is to show the bearing of science and the discoveries of archæology upon the hypotheses of the Higher Criticism. He treats the subject from the scientific standpoint, and his conclusions, from his reputation for accurate scholarship, are worthy of respectful consideration.

He has no sympathy for those " who are not ashamed to attribute fraud and even conspiracy to the authors of the early books of the Bible and yet profess to attach to these forged documents a certain religious value." He thinks it made out that the literary and general conditions in Egypt at the time Moses is said to have lived would have fitted him to be the author of Genesis and Israel's great leader and law-giver. Peculiarities in the Mosaic religion, also, agree with its origin in the place and time assigned it, and not in any later period. He concludes "that, as far as yet known to us from geological investigations, the details of the antediluvian world were present in the mind of the writers of Genesis, in a clear, definite, non-mythical manner, which bespeaks an early date and accurate sources of information. Further, they must have been collected and published by one who had exceptional means of access to the earliest records of the ancient Hebrews. All this points to Moses, etc." In reference to the account in Genesis of the dispersion and the growth and location of nations, in the area covered by it, Dr. Dawson declares that "all modern research has vindicated its accuracy." He also believes explorations in the Desert of the Exodus "have proved for all time that the narrative of the Exodus must have been written by an observant and highly intelligent contemporary."

The book discusses only a few of the questions involved in the Higher Criticism, but these are among the more important. Its tone is reverent but judicial. The treatment being from the scientific standpoint may not seem to some to give scope enough for the supernatural ; but it is wholesome and helpful for this time of unrest.

THOUGH many of the readers of the MCMASTER MONTHLY are doubtless familiar with the memorial volume of the late Principal McGregor, they will be none the less pleased to see his well-known face in our gallery of Canadian Baptist portraits. The writer of the accompanying article dates his acquaintance with Mr. McGregor from his earliest days at Woodstock, when an attachment was formed that grew closer and stronger as both came to work together in the Master's vineyard. Mr. Bates' tribute to the character and work of his beloved friend is inspired by the tenderest memories and will be read with grateful appreciation by all to whom the memory of D. A. McGregor is precious and sacred.

THE late Dr. Laughlin McFarlane, of Toronto University, who a short time ago was cut down so unexpectedly and under such distressing circumstances, began teaching school when still a mere lad. In the early sixties he taught as a graduate of the Toronto Normal School in the Boston Mills Public School, in the County of Peel. He was the first teacher of that school who ever made English grammar intelligible. He was also the first to introduce the subjects of Composition and History, his principal text book in the latter subject being the old National Fifth Reader, which contained an excellent compendium of Scripture History, followed by an outline of Grecian, Roman and Modern History. The pupils of that school, under his instructions, acquired a wider and more thorough knowledge of the historical parts of the Bible than is ever given in our Sunday Schools; and the writer, gratefully recalling those early privileges, cannot but regret that such instruction is no longer given in our schools of to-day. Algebra and Arithmetic were in those days taught largely on the principle of aiming at the printed answers. There was little of the elaborate blackboard explanations now demanded of the teacher, but as a consequence, the pupils were thrown more upon their own diligence and ingenuity, and thus early enjoyed the keen sense of triumph of him who discovers truth long hidden and patiently sought. It could not fail to be an advantage to a pupil in higher schools that he had been required to wade through Davies' and Colenzo's Algebras with no help but the rules and explanations found in the book. They do it otherwise to-day, but some of us older heads still think the former way was a good one.

HERE AND THERE.

O. G. LANGFORD, ED.

THE first Ph. D. given by the University of Chicago, was conferred upon a Japanese.—*Ex.*

PRESIDENT Harper, of Chicago University, has forbidden all students to join fraternities during their Freshmen year.—*The Madisonensis.*

THE libraries connected with Yale College contain over 220,000 volumes.—*Ex.*

Yale University has 2,415 students, and the University of Michigan 2,904.

"'TIS a queer woman that never asks a question," said the sage; "but the one that does is the *querist*," said the funny man.

Dr. Elvia F. Mosher has been appointed professor of Hygiene and Dean of the Women's Literary Department in the Univ, of Michigan.

BELOIT College became co-educational this Fall. There now remain only two colleges in the West which are not co-educational—Illinois and Wabash.—*Ex.*

SINCE the final settlement of the Stanford estate, Stanford University will have an income three times as large as that of Harvard. It is the richest University in America.—*Ex.*

Old lady in book store : "'Last Days of Pompeii !' So he's dead, poor fellow. I wonder what killed him ?" " He died of an eruption, madam," said the grave-faced clerk.—*Ex.*

" MAN's life means tender teens, teachable twenties, tireless thirties, fiery forties, forcible fifties, serious sixties, sacred seventies, aching eighties, shortening breath, death, the sod, God !"—JOSEPH COOK.

THE plan of student self-government worked so successfully last year at Rutger's that it will be tried again this fall. The student governors will include four from the Senior and Junior classes, and two each from the Sophomore and Freshman classes.—*The Adelbert.*

THE following is a list of the dates of founding of the oldest colleges in the United States : Harvard, 1636 ; Yale, 1700 ; Princeton, 1746 ; University of Pennsylvania, 1749 ; Columbia, 1754 ; Brown, 1764 ; Dartmouth, 1769 ; Rutger's, 1770.—*Amherst Student.*

KINDLY mention is made of the MCMASTER MONTHLY by several exchanges, notably the *Manitoba College Journal* which quotes Dr. T. H. Rand's poem, "The Dragon Fly," in full with many encomiums.

The Sunbeam gives more attention to exchanges than any other Canadian College Journal. It also makes appreciative mention of our magazine. We quote the following :—

Little Miss Snowflake dressed in white
Came down the dusty road one night.
Her dress was as white as a piece of chalk
And she pranced around but she did not walk,
For she was going to a ball that night,
And that was the reason she dressed in white.
There were fifty thousand and many more, too,
And they looked like the children that lived in the shoe.
They had for music, that happy night,
A little book that sang about flight.
They had for chorus the rustling of leaves
That came from the tops of the tallest trees.—*Ex.*

YE PRAISE OF OLDE BOOKES.

In these ye moderne daies whenas they singe
Their moderne ditties to ye poet's lyre,
Perchaunce their rollinge numbers often ringe
With ye true musick of ye minstrel quire.

But me is liever farre to sytte and pore
Upon ye auncient folio's yellowe page ;
To sytte and conne ye magic verses o'er,
Writ by ye haunde of some immortall sage.

These aged tomes that breathe with lyfe of elde
Have cheered ye wearie houres of manie a wyghte ;
For manie an hundred yeare have they been helde
Of every bookish clerke ye chief delite.

Then why sholde I through newer pastures fare,
When here are meadowes well y-proved and rare ?

W. HARVEY MCNAIRN.—In *'Varsity.*

A young Junior Chemistry tough
While mixing a compound of stough,
Dropped a match in the phial,
And in a brief whial,
They found his front teeth and one cough.—*Ex.*

" For me one hope in life I trace,"
A Senior said, "'Tis this:
That I may sometime find the place
Where ignorance is bliss."—*Ex.*

WISCONSIN University has lately adopted a set of very stringent rules preventing students from extending their vacation beyond the reported days of closing. A student absent more than three days without pre-arrangement will be disciplined.

Bishop College Monthly comes to us with renewed interest. The enrollment is 368. A new building has lately been erected, designed and superintended by F. Goble, well known to our Woodstock boys. A recent number chronicled the death of the son of Dr. M. McVicar, the first Chancellor of McMaster University.

McM. . in McGill University, was unfortunate enough to forget to put on his gown before entering one of the Dean's classes and was saluted with the order " Go out! Go out ! This lecture is not open to the public. Strangers are not allowed in here !" He tried to remonstrate, but that stern voice bade him depart. He went, and returned wearing the livery of the establishment, and naïvely remarking : " I came unto him as a stranger, and he took me not in."

WASTING TIME OVER NEWSPAPERS.—If I were asked to select what one influence more than another wastes the spare time of the modern man, I should be inclined to specify the reading of newspapers. The value of the modern daily newspaper as a short cut to knowledge of what is actually happening in two hemispheres is indisputable, providing it is read regularly so that one can eliminate from the consciousness those facts which are contracted or qualified on the following day. Of course it is indispensable to read the morning, and perhaps the evening newspaper, in order to know what is going on in the world. But the persistent reading of many newspapers, or the whole of almost any newspaper, is nearly as detrimental to the economy of time as the cigarette habit to health.—*Scribner's Magazine.*

The *University Monthly* of Fredericton is of unusual interest. Its articles are too good to pass off with a hurried glance, they require careful reading. Its matter is worthy of better paper and typography. The following has some sensible suggestions :

NECESSARY FOR SUCCESSFUL STUDY.—The first essential to successful study is the power of concentration of thought. This power is largely a matter of habit and cultivation. Read five pages of history in a lackadaisical manner. Close the book and write out all you can remember. Then compare your production with the printed matter, and you will be able to judge of your proficiency. Read five pages more with fixed attention and a resolution to retain the subject, and compare as before. You will find a marked improvement. If your memory is treacherous read but very little and always write on the subject. When you hear a sermon, or address, hear it, and afterwards reduce it to writing. Read no novels and do not read aloud to please others unless you care nothing for the article yourself. A practical reader can read aloud for hours and carry on an independent train of thought all the time. This ruins the faculty of study as well as the memory. Dismiss all other subjects but the one in hand. Let the ear be deaf to all sounds, and the eye blind to all sights. Let the sense of touch sleep, and smell and taste be as though they were not. A lesson learned in this state of mind will stay with you, and will not need to be " crammed " again the night before examination. It will be like lines carved deep into the rock, or chiseled on the Rosetta stone. The other method is the dim tracing of obscure letters in the sand, which the next wave obliterates.

" THE *Daily Princetonian* gives an interesting account of the plans for the great international Olympic games to be held at Athens next April.   Greece itself has raised a fund of nearly $200,000 to put the scheme through.   The Panatheniac Stadion, capable of seating 70,000 spectators, is being restored, largely through the munificence of an Athenian merchant named Averoff.   The Phaleric plain will witness bicycle races.   In the bay and gulf will be held swimming contests and yacht races.   The arena of the Stadion is in the form of a horseshoe, 670 feet long and 109 feet wide.   Grecian royalty is deeply interested in the enterprise; the king has promised to award the silver olive wreaths.   The festival will be closed by the production of a tragedy of Sophocles and the ' Lohengrin ' of Wagner."

VERB. SAP.

" It's a very good rule in cliniques,
When a prosy old lecturer spiques,
To close up your book
And silently hook
And never go back there for wiques.—*Ex.*

COLLEGE NEWS.

W. P. COHOE, '96,   R. D. GEORGE, 97
J. F. VICHERT, '97,   MISS E. WHITESIDE, '98·
Editors.

THE UNIVERSITY.

1ST STUDENT : " What is our telephone number ? "
JUNIOR : " 3557."
No wonder he lost his grip.

GREEN ribbons and bouquets of shamrock were very much in evidence on St. Patricks' day.

OVERHEARD in corridor at 12 p.m. Friday, 13th February: " Where was the ' old man ' to-night?   He wasn't at the ' At Home.' "

IN this age of new photography McMaster is not behind in discoveries.   The following chemical formula will fully describe some brilliant discoveries made by the science class of '96 :

1 $MeD + CaT = ScAt.$
1 $Cake + STu_2Dy = 7 (StAr).$

SHOULD the shade of Tennyson visit McMaster about this season of the year, he would perform some 'Limae Labor' upon that much quoted line

"In the spring a young man's fancy, etc.,"

he would not attempt to describe the form it would take, but the changed line would have involved in it the idea of a bicycle.

REV. DR. SAUNDERS, of Halifax, was present at prayers on Tuesday, March 17th, and spoke a few words to the students.

THE bicycle fever is raging here as elsewhere. The front entry and the basement hall have taken on the appearance of a bicycle emporium. Many and frequent are the wishes for spring and dry streets.

THOSE students who have been laboring so very arduously amid the intricacies of Hebrew hieroglyphics will appreciate the following remark made by the Hebrew professor:
"Cain killed Abel with a 'waw consecutive.'"

THE sympathy of the school goes out to Miss M. E. Burnette, '97, and Mr. J. J. Patterson, '97. On Thursday, March 12th, Miss Burnette was called home by the sudden death of her mother, and on the same day Mr. Patterson received a telegram announcing his father's decease.

WE would not forget the mention of the now many times renewed kindness of Mr. and Mrs. Newman in giving some of us the opportunity of meeting their friends at their home. Mrs. Newman is a very faithful friend, and her "At Home" is always very much enjoyed by all privileged to attend.

THE McMaster student has many friends. On the evening of Friday, Feb. 3th, Mr. and Mrs. C. J. Holman invited the graduating classes and all the post-graduates of the University to their beautiful home, 75 Lowther Ave. Needless to state, the invitation was generally accepted, and a delightful evening enjoyed. Nearly all the city pastors, our Faculty, and a large gathering of Baptist friends were present, who seemed as pleased to meet the students as the students were to meet them. These evenings are much appreciated, and the kindness of Mr. and Mrs. Holman and others who have helped to make the college life doubly happy will be remembered in the pleasantest way for a long time to come.

THROUGH some personal correspondence with one of our students, we have learned of the success attending the labors of our former fellow-student, Rev. Ralph Trotter, B.Th., of Victoria, B. C. He has begun along the line of the institutional church in establishing a reading room and parlour, a second hand clothing bureau, a free medical attendance bureau, and also a floating library for sailors of 1,600 volumes in 60 cases, which are put on board the outgoing sealing vessels and exchanged on their return. Recently he has opened a crusade against saloons, gambling dens, etc., and has succeeded in rousing public sentiment to resist the encroachment of these moral pest houses by a rigid enforcement of British law. In this he has made many enemies who even threaten personal injury, but he has the moral support of all philanthropic organizations in the city. We believe our friend Ralph is fully competent to prosecute war along such lines. We wish him success.

A PROSPEROUS farmer on the banks of the romantic Nashwaak in New Brunswick, a respected magistrate, the chief man of the neighborhood during the active years of his life, a pronounced Liberal in politics, and a warm advocate of taxation for the support of schools, the main support of the Nashwaak Baptist church, a deacon from the age of 24 until his death in his 92nd year, a period of nearly three score years and ten—such in brief is the record of the life of Calvin Luther Goodspeed, who died at Nashwaak, N. B., on the 5th day of February, 1896. Deacon Goodspeed was the father of our Professor Goodspeed, with whom all the members of the University sympathize in this hour of his bereavement.

THE death of Dr. Goodspeed's father was followed soon by the death of a brother of another member of our Faculty. Edward J. Farmer died in Perth, where for many years he had carried on a mercantile business in partnership with his brother George, on the 5th day of March, at the age of 46. Never a vigorous man physically, he found his health so far impaired a year and a half ago that he went to Michigan, hoping that a change of climate might benefit him. From there he returned a few months ago to die. In 1874, the year of Prof. Farmer's baptism, he was baptized into the fellowship of the Perth church. He died in great peace. The Faculty and students give to Prof. Farmer their heartfelt sympathy.

THEOLOGICAL SOCIETY.—On the evening of Friday, Mar. 13th, the Theological Society held a most enjoyable meeting in the chapel. The announcement had been well bulletined, and as a consequence a large number of the students were on hand to gather information regarding "Evangelistic work." Rev. Wm. Patterson, of Cooke's Presbyterian Church, who is in the midst of special work in his own congregation, was the first speaker. The subject assigned him was "How to Conduct Evangelistic Services," but apologizing for not keeping to his text, he roamed at will, gleaning many a handful of wheat, and beating it out for his audience. Mr. Patterson defined a revival as having its basis in *life*, and not a special work among the unconverted; the work might extend to them, but first and foremost a revival had to do with Christian men and women. The necessity of revivals to the life of the church was then dealt with and enforced by many illustrations, but it was when the speaker spoke of the after-meeting that he was especially happy. This department of the work was declared to be the key to the whole situation. Great care must be taken in the selection of workers ; the enquirer must be skilfully questioned concerning his hope, for if he rest on feeling, on desire, on anything short of Christ Himself, the arch-enemy will use these very soul-exercises through which he has been passing to contribute to his final ruin.   Dr. Goodspeed then spoke of "Sermons for Evangelistic Occasions." With great tenderness and power he opened up the subject.   He warned the students not to attempt evangelistic services over a cold church, for should young Christian life be born in such an atmosphere, it would be dwarfed by the cold, and would not attain the beauty and the power which God intended it to possess. Get the church right, and you can only do this as you yourself are living in constant communion with Jesus Christ.   Sermons for such occasions should be, to a great extent, born of the time.   Leave yourselves open to the leading of the spirit, and it is wonderful how He will lead and empower when a man is really living with God.   Preach the law of God ; show its claims upon the souls of men, make God very real, not an abstract law, but a person ; exhibit the exceeding sinfulness of sin, shut the sinner up without excuse ; then in tenderness of soul herald the love of God manifested in Christ, and exhort the hearers to turn to Him. Dig deep foundations or you cannot expect to build sturdy Christian characters.   After a brief season of prayer in which great nearness to the throne was experienced, the business of the Society was transacted. A very warm vote of thanks was tendered each of the speakers, and the meeting adjourned, the unanimous verdict being " It was the best yet."

THE latest meeting of the Tennysonian Society was one of exceptional interest.   The chief feature of the programme was an instructive and forceful address on " Remedial Legislation," by Dr. Rand, of which we present a summary :

After a word of encouragement to the Literary Societies, which he characterized as the thirteenth chair of the University, the Doctor said that young men should study to have sound views on public questions, that free institutions can live only by the breath of a free and independent people, that a free Parliament is only possible where there is a free electorate, and that principle, not party, was the touchstone of worthy citizenship.   The tyranny of opinion is especially powerful over young life, in colleges and elsewhere.   Popularity is thought to be a worthy test of conduct, but if one's manhood is to be real and true it must be free, and one must be content to pay the price of freedom, whatever it costs. He then sketched the condition of public education in all the Provinces previous to the union of Upper and Lower Canada.   Separate schools were then unknown to the law, save that the public schools of lower Canada were out and out Roman Catholic schools.   To make it possible for Protestants in that Province to secure a common school education for their children, "dissentient schools" were established for them by the united parliament, but only at the cost of giving separate religious schools by law to Roman Catholics in Upper Canada,—whose schools, be it remembered, had always been just as accessible to Catholics as to Protestants.   This was the entrance of the virus into our Canadian public school system.   At the Quebec Conference in 1864 it was provided that what had been accorded to Protestants in Quebec and to Roman Catholics in Ontario, should be made permanent in the Canadian Constitution for those Provinces.   That was the only educational provision in the Quebec scheme.   When the delegates subsequently met at Westminster to draw up the British North American Act, great pressure was, *without the knowledge of the public of Canada*, brought to bear by the Catholic Bishops, to make this provision apply in the Act to *all* the Provinces of Canada. This attempt, there is reason to believe, came very near succeeding in that form. It was successful to the extent of surreptitiously inserting the clause under which the Remedial Bill is now constitutionally before the House of Commons. New Brunswick was the first province to reconstruct its school system after confederation. As it was a non-sectarian system, the Roman Catholics claimed it to be unconstitutional—claimed it to be such under that surreptitious clause of the B. N. A. Act—and sought the interference of the Dominion Government and Parliament. The Government (1871-2-3) refused to interfere, but the Parliament entertained the question, and sought the interference of the Imperial authorities, by a majority of 35. This created great local trouble in N. B., but the N. B. Government and Parliament stood for their rights, and the courts and the Imperial authorities upheld them. Then followed P. E. Island. The action of the Roman Catholics was less violent in that Province, because the response at Ottawa—from previous experience—was not cordial. Then in 1875, an Act to amend and consolidate the Laws respecting the North-West was passed. Section eleven of that act provided for separate schools in any and all parts of Canada, from Manitoba to the Rockies, whenever any part or parts of the Territory should be organized. This was an extraordinary proceeding, clearly designed to take away by anticipation the freedom on this question of the Legislatures yet to be in one great wilderness. The Act seems to have passed the Commons very quietly, but was strenuously fought in the Senate by Hon. George Brown, where it passed by a majority of two. This is the legislation which is the source of the present trouble in Keewatin, and has entailed a legacy of strife for the future in all parts of the North-West. You all know the history of education legislation in Manitoba. It is a battle for free institutions against mediaeval institutions. We see by this review (1) the result of temporizing with false principles in state craft; (2) that the safety of Canadian institutions has not been insured by vigilance of either political party—that the vigilance of the people is our real hope; (3) that Canada is yet to be a great battle-ground on the relations of religion and the civil power, and that young men should reach clear convictions, and bear worthily their part in the struggle; and (4) that this is a pivitol hour in our history. The spirit which has unceasingly watched for aggression since 1840, and has seized strategically every opportunity to advance in Canada mediaeval institutions must be firmly and intelligently met. The conflict is impressible, and can have but one issue if we are true to our time. Believe me, the bottles of mediaevalism must burst when filled with the new wine of freedom—the life blood of a free people. If McMaster University has a mission—and I have always believed it had a special one—its hour has come. Our principles of religious and civil liberty should be sounded out by her sons from Cape Breton to Vancouver. We stand for these to the uttermost.

THE receipt of the following new books is acknowledged with thanks by the Librarian :

From the University : Bascom : Philosophy of English Literature ; Carus : The Religion of Science ; from Dr. T. H. Rand : N. Menschutkin : Analytical Chemistry ; from the University of Toronto : Examination Papers, 1895 ; from the Smithsonian Institution : Bulletins, Reports, and Proceedings of the U. S. National Museum ; from the U. S. A. Government : Report of the Commissioner of Education, Vol. II, 1892-93 ; from the Ontario Dept. of Education : Hodgins : Documentary History of Education in Upper Canada ; from E. C. Millard : What God hath Wrought ; The Same Lord.

Moulton College.

At our prayer-meeting Tuesday evening, March 17th, we had the Rev. Mr. Bishop to lead. He spoke to us on the subject of prayer, Luke xi. The thoughts he left with us were very helpful and inspiring.

Several of the students of M. L. C. had the privilege of listening to Handel's famous oratorio, "The Messiah," on Monday, March 23rd. The soloists were all celebrated artists, Albani taking soprano. Her rendering of the solo, "I know that my Redeemer liveth," was especially effective.

During the past month we have had Chancellor Wallace, Dr. Rand, Rev. Mr. Bishop, of the Central Methodist Church ; Rev. Mr. Weeks, of Walmer Road ; Rev. Mr. Eaton, of Bloor Street, and Rev. Mr. Neil, of Westminster Church, to lead our chapel exercises, and we have been much benefited by their encouraging words.

The students were all very much pleased when they learned that the vacation at Easter was to be longer by two days than heretofore. Some complaints were heard about the requirement that we should remain till the end of the day before the beginning of the vacation, and herein is verified the saying, "The more we have the more we want." However, our return will be very much brightened by the prospect of hearing in the near future the renowned pianist Paderewski.

Moulton has been very kindly remembered by her friends during the past weeks. On the afternoon of February 28th, Mrs. Newman entertained the graduating classes of Moulton and McMaster, and although the weather was unfavorable, a goodly number of guests were present, and a very pleasant afternoon was passed. Mrs. Holman also gave an "At Home" for the graduating classes and a large number of friends, on March 13th. The students enjoyed these "At Homes,' and appreciate the kind thought and interest which their friends show toward them.

Woodstock College.

The members of the class of '96, having striven through weary years of preparation, are at last approaching the time when they are to reap, as the fruits of their labors, class honors and certificates of various kinds. But these confidently expected attainments are by no means the only source of gratification to the learned seniors. Social privileges and enjoyments come apace. Two very pleasant receptions have already been tendered the class by some of the "better halves" of the Faculty. The first of those, on March 6th, was given by Mrs. McKechnie and Mrs. McCrimmon in their commodious rooms in the

East building.   Both ladies proved themselves to be model hostesses, and with games and various other modes of entertainment, the evening passed very happily, but all too quickly.

At the second reception, which was held at the home of the Principal, Mrs. Bates and Mrs. Smith were the entertainers.   In the highest sense of the word, they showed themselves worthy of all that the name " entertainer " implies ; for in a most charming manner, they succeeded in carrying out their purpose of giving their guests an enjoyable evening.

OPEN MEETING.—The concert given by the Literary Societies of the College, on the 28th of Feb., was a grand success.   The entertainment was novel in its character, consisting of a programme of genuine excellence in a humorous sitting.   It was announced as " Mr. and Mrs. Josiah Allen's reception to the College students."   Mr. Cornwall, both in voice and manner, enacted the part of Samantha to perfection ; and Mr. Elliott as Josiah, " proud he's a man," bore himself with a dignity becoming a person so celebrated as Mr. Allen.   Mr. Brophey as Thomas Jefferson Allen, introduced the students to his Pa and Ma, and it is needless to say performed his part to the delight of all.   After the reception ceremonies, the following programme was rendered, each number being informally introduced by some of the guests :

Orchestra	
Quartette	Messrs. Spidle, Bryant, W. Welch, and Bowyer.
Small Boy's Recitation	Mr. Gifford.
Chorus	Glee Club.
"The Oracle"	Messrs. Spidle and La Flair.
Duet " Excelsior " . . .	Messrs. Bryant and W. Welch.
Orchestra	
Pygmalion and Galatea . .	Messrs. Priccy, W. Lailey, O. Lailey and Henderson.
Solo	Mr. W. Welch.
Oration	Mr. Grigg.
Harmony Quartette . .	Messrs. Brophey, La Flair, Brownler, H. A. Smith.
College Quartette . . .	Messrs. Bryant, Spidle, W. Welch, Bowyer.
Debate	Messrs. Coumans and Bowyer.
Chorus.	

Space will not allow us to enumerate those who deserve honorable mention, which indeed is merited by all the performers, but we cannot forbear to speak of the Quartette, the Glee Club under the leadership of Mr. Spidle, the Orchestra directed by Mr. Mayberry, the rendering of Pygmalion and Galatea, and Mr. Grigg's mock-heroic but thoughtful oration as especially deserving of commendation.

ANOTHER painful accident has occurred in the College.   Mr. Wm. Bowyer, while exercising in the gymnasium, fell from one of the bars and broke his right arm.   He is now in the Woodstock hospital, where he will have our tender sympathy and care.

GRANDE LIGNE.

We miss from our halls and classes the familiar face of A. Pelletier, who has been laid aside by a severe illness.

We have just received the sad news of the death of Albin Jousse, one of our school-mates of last year. Albin was a pleasant and popular Christian boy of fourteen years of age. He had been ill for some time and was quite prepared for the end. His parents have our sincere sympathy in their deep affliction.

OUR Ladies' Society of Intellectual Culture seems to have completely eclipsed the Boys' Literary Society, for while the latter has suspended its meetings for a while, the former has developed unexpected strength. A week or two ago they gave us an evening's programme devoted to the life and works of Charles Dickens. The selections were well executed and the meeting was thoroughly enjoyed. We hope the ladies will be generous and soon give us another evening with another standard author.

Now that the allotment of taxes on the Catholic farmers for the new R. C. church is about to be made, many of the parishoners are beginning to think seriously of sending in their resignations to the priest, so as to escape the taxes that will fall very heavily upon their property. We have reliable information that already eight farmers have sent in legal notice of their resignations, and that others are about to do so. Others again are trying to take legal measures to prevent the re-partition of taxes being made at all. Would that these persons might not only throw off the bondage of Rome, but that they might also come into the true liberty of the gospel !

TUESDAY, Feb. 18th, was a day to be remembered in the Grande Ligne Baptist church. The evening train of that day brought to us Mr. and Mrs Mellick of Manitoba, and Mrs. Thos. Graham of Montreal. Of course Mr. Mellick was to speak to us on Manitoba missions. Using his large and splendid map, he portrayed for us the vastness, the wonderful growth, varied population, and the magnificent possibilities of that splendid country. He explained Manitoba's noble position on the School Question, and showed that the Gospel among the people is the only means of finally settling it. We were told of the number and character of the French Catholics of Manitoba, and how poorly they compared with their Protestant neighbors. The speaker hoped that another Madame Feller might be raised up to give this people the Gospel, and urged that Grande Ligne should reach out her hand to help the French of Manitoba as well as those of Nova Scotia. It is needless to say that every one who heard Mr. Mellick's address enjoyed it thoroughly. A collection of over thirteen dollars was taken. We believe we shall be more interested in Manitoba and the Baptist work there henceforth.

THE

McMASTER UNIVERSITY MONTHLY

APRIL, 1896.

THOMAS TROTTER.

Though I have not at my command such biographical facts as might lend special interest to a rapid sketch, I cannot decline the request of the Editor of the McMASTER MONTHLY to contribute a somewhat brief text to accompany the portrait of Thomas Trotter.

I recall but two families among the Baptists of Canada which have each given three sons to our Canadian Baptist ministry. In one, the sons were alumni of Acadia; in the other, of McMaster. Of these latter, one brother is the pastor of the Baptist church at Victoria, British Columbia; another, of the Baptist church at Peterboro, Ontario; and the third Thomas Trotter, is now the pastor of the historic Baptist church at Wolfville, Nova Scotia,—the seat of Acadia University. This recital suggests the wideness of the field in which the work of our Baptist educational institutions of Ontario is already felt, and the oneness of sympathy and realized fellowship of our Canadian Baptists.

Mr. Trotter is chiefly the product of our Canadian life and institutions. When but a lad, he, with his family, came from England to Toronto. Early deprived by death of his father, he found himself in that wonderful school of gracious discipline,—a member of a large family ardently devoted to a beloved mother begirt with manifold cares. A dutiful and affectionate son and brother, sharing bravely to the full the responsibilities which it was the increasing joy of his heart sympathetically to discharge, Mr. Trotter, doubtless ere he was aware of it, developed a firm, manly, frank, self-reliant, and sympathetic life. Subsequent training and experience enriched these qualities, and gave to them that balance and wise control which are so conspicuous in his personality. His school life at Woodstock allied him with Christian forces and interests to which he readily responded. To one of his quick responsiveness of spirit, it could not be that the earnestness of Christian purpose and loftiness of Christian aims embodied in Dr. Fyfe and Professor Wells, and in many worthy young lives engaged in study with him, should fail to quicken into generous impulse and life latent energies of heart and mind, and turn them into channels of noble service. A course in Arts at Toronto University was a natural result by way of will and process in further self-equipment. The personality of a teacher like Dr. Young stimulated him to patient and painstaking scholarship, and widened the horizon of thought. Then came his theological course at McMaster, from which he was graduated in 1885. The uniform testimony of his teachers is that Mr. Trotter was an earnest man and an able student, capable of entering with purposeful effort and zest into whatever subjects were before him, and of shaping results to the ends of practical service. During his protracted course of preparation, he was earnestly engaged during vacations in preaching on Home Mission fields. While a student of Toronto University, he preached one summer as far east as Shelburne County, Nova Scotia; and in August of that year made the long journey to Wolfville to hear Dr. Lorimer (then, as now, of Tremont Temple, Boston), and to be present at the annual Convention held there. It was then I first met him.

On graduation from McMaster, Mr. Trotter became the pastor of Woodstock church, one of the mother churches of this province. When I was pressed into the duties of the Principalship of Woodstock College, I found myself in close official and personal relations with him. He was the efficient Secretary to the Board of Trustees. The interests of the college were dear to him, and teachers and students could always reckon upon his helpful sympathy. No pastor of Woodstock church was ever more beloved, or loved his people more. It was never my privilege to sit under a pastor whose ministrations I more highly prized. I was much impressed with his unfailing exegetical instinct which enabled him to discover the truth of the Divine Word; while his warm spirit and fine imagination ministered that truth convincingly to the hearts of his hearers. Prayer, song, the reading of the Scriptures are meaningful and vital to him. In his relations to men the progress of moral and social reforms are of concern, but he regards them chiefly as the kindly fruitage of the publication of the gospel, essential alike to the time-life and the life eternal. He is ever ready to bear his part in all forms of coöperative service to these high ends.

As was well known to many at the time, I accepted the Principalship of Woodstock College solely because I deemed it possible that by so doing a way might in God's providence be opened by which the Baptists of Ontario and Quebec might become permanently possessed of a Christian college, and ultimately, as I ventured to hope, of a Christian University. The precedent conditions which I secured in this behalf, and which involved a charter revision, found a lodgment in none of the hearts of our Baptist ministers so quickly, or took such depth of root, as in that of Thomas Trotter's. The significance of a positively Christian University, with the Bible as an open text in every course of study, struck home to his heart. While some worthy brethren were unable to see what the denomination had to do with providing the higher education, and others characterized the proposed Christian University under Baptist control, as "a sort of Sunday-school University," which could not command the confidence either of students or of the public, Mr. Trotter coöperated, in all ways, and on all occasions, with those who were laboring to shape results to the gracious ends which have now been achieved.

In October, 1887, within less than a month after the sudden removal by death of Senátor McMaster, the annual meeting of the Convention took place in Toronto. The Charter Committee made a full report of its efforts, and presented to the Convention the charter of McMaster University, as it had passed the Legislative Assembly. The Will of Senator McMaster was also laid before the Convention, with its magnificent bequest in behalf of a Christian University, for its acceptance. On that occasion, Mr. Trotter preached the educational sermon, from Rom. xiv: 8, 9. His theme was "The Lordship of Christ in the Higher Education." The clearness of his convictions and the fervor of his spirit may be gathered from the following utterances in that historic hour:

Thank God, the ideal may be actualized. We are no longer trammeled with inability. The means have been placed within our reach. It is the hour of supreme opportunity. To enthrone Christ in the realm of learning and intellect, this is the honor to which we are invited. It may need courage to leave the beaten track and enter this highway which the Lord has opened up. But brethren, the centuries are before us; and as He points to us the purpose of His cross and tomb, God grant we may rally at His call, and pressing along His highway, plant His standard where, through perhaps centuries of years, His name shall be the Name above every name, and multitudes shall be blessed in Him. . . . . . To reach this ideal is the thought that lies behind that Charter recently obtained from the Legislature of the Province. I find in that charter every feature which I have sketched of the institution to be desired. The world-spirit may misunderstand and sometimes even sneer at its provisions, but depend upon it, it counts for something with the Lord of Glory that His Name and His Truth have been given their place, and that the institution projected is to be, in the fullest sense, a Christian University.

During the discussions of the Convention on the acceptance of the Trust contemplated by Senator McMaster's Will, Mr. Trotter moved the following resolution:

Resolved—That the Convention affirm its judgment that McMaster University should be organized and developed as an independent school of learning.

Educational decisions were not reached by the Convention during its meeting; but at the special Convention held at Guelph in the following March, the above resolution, with the addition of the word "permanently" before "independent," was carried by an overwhelming vote.

Loss of health compelled Mr. Trotter to seek rest for nearly two years. On resuming active duties he entered upon the pastorate of the Bloor Street Baptist Church, Toronto, in 1889. In the organization of the University, however, there was a general concensus of opinion that his services should be secured for the chair of Homiletics and Pastoral Theology. The carrying out of this decision was a severe strain on Bloor Street Church, into whose affections his life had entered with exceptional fervor and strength. I need not speak of his careful and laborious discharge of the duties of his professoriate. Students and Professors felt the fine enthusiasm which clothed him as with a garment. A good scholar, a good teacher, a good preacher, a good man! He is all these. He has head power, heart power, soul power. Life lives in him, and has its richest expression in a warm and biblical preaching, luminous with the gospel of the Son of Man who is the Son of God. He is a safe and wise man, quick with interpretative sympathy, loyal and true, incapable of betraying a trust, and delighting in open and manly thinking and living. As the recent head of the University, it may be permitted to me to say that no member of the Faculty responded more quickly and continuously to considerations involving the welfare of every side and phase of our complex organism than did Mr. Trotter. Nor was he quicker to perceive than willing to do. . That he should, on resigning his chair last spring to enter upon the duties of the pastorate at Wolfville, have the satisfaction of knowing that he retired from an institution, which, for its age and scope, is unique among the Universities of Canada in the elaborations of its courses and deft adjustment of educational means to ends, must in all justice be counted to his credit, as well as to the credit of those whom he left behind. His retirement was a sore loss to McMaster ; but it is some consolation to know that it was a great gain to Acadia.

On the re-assembling of the University Faculty in October last, an appreciative minute was made, which, as it has not been mentioned or recorded in the MONTHLY, I here record :

Resolved—That we place on record our personal esteem for Professor Trotter, and our appreciation of the excellent service he has rendered during the past five years. His genial manner and unfailing courtesy made him a very delightful companion ; whilst his clear views and sound judgment, his fine candor and genuine manliness rendered him a most useful member of the Faculty. We admired the hearty and conscientious interest which he took in every department, and in the general life of the University. Of his work as Professor of Homiletics and Pastoral Theology we have heard only words of praise. It was marked by painstaking thoroughness and a contagious enthusiasm that made his lectures a delight as well as a profit to the students. He enjoyed in a large measure the esteem, confidence and affection, not only of professors and students, but also of our people generally. Now that in obedience, as he believes, to the will of God, he has re-entered the work for which his heart always yearned, our prayer is that the Holy Spirit may crown with large blessing his pastorate in Wolfville—a pastorate for which he is eminently fitted.

On the 4th of September last, Mr. Trotter actively entered upon what has already proved to be one of the most influential and happy labors of his life. I was at the time resting at Partridge Island, on the opposite shore of the Basin of Minas, some thirty miles from the scene of his new duties, and where I spent my undergraduate life. With the memory of the past ten years of educational life and struggle in my heart, during almost all of which time Mr. Trotter had, in one aspect or another, been a companion-in-arms, I sent my heart in prayerful wish and welcome to him across the Basin, in words whose final numbers, I doubt not, expressed the fervent wish of every worthy reader of this sketch :—

TO T. T.

Sometimes the tide upon this beauteous shore,
　　With stealthy foot creeps silent to its goal,
　　Whelming in darksome death a trusting soul ;
　　Sometimes it moves with menacing rout and roar,
As who should venture through its open door
　　Must taste its vexing power to exact its toll ;
　　Most oft in smiles it brims its waiting bowl
And lavishes its love yet more and more.

O friend in sun and storm, by day, by night,
　　Whose heart has known the tides of human life,
　　And felt their weal or woe of destiny ;
Take thou my prayer that on thy sail a light
　　Fall sweet—His own Love's light for thee and wife—
　　As turns thy prow to meet a smiling sea.

THEODORE H. RAND.

THE HEPATICA.

Hail, first of the spring,
Pearly, sky-tinted thing,
  Touched with pencil of Him
Who rollest the year !
  Lo ! thy aureole rim
  No painter may limn—
Vision thou hast, and no fear !

Fair child of the light,
What fixes thy sight ?
  Wide open thy roll
From the seal of the clod,
  And thy heaven-writ scroll
  Glows, beautiful soul,
With the shining of God !

Thou look'st into heaven
As surely as Stephen,
  So steadfast thy will is !
And from earth's ingle-nook
  Seest Christ of the lilies
  And daffadowndillies,
And catchest His look.

And a portion is mine,
Rapt gazer divine,
  From thy countenance given—
Angel bliss in thy face !
  I've looked into heaven
  As surely as Stephen,
From out of my place !

THEODORE H. RAND.

In Massey's Magazine for April, 1896.

IS THE BAPTIST POSITION IN REFERENCE TO THE MANITOBA SCHOOL QUESTION CONSISTENT?

In view of the position taken by the Baptists in Convention in May last and of a more recent expression of opinion in regard to the Manitoba School question, the moment seems opportune to examine carefully such position and see whether it is consistent with those principles for which Baptists have in the past so strongly contended. If we shall find it does not accord with true Baptist belief, we ought at once and forever to cease expressing opinions and passing resolutions concerning State policy, and confine our work as Baptists within its legitimate sphere. For if our position is not a logical one and does not accord with our principles, we do ourselves a great injustice, and injure the good name of " Baptist." We hinder the growth of " the Kingdom of God." We have besides to bear an additional odium not only of having violated our principles but also of having injured the very movements our actions and resolutions were intended to promote. The observations and arguments which I shall make will not, however, be directed to all those subjects upon which the Baptists in conventions and in churches have seen proper to pass, but will be confined to the relation of the Church to the State, with especial reference to the attitude of the Baptists to the Manitoba School question as indicated in resolutions that have been passed as purporting to represent Baptist opinion and conviction.

Now it must be admitted that the Baptists more than the members of any other religious denomination should be especially careful of the position they take on any matter with which *prima facie* the State has a right to deal, inasmuch as they (the Baptists) have always been so strong in contending for the principle of complete separation of the functions of the State from those of the Church and *vice versa*.

The history of the Baptists in the past has shown indeed, that (with very few exceptions) they have acted consistently with their belief. With those who have less clearly defined views on this matter a *faux pas* might be excusable, but the Baptists have no excuse to offer; for their contention for such a principle implies surely that they know what the principle is. If they do know what the separation of Church and State really means, there should be no difficulty in determining when they are in the one or the other realm, when they have left the sphere of the one and entered that of the other, and if they do not know, their position is censurable ; for they have been sailing under false colours, contending for a principle and assuming they knew when they did not know what it was.

I venture to assert that there is no principle which has been so much heralded abroad and none more imperfectly understood than this one. We have heard so much of it, we have been fed on it so often, that it has almost been set up as a part of our religious faith. It has been spoken of as if it were a part and parcel of the inheritance of every Baptist, as if it were a principle belonging wholly, solely and exclusively to the Baptists and that none other could have the same. As if there were something in the name Baptist which carried with it a belief in the aforesaid principle.

Now as a matter of fact the principle can be logically arrived at by any one. It has no *especial* connection with Baptist belief. It does not grow out of one's relation to any church. It is a position which grows out of the very nature and existence of a church. Not something which a church or a member of such church believes, but what a church is. The principle of separation of Church and State is one which lies in the very nature of things. The Church has one sphere, the State has another sphere. With the true sphere of the one the other has nothing to do. It is not concerned with it.

Again, I think a good deal of confusion has been caused by the use of the words " State " and " Church," when we wished to assert a principle in which we believed. What we have often wished to assert is that the citizens acting through the State or through State power should not pass or endeavour to pass laws affecting individual liberty of conscience, and that the individuals banded together into a Church should not endeavour to force their religious belief upon the citizens of a State. When the citizens endeavour to legislate in the realm of conscience, they generally do wrong, and when religious belief is sought to be forced upon citizens there is equally a wrong done. Who is to decide where the realm of conscience begins and ends will be shown later on.

It must, however, be borne in mind in discussing the separation of Church and State, that there are certain duties and obligations which the individuals composing a Church owe to the State, and certain other or correlative duties and obligations which the citizens acting in the name of the State owe to members composing a Church. There is a certain union which must always exist between the Church and the State, inasmuch as in the one individual there is both a member of a Church and a member of the State. The duty of a Christian in reference to the State is set forth by Paul in the 13th chapter of his Epistle to the Romans. This chapter might well be very carefully studied, to see whether we sometimes do not push our Church ideas too far into the realm of the State. In some cases it is clearly seen what falls within the sphere of the one or of the other. In other cases it would appear a difficult matter to determine with accuracy just where the border line of the one begins and that of the other ends. If our ideas were logical and consistent, I think such difficulty would be found to be apparent rather than real, and that the difficulty has been caused, or at least enhanced, by the hazy views we have held of this important principle. In other words, if our position is a proper one, it will be found that the ability to distinguish between the things pertaining to the Church and those to the State will be made easy.

In order then to show more clearly what I conceive to be an improper position of the Baptists, let me call attention to the nature and constitution of a Baptist church. It is necessary for us sometimes to retrace our footsteps, to see whether we have not wandered from those foundation principles upon which the Baptists in the past have been so proud to stand. In these days when combination, unification, and organization on grand and broad bases seem to be the order of the day, when we have almost begun to frown down upon individual effort, when nothing is thought to be accomplished unless through committees or larger organizations, when Christian work runs largely into broad platitudes of moral teaching, it is necessary to consider whether we too have not caught this spirit of the age. If

we have, let us not justify ourselves, if for no other reason than
that the New Testament furnishes us with no such precedents·
I think all Baptists would be willing to follow the lead of the
late Dr. Armitage, and what he has to say with reference to a
church is as follows :—" In the apostolic age the church was a
a local body and each church was entirely independent of every
other church. It follows then that the New Testament nowhere
speaks of the 'Universal' Catholic or 'Invisible' church as
indicating a merely ideal existence separate from a real and
local body. There can be no distinction between the church and
the members who compose the church. Such a generalization is
a mere ideality incapable of organization under laws, doctrines,
ordinances and discipline." Further testimony on the same line
can be easily found; let me, however, merely refer to Dr. Carson's words :—" As to a visible, universal church it exists nowhere but in the ideas of polemical writers and the absurd
distinctions of scholastic divinity." These words should be carefully weighed and considered, for I believe they will be admitted
by all correctly to set forth those views that Baptists hold
regarding the constitution of a church. And especially should
they be considered by those who are ever ready to bring forward
on every occasion resolutions of all kinds, with the object that
the pronouncement of the Baptist body should be had thereon.
If I am right in assuming that these men correctly set forth
Baptist principles, then there can be no universal expression of
opinion of the Baptists on any question. There is no Baptist
church through which Baptist opinion can be voiced. What
then becomes of the resolutions and protests passed by the Baptists in convention ? Whose are they ? They are not resolutions
of " the Baptist church." There is none. They are not those of a
Baptist church. They can be nothing more than the expression
of opinion of some persons of the Baptist persuasion who are
gathered together in convention, and no church can be responsible for them, for their framers have no status. I do not think
it would be so bad if those who moved and passed resolutions should recognize that they did not speak for the Baptists.
The evil lies in the fact that they believe they do voice Baptist
opinion and conviction, and in addition, that they are quite
within the sphere of the church when they pass resolutions

memorializing the State to do this or do that, to carry out this or that reform, as being the proper thing to do, as being forsooth in accord with Baptist belief. Even supposing it were possible to express the opinion of " the Baptist Church " in the way indicated, there would still remain open the broad debatable ground of the wisdom or lack of wisdom of passing upon these questions at all, and the grave charge is laid against us that in so doing we violate our principles. If there is a liability to err in this way, we ought not to pass upon these questions at all. There is no doubt that, in regard to the Manitoba School question, the State has an undoubted right to act. It does not need to justify its jurisdiction in that behalf. It clearly has it. But can the same be said of any church ? Can it justify its jurisdiction ? It is necessary that it first should do so. It cannot be granted that it has any jurisdiction whatsoever. And then it is necessary to make a long and laborious argument to show that the church has any part or parcel in this matter, and in the end will it not be found that it has no right to interfere or protest ? It has touched a matter with which it has nothing to do. I repeat then, that if there are such unsurmountable difficulties in the way of establishing that we have *any* jurisdiction at all, we ought by all means to cease passing such resolutions.

Now let me refer more particularly to that which concerns the wisdom of passing resolutions upon those subjects with which the State has clearly a right to deal, and especially as shown in some recent opinions to which Baptists have given expression. A short time ago we witnessed the unhappy spectacle of a high dignitary of the Catholic church telling a member of Parliament of the attitude of his church toward the Manitoba School question. We were somewhat startled at this. We thought we saw in it the power of the church brought into the realm of the State. We thought in fact it was a violation of a principle by which we believed we were prepared unhesitatingly to condemn such action. We feared for our liberties and the independence of Parliament. We should have resisted such aggression to our utmost power. But suddenly our arm was paralyzed, we could see things only in a hazy manner. Our voices were silenced. We found to our amazement that our own denomination would do the thing we were wont to condemn.

Such action was justified in several letters in "The Canadian Baptist." The very leaders of our denomination were the foremost in anxiously endeavouring to show the members of the House of Commons and of the Senate that if one church would act in one way the Baptists, at least, would act in another. Thus they who demanded complete separation of Church and State, in the very same breath violated the principle. They said by their conduct, "we want the State not to interfere in that which concerns the Church only, but when we wish we will tell and show and effectively compel the State to do what we wish." It may be that some can draw nice subtle distinctions to justify their actions, and show that when a member of a religious body writes a letter to a member of Parliament stating the attitude his church will take towards a question, there is a violation of the principle of separation of Church and State; but that when many members of a church shall pass a resolution, showing the attitude of that church to the same question and transmit copies to the House of Commons and the Senate, there is no violation of such principle, their action is perfectly justifiable. I believe both are equally culpable. It was said, however, that this was a favorable opportunity to show to the world what the Baptist principles are; that we should not let such an occasion pass for making ourselves known. As if we had received a commission to propagate Baptist principles. As if the world were in need of knowing any other commission than the great one of "Go ye into all the world and preach the gospel to every creature."

Now, why have we wished to place ourselves on record on the Manitoba School question at all? What have been our reasons for passing resolutions on this subject? Is it that we are anxious to place on record our disapproval of the provisions of the Remedial Bill, and the methods adopted by the Dominion Parliament in forcing this Bill upon a free and sovereign people? Here the question is one which concerns us as citizens and not as members of a Baptist church. It is a question of political expediency with which no church, and least of all a Baptist church, has anything to do. Besides, it may be urged, as the Dominion Government do urge, that they have a right to pass this Bill to remedy what has been found to be a grievance of the

Catholic minority, and to this proposition we all must consent. The Dominion Government are quite within their rights when they pass this Bill. We may not agree with them as to whether an occasion has arisen for the exercise of that undoubted right. Yet once granted that the right exists, then the question falls, and we have no right as Baptists to interfere with what may be termed the inexpediency of such a course. So also with regard to the Provisions of this Bill. If we, as I have said, object to the Provisions of the Bill, it must be on the ground of political expediency and it must be by us as citizens, not as Baptists. This Bill may be very badly framed, but if the Dominion Parliament have the right, as they undoubtly have, to pass this measure, we cannot object to the Bill passing; for our actions would say that we believe that these men who have a right to pass a measure, and who sincerely wish to carry out the constitution should refuse to do so, even though the constitution be thereby violated, because forsooth it transgresses upon some supposed Baptist principle. Who will justify such a reason as this for opposing the Bill? There must be some other reason then why Baptists seek to prevent the passage of this Bill. Is it this, that if this Bill becomes a law and is enforced by the Dominion Parliament, the Baptist principle of the complete separation of Church and State will be violated?

Let me examine this assertion and see whether we, as Baptists, have anything over which to raise our hands in protest; to see whether our reasons for interference with what the State considers to be its duty to carry out are just and fair. Supposing the Remedial Bill becomes law, a system of Separate Schools in Manitoba will be the result. That is, the same thing will obtain in Manitoba that has for twenty-five years obtained in Ontario, and with what result? Are we in any way interfered with? Are our rights as Baptists trampled upon? Have any rights of conscience been violated? Are not we allowed to worship God in any way we choose? Is there anything whatsoever for which we, as Baptists, can condemn our Catholic fellow citizens except it be that they have and we have not Separate Schools?

But some say we object, because, we say, the State has no right to grant State money to assist any Church in propagating its peculiar tenets, and we object to our Baptist money going in support of any such church. This, I believe, is the strongest argument that the Baptists use and therefore should be examined most carefully. Let me examine the last clause, "that our Baptist money goes in support of separate schools!" I think this is clearly a fallacious statement; for the State does not attempt to, and does not, raise any money from any Church. It looks at citizenship as distinct and separate from membership of a church; levies taxes on all its citizens for the purposes of the State, and they pay taxes as citizens of the State. Because we happen to belong to the Baptist or Catholic church, we do not pay Baptist or Catholic taxes. I think this is clear. Now then, the State says, we want to raise a certain amount of money from our citizens and we will levy accordingly. It needs so much for schools and it levies upon all citizens, and in its discretion assigns it to the Separate and Public Schools in the proportion it deems advisable. Surely Baptist money does not support Separate Schools. It is the State's, the citizens', money.

Finally, let me ask who is to determine the functions of the State, both what it is and what it ought to be? Whose ideas are to prevail, the citizen's or the churchman's? Surely there can be no difficulty in deciding that it is the citizen's and his alone. And why? Because from the very nature of things a State could not otherwise exist. For what the Baptist says is not within the realm of conscience, the Catholic as stoutly affirms is within the realm of conscience, is within the realm of the Catholic church, and the State should not interfere. For example, the Catholic (and many a Protestant) says: we do not believe in "Godless" schools for our children; we believe the schools should provide religious instruction for our children and you violate our conscience if you banish religious instruction from our schools and allow our children to grow up under "Godless" teachers. The Baptist says we believe in schools in which there is no religious instruction; that should only be taught at home and by the parents, and when you compel me to support schools in which there is religious teaching you violate my conscience. Now who is to decide between these? Who is to say how far the rights of conscience shall be observed or violated? Who and what? Without doubt the citizens and the State. If necessary the State will in some cases have to disregard or violate the rights of conscience, or what are sometimes considered the rights of conscience. The State cannot exist unless in some cases it does do this. But the point is simply this: it is the citizens' privilege, right and duty to decide in *all* cases how far the rights of conscience shall or shall not be observed. We have just had a very good instance, and one strikingly pertinent to this point, in a case recently before the Courts, where three " Seventh Day Adventists " were fined for working on the Sabbath contrary to the Lord's Day Act. Their justification was that they considered they would be guilty of sin if they were idle on that day and did not work. They would violate their conscientious belief if they did not act in this manner. Is the State not to determine whether it will allow such conscientious scruples to prevail or whether or not it will recognize Sunday as different from other days of the week ? Surely there can be no argument on this point. The State must in some cases override the conscientious scruples of some. It ought always to be very careful in so doing. But the point is, the State has the right to to determine ; and so I think it will be found that other arguments which have been urged qualifying the action of the Baptists are not sound.

Let me now resume the position I have endeavoured to establish. I have tried to show :

1st. That the principle of separation of Church and State is not necessarily a Baptist position, but grows from a recognition of the fact that one is concerned with temporal, the other with spiritual, things.

2nd. That from the very nature and constitution of a "Baptist Church", there can be no universal expression of opinion of the Baptists.

3rd. That in any case with which the citizens have *prima facie* the right to legislate, the Baptist body should be careful in passing upon it.

4th. That in regard to the Manitoba Schools, citizens acting through the State have an undoubted right to deal, and there appears to be no good reason for Baptist interference.

5th. That it is the right of the State to say how far it will or will not recognize what sometimes appears to be within the realm of conscience.   W. A. Lamport.

PATIENCE.

What is patience ? sweet and quaintly
   Came the answer thus to me
From a little Scottish lassie,
   " Dinna weary, bide awee !"

Deepest wisdom in this meaning,
   Sweet as music may it be !
Ever in thy heart thus singing,
   " Dinna weary, bide awee !"

When with clouds the sky is darkened,
   And the sun thou canst not see;
Falter not, thy Father knoweth,—
   " Dinna weary, bide awee !"

When the path of life is toilsome,
   And thy steps drag heavily ;
Forward press, thy God is guiding,
   " Dinna weary, bide awee !"

When the heart grows faint with watching
   For the ships so long at sea;
Trust them in the Master's keeping,
   " Dinna weary, bide awee !"

Patience is the Queen of workers,
   Hinder not her work with thee !
Perfect its imperial beauty,
   " Dinna weary, bide awee !"

Patience then, my fellow pilgrim,
   Till the blessed face we see
Of the Christ, our living Pattern,
   " Dinna weary, bide awee !"

M. D. S

2

Students' Quarter.

AN IDEAL HOME.

" Home is the spot of earth supremely blest,
A dearer, sweeter spot than all the rest."
Montgomery.

The home of the Palmers stands just where the winding Arno river crowds the Elton turnpike against the southern spur of Wildwood mountain, about a mile from the city of Barton, in the Province of Ontario. The plain, square-built, stone house looks through the park-like clump of shapely elms and maples down over the valley toward the eastern sun. Away to the south on both sides of the river, as far as the eye can reach, field follows field like the blocks of an immense chess-board. Toward the north, rising in easy slopes and levels, the mountain wears her primal dress still unmarred by human hand. Behind the house the valley gradually rises higher and higher till it ends in a sheltered glen in the bosom of the mountain, where nature in wondering pause before her own handiwork had let fall the grace of Eden's bowers.

The immediate surroundings of the house were beautiful from the absence of that prim mathematical regularity and exactuess which is, for some inconceivable reason, called artistic and beautiful. Everywhere nature had been the master artist, and man her willing and teachable co-worker. In some places her too bountiful hand had been stayed, her wanton luxuriance checked; in others her more feeble efforts had been encouraged, and her fainting offspring cherished.

The wild ivy and the grape were not divorced from the elms to which nature had wed them. The hepatica and the trillium still loved the sun-kissed knoll, and the fragrance of the violet and the dog-rose still breathed from the margin of the rippling brook which washed the same channel as when its waters mirrored the thirsty deer. The painted orchids too and eglantine had forgotten to flee to the wilds at man's approach. Side by side with these children of the forest, grew the choicest products of the florist's art. The commonalty and the nobility of the flower race were here united in their mission of adding grace and beauty to the earth, delighting the eye, and refining the nature of man, and lifting his thoughts to Him who " so clothed the grass of the field."

The songbird had not given place to the quarrelsome sparrow, and the oriole's "bottle" still swung on the slender branch. The squirrel ran unharmed from tree to tree, and saucily chattered his right of domain.

The Palmers had no golden piles from the top of which they could presume to look in scorn upon their neighbors, but hearts, content and at peace with all the world, gave them greater wealth than all the glittering stores of Crœsus. Their farm furnished them an income which must be wisely used, and they had learned life's best lessons at the smallest cost. Wealth had never taught them that weak self-indulgence which leads to the worship of gold, and the contempt for all that is truest, noblest, best, in the discipline of life. A limited income had impressed the lessons of thrift and self-dependence. They had learnt to measure life and its realities by a truer standard than the gold dollar.

The furnishing of the large airy rooms told of comfort, but not luxury or wasteful wealth. Use rather than ornament had been the motto of those whose judgment had given each room its appointments, and the very apparent utility of every article gave the impression that elegance can never be separated from tasteful utility.

The library, though small, was selected with good judgment, and was composed of the standard poets, biographies, histories, and fiction in plain strong bindings, not too good to be used every day. Two or three shelves were devoted to the children. Here were found such works as would introduce the young mind to the best literature and at the same time give it a view of life, not as a fairy land of ease but as a reality which calls for the best and truest activities of mind and body. There were attractive biographies of the world's truly great men, easy histories, selections from the poets, wholesome travels, elevating fiction and elementary science and natural history. A few of the best periodicals furnished reading for spare moments, but by judicious care the parents directed the intellectual appetites of the family toward the stronger and more wholesome foods afforded by the library, rather than to the unsubstantial knicknacks and fragmentary literature of magazines.

The great value of music as an educator, and its power as a factor in character-building, were clearly recognized, and due provision was made for the study of both vocal and instrumental music.

Though their fortunes would not allow them to decorate their homes with costly paintings and statuary, the pictures and paintings on the walls showed a cultivated taste and a true appreciation of art. The older girls had already gained by their studies of art an intellectual relish for the artistic, and a keen insight into that which lies behind the painter's canvas and the sculptor's block—the soul of the artist speaking through brush and chisel. They had learnt to see in a picture more than a mere harmonious blending of purposeless colors ; they read the thought for whose expression words were hopelessly impotent— the thought which in its struggle for utterance drives the painter to his canvas and the sculptor to his marble.

From earliest childhood, both by precept and example, the members of the family were taught that life has its duties and its services. Each day has its part in the moulding of thought, the direction of activities, the suppression of wrong tendencies.

The spirit of Christ was the supreme rule of life. His example was the standard of conduct. The highest delight of all seemed to be to serve one another, and in these kindly efforts to bear one another's burdens they learnt to bear their own.

The gulf which so often divides the interests and delights of parents from those of their children was bridged in a hundred ways. After the day's duties were done, the evening hours were spent around the fireside. The parents would direct and encourage the studies and reading of the children, and the often difficult paths of learning were paved for their feet. Schoolbooks to them became a delight because they saw in them the key to the great kingdom of knowledge to whose gates they had been led and of whose shining fields they were day by day getting clearer glimpses. Each, as far as possible, contributed a part toward the evening's joys. The story of some gallant knight, the history of a famous deed of heroism, the recital of poetic gems, the study of some Bible character; music, games or songs, filled up the evening· hours.   Often the young people from the neighboring farms were called in to share the pleasures of their winter evenings, and they, too, caught the spirit of the home, and learnt to collect a rich revenue from what had before been idle hours.

Then round the family altar with hearts attuned and sacred joy they sing their praise to Him who has perfected praise out of the mouths of babes." They read. the Holy Word and are taught to take its precepts "as a lamp unto their feet," and to hide its counsels in their hearts that they may not transgress the laws of God.   Then kneeling to their Heavenly Father, in simple earnest childlike trust they confess the failings of the day, thank him for his bounties, and seek his grace and guidance.

Winter and summer bring their outdoor pleasures for all. The snow-covered hills attract happy coasting parties ; a merry sleigh-ride in the keen winter air, over the crisp creaking snow, is a delight unmeasured.

The Canadian frosts throw their icy mantle over the winding river, and away upon its glistening surface, the skaters shod with their ringing steel glide like the flitting swallows, above its summer waters.   Away they speed, down the valley and into the forest depths, where the pendent boughs with their sparkling winter jewels make a dim arcade through the echoing solitudes.

In the summer, boating and fishing were among the many pleasures.   But the chief outdoor delights of both parents and children were gardening, and rambling in the forests and up the mountain slopes, making friends of shrubs and flowers, trees and ferns, studying the habits of birds and animals, making natural history collections and revelling in nature's numberless unfoldings of the handiwork of God.   No modest flower could hide its blush in twilight dell, but they would know its opening hour. There was no bird of so retiring habit, but its nesting time and place were known.   The fox's den, the beaver's dome, the squirrel's retreat were known not as the haunts of enemies but as the ho.nes of nature's children who " divide her care."

From homes like this comes the full vigorous manhood of our land ; a manhood not simply of bodily vigor but of mental,

moral and spiritual worth, fashioned after the ideal manhood of
Jesus.   Such homes are the fountains from which all true
national life and worth must spring, for true patriotism is but
fraternal love with a national horizon.

R. D. GEORGE, '97·

THE VOICES OF THE DEEP.

The ocean in silent slumber lay,
   The sun burned low in the west;
What did the heaving waters say ?
   What is their endless quest ?
Said a stripling, buoyant with glowing health :
   "They surely whisper to me
Of the wells of love and the mines of wealth
   As deep as the soundless sea."

A strong man stood by the rock-bound shore,
   The billows were dashing high,
As the waters writhe and the wild winds roar
   And wildly the sea-gulls cry :
"Ah me !" he said, "What a scene is here
   Of the toilful pangs of life,
The wrathful tones of the surging mere
   Are pæans of woe and strife."

An old man sat by the quiet shore
   And gazed far over the deep,
The storm-king rides on the storm no more
   The moving tide is neap;
"The battle of life is o'er," he said,
   "The evening hour has come,
When the glory glows in the evening red
   The Pilot will take me home."

O. G. LANGFORD, 95.

A YARN.

Well, I say! I want to know! What kind of country are we in, anyway?

To enter into the general question why a Yankee always wants to know,—of course it was a Yankee asked this question —is not the present purpose. This particular Yankee certainly had a right to know, and a good purpose in knowing. The particular part of country we were in was not very prepossessing certainly, as far as present appearances went. Our position was not an enviable one either. We were snow-bound—on a train, several miles from a station. There were seven of us. First, a knight of the road, one of that class of men you meet everywhere. A farmer who was on his way home from town made the second member of the party. The third was an architect, evidently with high ideals. The fourth a lumberman, a-well-to do business man, intelligent, and one who had seen a good deal of life. The fifth member was a lecturer. He had hours ago given up all thought of delivering his lecture on that special occasion. The Yankee made the sixth. He was of the down east type, a business man evidently. The seventh, as you will no doubt have guessed, was myself. Of him I shall say no more.

We were *not* seated in orthodox style in the smoking room of a Pullman. There were various reasons for this; chief and most important of which was that being on a local train there was none. On that account we were seated around the heater in an ordinary "first-class" Grand Trunk day coach. Inside we were comfortable enough. It was warm and light, but as I said, outside the conditions were far from cheerful. The wind was blowing wildly. The low humming vibration of the wires along the track made a dismal accompaniment for the spectre-like motions of the drifting snow. Above us towered the black outlines of a high hill, almost a mountain, rising so precipitously that the snow had no place to cling. Below was a dark forest of pine, which, blown upon by the wind added its melancholy song to that of the wires. Before or behind we could not see. There were no works but those of nature in sight. As far as appearances went there was no human habitation near.

" Well, I say ! I want to know ? What kind of country are we in, anyway ? "

The question somewhat startled us.   We, like stolid sons of John Bull, had been keeping silence through the long tedious battle with the snow, and when snow had conquered the result was not a surprise.   For that reason we kept silence, knowing that there was nothing better to be done than to wait for the snow-plow.   This question, however, aroused us.   It was put as a challenge, not in form indeed, but in tone.   An ordinary question would not have aroused us from silence, but the implied challenge awoke every one of us.   Evidently, with the exception of the questioner, all were Canadians.

" It's a pretty good country, I tell you," replied one.

" Well, it doesn't look very much like it just now."

"That I will grant; but that is because we are placed by the weather in an uncomfortable position."

" I don't see how that affects it."

" It does, however.   On a clear day the view from this very position is magnificent.   We are situated on the edge of a series of ridges of which this is the highest and last.   From the top of this you may look back upon a country rocky but well wooded. Here and there streams cut their way.   The valleys are very beautiful.   On our front is a rolling country.   We have here within a few miles the beauties of mountain and lowland."

" That may all be, but what is it all good for ? "

" I wish I owned that pine down the hill here," responded the lumberman.   If it does not suit you as landscape, very little trouble will convert it into money."

" And that valley," interrupted the farmer, "is one of the richest farming countries you will find anywhere.   Why ! it is all clear, no broken land for miles, dotted all over with the substantial buildings of well-to-do farmers."

" Yes, but that's only half.   I don't see much use for this hill here and the rocks beyond."

" Wait until you get around the corner of this hill and you will see," replied the architect.   " The stone of which it consists has furnished the material for some of the finest buildings in Ontario."

" Well that *is* surprising.   I never was in Canada before, and I had always heard it was a wilderness, with a few people left here and there to take care of it."

It is needless to say that a smile went round the party. We thought of Canada as being anything but a wilderness.

"How did you get this far into Ontario without seeing anything of it, anyway?"

"Came in the night."

"That accounts for it. You will have a different opinion of it before you have been in it very long."

"Have you got any towns, anyway?"

"Yes," responded the commercial man, "we have, they are good business places too. Of course our Canadian cities cannot compare in size with some of the American cities, but for their population the business they do compares favorably with those of any other country. They have this advantage, also, that the foundations of trade are solid. What is known as mushroom growth is heard of but little. We Canadians are quite like the English in this way. We do not regard a business as a business until it is solvent."

"But why don't you go ahead then?"

"Well there are various reasons for that," said the lecturer. "Some contend that the present political policy is the cause. This may or may not be the reason. At all events, I believe with a well known politician, 'we have, without doubt, one of the finest countries in the world.'"

"Yes," said the lumberman, "I believe that is true. Lots of people, along with our friend here, don't believe it, and why? Just because they don't know. Now I was surprised myself. I was called away a year ago on a business trip up through our northern districts. Before this I had no idea of Ontario's natural resources. The natural wealth seems unlimited. Take, for instance, timber—thousands of square miles of it untouched. We have little idea either of the mineral wealth. Nearly all the minerals of value are found in paying quantities. There is any amount of farming land up there too. The Ontario Government has, I believe, lately started an Experimental Station in that district."

"This is true also," added the architect, "of every province in the Dominion; down by the sea, in Quebec, the North-west, and away out by the coast.   The natural resources seem bound-less."

" Now I've two sons in the North-west," said the farmer, " and I was out there a while ago to see them.   Such a country I never saw before.   The harvest was just being gathered.   It seemed to me that if the land was all settled up it would raise enough to feed the whole of North America."

" The prairies are a wonderful sight," continued the lecturer. " In places there is not a tree to be seen and it seems as if you were out at sea.   You may travel from Winnipeg west to the Rockies with prairie scenery all the way ; but when the Rockies are once reached all is changed.   You have then all the glory and solid massive grandeur of mountain scenery.   European scenery, though far-famed, does not surpass this.   ' Mass upon mass their summits pierce the sky.' "

" Yes the Rockies are a rare sight, but we have scenery nearer home."

" Niagara Falls aren't bad," interjected the Yankee.

" No, they are not.   On the contrary, they are one of the most wonderful sights eye can see," returned the architect, " but they are partly yours, so I did not refer to them especially. Take for instance the St. Lawrence scenery.   Commencing at the Thousand Islands—from there clear to the Gulf the beauties of nature are enchanting."

" Were you ever on the Saguenay ?" asked the lumberman.

" No, never."

" Well you have something yet to see.   I am a rather prosaic mortal myself, but when we steamed up that gorge into Ha Ha Bay I felt that I could write an epic."

" Some of the most beautiful sights I have ever seen," con-tinned the commercial man, " have been down by the sea in the Maritime Provinces.   They simply baffle description."

" Well, to my thinking," added the farmer, " there is nothing more pleasing to the eye than the rich rolling farming country of Ontario, watered by streams, dotted with small lakes, and here and there a village with its cluster of houses and its church spires."

" These natural advantages are all right in their way," said the Yankee," but I've been born and brought up in a town, and

I care more about men and cities than about natural advantages. After what you've told me, I'll admit you have been well provided for, but what good are natural advantages if you hav'nt men and cities?"

"The proper study of mankind is man," quoted the lecturer

"We were talking of cities and trade just now, I believe, weren't we?" said the commercial man, "and some one of you switched off. I'll admit that our trade isn't what it might be, and I predict that it isn't what it will be."

"Talking about cities," said the architect, "I don't know where in a new country you will find more variety. It is doubtless a result of our national history. Take Quebec for instance. You might suppose you had dropped into some corner of France, while in Winnipeg everything is new."

"We have some fine institutions in these cities too," added the lecturer. "You, my friend, will speak of them from an architectural standpoint."

"Yes, we have some fine buildings. Take for instance the Dominion Parliament Buildings, and many of our other structures I could name. Canadians are certainly lovers of fine architecture.

"I was much interested," interrupted the commercialman, "in listening to the praises of some American tourists in Toronto last summer. They were completely delighted with the city, praising its streets, its parks, its residences, its public institutions to an extent which I, a Canadian, would not have risked my reputation upon, if abroad, even although I know it all to be true."

"Canadians are well educated too," remarked the lecturer. "As I heard a prominent man remark the other day, 'in Canada any one may obtain an education practically without money and without price.'

"That's a broad statement," replied the architect, "but I believe it is true. The public school system is a very complete one, and the higher education is well looked after. The work done is well done, and the Canadian has no need to be ashamed of his educational advantages. If he is ashamed, it can only be because he had not availed himself of the offered privileges, and even a case of that is somewhat rare."

"Well you seem to have a pretty fair country," half admitted the Yankee, "but why don't you join with the United States ?"

"Ah," replied the lecturer, "we think too much of our country to do that. We are Canadians, and loyal to our flag. We prize that flag and honor it. 'Canada for the Canadians,' is not merely a party cry to us. It means every thing to every son of Canada. We have a country of lakes and rivers, of woods and forests, mountains and valleys, fields and mines. There is wealth for the farmer, and the miner, the hunter and the fisherman, the woodsman and the mechanic. We have beautiful cities containing great institutions. Our legislation is administered by men who have the good of the country at heart. Our schools are located everywhere. They are taught by teachers who are qualified for the most thorough work. Ours is a land where men may worship as they will, where any attempt to interfere with a man's religion is frowned and hissed upon, a country where God is worshipped as the Giver of all. What more could a nation desire ? If every Canadian is true to himself, his inheritance and his flag, we shall be a great nation."

"You said you were a lecturer, did you not ?" enquired the Yankee.

"Yes."

"Well, isn't that a part of the lecture you couldn't deliver to-night ?"

.   .   .   .

The humming wires and the howling wind finally had their effect. Somnus has power even under such conditions. This was all I heard of the conversation. At all events, just as the sky was getting grey I awoke with a jerk. The snow-plow had got through to us, and soon we were enjoying ourselves in a country hotel of the old type. Our Yankee friend in his own style was having "something hot." I do not know whether it was this latter or the conversation that called forth the remark, but between sips he was heard to say, "Well, this isn't a bad country, after all."

WALLACE P. COHOE, '96·

COMMENT ON HAMLET, ACT I, SCENE III.

ROOM IN POLONIUS'S HOUSE.

In this scene a new family is introduced, consisting of three; father, son, and daughter; Polonius, Laertes and Ophelia; affording fruitful sources of comparison with Hamlet's deceased sire, Hamlet himself, and Gertrude.

As to its bearing on the plot, the scene is, in any case, inserted with taste and judgment.   Some intervening action is necessary between the appearances of the Ghost in Scenes Two and Four respectively, else the effect would be monotonous and displeasing.   We know, furthermore, at the conclusion of this scene, several important factors in the development of the play, which were, some unrecognizable, some not manifest, previously. Briefly, Laertes leaves for France; Laertes is loving and high-spirited; Hamlet loves Ophelia; Ophelia loves Hamlet; Polonius is henceforth to be considered: the elements of his character; Laertes and Polonius oppose the loves of Hamlet and Ophelia.

With regard to artistic qualities, and evidence affirmative of family failings, we propose to touch upon these as we proceed with the synopsis.

Laertes, on the eve of his departure for France, undertakes to admonish his sister against the importunity of Hamlet; to play the monitor, lovingly, no doubt, yet, perchance, with undue assumption of innate superiority :

> " For Hamlet and the trifling of his favour,
> Hold it a fashion and a toy in blood,
> A violet in the youth of primy nature,
> Forward, not permanent, sweet, not lasting,
> The perfume and suppliance of a minute,
> No more."

Ophelia replies with semi-acquiescence :—

> " No more but so ? "
>   " Think it no more,"

answers Laertes, 'for Hamlet has not yet attained to soundness of judgment and obduracy of will.   He may, indeed, love you truly, but he is not his own master, being a prince of the royal blood.   The disposition of his life is in other hands than his.   So be careful, my sister!' Then follows the climax of his expression, which, though it displays much of the sententious proverbialism we find in Polonius later on, is nevertheless apt and apposite :

> " The chariest maid is prodigal enough,
> If she unmask her beauty to the moon."
>
> . . . . .
>
> " The canker galls the infants of the spring,
> Too oft before their buttons be disclos'd ;
> And in the morn and liquid dew of youth,
> Contagious blastments are most imminent."

Gently Ophelia replies. She appreciates the fraternal advice ; but, with an indefinite desire to tender 'tit for tat'; she retorts, yet gravely and demurely,

> " good my brother,
> Do not, as some ungracious pastors do,
> Show me the steep and thorny way to heaven,
> Whiles, like a puff'd and reckless libertine,
> Himself the primrose path of dalliance treads,
> And recks not his own rede,"

' Let him that thinketh he standeth,' brother Laertes, ' take heed lest he fall.'

Laertes grows impatient; he has no relish for what he deems a most unjust suggestion. Though he loves Ophelia dearly ; surely, surely, 'tis half-unbearable. He almost suspects that

> ' Her wit is more than man, tho' her innocence a child.'

But the possible crisis is averted ; harmony is restored ; the imp Doubt makes a hurried exit, for,—

> " *Enter Polonius.*"

In the nick of time ! " Marry, well bethought!" What could be better ?

> " *Enter Polonius.*"

Instantly Laretes changes the subject, and remarks upon the happy omen which the repetition of farewells must prove. Polonius exhorts him to hasten abroad ; ransacks his memory ; discovers some ' gem ' aphorisms ; brings them forth ; polishes, mixes, jumbles them into a sort of tesselated pavement whereon to enact the moralities ; and concludes with a self-satisfied, condescending smirk of dismissal.   Laertes departs, but flings 'the last word' at Ophelia, bidding her remember his advice.

Polonius surmises secrets.   Ah !

> " What is't, Ophelia, he hath said to you ? "

' He spoke with me concerning Hamlet,' says Ophelia.   'Good,' cries Polonius, ' I, too, have heard of you and Hamlet,—what means it, eh ? '   Dutifully Ophelia declares Hamlet's affection ; dutifully, yet with maidenly reluctance.   Polonius pooh-poohs such absurdity.   ' Come, tell me *your* mind,' says he, ' surely you don't believe his vapourings.'   You do not know ?   Come, come, then, you must know he's false ; he's light of heart and head.   Speak never more to him.   Think not aught good of him.   Take care.   Obey !'

How filial and sad and solemn it is,—that answering utterance of Ophelia's ; the submission of a pure soul, unable to satisfy its yearning, to fling aside the clogs of weariness and perplexity ; ground down by fate, harshly, remorselessly, into the ' stale, flat, unprofitable ' world :—

> " I shall obey, my lord."

HAMFRITH.

PEACE.

The moonbeams fall aslant the lake
And fling soft shadows from the cliffs,
The blossoms now in dreamland, take
Long draughts of dew on thirsty lips,
The soft winds whisper 'mong the leaves
Love's long low tale in shady bowers,
And on the lake and land he breathes
His passing spell, while night's calm hours
Bid beat in nature's breast the tranquil pulse of peace.

Softly the falling waters flow
Their joyous lives they babble forth,
And in the moonlight, beam aglow
As from a glorious inward birth—
And o'er my life there rests a calm
Peaceful, like music's soft sweet sound
Hushing the waves, that roll alarm
Around my bark.   My soul has found
And loves, the breathing, pulsing, angel form of Peace.

I. G. MATTHEWS, '97.

ELIZABETHAN CATCHES.

I.

Bees buzzing overhead,
   Dreamily I lie,
      Idly and dreamily,
   A lazy fellow I !
Flowers their perfume shed
Sweet is my clover-bed,
While by bright Fancy led,
   Dreamily I lie,
      Idly and dreamily,
   A lazy fellow I !

II.

Life and Death,
   Deceit, despair,
      So shall the varlets vary ;
A stifling breath
   Cuts off our care,—
      Now by 'r Lady Mary,
Life, Death,
   Everywhere,
      Must take us all unwary !

C. C.

EDITORIAL NOTES.

WE recommend all readers of the MONTHLY to peruse attentively Mr. Lamport's article in the present number. The writer has thought out his subject carefully, and presents with great force some views of the relations of citizen and church member which are well worth consideration. It is well to look at all sides of this question, to see ourselves as others see us, and thereby to avoid assuming positions that are not tenable, or claiming as peculiarly ours principles that are far more widely active than we are wont to believe.

As student, pastor and professor, Thomas Trotter has been long and closely identified with our educational work, and no name is held in higher esteem within our walls, or awakens more pleasing memories than his. Dr. Rand sets a high value on the part which Mr. Trotter has contributed to the realization of the gratifying position which Mc-Master holds among Toronto Universities to-day, an estimate which we feel sure all friends of the University will heartily approve. Though no longer a member of our Faculty, Mr. Trotter is still closely connected with University work, and long may his life and strength be spared to wield that influence for moral good in which few are so powerful as he.

THE indebtedness of the University to Dr. Gifford for his able and inspiring sermon before the Fyfe Missionary Society was increased by his address before the students on the following morning in the College chapel. The address was a fitting supplement to the sermon, and served to enforce its truths. In the sermon he expounded the doctrine of Christian stewardship ; in his address he showed how the steward would be paid according to the quality of the service performed. The moral universe was so constructed that every reaping would be according to the sowing, whether of the flesh unto corruption, or of the Spirit unto eternal life. The spirit of unselfishness lay at the heart of the kingdom of Jesus Christ—constituted the very essence of acceptable service for Him. It was of the very nature of the Christian religion that those who gave the most of it away to others had the most of it left for themselves. Those who acted on the principle of saving their lives would lose them, while those who lost them in self-denying effort for the spiritual good of their fellows, would find them again on earth reproduced in the lives whom they had thus saved, and finally glorified in heaven. Dr. Gifford's pithy, antithetical sentences will linger in the memory of the students, and the important truths which these sentences enshrined, in all their hearts.

CHAON ORR, by Mrs. Eva Rose York, is an attractive little volume of rather more than a hundred pages. It takes the form of a novel, though the author in her preface disclaims any attempt at producing a novel. All the same, young and old alike will find here a very interesting story. The spirit of poetry throws its charm over the style, so that it abounds in striking sentences and descriptive passages of great beauty. The main purpose of the book, however, is not to furnish us with a few hours' entertainment. It is more serious than that, and seeks to aid the reader in dealing with life's greatest questions by tracing the " development of the real life of Chaon Orr." Where can true rest and highest freedom be found? What is life's true centre? What the place of strength and courage, of intellectual culture, of poetry and art and music? These are the questions that confront young Orr. His early experiences, at home, college days with their entanglement in false views of life, the finding at last of a " blissful centre " in which his heart might rest, and the later adjustment of other things to that, are sketched sympathetically, and reveals a good deal of insight, careful analysis, and a high degree of literary skill. The book will bear, may almost demand, re-reading : for it is perhaps, too highly condensed. The transitions are abrupt, and seem at times unnatural ; the language occasionally strikes one as extravagant—indicating feelings that the situation does not seems to warrant ; and the discussions are not as clear and satisfying to the average reader as a fuller treatment might make them. The nature of the argument too is poetic rather than severely logical, and so will repay a second reading if one is to have the same assurance of the soundness of the reasoning that he has of the soundness of the conclusion. That conclusion is that only in Jesus, the Saviour, can the soul find safe rest, and that the knowledge of Him is the key to the truest appreciation and use of all that is beautiful in nature and life, in literature and art. We believe that this book will have a very useful mission in the world. In that hope we cordially commend it to our readers.

HERE AND THERE.

O. G. LANGFORD, ED.

CORNELL offers a course in the Russian language and literature.

IAN MACLAREN (Rev. John Watson) has been lecturing at Yale.

BROWN is the only college in America which offers a course in Dutch.

THERE was sold in one year in the college town of New Haven, 25,000,000 cigarettes.

THE Faculty of Boston University has decided to allow work on the college papers to count for English in the regular course.

THE *University of Michigan Daily* is authority for the statement that the degree of A.B. will be required for entrance to the Medical Department in a few years.

SEVERAL of our exchanges have printed excellent pictures of their Editorial Staff, Foot ball Team, and the *Transylvanian* has in addition excellent pictures of the presidents of its four Literary Societies.

The Echo wishes to place Olivet on the list of those colleges which appreciate the value of work on college publications. A year's work is accepted for a year of rhetorical work.—*Ex.*

THE women of Cornell University have decided to form a rowing crew. The Faculty are in favor of the movement, and Mr. Courtney, the Cornell coach, is to instruct them in rowing.

A letter by Miss A. L. Dicklow, Ph. M., appears in a late number of the *Ottawa Campus.* The writer, in a chatty conversational style, describes Canada and Toronto in general, and Moulton College life in particular.

KINDLY notices of our MONTHLY have appeared in many of our valued exchanges. Notably *Manitoba College Monthly, McGill Fortnightly, Acta Victoriana, The Student, Delphic University Monthly, Sunbeam* and others.

A MUSICAL combine has been effected of the great Choral Union of the Western Universities. The intention is to render the oratorios of the great masters in the town and cities where the colleges are located in succession, producing one oratorio or two each college year.

Queen's University Journal is uniformly good, the typography is of the best, the matter dignified and worthy of careful reading. A recent number contained an excellent portrait of the late Rev. D. J. McDonnell, with an appreciative memoir.

IT is evident that an agricultural college student produced the following : "When you talk about there being a better state than Ohio, every potato winks his eye, every cabbage shakes its head, every beet gets red in the face, every onion feels stronger, every oat field is shocked, rye strokes its beard, corn pricks up its ears, and every foot of ground kicks."—*College Days.*

THE late H. A. Massey, of Toronto, has made the following bequests to educational institutions :—Mount Allison College, $100,000 ; Victoria College, $200,000 ; Wesley College, $100,000 ; Wesleyan Theological College, $50,000 ; the American University, Washington, $50,-000 ; Alma Ladies' College, $10,000 ; Stanstead Wesley College, $10,-000.

PROF. HENRY A. ROWLAND, of Johns Hopkins University, after nearly a year's labor, has obtained successful results from a remarkable invention for transmitting telegrams written upon a typewriter at the place of sending and reproduced in typewritten form at the receiving part of the invention. Prof. Rowland, with his new machine, can send over the same wire five or six different messages at the same time in one direction.— *Yale News.*

WE live, not for the final scene of life, but for the whole course of living. Life, as a life, never can be wholly right unless it is begun right. " If you miss the first buttonhole you will not succeed in buttoning up your coat," says Goethe. Things may even up at the end, but it will not be without an ugly buckle in the cloth somewhere. Nor is it enough to have begun right. Any button in the row may make the trouble. A right is a life of right living all the way through.

HOPE is a duty. Despair is a sin. There is a bright side and a dark side to life itself, and to every event in life. We can choose our point of view, it is not forced upon us. We can resolutely look toward the light, or away from it. There is no cheer in gloom ; there is no gloom in cheer. Our duty toward God, toward others, and toward ourselves, demands that we should always recognize and be grateful for the light that is, and thus honor God, help others, and be glad ourselves.— *S. S. Times.*

OF all the popular American airs, the favorites of Edouard Remenyi, the great violinist, are "Suanee River" and " Dixey." It recently came to the notice of Mr. Remenyi that the author of " Dixey," Mr. Dan Emmett, was living in poverty in an obscure town in Ohio. The fact so touched the heart of the genial genius, that he immediately set about raising a fund for relief, and started it himself with a contribution of $50. That a man who could compose " Dixey " should live in poverty in enlightened America is something unaccountable.

IT is a matter of regret that the University never has had enough spirit to give a Greek play, and has let this honor stay in the west with several institutions of a quarter her size in point of numbers. The Latin play, " The Menaechmi," which was given here a few years ago was a great success, and there is plenty of ability to accomplish the greater task of presenting a comedy or tragedy in the original Greek. Prof. D'Ooge witnessed the Antigone of Sophocles, at Toronto two years ago and would undoubtedly give the benefit of his support and experience to the project. The sophomore classes in Greek are now larger than ever before and there is an excellent chance for '98 to show its spirit and scholarship in this affair.— *University of Michigan Daily.*

IN reading the accounts of the desperate efforts of the American and Australian prize fighters to get at each other, we wonder if these columns of blow and bluster are demanded or relished by newspaper readers. Both of these gentlemen have given a half dozen " ultimatums " couched in language made extremely disgusting and nauseating by a prolific use of personal pronouns and a generous indulgence in the common vernacular of braggadocios. It is extremely doubtful if the intelligent reader be interested in such. When Mr. John Sullivan, in a half drunken condition, arises at a banquet in New York and delivers himself of a " speech " bristling with complimentary references to his own prowess and heaping abuse upon his fellow-craftsmen, it may be seriously questioned whether or not the American public cares anything about such maudlin expressions. While it is doudtless true that the newspapers are led to publish much that is really objectionable because it is demanded by the public, yet we believe that the average newspaper reader would prefer not to have such rubbish as we have mentioned constantly thrust upon his notice. We can easily get along without it.

A DEADLY blow has been struck at Mohammedanism in India by the translation of the Koran into simple, idiomatic Urdu, the language of the common people of a large part of Northern India. Mohammed forbade the translation of his book, and his superstitious followers have believed it could not be put into any language except Arabic, the language in which it was written. The translation into Urdu is the work of an able Mohammedan convert to Christianity, and it has caused consternation to the defenders of Islam. The power of Islam has been that its Book existed only in Arabic, which few in India understand, or in ambiguous paraphrases. Now that it is in form to be read by the common people there is a panic in the camp of Islam. Two Mohammedan copyists engaged on the translation have abandoned Islam in disgust. " The Word of God ! it is not even the word of a decent man," they said. This indicates a most encouraging break in the solid ranks of Mohammedanism.— *Albert College Times.*

THE American school at Athens, which has been so instrumental in helping on the exploration and excavation of Greek remains in Greece and thereabouts, has received permission from the Greek government to excavate and explore the Isthmus of Corinth, says the *Pennsylvanian.*

This is a most important concession and one of great moment at this time, for the Isthmus of Corinth and the site of the ancient city of that name have never been excavated. This region, therefore, promises to be a most fruitful field of research. The point which renders it exceptionally promising is the fact that the site of the city of Corinth is now a flat plain with no buildings of any kind about ; not as in too many cases the site of some new town or city, rendering excavation almost impossible or only at great cost. So those in charge have every facility to aid them in their search, for Corinth presents a chance of finding remains the equals of any yet discovered. This city, for years one of the leading powers in Greece, was the trade centre and mart for all land traffic between Northern Greece and the Peloponnesus. Here, too, were held the famous Pythian games, which drew together people from all Greece, who contributed each their part to make the city wealthy and beautiful. Corinth was also a great center of art, and held within its walls many masterpieces of sculpture and architecture. It is true that many of these works were destroyed or taken away to Rome by Mummius when he sacked the city in the second century, B.C., but many must have escaped him, and these are now within the grasp of American explorers. If all goes well the result of their work should prove of incalculable·value and throw new light on many points of Greek art and history now dark.

THE improvements which W. H. Soulby has lately added to the microphone, or " sound magnifier," make it one of the most marvellous mechanical contrivances of the age. The special construction of this instrument is of no particular interest to any one except experts, but what is told of its wonderful powers as a magnifier of sounds will entertain young and old, as well as the scientific and unscientific readers of " Notes for the Curious." After the instrument had been completed with the exception of a few finishing touches, Soulby found it absolutely necessary to keep the door of his workshop tightly closed, so as to admit no sounds from the outside, otherwise the inarticulate rumblings given off by the "ejector" would have become unbearable. Even with closed doors the cap had to be kept constantly in place on the receiver to keep the instrument from sending forth a roar, which previous investigation had proved to be a combination of sounds produced by watch beats, breathing, the hum of flies, etc. A fly walking across the receiver of the instrument made a sound equal to a horse crossing a bridge, and when Mr. Soulby laid his arm across the box the blood rushing in his veins gave forth a sound which much resembled that made by the pump of a large steam engine. The playing of a piano in a house across the street was, when ejected from Soulby's machine, like the roar of an avalanche, and the washing of dishes in the kitchen of a house across the alley made a sound which the inventor says was a " burden to his soul." When anyone entered the room, walked about, coughed, touched the table or door handles, the shriek which issued from the ejector was most painful to hear. Hundreds of uses have been suggested for the microphone, the most practical being those of blood circulation and lung test.

A SERIOUS LOVE SPELL.

A young lady sings in our choir
Whose hair is the color of phoir,
    But her charm is unique,
    She has such a fair chique
It is really a charm to be nhoir.

Whenever she looks down the aisle
She gives me a beautiful smaisle,
    And of all her beaux
    I am certain she sheaux
She likes me the best all the whaisle,

Last Sunday she wore a new sacque,
Low-cut at the front and the bacque
    And a lovely boquet
    Worn in such a cute wuet
As only a few girls have the knacque.

Some day, ere she grows to antique,
In marriage her hand I shall sique ;
    If she's not a coquette
    Which I'd greatly regruette,
She shall share my six dollars a wique.

————

THE *Independent,* of New York ; *Sunday-School Times,* of Philadelphia ; and *Massey's Magazine* will publish poems by Mr. G. H. Clarke, '95. THE *Ram's Horn* has accepted a short story from Mr. S. R. Tarr, '95.

THE *Owl* has said a good many cross words since the Manitoba school question was mooted. It is not at all strange that the *Owl* cannot agree with everything expressed in the exchanges. Catholics do not seem to be able to distinguish between things that differ. It is surely not necessary to make every question a religious one, and yet it would seem that our Catholic exchange can see in every sentence uttered by a Protestant, whether it be scientific, historic or political, some secret intrigue, or some covert criticism of the HOLY ROMAN CHURCH. The following admirable reply to one of these growls is clipped from *Queen's College Journal :*—" Our grave friend the *Owl* was very cross last week and apparently very sleepy too. After reading into our report of Prof. Marshall's address on Galileo, something which was not there, he ruffled up his feathers and gave our whole institution a severed rubbing. If our irate friend will consult his history, he will find that in the time of Galileo the church did believe in the Ptolemaic theory, and if that implies a fault, though we fail to see that it does, history, and not our respected professor, is to be blamed for the reproach. The church, Protestant as well as Roman Catholic, has ever been slow to admit the claims of advancing science, and even to-day certain scientific theories are mooted questions with the church. We thank our friend the *Owl* for his solicitude for our Roman Catholic

students, than whom there are no more loyal sons of Queen's.   But
the solicitude is uncalled for.   These men will let us know when their
religion has been insulted or the tenets of their church misrepresented.
But they are not looking out as is the *Owl*—from its watch-tower—for
fancied insults, and being reasonable men, they do not object to the
statement of a plain historical fact nearly three centuries old, nor do
they take it as a reflection upon the church which they love and revere
as devotedly as do their brethren of Ottawa College.   The 'many such
instances' are, no doubt, of a piece with the one that has called forth
this hooting of our nocturnal friend.   As for the attack upon our
Principal, no comment is necessary.   It must be merely the moulting
season with this *rara avis*, which is, after all, one of our most valued
exchanges."

AN old Varsity boy writes a most interesting letter regarding
Stanford University.   It is so racy we cannot forbear clipping a paragraph or two :—" Here we are, in the middle of February.   I suppose
you are all, by this time, getting slightly tired of frost and snow, and
longing occasionally for the bursting buds, the robins, and the young
grass of triumphant spring.   How odd it is to think of you trudging to
and fro between library and lecture rooms, muffled to the ears and
'hustling' along to keep circulation up.   With the exception of a
couple of weeks' rain, we have been enjoying the most splendid weather
ever since I reached here on Sept. 9th.   I wish you all could have a
peep at the green fields, the leafy trees, the cloudless skies, the flowers,
fruits, and birds of the Santa Clara Valley.   Only twice since last
March have I seen snow : first, as I came through the Rocky Moun
tains over the C.P.R. ; and again when a light mantle of 'the beautiful' wrapped for a day or two the rugged sides of Mount Hamilton, on
which stands the Lick Observatory, plainly visible, though some forty
miles to the eastward of Palo Alto.
   "When this reaches you, the Conversazione will be a thing of the
past, and only the election contests in the various societies and the
swift-approaching 'exams.' will remain to cheer the uneventful way.
It seems hard to realize that I shall have no long-drawn agony in May
this year.   Here, there are no finals ; every Stanford student already
has the majority of his examinations over and done with.   It is
marvellous that the old system should still exist in Toronto and other
Canadian universities.   The fact that it does, proves the conservatism
and long-suffering of our people, for it has long ago been condemned
root and branch by the most advanced educationists ; and truly it has
many evils.   Another thing hard for me to realize is that I shall see
nothing this year corresponding in the smallest degree to the great
annual election contest of Toronto.   If our beloved old university has
one institution peculiarly and entirely its own, it is the Literary Society
election.   Whenever I describe that feature of our life to the fellows
here, they listen in open-mouthed wonderment ; but afterwards, upon
mature reflection, invariably set me down as a would-be rival of Baron
Munchausen.   They cannot understand it at all.   They want to know
what our parties fight about.   But I, like Peterkin's grandfather, can
only shake my head and say : 'It was a famous victory.' "

COLLEGE NEWS.

W. P. COHOE, '96,   R. D. GEORGE, '97

J. F. VICHERT, '97,   MISS E. WHITESIDE, '98

Editors.

THE UNIVERSITY.

THE Library received nearly 300 books during March.   Dr. Newman was the chief donor.

THERE is said to be *circum*-stand-ial evidence that one of our men was out for a walk the other night.

EVERYONE was pleased to welcome Mr. G. N. Simmons, '96, back again well and strong after his recent illness.

MESSRS. A. R. Park, Th. '98, and D. B. Harkness, '97, have had to give up work for the present on account of illness.

We are much pleased to learn that Dr. Rand is to deliver the Oration at the Enccœnia of New Brunswick on the 28th of May.

GENTLEMEN desiring the new silent ring attachment on their bicycles should not fail to call on Mr. McKechnie.

MR. W. P. SPOTTS has the sympathy of the school in the sore bereavement which he has sustained in the death of his mother in Victoria, B.C.

MANY of our students were visibly affected the other day on hearing the strains of "Sweet Bye and Bye" from a street organ playing outside the Examination Hall.

SAID one metaphysician to another: "If you want an adequate idea of eternity, come to my boarding house and hear for one night my landlady's daughter play the piano."

THE "Argosy," laden with a rich and varied cargo, gathered from many sources, under the direction of Messrs. H. W. Newman, '99, and W. B. Teakles, '98, furnished an abundance of amusement, pleasure and instruction for the closing meeting of the Tennysonian Society.

THE students were very happy to entertain Dr. Neff, of the Neff College of Oratory, Philadelphia, Pa., at tea one evening this month. After tea Dr. Neff was kind enough to talk to us on the subject, "Education and Everyday Oratory." Dr. Neff managed this subject in a very interesting and instructive manner.   All present were very much delighted that they had availed themselves of this opportunity. We can assure Dr. Neff of a warm welcome when he again visits McMaster.

THE closing meeting of the Literary and Scientific Society was held on the evening of Friday, April 3rd. The Society under the able presidency of Mr. J. J. McNeill, '96, has had a very successful term, and the president and officers deserve congratulations for the success which has attended their efforts. The chief interest of the last meeting centered in the reading of the " Student" by its efficient editor-in chief, Mr. I. G. Matthews, '97. Needless to say it was brimful of bright jokes, articles containing more or less sense, and effective local hits, all of which were thoroughly enjoyed by the members present.

AN open meeting of the Literary and Scientific Society was held on Friday evening, March 20th. Resolved—" That the so-called balance of power is the best means for maintaining and promoting peace and justice among the European powers," was the subject in hand for debate, and after able discussion on both sides was decided in favour of the affirmative. Messrs. R. D. George, '97, and J. C. McFarlane, '99, upheld the affirmative, and Messrs. L. Brown, '96, and F. J. Scott, the negative. The readings by Miss Jessie Dryden and Mr. W. J. Thorold, B.A., were well received, as was evinced by the hearty encores. The musical part of the programme consisted of an instrumental selection by Miss V. Kirk, of Moulton College, a song by Mr. McAlpine, B.A., and selections by the University Orchestra and Glee Club. Mr. C. J. Holman, M.A., one of the Board of Governors, kindly acted as Judge of the debate.

THE Philosophical Club, under the Presidency of Prof. Ten Broeke, has had a very interesting and profitable session. The president has taken great pains to make all the meetings a success, and he has accomplished his purpose. The problems in the philosophical world which have been brought before the Club and discussed have been both interesting and instructive. The meetings have been well attended both by professors and students, and although the last to find its place among the numerous clubs of this institution, it is one of the largest and most thriving.

THE Camelot Club held its last meeting for this college year on Saturday, April 11th. Dr. Rand, the Honorary President, gave us a very interesting hour in reading and talking about poetry. Many of his beautiful poems of various types were read and commented upon, much to the delight and profit of all present. Dr. Rand's reading of poetry and stimulating lectures are always peculiarly interesting to all lovers of English song and the Camelot Club during the past session has been peculiarly favored by his presence and help. An earnest and hearty vote of thanks was moved by Mr. G. H. Clarke, '95, and seconded by J. C. Sycamore, '96. Our meetings from month to month have been very interesting and helpful, our last meeting certainly was a very fitting climax, and the hour will not soon be forgotten.

DEEP earnestness of spirit characterized the closing meeting of the Fyfe Missionary Society held on Tuesday, March 31st. The addresses were full of practical, helpful suggestions for the summer's work on the Mission fields. The morning session began at 10 o'clock with a devotional service conducted by Vice-President Reeve. During the business meeting which followed an interesting letter full of bright hopes was read from Missionary H. Stillwell. Missionary Laflamme then gave a most instructive address on the work in India. After giving a few statistics showing the great number of young men who have never heard of the Christ, the present rapid increase in population and the vast number of the gods (330,000,000), Bro. Laflamme gave us a bird's-eye view of the Akidu field, and related the various incidents of an inquiry meeting. This account gave a more vivid conception of the work and, spite of difficulties, inspired us with a longing to be working where the need is so great. City Missionary Hall, by special request of the Society, then spoke on " Personal work among Roman Catholics." From his varied experience Bro. Hall related many touching and thrilling incidents connected with the conversion of many who had been won by the simple telling of the Gospel story in love and in the power of the Spirit. Many of the students will do better work this summer for these helpful words. The President, Professor Farmer, took charge of the afternoon session. After an earnest devotional service, Bro. F. L. Fowke, of Oshawa, gave a stirring practical address on "The Business Man and Christian Work." Many earnest suggestions were given as to the way in which wide-awake pastors might avail themselves of the wealth, talent, and executive ability of the business members of the church. Bro. Fowke has laid the society under deep obligation for his manly and instructive words. Pastor Eaton of the Bloor street Church followed with an address on " Spiritual Quickening." The subject was dealt with under the headings of a Gospel of (1) Largeness, (2) Life, (3) Love. In enlarging on the last heading Bro. Eaton emphasized the necessity of being filled with the Spirit of Love in all the largeness revealed in the word and obtained by secret prayer and communion. Then indeed should we be spirit-quickened and our lives made fruitful. Bro. McEwen then closed these most earnest meetings by commending the students to the care of the loving Father, for the summer months.

ON Sunday evening, April 12th, in Bloor St. Baptist church, Rev. O. P. Gifford preached the annual sermon of the Fyfe Missionary Society. The subject of the sermon was " Stewardship," taken from 1 Pet. iv. 10 : "As good stewards of the manifest grace of God." This Oriental term, which has no parallel in Western languages, was aptly and humorously illustrated by the office and work of Abraham's servant, Eliezer. Out of the stewardship of the Old Testament came the idea of the New—absolute ownership.

The Christian belongs absolutely to God. When the speaker was touched by the finger of God, he began to speak in the prayer meeting. The deacons said, " You ought to study for the ministry. These talents belong to God." But no one had said, when he was a clerk in a warehouse, " Your money belongs to God." God made *men*, not ministers.

It is an infamous doctrine, that a man has anything, when he himself belongs to God.

Absolute ownership involves control of— .

(1) Time, (2) Talent, (3) Acquisition, (4) Communion with God, (5) Service for God.

As well might the violinist in the orchestra tell the leader, "This instrument is mine, I will use it or not, as I please,"—as for a business man to break the harmony of Christ's church by hugging his wealth.

How few know their *Time* belongs to God !

When the speaker's father was a boy, a neighbor came to his grandfather and offered him a position in which he might be fitted in time for great usefulness. "No" was the reply: "his time is mine till he is twenty-one"; and thus a life was wrecked on the reef of his father's selfishness. But a Christian never comes of age.

When Lazarus was raised from the dead, no doubt he regarded the years that followed as sacred. But what of the years before his resurrection? And when we step down to the black water and dip our finger into its tide, and are recalled, how real life becomes !

Mr. Gifford preached in College St. Baptist church on the morning of the same day, giving a strong and helpful exposition of "Comforter" John xiv. 16. The sermon consisted of a series of well selected illustrations, showing that the Scriptural meaning of "comfort" is strengthen.

On Monday morning, after chapel service, our Chancellor, in a happy speech, introduced Mr. Gifford as One Peculiarly Gifted.

Mr. Gifford, in response, gave a brief address, based upon the parable of the Unjust Steward. Selfishness and sacrifice, he said, are the two possible centres of every man's life. It does not pay to be selfish, *e.g.*, Æsop's Fables—Fox and Stork Dining—Monkey and Roasted Chestnuts. Selfishness is the thing Christ came to destroy.

> " Who gives himself with his alms feeds three,
> Himself, his hungering neighbor, and Me."

MOULTON COLLEGE.

OWING to ill-health, Miss Spowers Graham was unable to finish her year's work, so left for her home in Lindsay on Friday last.

WE were pleased to have a short visit from one of the '95 graduates, Miss Carrie Fisher, who came down to attend the Paderewski Concert.

WE residents of Moulton have been pursuing our usual routine in life, only relieved now and then by occasional and much-welcomed events. At the thought of approaching examinations, our faces become lengthened, and we no longer care for the gaities of life, but our burdened minds are kept from despondency by the anticipation of our well-earned reward—the holidays.

On Friday evening, April 10th, the class of '99 provided the entire programme for the Heliconian Society. Several musical numbers and a very amusing dialogue were given, and the final number, the "Sunflower Chorus," was entirely beyond criticism. The audience was quite delighted with the manner in which the programme was rendered, and we have great hopes for the future of our youngest class.

As a substitute for the regular open Heliconian meeting, which has usually taken place after the Easter holidays, the Faculty, this year, gave the students of the College a reception. During the evening a number of musical selections and two or three short recitations were given. This social manner of passing the time was an agreeable change from the ordinary formal literary, and all the students enjoyed the entertainment exceedingly.

It was with extreme pleasure and benefit that we listened to the famous pianist, Paderewski, on April 9th. It is quite unnecessary to speak at length of his great genius and wonderful execution. The papers and magazines of the day have already almost exhausted the musical vocabulary in endeavoring to do him justice. Suffice it to say that he aroused even in the minds of the least sympathetic of his hearers, every emotion which true music is capable of expressing, and surpassed our highest expectations.

On Friday and Saturday afternoons, May 1st and 2nd, our Studio was opened for the inspection of the work done by the art-students during the term. It was thronged with visitors, who passed many favorable comments on the work displayed. Besides flower-studies in oil and water-color, and work from the antique, some clever pen-and-ink sketches and some remarkably good modelling in clay were exhibited. Mrs. Dignam is to be congratulated on the way in which she inspires her pupils, and Moulton is fortunate in having a teacher who is able to arouse such enthusiasm among them, and who has such a high conception of the educative value of art.

Woodstock College.

At the last meeting of the Judson Missionary Society, Rev. Dr. Dadson addressed us with his usual force and freshness, on the subject, "The Oratory of Jesus," "Never Man Spake like this Man."

Friday morning, April 17, brought us the pleasure of Rev. R. G. Boville's presence at our chapel service. In a few happy remarks he won the interest and applause of all. Nor was it with less pleasure that we followed him on a camel ride to Mount Sinai, and along the route travelled by the emigrant Israelites. This trip was made vivid and instructive by the aid of lime-light views, charming description and many personal incidents.

ON April 21st a very enthusiastic meeting of the bicycle riders was held for the purpose of organizing a club for the term. It was decided to call our club the Woodstock College Bicycle Club, having for its badge streamers of red, white and college colors, and the time for runs, Monday and Thursday evenings. The following officers were then elected: Hon. Pres., Chancellor O. C. S. Wallace; Pres., W. R. Smith, B.A.; Vice-Pres., F. C. Elliott; Sec.-Treas., H. A. Smith; Captain, E. E. Howell; Lieutenant, W. Grant.

THE members of the First Baptist Church were fortunate in securing Dr. Thomas, of Jarvis St. Church, to preach at their anniversary services which were held on Sunday, 19th inst. We were all greatly delighted and withal profited by the sermons, which were full of fresh and original thought. And this being clothed in most elegant language spoken with force and eloquence, made the Dr.'s visit one that shall be long remembered by those who availed themselves of the opportunity of hearing him. On the following Monday evening the Dr. delivered his popular lecture on " Living in a Hurry." The points made, and driven home by interesting and witty stories, by way of illustration, did not fail to make the hour spent with the lecturer a most enjoyable one. We shall always hail with delight a visit from this popular divine.

GRANDE LIGNE.

Our gymnasium has found a new use. The boys have lately devoted it to the game of basket-ball, which to Feller Institute is a new and exceedingly popular game. The students are quite enthusiastic in their devotion to it.

The religious interest in the school that we mentioned last month, has been bearing fruit. The spiritual life of the school has been much quickened. About twenty students have professed conversion, while last Sunday evening our pastor had the joy of baptizing seven. Of these six were students of the school.

The Society of Intellectual Culture, having had such a successful Dickens Evening last month, determined to try the same plan for a French programme, devoted to Victor Hugo. The ladies worked hard and success crowned their labors. The amount of reading and composition to be done, in order to make such a programme interesting and instructive, must surely result in great good to the students that do it. At the same time our interest in these authors is increased. We assure the ladies that their efforts in this direction are heartily appreciated.

OF our two rival papers, " The Monitor" and " La Vérité," which for the last two years have been so bitterly assailing one another, each has at last accomplished its object, viz. : the other's destruction. Both fought bravely, and we congratulate them upon their success ; may they now rest in peace ! From their ruins, however, Wm. Cotton has succeeded in resurrecting an independent publication called " The Rising Bell," whose editor we often see around with pencil and note-book soliciting information. We wish the new paper a better fate than its predecessors have had.

" La Grippe " has been busy at Feller Institute again. Being free from it so long during the winter we thought it had forgotten us. We were mistaken. It was only waiting for a favorable opportunity of attack. This was found just before exams., when one after another of the students felt its grasp. Nor were its effects felt by students alone. Teachers were not passed by. In one instance all the lady teachers were in its hold at once. We are glad to say that all the teachers have recovered, and that only one student, who had a very severe, attack is still confined to his room. The doctor says this one also will soon be around again.

The Final Examinations for the Winter Term have come and gone, with the usual successes and failures. Some of the students who have been so happy and light-hearted all the year are now mourning over the fact that they did not settle down to work soon enough. Others who have more soberly wrestled with the difficulties of every day are now rejoicing over the victories won. Four of our boys we expect to go to McMaster University next year. One will take the Arts Course in McGill, and another will probably be found studying Medicine at Laval. After a little further study, during the Spring Term, we expect these to be prepared to enter upon their respective Courses.

On April 2nd our closing exercises for the school year were held in Feller Institute. Owing to the almost impassable condition of the roads, and the stormy weather, very few visitors were present. A good programme of music and recitations was provided, which, with the reading of the marks obtained in examinations, made the day pass very pleasantly. In the evening a good many of the students left for home for the Easter vacation. We still have another term of seven weeks before the end of the school year. During the Spring Term we expect to have about fifty students left with us. Many others would remain, but are compelled by financial circumstances to leave now, in order that they may earn enough money to enable them to come back again next winter.

The annual meeting of the Students' Society of Feller Institute took place on Feb. 27th. There were present nearly all our missionary pastors, and a larger number of old students than usual. We were very pleased to have so many missionaries with us at one time. The Wednesday evening prayer-meeting was taken charge of almost entirely by the pastor, so that it amounted almost to a missionary conference, which was a change thoroughly enjoyed by all. Thursday morning the pastors spent in discussing plans and suggestions for future work. Some important changes in the work were suggested which no doubt will be adopted in due time.   In the afternoon came the business meeting of the Student Society. The President, Mr. Leonard Therrien, occupied the chair. The Society showed improvement in several directions, but especially in its finances. A desire to bind the old students more closely to the Alma Mater being felt, the Society voted money for the the purchase of a printing-press, with which to publish monthly reports and items of interest, to be distributed among the members of the Society.   In the evening a good miscellaneous programme was provided by the school.   A paper by Rev. Mr. Roux, a former Principal of Feller Institute, occupied a prominent place on the programme. This meeting was one of the most enthusiastic gatherings of old students that we have ever had.   Our accommodation was taxed to its utmost.   It was truly an encouraging sight to see so many French Baptists crowding our halls.   The efforts of the past have not been fruitless, May we not hope, now that the work is well established, that progress will be much more rapid ?

336

N. Wolverton

THE

McMASTER UNIVERSITY MONTHLY

MAY, 1896.

NEWTON WOLVERTON.

To hundreds of young men and women who thronged the halls of Woodstock College during the seventies and eighties, as well as to many of the oldest and best friends of our educational work, the likeness which we present this month will be both familiar and heartily welcome. Canadian Baptists have had a goodly succession of able and devoted leaders in their educational work, and in that list the subject of this sketch should always have an honored place. The death of the imperial Fyfe, and the removal shortly afterward of the Theological Department from Woodstock introduced a grave crisis in the history of the Literary Department. For that crisis, with its peculiar difficulties and pressing financial problems, God gave us in the person of Newton Wolverton a man possessed in a very eminent degree of the qualifications that were then most needed. His was the privilege and the honor of tiding us over that crisis and saving the foundations for the building of the brighter day that was yet to dawn.

Mr. Wolverton has just reached his jubilee year, having been born Feb. 5th, 1846, in the County of Oxford. When he was three years old, the family moved to the village of Wolverton. Seven years later his mother died, and soon after that the lad went into the lumber-woods of Walsingham. In the fall of

1859 he went to Cleveland, Ohio, to attend school ; caught the war-fever two years later, enlisted the very day the first battle of Bull's Run was fought, served two years, and then returned to Canada to spend a year at the front with the Canadian Volunteers, watching for the Fenians. The next few years were spent in business, farming and carpentry at Wolverton.

His conversion took place shortly after his return from the army. He first united with the old River Church, but afterwards became one of the thirty-two constituent members of the church at Wolverton. During these years Rev. T. Booker helped him much, and was largely influential in leading him to decide upon studying for the ministry.

In accordance with this decision he entered Woodstock College in January, 1870, and after a course of four years, won the mathematical scholarship at senior matriculation in Toronto University. Graduation followed in regular course with honors in metaphysics and ethics and oriental languages.

During these student days, summer vacations were spent with the churches in Petrolia, Dorchester, Sarnia and Onondaga. In the first he broke ground and organized the church; to the permanent pastorate of the last he was called the summer before graduating, supplied there during that winter, and the following summer was by them ordained.

Mr. Wolverton's connection with our educational work was certainly not of his own choosing. He was looking forward to years of happy usefulness in his Onondaga pastorate, when an urgent invitation came to him from Dr. Fyfe to go to Woodstock to teach mathematics. When he declined, the request became almost a command, and, in deference to the wish of his revered preceptor, he yielded. The following year the great leader lay dying, and, pressed by him, Mr. Wolverton promised that he would stand by that school as long as he believed it needed him. That promise he always held sacred and carried out to the letter.

His history since that time is so well-known to most of us that I need not detail it here. It is enough to say that the quality of his work during the first four years warranted the Board of Trustees in calling him to the Principalship in 1881 ; that his five years' Principalship was, in many respects, a distinguished success ; that his services during the following four

years, as Financial Manager, Teacher and Founder of the Manual
Training Department, were simply invaluable; and that his
Presidency during the past five years of Bishop's College, Texas,
with its four hundred students, has been marked by such progress and efficiency as to have won the warmest approval of the
Board of the American Baptist Home Mission Society, under
whom he labors.

In 1879 Mr. Wolverton was married to Miss I. Cowie, of
Caledonia. Her beautiful life closed in 1890, her memory is a
benediction still. The present Mrs. Wolverton is a worthy
daughter of our honored brother Mr. Geo. Matthews, of Lindsay.

I cannot close this brief sketch without a few words of a
more personal nature. My own acquaintance with Mr. Wolverton goes back into University days. That acquaintance was but
casual, and my impressions were not particularly favorable.
When, however, four years later, I became associated with him
intimately in Woodstock, I found a vastly stronger and better
man than I had known in college days. Either my first impressions had done him great injustice, or he had wonderfully improved in the meantime. Indeed, both were true. The influence
of a noble woman and the serious responsibilities of a great work
had mellowed and toned down a somewhat rugged and, at times,
frivolous exterior, and called into fuller play and truer poise the
wealth of real strength and goodness that lay within. I have
often wished that others of his earlier associates had been conditioned to make the same discovery. His heart was true to
Jesus Christ, his conception of Christian education sound; he
longed for spiritual blessings on the school and none was more
rejoiced than he when they came, as come they often did in
gladdening richness.

In the varied duties that devolved upon him he evinced a
conscientious devotion, large teaching power, great business
capacity with a remarkable mastery of details, and fine administrative ability. His early exuberance of spirits stood him in
good stead, and, joined to a strong will, enabled him to be cheerful and hopeful under heavy burdens and in the face of the
gravest difficulties. No Principal ever worked more harmon-
iously with his Faculty, or more fully succeeded in enlisting
their sympathy and making the most of their varied gifts.

Of course he had imperfections, as we all have, and imperfections of the kind that run before to judgment. But he was sound at heart, and, wore well. During our eight years of association in Woodstock, I grew to have for him the sincerest respect and strong brotherly affection. And now, after seven years of separation, my heart still beats warm toward him, and I am happy to join with his hosts of friends in wishing him length of days and still increasing usefulness.

J. H. FARMER.

THE MEANING OF PHILOSOPHY AND ITS APPLICATION TO EDUCATION.*

I desire to present some thoughts upon the meaning of philosophy and its application to education.

It is sometimes said that those who study philosophy do not know what they are studying, and at best gain nothing for their pains except useless lumber; that it is still worse with the teacher of philosophy, who talks much about many things, but there are only "two kernels of wheat" in the two bushels of chaff—only two kernels, and these probably would not grow or nourish life.

These words imply more; they imply that philosophy itself is unsatisfactory, that the same ground is traversed again and again without essential progress; that the philosophy of one generation overthrows that of the preceding; and so the contest goes—a fencing with wooden swords, a mock battle in which no one is killed or injured. Indeed, philosophy is only a holiday affair, to be dismissed, like the fool with cap and bells, from the king's presence when the serious business of life is to be undertaken.

But who is this king? Why is he so revered to-day? His name is natural science. He is respected because he is equipped with a so-called *scientific* method; he speaks very wisely concerning laws, atoms, forces; he is armed with the microscope, the crucible, the scalpel. Therefore, exalt science. Accept unquestioningly the teaching as truth.

*An address delivered at the opening exercises of McMaster University, October 18th, 1895.

Is the case so serious, after all, with philosophy? It may be that this old friend and playmate of idle moments can, like the fool in *King Lear*, speak wisdom, which, if the king would heed, might save his life and his happiness.

First of all, the field of philosophy differs from that of the sciences. Theirs remains for the most part fixed and a quiet building up of knowledge is the rule, as soon as they have gained a sure methodical footing. Each investigator starts where his predecessor laid down the work and his advance in the science depends largely on his own patient toil and the keenness of his insight.

In philosophy, it is different. As one says: "There it is the exception that successors gratefully develop what has already been achieved, and each of the great systems of philosophy begins to solve its newly formulated problem *ab 000*, as if the other systems had scarcely existed."* To say that philosophy makes no advance and is simply a harmless war of words is to misconceive its nature. Its problems are constantly recurring; they are tasks which the human mind cannot escape and does not wish to escape. Nor will philosophy cease to ponder these problems with intense interest till the last soul has passed from the earth to the world where the substance of faith and hope is found.

I desire to remove all thought of philosophy as mysterious and unknown, as the peculiar possession of the schools and the lecture-room. Philosophy must be defined in terms of life—life in the highest sense of all we hold most dear and true. Look abroad over human knowledge; what have we? Gratefully do we receive the teachings of the sciences. We reverence those discoverers who have made biology, chemistry and physics what they are to-day. The geologist, the botanist, the astronomer, have each also a marvellous story to tell and we can only listen with profound humility and gratitude. Sweet music awes us into silent aspiration after an as yet unrealized harmony of soul; we look upon art and see more than paint and canvas or marble. A beautiful character arouses hopes too large for earth's possibilities. Think of the comedy, the tragedy, of each life; its hopes and fears, its struggles after ideals, its joys, its sorrows

*Windelband, History of Philosophy, p. 9.

If one little life has such problems, how complex they become for the race!

Have the sciences, then, spoken the last and only word that can give any peace to the questioning mind? Let us not undervalue what they have done and are doing, for all of which we need to be deeply thankful. But the sciences themselves need to be explained; for, while they may speak with implicit confidence, within their proper sphere, of laws, forces, atoms, matter, substance, action and reaction, space, time and motion—what do they after all mean by these terms? Is reason's work finished while these words remain unexplained? And, besides, the special sciences do not even attempt further definition of these terms and give no account whatever of the true, the beautiful, and the good, and the postulates of the Practical Reason, to use Kant's somewhat awkward expression.

More must then be done before the mind can rest satisfied; and what is this additional task? It is to gain some consistent, reason-satisfying view of the general questions concerning the universe and human life. We each strive to accomplish this. We have grown into good or bad terms with the world. In some sense, the earth is our mother, the skies our home; we are not in chaos but cosmos, an orderly, beautiful whole. But what is this way of looking at things? Philosophy; vague, it may be; impossible of exact expression; yet it is there, our philosophy, yours and mine, our understanding of nature, of life, of destiny. It may be as fanciful as the Greek mythology; yet Homer and Hesiod had the germs of philosophical conceptions in their poetry. But shall anyone dictate to you just how you shall think of these things? Instead, must you not work out the problem patiently as you are taught by life's experiences in connection with your own mental development and training? It is thus that philosophy is not limited to the lecture-room. We each have a philosophy of our own because we have minds that must think—a philosophy freely formed and defined in terms of our own life—a necessary part of our rational existence.

It is only necessary to bring the questions which each one attempts to answer, and somehow does answer, into a clearer light and more sharply determine them in order to have before us the problems with which philosophy has for ages been occupied and with which it will continue to wrestle. This is none the less true when it is admitted that philosophy is critically analytic and synthetic in its method, and postulates, as Lotze says, "the existence in the world at large of a truth which affords a sure object for cognition" and also assumes a unitary Ground of all that is, whatever its nature may be. Remember that it is the mind approaching its materials to relate them all, according to its own modes of action, into a consistent whole in relation to some ultimate, unitary Ground of all that is.

At this point, I can only state several great truths. One is that the materials which the mind seeks to bring into a comprehensive, consistent whole are all that is known and experienced with reference to the universe and to life.

Another is that philosophy is final truth only for its particular time. Why? Because philosophy is the formal expression of the collective knowledge of a given age. This knowledge, or material for synthesis, having its origin largely in the continual advance of the sciences, is constantly changing. Therefore, a philosophy which synthesizes the whole cannot be final, but has in it rather premises which another age with its fresh discoveries may have to correct; or, premises whose legitimate conclusions only other and later thinkers will be able to recognize and set forth.*

Descartes did not teach a final philosophy, whatever he himself may have thought of it. It was corrected and improved by Spinoza. The rationalists and empiricists preceding Kant were in conflict. Kant mediated between them. Darwin, in the laboratory, unfolded the laws of development, survival of the fittest and variation. A new philosophy, a new statement of old problems, was demanded, which should do justice to this newly discovered principle. Herbert Spencer attempted to meet the need with his Synthetic Philosophy.

These are only a few illustrations of the fact that a given philosophy is final truth only for its particular time, and the men who seize upon and give formal expression to newly discovered principles become the philosophers of their generation.

I would emphasize the fact that philosophy is reason's grasp upon all its materials of knowledge rather than any particular

---

*Erdmann, History of Philosophy, Introduction. Also Windelband.

set of doctrines which may be bequeathed to succeeding generations, except so far as they are to enter into a fresh, formal expression of the sum-total of the knowledge of those later times
which shall be, if not an advance upon, yet a re-adjustment of,
preceding thought to the changed phases of the problems
considered.

Forgetting that every age, and, indeed, every man to some
extent, must struggle with this problem of synthesis of all that
is then known and experienced concerning the world and life,
fears sometimes arise that philosophy is opposed to religion.
Far from it. Philosophy must, according to its nature, approach
religion analytically and critically. But it does not stop with
the analysis and the criticism ; they are made simply to ascertain
the essential factors in the religious nature of man·that, after
they are clearly understood, the grand synthesis of these with
all the rest that is known and experienced may be made. By
religion, I do not mean theology, but the religious nature of man,
whether he be in the jungles of Africa or in the midst of European civilization. Indeed, were it possible, as it is not, for the
ethical and religious nature of man to withdraw itself from such
critical analysis and universal synthesis of its factors, I fear
philosophy would grope in darkness and be lost in the confusion
of atheism; and yet, these factors of the religious nature are at
best often vague and indefinite, easily rising into the fanciful
and the mystical, although we may not agree with Matthew
Arnold, who said, "take away mystery and you take away our
religion."

Nevertheless, as Shadworth Hodgson says : "the passionate
religious tendency is not a sentiment fluttering round a fancy,
but is a feeling rooted deep in the structure and mechanism of
consciousness." In general, it may be said that the sources of
religion are in those profound feelings and longings after ideals
to which it has been possible to give, thus far, only a partial
expression. These philosophy strives with keen, loving insight,
to discern, and with tenderness and sympathy to appreciate the
significance and value of the heart's insatiable longing after
good, its unceasing dissatisfaction with the finite, its pleading
cry for an ethical and æsthetical basis or ' *Ground* ' of all
that is.*

---

*Ladd's Introduction to Philosophy, pp. 381-2 ; also 288-394.

" In die Welt hinausgestossen,
Steht der Mensch, verlassen da "

until he reaches some heart-satisfying conception of the world, himself and God. Speed rather than hinder his effort! Let him think, let him pray, let him weigh carefully and critically till the light of truth dispels the gloom, hushes the distressful cry, till he rests with unshaken trust and peace in the "Nature" of science, in the "Absolute" of philosophy, in the Supreme God and loving Father of religion.

In the second place and in view of what has been said concerning the nature of philosophy, permit me to add some considerations of the problem, the aim of education.

Here man must be regarded in relation to all that has existence. No view can be accepted which considers him as less than a real personality. He must be real, I might say, immortal, to be worth educating. How can anyone ever forget the reality of himself! And yet Von Hartmann, in his Philosophy of the Unconscious, says: "Let the Unconscious change the combination of activities or acts of will which constitute *me* and I have become another. I am a phenomenon like the rainbow in the cloud. Like it, I am born of the coincidence of relations, become other in every second and shall dissolve when these relations are dissolved. The sun alone is always shining which is transiently reflected from yonder cloud; only the Unconscious forever rules which is also mirrored in my brain."*

But such teaching as this repels us. We are so real to ourselves that we can never believe our relation to the Supreme Being is fitly represented by the comparison of ourselves, with Spinoza, to a ripple upon the ocean's wave; with Hartmann, to the rainbow of the cloud, "the transient product of the coincidence of relations." The prospect of sometime losing our self-conscious existence is unbearable. We cannot with any patience face the eternal void. Grave though the responsibility may be, we prefer to have our destiny, in some measure at least, in our own hands. Consequently, we must hold that man is a real personality and his education must be suited to his nature in relation to the great whole.

*Trans., II, 243.

Although Hegel did not sufficiently recognize finite personality, yet in his work entitled, " The Phenomenology of Spirit," he gave expression to an idea of much importance in the philosophy of education, the idea of self-estrangement. It will be readily seen that this idea is the application of his philosophy to the individual. First, there is the undeveloped mind full of possibilities as yet unrealized. In this first stage, the mind has not yet learned to regard itself as set over against the world in which it is. The early Greeks furnish an illustration. At first, the Greek mind dwelt in unquestioning fellowship with the natural world, understanding it in terms of its own life. But this first stage was soon followed by a second in which the mind began to assert itself, to make itself real. The world assumes a new rôle; it appears strange and other than the mind which contemplates it with that feeling of wonder of which Plato wrote. This vivid consciousness of self leads to an effort on the part of mind to remove this estrangement, to bring itself again into perfect harmony with that which for the time being is apparently so different from its own nature. So the third stage is the removal of this self-estrangement, in which the awakened mind seeks to go beneath that which is foreign to it, discover the underlying laws and recognize in that other as in itself reason as the basis of all. Three stages : first, mind, potential, full of possibilities; secondly, mind sharply distinguishing itself from that which is other than itself; thirdly, mind again bringing itself into harmony with this other because in it are recognized rational principles.

What I have said thus far concerns chiefly the intellectual side of education. Expressed very simply, it means that we begin life with almost no reasoning concerning the world about us. We ought to be so educated as to find everywhere manifested those laws which lead us directly to the infinite Reason. So one factor in the problem of education is to bring the human mind to a clear recognition of and intimate communion with the infinite Reason in whom all that exists is grounded.

Again, the mind is in itself free. This freedom, inherent in its nature, sets before it great possibilities which ought to be actualized. Man's true nature is not found in him already realized at birth. His true nature is his ideal, and it lies with him and those who have influence over him how much or how little of this ideal nature is made actual. We begin at the foot of the ladder with the animal nature dominant. The problem for each is to subordinate the animal, the physical, and give supremacy to the rational and the spiritual. If we are to educate and be educated, it must be done in view of the fact that, not our present but our ideal, our spiritual, nature is in the highest sense our very own.*

One of the factors in this ideal is the æsthetic. There is a great need of deepening appreciation of the beautiful and the sublime into which the beautiful merges. We over-estimate the culture of the present age. Matthew Arnold was not altogether wrong in his criticism of the people of his own country and beyond the seas. It is only an occasional poet or artist who looks upon the beauties of nature with emotions at all adequate. The best music, the noblest plays, cannot be given the public with financial success; and it does not require a Schopenhauer or a Von Hartmann to make it clear that many of those who are apparently so devoted to music and art, and go into ecstacies over a beautiful landscape, are prompted more by the fact that it is the thing to do than by any genuine love of the æsthetic.

On the other hand, there are delicately sensitive spirits for whom a noble painting, grand music, the beauties of nature, occasion emotions too deep for expression, except as the tears that come unbidden bear silent witness to the profoundest appreciation, as they see, like those who look upon Raphael's Madonna aright, beyond the physical,—the spiritual, the divine. And why cannot we all be so ? Isn't it, then, one of the purposes of education to make us increasingly appreciative of the beautiful and the sublime ?

The other factors in the ideal nature are the ethical and religious. Here I must not pass by that philosophic teacher, Froebel, who, in 1840, gave to his school the name Kindergarten. Froebel conceived most clearly the ethical and religious aim of education. His teaching was grounded in his view of the world. He believed that there is one divine unity in nature and in spirit, God within the inner world, God in the outer world, while

---

*On Hegel and this section, see especially Rosenkranz's Philosophy of Education, pp. 1-50. Also Histories of Philosophy, *in loco.*

life, human life, unites the natural and the spiritual, and has for
its goal the clear recognition of and communion with the fundamental Reality, God Himself.

Froebel said: "It is the special destiny and life work of
man to become fully, vividly and clearly conscious of his essence,
of the divine effluence in him, and, therefore, of God, to become
fully, vividly and clearly conscious of his destiny and life work."
With this high conception of what man has to accomplish,
Froebel thus speaks of himself as a teacher: "I would educate
human beings, who, with their feet, stand rooted in God's earth,
in nature, whose heads reach even into heaven and there behold
truth, in whose hearts are united both earth and heaven, the
varied life of earth and nature, and the glory and peace of
heaven, God's earth and God's heaven." Thus Froebel regarded
education as leading and guiding man to clearness concerning
himself and in himself, to peace with nature, to unity with God,
to a faithful, pure, inviolate and, hence, holy life. He would
have us believe that each has one thought peculiarly and pre-
dominantly his own, the fundamental thought as it were of his
whole being, divinely given, the key-note of his life-sympathy,
and the purpose of each should be the clear expression of that
thought, that note in the universal melody.

Thus it is that the name Froebel gave to his school was
highly fitting—the garden of the children, in which their spirits
grew and bore choice fruit, for it was, in very truth, the garden
of the Lord.*

And now, in view of these teachings and in view of the
truths which we must hold at the present day, how may we
understand the problem of education ?

First, we must think of man as real personality, in a real
world which may be known and which he is fitted to know. In
view of what physics teaches, mind appears as possessed of the
wonderful power of interpreting the world of motion and change
in terms of self-conscious life. · Mind in a very real sense completes the universe, and is that for which all else exists.

I like to think of the natural world as grounded in the
divine mind, in whom thought and will are so united that what
is divinely thought is made actual through the energizing of the

---

*Education of Man, by Froebel, pp. 1-200.

divine will. What then is this natural world? The divine thought made real through the divine will according to a fixed order of activity. Reality can be known because it finds an expression united to the interpreting mind.

I admit that this is only a belief which prevents me from stopping in the idealism of Berkeley, still less in the absolute idealism of Fichte, and leads me to go beyond the world of consciousness to a world of reality. I admit that I may ultimately have to rest this belief on ethical grounds, nevertheless, it is an abiding belief. If it is well founded, then we should be so educated intellectually that we shall cease to regard the world as so much dead matter, and everywhere look beyond the sensuous to living Reality. Kepler's exclamation as he beheld the heavens, " I read thy thoughts after thee, O God," may well be ours wherever we turn. Whether we are students and teachers in the lecture-room, tracing the delicate shading of colors on the petals of a flower, or woodsmen in the forest, we may see everywhere manifestation of the Supreme Reason.

But he who lives in such constant communion with the divine Mind beyond the sensuous will quickly see that the goal of his life is an ideal which he has not yet realized. He will soon discover that to sin, to be unspiritual in the clear, steady light of Reason shining everywhere, is not his true state, and, as Lyman Abbott says, his redemption will begin when he strives to shake off the animal, the physical, and give supremacy to the spiritual nature. He will become, not only ethical, as Hegel said, but devout.

The life of the poet Whittier illustrates my meaning. He saw more in this world than ordinary men see because he looked beyond the physical, to the spiritual, the divine. Who can read his poem on " The Eternal Goodness " without feeling that here is a soul almost as spotless as the snow about his New England home, itself the occasion of a lovely poem, a soul that lives in closest communion with the Father of spirits.

Thus it is that philosophy of her own choice goes beyond the Greek intellectualism towards the fervent spiritualism of the Hebrews, who saw God in the whirlwind and the storm, who worshipped Him in the temple, who " lived and moved and had their being in Him." Though unable to walk with the same confidence in the paths which are peculiarly those of faith, yet philosophy turns her face towards them, offering hope and encouragement to go forward with trust in the eternal verities of religion.

Finally, let me utter an earnest word in behalf of the study of philosophy. It seems to me that a fresh and vigorous treatment of its problems is greatly needed. The need is apparent the moment we ask what system we shall make our own, if we are to adopt one. We do not wish to give our adherence to Herbert Spencer. Hegel's teachings are not satisfactory, however fascinating they may be. Many regard Lotze as in error, while Wundt's system is in some respects a revival of the doctrines of Spinoza. Besides, the material for philosophical treatment furnished by the sciences is rapidly accumulating.

To you who are interested in this subject, and we all ought to be, let me say: grapple with the great problems of the universe and of life afresh! Recognize the need of the age in which you are living! It may be your privilege, it is not too high an aim, to lead the human mind one step nearer the Eternal Truth than it has ever gone.

To those of us who occupy the humble office of teacher is granted the priceless privilege of promoting and stimulating the unfolding of the minds entrusted to us in order that they may attain unto their ideal nature, free from error, therefore free from sin, fully consecrated to that heavenly Father who values more highly the willing, loving service of his children than "the music of the spheres which cannot choose but play."

JAMES TEN BROEKE.

A DAY ON THE UPPER OTTAWA.

I.

Morn on the bosom of Allumette Lake!
The sunbeams are sparkling, the breeze is awake,
Stirring the ripples that flash in the beams
That have waked them so early from peacefulest dreams.

Wandering cloudlets that aimlessly stray
Up from the golden-barred gateway of day,
Smile, as they watch on the calm waters' breast,
Their fair-mirrored faces afloat or at rest.

Gently coquetting with innocent guile
With the bright laughing waters that woo her the while—
Woo her to glide from the place of her rest
To sunshine, and freedom, and joy on her breast—
Still, at her anchorage, lingers our boat,
Waiting the signal that sets her afloat,—
Waiting the word to be up and away.
Like a fetterless bird with the billows at play—
Waiting, with welcoming curt'sey and bow,
The youths and the maidens that flock to her now,—
The fathers, the mothers, the sisters, the sons,
The wondering babies and bright little ones,
Coming, still coming with laughter and song,
A motley, a mingling, a joyous throng,
With baskets and boxes, a deftly-packed store
From many a generous larder—and more,
Far more than all else to the little ones dear
The swing and the boats, with their promise of cheer,
Such swinging, such rowing, such fun and such glee,
Such good things to dine on, such marvels to see,

NOTE.—This poem is an attempt to describe fairly and faithfully the sights and scenes of one never-to-be-forgotten day—August 4th, 1882. Lake Allumette is formed by the widening out of the Ottawa river, and covers a large number of square miles. Pembroke is situated on this lake, and enjoys an unobstructed river run of some fifty miles to Des Joachims, a short distance below the famous rapid of the same name. One such day as that, here described, seldom enters into any life, when sky, air, water, and scenery all combine to make "perfection so nearly perfect."

P. S. V. Y.

No wonder the young ones are gleesome and gay,
And the older ones hopeful and happy as they—
God grant that no sorrow may darken the light
That gilds the first hour of this holiday bright !

And now we're afloat on the beautiful lake .
Whose bright ripples sparkle and flash in our wake,
As the boat cuts her way through the waters that lie
Like a vast shining mirror beneath the blue sky ;
With the sun in the east, and the moon in the west,
And the soft, fleecy cloudlets above us at rest,
Or trailing their garments of dazzling snow
Far behind them as dreamily onward they go ;
The while, with the murmur of voices anear,
The prattle of children, and loud, and more clear
The musical ringing of laughter and jest,
And fresh in our faces the wind of the west,
Past regions still bright in the garlands of spring
We sweep on our way like a bird on the wing.

Behind, in the distance, the town is yet seen,
Faintly outlined against the soft back-ground of green ;
Boldly, to right of us stretching away,
Blue in the light of the new-risen day,
Rank behind rank, rise the forest-clad hills
Craggy and seamed by the spring-swollen rills ;
Calmly, to left of us, hamlet or farm
Lends to the landscape its varying charm ;—
While beyond and around us, on every side,
Like emeralds set in the blue of the tide,
Isle after isle, undisturbed and serene
In its calmness and loveliness reigneth a queen,
And smiles from her throne on the waters that meet
With murmuring music to kiss her fair feet,
And every charm of her beautiful face
Again and again in their mirror to trace.

II.

Noon on the blue-bosomed Ottawa smiles !—
Past are the beautiful summer-crowned isles ;

Left are the joyous, holiday throng
To their feast and their pastime, their mirth and their
      song—
Whispers of lovers and blushes of maids
Under the covers of evergreen shades,
Laughter and gambols of little ones free
To sport for a while unrestrained in their glee,
And fathers and mothers released for a day
From toil and from business as happy as they.

We, thoughtful and silent, our journey pursue,
Entranced with the beauties that crowd on our view,
And folding our arms bid our thoughts wander free,
And revel unchecked in the wonders we see.

The hills that, at sunrise, so distant were seen,
With many a valley and upland between,
Ever nearer and nearer have drawn as we passed,
Till only the river divides them at last;
And their old granite bases are lapped by the tide
Of the vast silent river that washes their side.

O, deep-rooted mountains, O, sentinel hills,
Calm watchers and silent, whose majesty stills
The voice of ambition, the whispers of pride,
As here, at your feet, like awed children we glide,
And look rev'rently up to your towering forms
Where, ages on ages, wild tempests and storms
Have battered and beaten in impotent wrath,
And their floods down your bosoms plowed many a path—
O, wood-crested summits, blue, silent and far,
Where clouds rest serene, and the calm sunbeams are,
Our thoughts wander past you, ye strong-rooted hills,
Past the clouds that brood o'er you, the vast sun that fills
Your hollows and heights with such glory to-day,
To Him who upreared you our homage to pay !
We worship the Hand that, long ages ago,
Sank your sunless foundations the waters below,
Compacted, and massed you, and lifted you high,
Till your towering peaks kissed the blue, upper sky,

2

And your huge, massive columns, firm-planted and
    proud,
Loomed up to the regions of sunshine and cloud !

And thou, peaceful river, fair child of the hills
God-bidden to feed thee with numberless rills—
To feed, and protect, and at night's dewy close
Like guardian angels watch o'er thy repose,
Calm river, unswerving, untiring and free,
Bearing ever thy tribute of floods to the sea,
Nor grudging thyself and thy treasures so rife
To the vast, parent ocean whence floweth thy life,—
Our thoughts, at this hour, wander past even thee
To Him who from cavernous gloom set thee free ;—
Who hollowed the channels, deep, darksome and lone,
Fathoms deep in the ancient enduring stone,
And walled thee with granite-ribbed mountains, that so,
"Thus far, and no farther" thy waters might go ;
Who commanded the light on thy mirroring face
His sun, and His clouds, and His mountains to trace,
Till forests and cliffs, and the mosses that cling
To the rocks' craggy feet, and each fair wilding thing,
In picture should smile from the depths in our sight,
Reproduced by the marvellous pencil of light ;
And every fair picture be filled with the praise
Of Him who is wondrous in works and in ways !

III.

Eve on the beautiful Ottawa's breast !
The sunbeams fall slant from the radiant west ;
"Des Joachims" behind us has faded away,
And the "Oviseau" is seen for the last time to-day ;—
Each mountain and headland, and bold, rocky height,
In the widening distance has faded from sight ;—
But the sun's matchless splendors are coloring yet
The scarce-heaving bosom of Lake Allumette,
As once more, in their setting of soft, changeful green,
Through beautiful vistas her waters are seen.

They of the morning, our holiday-band—

We have welcomed them back from the green island-
    strand;
Little ones tired of the long day's unrest,
Are wearying now for the quiet home-nest;
All have grown calmer and graver to-night
Than they were in the flush of morn's kindling light,
Yet every face wears a look of content
As if happier grown for the day that's been spent,
And in the soft azure of many an eye
Some sweet hoarded mem'ries seem calmly to lie ;—
But whatever they are that so gladden and bless,
There's no one will tell you, and you may not guess !

How rapidly changes the scene, as the sun
Glides away down the west, and the hills, one by one,
Catch his dazzling splendors on every steep,
And reflect them again in the mirroring deep !
How the Lake laughs in light as the monarch of day
Aslant o'er her breast pours his long, level ray,
While his gorgeous curtains of crimson and gold
Around him he gathereth fold upon fold !—
How each isle seems to lift its strong anchor, and glide
Elate in its freedom away on the tide,
As in haste to escape from the place of its rest
Its homage to pay to the king in the west,
While each tree and each shrub clearly pictured below,
Itself is aflame in the sunset's red glow !

Home again ! Home again ! safe upon shore,
Glad that the day and its pastimes are o'er,
Yet we pause, ere we turn from the waters away,
To watch on their bosom the last sunset ray,—
To trace the long, roseate lines that yet lie
'Neath the tintings far richer that glow in the sky,
To glean them, and gather them up as we may,
With the beautiful things we have looked on to-day,
And hoard them away in the heart and the brain,
In the years that are coming to look on again ;
When memory's pencil shall hap'ly restore
The long-vanished scenes we may see nevermore !

And now, fellow voyagers, each one, adieu !
The day has been brighter and fairer for you,
And many a face we have looked on to-day
Will live on in memory's pictures alway.
But the long day is ended, the bright sun is set,
And pale grow the waters of calm Allumette ;
O'er the slow-fading hills glints the soft evening star,
And twilight is draping the mountains afar ;
Earth draws her close curtains and shuts out the light,
And, whether we will or not, bids us good-night !

Mrs. J. C. Yule.

Students' Quarter.

*ROBERT BROWNING,

THE POET OF THE FUTURE.

History proves nothing more clearly than that human nature
scorns a golden mean.   Impressed by the sense of one evil, men
rush to the opposite extreme, where an evil equally great awaits
them.   Like some vast pendulum, civilization swings to and fro,
now influenced by this new thought, now swayed by that, but
always unable to rest at the central point and possess the happy
medium of truth.   Thus, after long ages during which men had
contentedly trusted the opinions of their predecessors, and blindly
obeyed the dictates of tradition, there came a time of mental
and spiritual quickening, when the dogma which had been binding in the past must justify itself if it would remain so for the
future.   And as a result, we have the nineteenth century truth-
seeker, tortured by questionings which no man can answer and
filled with longings for the old hopes on which his soul once
rested.   The foundations of his faith rent away, he has grown
pessimistic, but if we may trust history, a reaction will usher in
optimism with a new era, the frown of despair to-day will be

---

*Read before the University at the Annual Commencement, 1896.

replaced by a smile of hope to-morrow. And since men desire most to hear proclaimed the doctrines they themselves believe, Robert Browning will be the loved among poets in that day, for he is the cheerful philosopher who will best express the spirit of the age. Have mechanical theories wrecked our faith in the good, lost for us our hope of immortality? Has the hard struggle for existence induced us to dispense with the sentimentality of ideals, or the weight of evil around us crushed out our belief that there is any God above "who made and loves us all"? Then it is for us that Browning has a special message. He has found the answer to our questionings where the future years will find it, not in reason, but in faith. And we may share his prophetic insight and find it there with him this afternoon.

He tells us first, and repeats it again and again in his poetry, that man's soul is in its nature *divine.* It belongs to the Infinite life, takes its rise there, is 'cooped up and kept down on earth a space' in the flesh, but is destined at the last to be free. Yet, his spirit being thus tenanted in a house of clay, man is intensely human. A veil of flesh screens his soul from that clear perception of truth which, by its right of divine birth, it ought to possess. So, in spite of all effort, man can never attain perfection here. Life is one long school of discipline. Yet, let him strive for the better, even though he meet constant failure! The fact that he attempts to be and do great things is the one thing that distinguishes him from, and raises him above, the brute creation. The lower creatures never fail because they never try. God never fails because He is omnipotent. But man is neither God nor beast. His nature partakes of both the highest and the lowest, and the consequence is for this life, an ever unsatisfied yearning, an endless struggle for the good, yet a struggle in which he is never quite victor. And in so far as a man strives, in so far he fulfils his destiny, for the soul grows by overcoming barriers, and "why stay we on the earth, unless to grow?" Let failure, therefore, never discourage us. It proves to us at least that we are capable of trying, and that very capability makes us men.

> . . . . "Man is not God, but hath God's end to serve,
> A master to obey, a course to take,
> Somewhat to cast off, somewhat to become!

Grant this, then man must pass from old to new,
From vain to real, from mistake to fact,
From what once seemed good to what now proves best.
How could man have progression otherwise?

. . . .

And say, by such confession, straight he falls
Into man's place, a thing nor God nor beast,
Made to know that he can know and not more;
Lower than God who knows all and can all,
Higher than beasts which know and can so far
As each beast's limit perfect to an end,
Nor conscious that they know, nor craving more;
While man knows partly but conceives beside,
Creeps ever on from fancies to the fact,
And in this striving, this converting air
Into a solid he may grasp and use,
Finds progress, man's distinctive mark alone.
Not God's and not the beasts'; God is, they are,
Man partly is and wholly hopes to be."

The aim of life then, being growth, soul-development, ought we to dread old age? Does it not mean more progress, doubts answered by experience, life's lessons learned?

"What's a man's age? He must hurry more, that's all."

Age, for Browning, is "the last of life for which the first was made."

And what is death? Something to be feared? Rather it is the setting free of a soul, the bringing it into full vision of that Absolute Truth, Beauty and Goodness, to which all the relatively good below has been pointing. And as we near the end and look back on life from our death-bed, we see the world and its sorrow in a softened light. Things begin to assume their right relations, for the light from Heaven penetrates the veil of flesh worn thin, and dark places are all brightened for the soul. Death but completes the work which life's long struggle failed to accomplish.

"Freed by the throbbing impulse we call death,
We burst there as the worm into the fly,
Who while a worm still, wants his wings."

What then does Browning say comes after death? What could he say but immortality? Why should the soul be freed if not to enjoy its freedom forever? Why should all here be

incomplete, imperfect, a restless yearning, if not to point beyond
to a complete, a perfect, and a joy of, satisfaction ?   Must the
soul spend all this life in learning how to live, yet never use the
knowledge gained, hereafter ?   "The world and life's too big to
pass for a dream," but how explain it without an after-life ?
The very fact that the soul longs for such life, and that this life
is meaningless else, ought to be sufficient proof to us that immortality is certain.   Otherwise, "most progress is most failure,"
for the soul climbs higher and higher in its search for truth, only
to perish at last, only to find the hopes its broader outlook has
given it, more and more incapable of realization.   Thus it is that
simple Christian faith can tell us more than all the learning of a
Greek philosopher, for it is the story of Christ revealing God as
a God of love, which after all is the sweet proof that He who
loves will grant the soul a "future state"

> "Unlimited in capability
> For joy, as this is in desire for joy."

Pain and sorrow are sent us that we may the better prize
the painless life to come.

> "What is our failure here but a triumph's evidence
> For the fulness of the days?   Have we withered or agonized?
> Why else was the pause prolonged but that singing might issue thence?
> Why rushed the discords in but that harmony should be prized?"
>
> .   .   .   .   .   "a new harmony yet
> To be run, and continued and ended,—who knows?—or endure!
> The man taught enough by life's dream of the rest to make sure:
> By the pain-throb triumphantly winning intensified bliss,
> And the next world's reward and repose, by the struggle in this."

But though the after-life will mean to us perfect revelation
of the true, the beautiful, the good, yet there are partial revelations in this life and goodness and truth, in whatever degree
attained, will last forever.   We have our moments of aspiration or of rapture, a noble thought, a lofty purpose, we speak a
kind word, we produce something of beauty ; do we sigh because
music and sweetness die away, when the sound lapses back into
silence ?   Do we fear it has perished forever ?   "No," says
Browning,

> "There shall never be one lost good.   What was shall live as before ;
> The evil is null, is nought, is silence implying sound ;

What was good, shall be good, with for evil so much good more ;
  On the earth the broken arcs ; in the heaven a perfect round.

.   .   .   .   .   .

The high that proved too high, the heroic for earth too hard,
  The passion that left the ground to lose itself in the sky,
Are music sent up to God by the lover and the bard ;
  Enough that He heard it once : we shall hear it by-and-by."

In view of Browning's thought of immortality, and his interpretation of the meaning of life, we are not surprised that he should lay great stress upon ideals. A high ideal is worth vastly more than its attainment. Only the little soul attains, and attains because its ideal is low.

> " That low man seeks a little thing to do,
>   Sees it and does it :
> This high man with a great thing to pursue,
>   Dies ere he knows it."

Attainment is not what we must look for in this life, but growth by striving, and the higher our ideal here, the grander our success hereafter, when effort shall give place to achievement.

> "'Tis not what man does which exalts him, but what man would do."
> " A man's reach should exceed his grasp,
> Or what's heaven for ? "

Browning's philosophy of life, however, holds something for us which is yet more beautiful than his thought of immortality, of ideals, or of the endurance of the good. This is his argument for Christianity, if that may be called an "argument" which is faith rather than reason. Browning believes in God, in a personal God, a God who may indeed be recognized in Nature as a Being of Infinite Power and Intelligence, but who is fully revealed as a *loving* God only in Jesus Christ, and in the testimony of our own hearts. God's power and intelligence are evident to all. Is His love not as evident ? The psalmist David asked :

> " He that planted the ear, shall He not hear? He that teacheth man knowledge, shall not He know ? "

And Browning but adds a line and says :

> " He that made man to love, shall not He love ? "

Does not the fact that God made us able to love, and with

natures craving love, prove to us that He Himself loved?
Would not the creature surpass the creator else?

> " For the loving worm within its clod,
>   Were diviner than a loveless god,
>   Amid his worlds, I will dare to say."

We need no mathematical or metaphysical proof. Enough
that human need can find comfort in no other God. Do we
"doubt that His power can fill the heart that His power
expands?" Man requires just that full revelation of love
which is given in Christ. Because he can be satisfied with
nothing else, he must believe the story of the cross.

> " 'Tis the weakness in strength that I cry for! My flesh that I seek
>   In the Godhead! I seek and I find it—"

> " So through the thunder comes a human voice
>   Saying, ' O heart I made, a heart beats here!
>   Face, my hands fashioned, see it in myself!
>   Thou hast no power, nor may'st conceive of mine,
>   But love I gave thee, with myself to love,
>   And thou must love me who have died for thee!'"

Where then is the agnostic who can destroy the faith that
reasons thus:—"My own heart can love. Therefore the God
who made it loves. A loving God means to me, Christ. It
is Christ I need. I believe then that this story of the cross is
true, that it is the satisfaction a loving God has provided, so
that the heart He made to love might never crave in vain!"

The presence of the spirit of Christ-love, Browning tell us,
is the completion of the Universe. Even in Nature it is the
transforming power.

> " Wanting is—what?
>   Summer redundant,
>   Blueness abundant,
>   —— Where is the blot?
>   Beamy the world yet a blank all the same,
>   Framework which waits for a picture to frame:
>   What of the leafage, what of the flower?
>   Roses embowering with naught they embower!
>   Come then, complete incompleteness, O Comer,
>   Pant thro' the blueness, perfect the summer!
>   Breathe but one breath,
>   Rose-beauty above,
>   And all that was death
>   Grows life, grows love,
>   Grows love!"

And to learn love's lesson is to know God, and to fulfil the end of life.

> " For life with all it yields of joy or woe,
>   And hope and fear,—believe the aged friend,—
> Is just our chance o' the prize of learning love,
>   How love might be, hath been indeed, and is ;
>
> .   .   .   .
>
>   The love that tops the might, the Christ in God."

What then of the outlook, if Browning's philosophy be true ? Shall we still be pessimists ? Or shall not firm faith in the immortality of all that is good, and in the power of the love of God, make us optimists with Browning ? Shall we look out upon the evil of this world and feel that good is conquered, and that even Christ will not interpose to save, the Christ

> " Whose sad face on the cross sees only this
> After the passion of a thousand years ? "

Rather let us say with this poet of the future :—

> " My own hope is, a sun will pierce
>   The thickest cloud earth ever stretched ;
> That after Last returns the First,
>   Though a wide compass round be fetched ;
> That what began best, can't end worst,
>   Nor what God blessed once prove accurst ! "

A little song from one of his longer poems gives us in small compass an example of Browning's poetic expression, his appreciation of the beauty of Nature, his optimistic philosophy, with the reasons for it :—

> " The year's at the spring,
>   And day's at the morn,
>   Morning's at seven ;
> The hillside's dew-pearled,
> The lark's on the wing,
>   The snail's on the thorn ;
>   God's in His heaven—-
> All's right with the world ! "

M. E. DRYDEN, '96.

THE GALE.

The wind came down on the waves that drew
    A midnight breath,
O the wind came down and as he flew
He laughed within himself and knew
    The end was death.

Out darted his long cruel arms,
    Persuading sore,
He roughly kissed as the snake that charms
And wakened all the wild alarms
    Of sea and shore.

He whispered, hissing: "See delight
    Not far, not far!"
O the sad waves shuddered that midnight
And shrieked and moaned at the sudden might
    Of the hidden bar.

Outshrilled a voice above the lash?
    The bitter mock?
"Woe! for the waves they flee and flash
In the flood of the moon till they die and crash
    On the birth-blind rock!"

G. HERBERT CLARKE, '95·

In Massey's Magazine for May.

ON MILTON'S DESCRIPTION OF EVENING.

(BK. IV., *Paradise Lost.*)

"That I may assert Eternal Providence" is the impulse which, as Milton declares, prompts him to poetic utterance. He must, in some way, reveal to others the spiritual significance which he, with larger faith and vision, has found in God's universe. In *Paradise Lost*, he has imaged forth, by the creative power of his own mind, truths and beauties, a realization of which might else be unattainable for us. If such be the grand purpose, the controlling life, of the poem, each minor part must have its essential office in the expression of this thought. What, then, in the light of the whole, is the purpose of this description of Evening, and by what artistic devices is it fitly expressed ?

How wonderful is God ! How perfect His handiwork !— this, in brief, is the controlling emotion of the entire poem. The inspiration of this feeling he finds in the beauty and economy of the creative work—nature and man. If in a description of evening he can make us feel, as *he* feels it, the beauty and the purpose of this one aspect of Divine order in the universe, then has he given adequate expression to a thought which is essential in its bearing upon his soul's purpose. Without doubt, then, in this product of his imagination he has sought to put in definite form, for himself and for others, those principles of economy and beauty — Divine law and love— which have been revealed to him as underlying all the manifestations of Nature.

The most utilitarian purpose that night serves is referred to in the lines which speak of the resting birds and beasts. But, one might ask, would not utter gloom and unbroken silence serve these as well ? The poet, however, sees more meaning than this in the aspect of God's universe which he describes. The Beauty of Night becomes his theme, and it is in beauty itself that the Divine purpose and economy are realized. Even though night's glories were forever unobserved by earthly creatures, God's plan would still be all-beneficent.

As Virtue is its own reward, so Harmony is its own economy, and Beauty its own purpose.   To bring more clearly to the minds of others this essential truth, the poet endows the elements of his picture with varying degrees of personality. By making each of these participate actively and consciously in this heavenly panorama, he gives forceful expression to the great principle that the universe is not a dull insensate mechanism, but a God-inspired Cosmos, throbbing with divine life and energy.   Like Wordsworth, Milton could be " a pagan " and

> " Have sight of Proteus rising from the sea
> Or hear old Triton blow his wreathèd horn,"

rather than look upon Nature as meaningless and lifeless.   We may imagine that, in the present day (while his intense devotional spirit would avoid the extreme of Pantheism), he would identify himself with the school of Idealistic Monists, whose philosophy thinks of all that is material as being an *aspect* of the one abiding spiritual force.

Let us examine this beautiful scene, as described by the poet, in some detail.   The approach of evening, following in the path of twilight, and accompanied by Silence, contains for the poet nothing of the inanimate—there is activity and personality. And, now, bird and beast have slunk to their sylvan retreats. But, hark !—" the wakeful nightingale."   ' And, here (exclaims some soulless one), there is beauty wasted.'   " Silence is pleased," answers the poet, sublimely.   In order that the resultant beauty of night might be made more harmonious than it otherwise would be, self-abnegating Silence yields up her exclusive sway. The poet does not view the stars as mere lamps in the heavens. They are " *living* sapphires," each riding in conscious glory amid heavenly splendours.   Now they are led by bright Hesperus, but she, faithful lieutenant, soon yields her authority upon the appearance of the peerless light of heaven's queen—the moon. She, sovereign of the night, reveals her calm power, and spreads over the darkened earth her silver ægis.

STAMBURY R. TARR, '95·

THE EDITOR'S RETALIATION.

Cicero Perkins was a very nice young man—not nice in the sense of fastidious, but nice in the sense of pleasant. His cheerful demeanor, however, was chiefly due, no doubt, to his excellent regard for him who is generally every man's most cherished friend, and is therefore known in calm and dispassionate grammar as the first person singular.

But a steady breeze may blow against a sturdy structure till it falls; a contemptible obstacle sometimes derails a huge and mighty train. Alas! The disturbance of self-esteem brings about a sea of fury, which, whether it afterwards subsides or not into the low, still tide of repentant humiliation, has waves that beat and spray to sting.

Cicero Perkins did not hope to win for himself a resounding fame in literature. He philanthropically *intended* to accomplish this enterprise for the lasting benefit of an eager world. A few weeks only need they wait. He abode his majestic time. Meanwhile, with a keen eye to self-improvement, and a discernment that now proves triumphantly the absence of conceit, he determined to read at least one page of the New Continental Dictionary every day before breakfast. He had heard of this plan before. He knew it would add zest to his resolution, and well up within him as a seething earnest of future glorification.

The plan worked admirably, and Cicero was really painstaking and conscientious.

.   .   .   .   .   .   , ...

"Hum," growled the editor, "this idiot says nothing, but he's stocked himself with words of a feather, and he's flocked them together with a vengeance. Lesse :

"'Accurate acknowledgments of acumen are adduced as the antipodes of amateur amenities. The Æneid is an allegory achieved by an a priori architect. Apropos of analogy, ancestry is advertised in æsthetic alternatives by alienating the amiable affections of antiquity, who aid aspiration with an arduous accent on the antepenult.'"

"Balder ——— !" was the enigmatic verdict rendered by the critical registering apparatus of the editor's weather hemisphere The proof-reader would have heaved a hollow laugh.

Scratching hastily on a pad before him, he tore the resulting note from its position, seized a printed slip from a pile on the right, thrust these with the manuscript into a long official envelope, and cast the lot aside to await the coming of the first instrument of Nemesis' reacting force, the office-boy.

.   .   .   .

Curiously we glance over Cicero's shoulder as he reads:

" Cicero Perkins, Esq:

Dear Sir: We regret that we do not find it possible at present to accept your article so kindly submitted for publication in the *Mammoth Monthly Magazine.* The rejection of a manuscript does not necessarily imply that it lacks merit. Thanking you for your courtesy, etc.,

We are very truly yours,

Tryem A. Gane, Editor."

Cicero madly tears open the accompanying slip, which, we perceive, reads as follows:

Cut up your stuff into feet and lines. It'll make a great hit as alliterative verse.

T. A. G.

Our hero Perkins howls vindictively, scatters fragments to the ceiling, pounds the wall, and bursts into a series of prolonged and awful objurgations, mostly beginning with the first letter of the alphabet, although as yet he had not mastered the first forty pages of the New Continental Dictionary.

Having become rather calmer and more bitter in a week or two, he one day seized the pen, broke it, seized another, grasped the ink-bottle, spilt it, laughed ironically, and reached for the red ink as better adapted for his purpose, anyway, and, thus bestirred himself to write. This is the letter he sent:

"T. A. Gane, Animal :—I defy you and assert your abominable absence of appreciation. Ardent ambition I have, nor is it blighted by the asinine ailing with which you are afflicted. Ah, arrogant anomaly, shudder ! for the day will dawn ere long when ample acclamation and applause shall drown your anxious cries, and anger destroy your apparatus. Avaunt, I say !

Anonymous."

This was perhaps rather mild after such treatment, yet restricted somewhat noticeably by a certain peculiar tendency.

But psychology can never analyze the emotions of Cicero two days after. For this is the letter he received—only a printed slip, yet a model of appropriateness and a masterpiece of retort:

"Dear Sir:—We regret that we do not find it possible at present to accept your article so kindly submitted for publication in the *Mammoth Monthly Magazine*. The rejection of a manuscript does not necessarily imply that it lacks merit. Thanking you for your courtesy, etc.,

We are very truly yours,
Tryem A. Gane, Editor,
Per Tryem Nomore."

Cicero Perkins, Esq.

PLASHET.

In Toronto Saturday Night.

THE JERUSALEM CROSS.

It was, I think, in reading General Gordon's " Letters to his Sister," or some other work on Palestine, that the fact that the interior of Jerusalem is divided by a cross was stated or suggested to my father's* mind, and it has occurred to me that perhaps the readers of the McMaster University Monthly might like to get the benefit of his thoughts on the subject.

Every writer says, and every visitor sees indubitably, that the city is divided by a deep valley or ravine, much deeper in ancient times, from north to south—from the Damascus gate to the pool and village of Siloam, which Josephus designates the Tyropœon or Valley of the Cheesemakers. Everybody also knows that from the Jaffa Gate, facing west, down to the Haram, or Temple Area, on the east, is another valley, even more filled up than the former with the debris of the successive destructions of the city. The question is, did it continue until it reached the Kidron, or Valley of Jehoshaphat, beyond the city? There are indications, outside the walls, that it did; my father firmly maintains that it did, and that it is the valley separating Moriah from Zion and the Akra, which Simon the Maccabee cut down to a lower level than Moriah, filling up the valley with the debris. Josephus xiii. vi. 7.

---

*Resident Missionary in Jerusalem.

I am well aware that this is encroaching on debatable ground. At present it is the south-west part of the western range that is commonly called Zion. Naturally enough, the Episcopalians with their chapel and the Armenians with their large convent and church, both situated on that part of the range, love to believe that it is indeed Mount Zion ; just as the Roman Catholics, the Greek Church, and many others, love to believe that their Church of the Holy Sepulchre contains Golgotha and the tomb where the Lord's body lay ; as also the spot whence God took the earth for the formation of Adam's body, the tomb of Melchizedek, the centre of the world and what not ! Whereas the mound outside the Damascus Gate is continually crying out with dumb pathos : " Golgotha ! a skull ! " and is, as I could abundantly prove, the true site of the crucifixion.

Psalm xlviii : 2, says Mount Zion was " on the sides of the north "—north of what ? Clearly, of " the mountain of His holiness "—Moriah. However, it is not deemed fitting to argue this question here.

Once my father had grasped the fact that Jerusalem had been divided by a cross of valleys, he began to consider that there was surely some meaning in it. It soon dawned on him that there was ; and he told me that as the facts flashed through his mind he felt a thrill of inexpressible delight, I might almost say of ecstacy, and the communication of his thought had much the same effect on me.

We find, then, upon examination : Siloam, south ; Golgotha, north ; Bethlehem, west ; Olivet, east. Siloam from the same root as Shiloh, the first name given to the Messiah, Gen. xlix : 10, " One to be sent." Siloam, south, had a pool of healing waters (John ix : 7) ; and He who came to save man from the consequence of sin was sent for what ? To ascend the cross on Golgotha, north, to expiate sin. That is the main upright beam of the cross.

The shorter beam points to Bethlehem on the west and the Mount of Olives on the east, the rising sun. Bethlehem, " house of bread." In it was born He who said, " I am the bread of life." The olive-branch is the emblem of conquest and triumph ; and He, " the Sun of Righteousness," who conquered death and

3

the grave, ascended triumphant from the Mount of Olives to heaven to sit at God's right hand, as was predicted (Ps. xc.); and thence He shall come again, "in like manner," as He was seen ascending; and "His feet shall stand in that day upon the Mount of Olives" (Zec. xiv: 4) as they stood at His ascension day.

Jerusalem, the city of "Peace," saw "The Prince of Peace" traverse the cross from Siloam to Golgotha, and from Bethlehem to Olivet—for what? To obtain, secure, and bestow peace on man. "Peace I leave with you, my peace I give unto you." (John xiv: 27.) Peace with God, peace of conscience, peace with all men; "the peace of God that passeth all understanding."

"Pray for the peace of Jerusalem, they shall prosper that love thee."

HERBERT A. BEN-OLIEL, '98.

EDITORIAL NOTES.

WITH the present issue we complete Volume V. of the McMASTER UNIVERSITY MONTHLY, which will be found in every respect to have maintained the high standard of excellence of its predecessors. The Managing Committee are grateful to all readers and friends of the MONTHLY, not only for their many and hearty expressions of appreciation, but also for their generous financial support, which has enabled the business managers to meet promptly and fully all their obligations during the year. We trust the experiences of the next and following years may continue to be at least equally gratifying.

FROM a cabinet photograph kindly placed at our disposal by Mr. Carson Cameron, B.A., we have obtained an excellent photogravure portrait of the late Rev. John King, which will be substituted in all our bound copies of Volume V., for the inferior picture which accompanied the biographical sketch by Bro. Higgins, of Ottawa, published a few months ago. Readers of the MONTHLY who desire it, may have one of these bound copies in exchange for their old numbers and the price of binding. Send to Mr. G. H. Clarke, M.A., Librarian, McMaster University.

THE five volumes of the McMASTER MONTHLY, handsomely bound in half morocco, and standing side by side on the shelf, will be among the most attractive and highly valued books in the library. With their forty portraits and biographies of distinguished Canadian Baptists, and hundreds of bright, instructive and entertaining articles by friends and acquaintances whose names are linked with their happiest memories of college life. They will mean more to Canadian Baptist students for many years to come than any other volume in their possession. So let every student of McMaster University see that they are all on his shelves, and so placed too that his eyes may frequently and fondly rest on their familiar bindings. We predict that these volumes at least will never, even under the most trying circumstances, be sent off to the dust and ignominy of the second-hand book stalls.

NEWTON WOLVERTON has long been absent from Canada in consequence of his educational work in the South, but his name has by no means ceased to be held in high esteem by his large circle of friends in his native province. There can be no doubt that Woodstock College would hardly have weathered the difficulties and discouragements that gathered about her at a certain period in her history, had it not been for Mr. Wolverton's unflagging energy and unusual administrative ability, and the confidence which his wise and practical educational policy inspired in the minds of friends and patrons of the college throughout the province, The brief but appreciative sketch by Prof. Farmer of his life and work in Ontario, as pastor and teacher, will be read with interest by all Mr. Wolverton's friends, and will remind them how high his eminent services entitle him to rank in the long line of ardent workers to whom the prosperity and happiness of to-day are due.

WE have heard it said, on all sides, that the commencement exercises of 1896, of which a detailed account is given elsewhere, were the most successful and enjoyable in the history of the University. It was a happy inspiration on the part of the Committee of Management to give to Dr. Lorimer, of Boston, Mass., so prominent a part in the exercises on several occasions. Nothing could have added more to the enjoyment of all the various exercises, or contributed more largely to make '96 so memorable in the Annals of McMaster University, than Dr. Lorimer's baccalaureate sermon and his stirring addresses at the collation and the conferring of degrees. We believe Dr. Lorimer has learned to love Toronto and the brethren whom he met during this brief visit; he certainly has won a large and permanent place in our hearts, and we shall give him the heartiest of welcomes and the largest congregations when he comes over again to see us.   Will ye' no' come back again?   Dr. Lorimer was born in Edinburgh, Scotland, in 1838, where he spent the early part of his life and attended school.   He came to the United States when about 18 years of age, and while on a professional visit to Louisville, Ky., he came under the spiritual influence of Rev. W. W. Evarts, D.D., and family, through whom, by God's blessing, he was led to Christ and communion with His people.   After his baptism, he entered upon a course of study at Georgetown College, Ky., was ordained in 1856 at the Baptist Church in Harrodsburgh, Ky.   Since that time he has had a number of important and successful pastorates in different American cities.   At present he is in charge of the Tremont Temple in Boston, Mass.

HERE AND THERE.

O. G. LANGFORD, ED.

GLADSTONE.

England, what is thy greatest glory now?
  Is it thy fleet, thy cannon, or thy gold?
  Thine empire millioned over lands untold?
Thy commerce world-wide on old Ocean's brow?

The current of a hundred years, whose flow
  O'er dynasties and empires darkly rolled,
  Draws to the deep; but mighty as of old
Thy nerves of conquest thrill at battle's blow!

And yet bethink thee, England; many a throne
  Has ruled the world and fallen, and a time
Shall come in Earth's far ages, when alone,
The fabric of thy glory passed away,
  Above thy wreck one name shall rest sublime,—
His who now stands upon the brink of day!

                    —JAMES T. SHOTWELL, in *The 'Varsity.*

THE University of Missouri has abolished compulsory attendance at prayers and has inaugurated a plan of inviting prominent ministers of the State to take in turn the duty of chaplain.

"YOU seem sad, my red-skinned brother," said the missionary. "Red-skinned brother's heart heap sad," said the noble son of the prairie, "white man shoot better, fight better, and now Injun hear college yell, he know Injun can't war-whoop any more.   Waugh?"

AN exchange says: "Chaucer describes men and things as they are; Shakespeare, as they would be under the circumstances proposed;

Spenser, as he would wish them to be ; Milton, as they ought to be ; Byron, as they ought not to be ; Shelley, as they never can be."

> " What a beautiful thing is thought," said she ;
> " A boon it is to myself and Jim.
> I sit and think he is thinking of me,
> And he sits and thinks I am thinking of him."
>
> *—Cornell Era.*

Knox College Monthly, enlarged to 60 pp., keeps up a very high standard of literary excellence. Its articles are stately and dignified. ....*Acta Victoriana* has taken a long step in advance this year in form, typography and size..... *Queen's College Journal*, always good, has made substantial progress.

IN college journalism this year one feature has been particularly noticeable,—illustration. Many of our esteemed contemporaries have given us engravings of their Editorial Staff, Glee Club, College Quartette, Football, Baseball, Hockey and Lacrosse teams. Some have printed excellent portraits of their prominent lecturers, their professors and presidents, of specially clever students that have won prizes, etc. This has added largely to the interest of the Exchange department, and we think to the value of the College paper generally.

The Madisonian is a new publication, the first number that reaches our office has a very pretty photogravure of the seven ladies of the Editorial staff. The number is a good one and we shall look with pleasure for subsequent issues. A poem entitled "Night," by Eugenia Parkham, has some good verses ; we have only space for three :—

> The wonder world of Thought
> Unbends beneath thy power ;
> Her grandest dreams are wrought
> Within thy deepest hour.
>
> Thy silence and thy dark,
> Lonely companions twain,
> The bounds of ages mark
> In Heaven's divinest strain.
>
> And yet in Heaven, they say,
> Thou shalt not ever be ;
> No night shall break the day
> Of that eternity.

THE following composition, according to a writer in the *Homiletical Review*, came from a teachers' institute in Pennsylvania. He asserts that not one in fifty will read it correctly at sight. Submitted to bishops, editors, professors, authors, etc., it has never been read, in his hearing, with less than five errors, while he has known ministers of considerable prominence to miss twenty-eight of these common words :—

A sacrilegious son of Belial, who suffered from bronchitis, having exhausted his finances, in order to make good the deficit, resolved to ally himself to a comely, lenient and docile young lady of the Malay or Caucasian race. He accordingly purchased a calliope, and a neck-lace of a chameleon hue, and having secured a suite of rooms at a leading hotel near the depôt, he engaged the head waiter as his coad-jutor. He then dispatched a letter of the most unexceptional cali-graphy extant, inviting the young lady to a matinee. She revolted at the idea, refused to consider herself sacrificeable to his designs, and sent a polite note of refusal; on receiving which he said he would now forge fetters hymeneal with the Queen. He then procured a carbine and a bowie-knife, went to an isolated spot behind an abode of squalor, severed his jugular vein, and discharged the contents of the carbine into his abdomen. The debris was removed by the coroner, who, from leading a life in the culture of belles-lettres and literature, has become a sergeant-at-arms in the Legislature of Arkansas.

NATURE AND LOVE.

This I learned from the birds,
        Dear heart,
And they told me in woodland words,
        Apart.
And they told me true—
That all their singing the summer through
Was of you, of you.

This I learned from the flowers,
        Dear heart,
In the dewy morning hours
        Apart—
And they sware it, too,
That all their sweetness the summer through
Was for you, for you.

This I learned from the leaves,
        Dear heart,
On stilly, starry eves
        Apart—
Though their words were few—
That all their sighing the summer through
Was for you, for you.

—*Nassau Lit. Magazine.*

A Song.—We had gone fishing, the boys and I, and blue-eyed seven-year-old—called "Judge," because of his seriousness—was the proud possessor of a string of sunfish and perch. The sun was hidden behind the thick wood across the stream, leaving us with the mystic charm of a midsummer twilight. Turning our faces homewards, we saw before us a group of boys playing La Crosse upon the common; and seven-year-old, who had never seen the game, took his position to witness it, one hand grasping firmly the rod and line and little tin pail of earth-worms, and the other holding the string of sunfish and perch.

As the design of the performance began to present itself to his mind, I heard his low rippling laugh, checked now and then by sus-pended breathing as arms, legs and cross-sticks were hopelessly inter laced. This disconnected music was the prelude of the song which soon burst forth full and free. Up and down the laughing scale ran the voice, clear as a high-keyed bell, and sweet as the singing of a bird at daybreak. Ripple on ripple, wave on wave, came the music, now rising ecstatically to the highest note, lingering and swelling, and now running the downward scale in a soft tremulous cadenza. The climax was reached as the game ended, then the song rolled across the stream in silver rings that chased one another in and out among the trees and sped on to lull, in their decline, the sinking sun.

That was before the day of the phonograph, or I should have enlisted its good offices to preserve, for the solace of my lonely hours, the sweetest song I have ever heard.

Eva Rose York.

COLLEGE NEWS.

W. P. Cohoe, '96,   R. D. George, '97,
J. F. Vichert, '97,   Miss E. Whiteside, '98,
Editors.

The University.

Lack of space prevents a full report of the student meeting for the election of new officers and the farewell dinner given to '96 by their hopeful successors, the new seniors. Both meetings were entirely successful. Mr. J. F. Vichert, '97, was elected High Kakiac for 1896-'97 and was installed at the dinner in the evening. Mr. H. N. McKechnie, '97, presided. Many excellent speeches were made laudatory of the departing classes and were graciously responded to by the representatives of the recent graduates. The retiring High Kakiac, Mr. C. J. Cameron, B. A., was presented with a handsome miniature gavel, in memory of his well-wielded authority. The enjoyment of the evening was greatly enhanced by the presence of Chancellor and Mrs. Wallace, and the ladies of the University. '97 deserves congratulations. That dinnner will not readily be forgotten.

During vacation our professors are by no means idle or

> " Free to sit with folded hands
> And gaze upon the meadow-lands."

Chancellor Wallace, after the Convention, will attend the Woodstock closing during the first week in June, and the Moulton closing during the following week. At the same time he will visit various Associations. In the last week of July and the first week of August, he will deliver a course of ten lectures at Pine Lake, Indiana, U. S. A., and then the same number at Luray, Virginia, on " The Life and Teachings of Christ." He will return to Toronto by the first of September to make preparations for the opening of the University in October.

Dr. Rand delivered an eloquent and masterly address upon " The Educational Ideal, how it is Realizing itself, and Whither it Tends," at the Encoenia of the University of New Brunswick on May 28th. He will visit in Fredericton and Wolfville and proceed to Partridge Island, Parrsboro', N. S. Dr. Newman is hard at work as usual among his books and MSS. He will sojourn at Hamill's Point, Muskoka. Dr. Welton is in the city revising old work and planning new. Prof. Campbell is studying at the University of Chicago. Prof. Farmer is visiting Manitoba and the North West, and doing work that tells on behalf of the University and denomination.

Prof. McKay will leave shortly for Cambridge University, England, where he will remain for a year engaged in mathematical work. Dr. Goodspeed will recuperate at Stanley Park and take charge of the Belfountain church. Prof. Clark has just concluded his arduous labours in connection with the examinations of various institutions and will take a brief holiday at Long Point. Prof. Willmott and Mr. Piersol are still at work in town. The former has been appointed by the Ontario Government to visit the Rainy Lake region in company with Prof. Coleman. Dr. Ten Broeke preached the Educational sermon before the Convention at Montreal. He returns home to Panton, on the shores of Lake Champlain. Mr. McLay is in Woodstock, and will return for his duties with regard to departmental examinations. Mr. Russell is taking graduate work in mathematics at Harvard University, Cambridge, Mass.

The Third Annual Commencement.

Commencement week with all its glories is now past and gone. '96 has been hooded, has been admitted " *ad gradum Bacalaurei in Artibus* " with long Latin names and " the rights and dignities pertaining thereunto." Everything was a perfect success. Nature and the Senate smiled favorably upon '96 and granted them a successful graduation. The new Chancellor is certainly well versed in the lore of commencements and makes ours not only second to none but superior to all. McMaster's commencement week is peculiar, in that nearly all her students remain to it, and in that way by their loyalty to *alma mater* make it a week always to be remembered by the graduate and looked forward to by the freshman.

The University is to be congratulated upon its good fortune in securing Rev. Dr. Lorimer, the distinguished pastor of Tremont Temple, Boston, Mass., to preach the Baccalaureate sermon. His presence at the various academic functions added much to the enjoyment of those who were fortunate enough to be present.

The annual meeting of the Associated Alumni was the first meeting of the series, and was attended by a goodly number of the graduates and friends. The President, Rev. A. P. McDiarmid, delivered an excellent address on " The Aim of Education." This he considered to be service, service for humanity and God, rather than self-aggrandizement.   Rev. J. B. Kennedy's address on "The Relation of Education to Missions " dealt with the importance of Education in the evangel·ization of the world.   Miss Bœhmer, of Moulton College, sang Gounod's "The King of Love" in a charming manner, and the University Glee Club gave an admirable rendering of the grand old hymn *Te Deum*.

The following officers were elected for the ensuing term :—President, Rev. W. M. Walker, B.A., London ; First Vice President, Prof. Clark, M.A., Toronto ; Second Vice-President, Rev. E. Hooper, M.D.; Third Vice President, Linus Woolverton, M.A., Grimsby ; Fourth Vice-President, Miss Eliza P. Wells, B.A., Toronto ; Secretary-Treasurer, W. S. W. McLay, B.A.; Corresponding Secretary, W.S.S. McAlpine, B.A.   Mr A. K. Blackadar, M.A., Ottawa, and Mr. A. P. McDonald, B.A., B.Th., were appointed representatives on the Senate of the graduates in Arts and Theology respectively.

The Committee appointed to report *re* Memorials in McMaster Hall to Dr. Fyfe and Principal McGregor, was continued.   A committee was appointed to draft a plan whereby all graduates, whether present at the annual meeting of the association or not, may be enabled to vote for representatives to the Senate.

DELIVERY OF ESSAYS.—On Tuesday afternoon members of the graduating classes read essays to the public.   The attendance was good for an afternoon.   All those present felt themselves more than repaid for going.   The essays were five : "Ideals : Their Nature and Value," Geo. John Menge, (Arts) ; "The Greatest Frenchman," Horatio Hackett Newman, (Arts) ; "Browning, the Poet of the Future," Mary Elizabeth Dryden, (Arts) ; "Christianity in the Nineteenth Century," William Wardley McMaster, B A., (Theology) ; "Christian Missions in Relation to Civilization," Bert Ward Merrill, B A., (Theology.)   The Glee Club sang "The Hunter's Call," and Mr. W. S. S. McAlpine, B.A., sang "The Ivy Green," in his usual acceptable style.

THE BACCALAUREATE SERMON will long be remembered by those who were privileged to hear it.   The large audience room of Walmer Road church was filled with an intensely interested audience of students and friends of McMaster.   On the platform were Chancellor Wallace presiding ; Rev. Dr. Lorimer, the University professoriate, Pastor W. W. Weeks, Rev. E. J. Stobo, Senr., and others.

We are indebted to the *Globe* for the following excellent digest of the sermon.   No apology is needed for its length :—

After a few words of welcome by the Chancellor short musical selections were rendered, and Rev. Dr. Lorimer was called upon to deliver the Baccalau-reate Sermon.   Dr. Lorimer spoke for over an hour, but the magnificent manner in which he dealt with his subject, combined with his eloquent delivery, made the time pass far too rapidly.   He is an orator of exceptional ability, and his address of last night will long be remembered by the graduates and friends of McMaster University.   From beginning to end his remarks were most impressive and inspiring, and delivered with a charm and grace of language possessed only by the most gifted speakers.

DR. LORIMER'S SERMON.—The words on which he spoke were taken from the Gospel of St. Matthew, chap. vi., verse 23.   "If, therefore, the light that is in thee be darkness, how great is the darkness."   Speaking on this text he said :—" This language forms part of a most striking analogy. Some commentators fancy that it was suggested by the relationship existing between the sun and our planet. Were a calamity to quench the fires of the chief splendor of the solar system earth would be hopelessly enswathed in endless night. As is the sun to our globe, so is the eye to the body, and were it to suffer an eclipse the entire body would be veiled in darkness. But with due respect to the expositors, the Saviour's comparison is less pretentious than this. He simply likens vision to a lamp, a lamp which may be the hope of some wanderer through a dangerous mountain defile, or the flickering beacon on the shore to guide the wet sailor on stormy Galilee, and which if it goes out leaves the pilgrim and mariner in despair. The terms he employs, however, in contemplating so sad a contingency do not describe actual blindness so much as prove perversion of vision. If the eye is single, if it sees straight, has in view one object and keeps it in view, then the path will be clear and bright, but if it is divergent, looks two ways at once, confusion, indistinctness and obscurity must prevail. Swiftly the application comes that throws light on the figure, "No man can serve two masters." "Ye cannot serve God and mammon."

The careful reader ought to note that the analogy in this passage is double. First, it is between the lamp and the eye; and secondly, between the eye and something corresponding to it within described as " light." To what does Christ refer ? It has been held by several writers that the eye of the soul is manifestly reason, which has to see for the whole body. But others insist that as He was discussing ethical principles He must necessarily have meant the conscience. As we are disposed to read our psychologies and metaphysics into the terminology of our Lord, and as there are conflicting schools on these high subjects, naturally enough we fail of agreement. Personally I hold that He did not intend to designate constitutional functions of the intellectual or moral nature of man, but primarily and exclusively the illumination, original or acquired, native or attained, of the soul. If we must find an exact analogy to the eye it exists in the soul itself taken as a whole. That is the seat of all intelligence, knowledge, radiance, brightness. Gœthe says, " The eye receives the sun because it is sunny," and so the mind is in a similar manner capable of receiving light because it is light. The Master discloses a most solemn contingency, paradoxical in form, and yet thoroughly philosophical in character. He affirms that the light may be darkness, and hints at the awful and pitiful immeasurableness of such darkness. It is to the force and significance of this teaching that we must look.

AN ENLIGHTENED PEOPLE.—The Great Teacher is thinking of those who prize reason, culture, knowledge and all that goes to make an enlightened people. In addition He is proceeding on the supposition that the inner light governs and determines a man's outward life. What are schools, public libraries, churches and newspapers to us if they are not appropriated and used ? The public library only benefits as it is utilized by the mind, nor are books a radiance on our pathway until they have been read. Two sad sights—a blind man stumbling along in the radiance of meridian splendor and a mind confronting the volumes in the library without the least conception of what they mean. Remember, we are governed directly from within, only indirectly from without. As the Deity gazing on this potential planet enveloped in darkness called on light to penetrate the thick blackness, so should every human being, realizing that without it there can be neither grass nor flowers nor beauty, make a way for his soul to be flooded with light. But what if the light be darkness ? How is such a thing possible ? It is always possible when reason is misdirected. When we stop to consider the part played by the mind of man in civilization and Christianity we are filled with amazement, and while we condemn the worship of reason impersonated in a frail woman at Notre Dame, we admit, if anything human is entitled to such homage, it is reason. And yet when we find it crowning a sinful woman, the sign of folly, viciousness and indecency, we have furnished to hand an illustration of light being darkness. Signs also have we of this grave miscarriage of the highest faculty in the religious mystic who interprets shadowy impressions into revelations from God ; in the technologist who devotes himself to the arrangement of impossible or superfluous inventions, in the astronomer who runs into astrology ; in the chemist who is secretly hoping to discover the elixir of life, and in the social reformer, who believes that the

hope of society lies in building it on a foundation that is contrary to every law
of human nature. So likewise is this faculty darkness, when individuals use it
to find excuses for idleness, restlessness and disdain for the ordinary obligations
of life.

When men like Mr. Gladstone and Mr. Balfour, though immersed in political affairs, devote their trained intellects to the cause of religion, we all seem to
feel the light of their thought. But, on the other hand, when we note writers of
a different type, well read, ever brilliant, setting forth doctrines which undermine man's trust in God and in faith, who are the very torquemadas of infidelity,
we do not impugn their motives, but we see how strong reasoning powers may
propagate darkness.

MISCONCEPTION OF RELIGION.—But again, the light within us is darkness
when religion is misconceived and misrepresented. We are to remember that
religion is a larger term than Christianity. Nicodemus was religious, as was the
devout centurion, before they became Christians. So we have no right to say
that Mohammedans, Buddhists and multitudes of reverent rationalists are not
religious. Of course we hold that the follower of Jesus is pre-eminently so.
However kindled, whether by the working of a necessary law of our being, or by
tradition and early education, a light springs up in the soul that points to God,
to the duty of worship and to the possibility of a future life. This light has
been increased by reflection, as in eastern lands, and by revelation and reflection,
as in the west. Moreover, it ought still to grow through experience and study.
But, alas ! it may be perverted, it may be misapprehended and misapplied.
When such is the case it becomes darkness, and the more there is of it the greater
the darkness. To illustrate : We are specially interested to-day in the attitude
of Mohammedanism towards Christianity. From the beginning that creed has
sought the extermination of our faith and has never restrained its barbarous
cruelties. Now the streets of Constantinople run red with blood. A Turk
stands with a dripping spear over a murdered woman. The world looks on and
exclaims, " That is religion ! No, I prefer none of it." I answer, yes, but the
light has become darkness. So, too, with the exception of a few Protestants
here and there, the church stands aloof, more afraid to do something impolitic
than to be guilty of inhuman apathy, and the great mass of unbelievers exclaim,
" and this is religion ! " It is another case of the traveller fallen among thieves.
The Levite and the Priest, State and Church, pass that way and no good
Samaritan has yet paused and poured in oil and wine This sad tragedy does
not prove the unreality of religion, only the conversion of its light into darkness.

And how great is the darkness ? Who can estimate it ? Our Lord uses a
form of speech that at once suggests superlativeness, incomparableness, excessive-
ness. It is as though He said it is greater than any other kind of darkness and
more impregnable. When men have never learned and are seeking the day,
though their state is sad, it is hopeful. They are in a fair way to a better condition. But when men are wrong, believing themselves right, irrational, believing themselves rational, wise when unwise, and thinking themselves truly
religious, when they are falsely religious, the difficulty of saving them is
immense. It is harder to overcome miseducation than no education, and more
difficult to counteract the errors of religion than to overcome the evils of
no religion. When dogmatism, when vanity, pride and self-confidence are
allied on behalf of a position, it becomes next to impossible to storm it, and
capture it by assault. These are entrenchments not readily taken. Consider
how traditions, habit, associations, intellectual pride and love of consistency
keep you from changing ground, and then think if you are in darkness how
great, how hopeless, how impregnable that darkness must be.

THE COLLATION.—When are students so happy as when they are
seated before a table loaded—not with books ? This fact was demonstrated at the annual collation held on Wednesday afternoon.

Shortly after 4 o'clock nearly 300 guests, including many ladies,
sat down to an elaborate repast, which had been prepared for the
occasion. The tables, which were arranged in six rows, with a long
head table, were tastefully decorated with flowers and ornamental dishes.

At the head table were the following invited guests:—President and
Mrs. Loudon (Toronto), Chancellor and Mrs. Burwash (Victoria), Dr.
Lorimer, Mrs. Holman, Principal Sheraton (Wycliffe), ex-Chancellor
and Mrs. Rand, Prof. and Mrs. Bell, and Mrs. Wallace.   Rev. Chancellor Wallace presided.   Among others present were Messrs. J. Short
McMaster, Rev. Jesse Gibson, Rev. D. E. Hutchinson (Brantford),
Principal Bates (Woodstock), Hon. John Dryden and Mr. Holman.
Shortly after 5 o'clock the toast list was entered upon with a toast to
the Queen, which was honored by the national anthem.   Next came
the "Sister Universities," which was proposed by the Chancellor and
responded to by Dr. Loudon, Chancellor Burwash, Principal Sheraton
and Prof. Bell.   All these gentlemen delivered excellent adresses, in all
of which they emphasized especially the good feeling which exists between the different colleges, and the mutual advantages which are to be
derived from their close connection.   "The Graduating Class in Arts"
was proposed by Mr. Linus Wolverton, M. A., representing the Senate
of McMaster University, and replied to by Mr J. C. Sycamore of the
graduating class in an able and eloquent manner.   "The Graduating Class in Theology" was proposed by Dr. Calvin Goodspeed and
responded to by Mr. J. J. Reeve, '96, who made many well-pointed and
humorous remarks.   The other toasts were : "The Governors," proposed by Prof. McKay, responded to by Mr. Dryden, "The Alumni,"
proposed by Prof. Willmott, replied to by Rev. W. M. Walker, President of the Alumni Association ; "Our Pastors," proposed by Mr. D.
E. Thomson, Q. C., and responded to by Revs. D. B. Cohoe and A. C.
Baker, and a toast to "The Preacher of the Baccalaureate Sermon,"
proposed by Rev. C. A. Eaton, and replied to by Rev. Dr. Lorimer in
an address which was marked with humor and eloquence from beginning
to end.   During the afternoon many excellent college songs were
rendered by the Glee Club and members of the graduating class of '96.
"McMaster men" was an especial success.

CONFERRING OF DEGREES AND DIPLOMAS.—But the culmination
of all things was on commencement night—Wednesday.   Every Mc-
Master man and woman turned out to the procession.   The solemn,
slow and majestic progress having been made, permission was asked of
the Chancellor that the graduates might be admitted to their degrees
This   given, each graduate mounted the platform, bowed profoundly and profusely, heard the mystic words pronounced, had the
hood placed over his head, received his "sheep-skin" and marched
down feeling himself not educated but a B. A. The one break in this
programme was when '96's lady, Miss Dryden, received her degree.
The applause testified to Miss Dryden's popularity, as the large number
of bouquets she received testified to the esteem of her many friends.

The degrees and diplomas were awarded as follows :

Ad eundem—Master of Arts Degree—Rev. Charles Aubrey Eaton,
Professor James Ten Broeke.

Bachelor of Arts Degree—Arthur Baker, William Hunter Piersol,
Alexander Robertson McDonald.

In Course—Master of Arts Degree—George Herbert Clarke, Geo. Cross, Philo Kilborn Dayfoot.

In Course—Bachelor of Arts Degree—Archibald Gillies Baker, Sawyerville, Que. ; Llewellyn Brown, Belmont ; Wallace Patten Cohoe, Scotland ; Archibald Darroch, Arkwright ; Mary Elizabeth Dryden, Brooklin ; William Findlay, Toronto ; Samuel Thomas Foster, Pembroke ; Andrew Imrie, Brockville ; Albourn Newcomb Marshall, Bridgetown, N. S. ; George John Menge, Toronto ; John James McNeill, Paisley; Horatio Hackett Newman, Toronto ; James Baxter Paterson, Montreal ; Canby Edwin Scott, New Sarum ; George Nowell Simmons, Ronson ; John Charles Sycamore, Brockville.

Bachelor of Divinity—Lyman Stanley Hughson.

Bachelor of Theology—Carson John Cameron, Tiverton ; William Wardley McMaster, Toronto ; Bert Ward Merrill, Hartford ; James Josiah Reeve, Guelph ; Edward John Stobo, Quebec ; Alexander Robertson McDonald (T. B. C., 1885), Lakefield.

Diplomas, English Theological Course—William Thomas Bunt, Hampton ; Andrew Fuller Hammett, Mount Albert ; James William Kirkpatrick, Brownsville.

ADDRESSES.—The address to the Graduates was delivered by Professor Daniel Morse Welton, Ph.D,, D.D. He briefly reviewed the work of the successful students in the different branches of study— mathematics, classics, natural and physical science, philosophy and theology. Four years ago, he said, the University course lay before them ; now it was behind them, an accomplished fact. With it they had grappled in a manly way. In one particular this was not a correct statement, for, to be more literally accurate, in one instance the grappling had been rather in a womanly way. He tendered some valuable counsel to those who were about to enter the larger school of life and contend with its problems and perplexities. Dr. Welton warmly commended the judgment of those who would return to take up the theological course. In answer to the criticism that the influence of the pulpit is not what it once was, he said that the pulpit could never decline ; those who entered it might. To those about to enter upon the ministry he appealed not to resort to mountebankism in order to draw the crowd.

Chancellor Wallace followed with an admirable address, of the high quality of which the following digest can give but an imperfect conception —:

The present is the age of the crucible. Beliefs of all kinds are subjected to the fires of relentless criticism, and there is a demand that doctrines shall be shaped anew. Because of this there is exigent need of leaders who are constructive in purpose and masterful by reason of intelligence and spiritual force. The advanced thinkers of to-day, with few exceptions, are men of conjectures rather than convictions. There is a field for men who are competent to build on the ruins which destructive critics have made. Self-control is the first qualification in a leader. If morally strong and mentally capable and equipped, he may hope to be ready and puissant in the field of opportunity. A man will be controlled for great purposes only when he is subject to a great thought. Such subjection may involve infinite sacrifice, as it has often done in past days of crisis and extraordinary service. No one can rise to the highest service who does not receive the great thought and inspiration of his life from conscious communion with God. As from Him came forth the Logos, so from Him must always come the thought-message which shall bring illumination and work redemption among men. He who does not worship God is incompetent to lead men to the highest things. The existence of the University shows progress from that state of society in which the leader of men carries a club or sword to that in which convictions and spiritual force are his weapons. With few exceptions, the universities of the world have been founded in response to a call for trained leaders, and a University is realizing its true aim only when it is sending forth graduates who are strong in self-control, filled with a great and holy purpose, and willing servants of the most high God. The University must not covet for her graduates places of worldly distinction, but must desire earnestly that they may find positions in which their qualifications will enable them to give help and guidance to those who have need.

Provost Welch, of Trinity University, followed with a short, practical address, in which he quoted the advice given to himself and fellow-graduates at Cambridge, advice which he tendered to the graduates of McMaster. This was to "study liberally, think seriously, work honestly, *epekteinomenoi*—pressing forward towards (the goal).

Dr. Lorimer was the last speaker. He took as the keynote for his speech the idea of " Progress," enunciated by Provost Welch, and reinforced the latter by a quotation from Robert Browning. He spoke of the many social injustices that are prevalent, and was cheered to the echo when he declared that society needs more justice and less charity, for more justice would mean that less charity would be required.

The Third Annual Commencement was then declared by the Chancellor at an end.

Moulton College.

Mrs. Dignam has finished her year's work, and has gone to spend the holidays in a Paris studio. We wish her a very pleasant and successful summer, and a safe return to Moulton in the fall.

Per Ardua is the watchword at Moulton at all times, but just now the girls are living up to it even more earnestly than usual. Early rising is the order of the day for the diligent ones who hope to distinguish themselves in the closing examinations, and if the proverbial saying about "early birds" is to be relied upon, there are some Moulton girls who will not stand low on the class-lists.

THE annual gathering of the Moulton Alumnæ is being anticipated with great interest. Every effort is being made to secure the attendance of all the members who can possibly come, and the programme for their entertainment contains several novel and interesting features

THE final meeting of the Heliconian was held on May 22nd, when the following programme was presented; Song, Miss Boehmer; Recitation, Miss Cornell; Story, Miss Rosser; Observation Contest, members of the society; Piano Solo, Miss McKay; Heliconian Paper, Misses Cornell and Dyer.

THE final meeting of our Mission Circle took place on May 15th, when the following exercises, interspersed with music, were rendered: Paper on "The Condition of the Indians," by Miss Wallace; Reading, "A General Presentation of Scandinavian Work," by Miss Rosser; Paper on "Our Missionary Among the Indians," by Miss Cornell; Reading, "A Foreign Missionary at Home," by Miss Mayberry. The meeting was both interesting and helpful, and the Treasurer's Report for the year, which was read during the evening, was very encouraging.

THE following letter, issued on May 20th, by Rev. Donald Grant, of Montreal, to his church and congregation, will possess much interest for our readers: "Your pastor takes pleasure in announcing to you and your friends that on the 17th of June next, he will, D.V., be united in marriage to Miss Alice Maud Dunning Fitch, of Wolfville, Nova Scotia, at the residence of the bride's parents. He sincerely hopes that the contemplated union may be for the glory of our Common Lord and the welfare of the Church, as well as for the happiness of those entering upon it."

WOODSTOCK COLLEGE.

"Kith and Kin Across the Sea" was the theme of a delightfully entertaining lecture on Friday evening, May 1st, by Rev. Chas. A. Eaton, pastor of the Bloor St. Baptist church, Toronto. In rapid sketches the speaker took his hearers across the green fields of old England, into her famous halls of learning, north into the land of Burns, to Glasgow, Edinburgh and back to London, the world's emporium. Conditions social, political and religious were outlined and commented on; and the lecturer closed with an earnestly eloquent and patriotic appeal, especially to young men, as an aim worthy of their highest ambition, to lend a hand in consolidating the peace and good-will of the great English-speaking peoples. The lecture was listened to throughout with the most intense interest and delight by the large audience present. Mr. Eaton made many friends during his short stay in Woodstock.

GRANDE LIGNE

NEXT year, if all is well, four of our students, E. Rossier, J. J. Nicol, P. Baker, and F. Therrien will begin the struggle with the Arts Course of McMaster University. Philip Nicol will study Medicine at Laval, Goodhue, Arts at McGill, and H. Sené will enter Theology at Newton. We wish them all success.

WE regret to say that Miss Laporte, who came in such good spirits to help us last October, was compelled, by failing health, to relinquish her work here at the end of the winter term. Since then she has been under treatment in a hospital in Montreal. We hope that her health may be speedily and completely restored to her.

Now that the warm weather and dry roads have come, the bicycle is becoming a very common sight. Almost every recreation the " oval " in front of the school would present the appearance of a regular race course. An increasing number of our students become devotees of the wheel every year. We fear, though, that lessons very often suffer from this devotedness. In fact, some students can hardly leave the bicycle long enough to come to their meals, much less to study.

WITH us " Arbor Day " was this year celebrated a little more extensively than usual. Not content with planting trees merely on our own grounds, we, this year, set out maples and elms along the whole front of the farm. Quite a number of apple trees, grape vines and currant bushes were also set out in our orchard and garden. The mission will reap the benefit of these trees in future years, and will thank a past generation for their generous forethought. If only some more of our neighbors would follow our example in setting trees along the front of their farms, Grande Ligne would soon present a very beautiful appearance.

ON April 10th it was our sad duty to lay to rest the remains of Mrs. Brouillet, the wife of our Missionary Brouillet, at Roxton Pond, and sister of our pastor, M. B. Parent. Five days later also we were called to follow the remains of our school-mate Aaron Pelletier to the same little cemetery behind the College. Both had been suffering for some months previous to their death, and both had a strong hope in Jesus Christ. Mrs. Brouillet leaves to mourn a husband and one daughter, while Aaron was the only son of a widowed mother. The bereaved ones have our sincerest sympathy in their loneliness.

ACCORDING to his usual custom in the spring time, Mr. A. E. Massé had on hand this year a large pile of cord-wood to be sawn and split. Every fine holiday some boys would tremble lest they should be called upon to work at the wood-pile. Nearly all of us have had our share of this work to do. Sometimes, when all could not work at once at the wood, different boys would be told off to rake or mow the lawn, pick up bits of paper, trim the apple trees and dig about them, or do various other jobs. While, however, these tasks were being performed, the bicycles enjoyed a much needed rest.

CPSIA information can be obtained
at www.ICGtesting.com
Printed in the USA
BVHW082052201118
533619BV00011B/1654/P